# ORTHOGRAPHIA
## DA LINGOA
### PORTVGVESA.

Obra vtil, & neceſſaria, aſsi pera bem ſcreuer a lingoa
Heſpanhol, como a Latina, & quaeſquer outras,
que da Latina teem origem.

¶ Item hum tractado dos pontos das clauſulas.

Pelo Licenciado Duarte Nunez do Liáo.

### EM LISBOA,
## Per Ioáo de Barreira impreſſor delRei N. S.

**M. D. LXXVI.**

TITLE-PAGE OF FIRST TREATISE ON PORTUGUESE
SPELLING
1576
*By Duarte Nunes de Leão*

# FROM LATIN TO POR

# FROM LATIN TO PORTUGUESE

## Historical Phonology and Morphology of the Portuguese Language

By

### EDWIN B. WILLIAMS

*Professor of Romance Languages*
*University of Pennsylvania*

SECOND EDITION

Philadelphia

UNIVERSITY OF PENNSYLVANIA PRESS

1962

Printed in the United States of America

*To*

LEONORE ROWE WILLIAMS

# PREFACE

SINCE the publication of Cornu's treatment of Portuguese phonology and morphology in Gröber's *Grundriss* (2d ed., 1904–1906), much new material has become available through editions of medieval manuscripts, dialect studies, and investigations of individual problems. But no new synthesis of this material has been presented. Nunes and Huber have worked in this direction, but while they have brought together the results of much research, they have left unsolved many of the major problems. The present book is an effort to present in systematic form the phonological and morphological history of the Portuguese language in the light of the most recent scholarship in the field. The author's own previously published studies have been utilized freely, but generally in a form somewhat modified or elaborated, and many new studies appear here for the first time. While most of the solutions arrived at apply only to the field of Portuguese, it is hoped that some will prove significant in the broader fields of Hispanic and general Romance philology. It is also hoped that theories which are but roughly outlined here will inspire other searchers to further speculation and the collection of additional data that may confirm or disprove them and thus lead to definitive solutions.

A word or two may be said concerning practical matters. The author has striven to maintain a rigid line of demarcation between phonology and morphology and to base the latter rigorously on the former with the intervention of no other factor than analogy. A knowledge of Modern Portuguese phonetics is presupposed. Phonetic symbols and diacritical marks are used where necessary to the exposition of phonological and analogical development. Modern dialect forms are quoted simply to show the continuance of tendencies found in Old Portuguese and the wider occurrence of changes found in standard Modern Portuguese. The author asks indulgence for the dogmatic tone of many assertions. Reservations are obvious. To express them always would consume too much space.

It is a pleasure to acknowledge my obligations to numerous friends: to Professor J. P. Wickersham Crawford for my first training and sustained interest in Romance philology; to Professor Roland G. Kent for advice and guidance in the solution of many difficult problems; to Mr. Alexandre de Seabra for information on special points in Modern Portuguese; to Professor Albert C. Baugh for constant encouragement and helpful suggestions; and to many graduate students over a period of more than ten years, who by cold logic or warm flashes of insight in classroom discussions have step by step helped me forward toward my goal. The scholars on whose writings I have drawn most freely are Leite de Vasconcellos, Nunes, Meyer-Lübke, and Grandgent, but a glance at the bibliography will show to what length this list might be extended. I am especially indebted to the Faculty Research Committee of the University of Pennsylvania for several grants, and particularly for one which made possible a summer of study and investigation in Portugal.

E. B. W.

# PREFACE TO THE SECOND EDITION

The new discoveries and the principles based on them that were set forth in the first edition of this book in 1938 (such as syncope in Portuguese, particularly as contrasted with Spanish—§ 51-§ 59; the fate of intervocalic *n* in all its ramifications—§ 78; assimilation, dissimilation, and contraction of vowels in hiatus—§ 99; the final *-ão*—§ 157; radical-changing verbs—§ 174) have not been challenged by reviews or by the research that has been carried out since that time. All the reviews have been in general favorable. What they have criticized has been the restricted scope of the book to the study of historical phonology and morphology and heterogeneous minor matters, varying from one reviewer to another, that have no bearing on the fundamental findings and conclusions. In the present edition, accordingly, there are no basic changes, but some adjustments have been made in the light of the reviews, the bibliography has been brought up to date, and all available resources have been used to support and strengthen the principal arguments. It is hoped that the book will continue to serve as a guide for the study of the development of Latin into Portuguese.

E. B. W.

# CONTENTS

# PHONETIC SYMBOLS, DIACRITICAL MARKS, AND OTHER SIGNS

These equivalents are obviously only approximate.

[a] (open *a*) English *a* in *father*

[ɐ] (close *a*) English *a* in *about*

[ɐ̃] (nasal *a*) close *a* nasalized

[b] English *b*

[ƀ] Spanish *b* in *cabo*

[d] English *d*

[đ] Spanish *d* in *nada*

[ɛ] (open *e*) English *e* in *met*

[e] (close *e*) French *é*

[ə] (neutral *e*) French *e* in *tenir*

[ẽ] (nasal *e*) close *e* nasalized

[f] English *f*

[g] English *g* in *good*

[ı] (open *i*) English *i* in *perish*

[i] (close *i*) English *i* in *machine*

[ĩ] (nasal *i*) close *i* nasalized

[j] (yod) English *y* in *yet*

[k] English *k*

[l] English *l* in *look*

[ł] (velarized *l*) English *l* in *old*

[ʎ] (palatalized *l*) Italian *gli* in *paglia*

[m] English *m*

[n] English *n* in *now*

[ŋ] (velarized *n*) English *n* in *bank*

[ɲ] (palatalized *n*) French *gn* in *enseigner*

[ɔ] (open *o*) French *o* in *école*

[o] (close *o*) English *o* in *note*

[õ] (nasal *o*) close *o* nasalized

[p] English *p*

[r] slightly trilled with tip of tongue

[s] English *s*

[ś] (cacuminal *s*) pronounced with tip of tongue raised to roof of mouth

[t] English *t*

[u] (close *u*) English *oo* in *food*

[ũ] (nasal *u*) close *u* nasalized

[v] English *v*

[w] (consonantal *u*) English *w* in *well*

[z] English *z*

[ź] (cacuminal *z*) pronounced with tip of tongue raised to roof of mouth

[ʃ] English *sh* in *shall*

[ʒ] French *j*

[χ] German *ch* in *ach*

| | |
|---|---|
| *ą* same as [a] | *ǫ* same as [ɔ] |
| *ạ* same as [ɐ] | *ọ* same as [o] |
| *ę* same as [ɛ] | *ụ* same as [u] |
| *ẹ* same as [e] | *i̯* same as [j] |
| *ị* same as [i] | *u̯* same as [w] |

The long and short marks ¯ and ˘ are used to indicate the quantity of Classical Latin vowels.

The acute accent is used to indicate stress except on close *a*, *e*, and *o* in Portuguese words, where the circumflex accent is used according to the rules of the *nova ortografia.*

The sign > means "becomes" and the sign < means "comes from." Both are used to indicate analogical change as well as phonological change.

Words not found in *Harpers' Latin Dictionary* are either marked with an asterisk or accompanied by an indication of their source in Vulgar Latin or Medieval Latin, even though they may be of late occurrence. In accordance with common practice, hypothetical etyma, i.e., words marked with an asterisk, are generally given in the form they would have had in Classical Latin.

# FROM LATIN TO PORTUGUESE

# INTRODUCTION

## VULGAR LATIN

### 1. KNOWLEDGE OF VULGAR LATIN.

Latin as a living language was subject to constant change. While the language of the cultivated classes (Classical Latin) became more and more uniform under the stabilizing influence of culture and learning, the language of the people (Vulgar Latin) became more and more diversified as it spread with the expansion of the vast Roman Empire. Classical Latin became a dead language while Vulgar Latin developed into the so-called Neo-Latin or Romance languages.

No great literature has been handed down to us to attest the existence of Vulgar Latin. Our knowledge of it is derived from the following sources: a) popular elements, of intentional or accidental origin, in Classical and Medieval Latin; b) linguistic observations in Classical and Medieval Latin; c) Latin elements in the languages of the peoples with whom the Romans came in contact; d) the Romance languages. Vulgar Latin is, therefore, a language reconstructed from heterogeneous fragments and largely on the basis of hypothesis.

### 2. CLASSICAL LATIN ACCENT.

The place of the accent in Classical Latin is determined by quantity, according to the following principles:

a) In words of two syllables the penult is accented: *hómo*.

b) In words of three or more syllables the penult is accented if it is long, that is, if it contains a long vowel: *imperatôrem*, a diphthong: *incaûtum*, or a short vowel followed by two or more consonants: *inténdo* (except a mute plus *l* or *r: ténĕbras*).

1

c) In words of three or more syllables, the antepenult is accented if the penult is short: *hóminem.*

### 3. VULGAR LATIN ACCENT.

The accent falls on the same syllable in Vulgar Latin as in Classical Latin, with the following exceptions:

a) In words of three or more syllables the penult is accented if it contains a vowel which was short in Classical Latin, followed by a mute plus *l* or *r*: *tenĕbras.*

b) In compound verb forms of three syllables which would be accented on the antepenult in Classical Latin, the penult is accented; in other words, the accent falls on the radical vowel of the simple verb and not on the prefix: *\*recípit,* not *récipit.* Usually the vowel of the simple verb is restored: *réficit > \*refăcit.*

c) Where an *i* or *e,* accented in Classical Latin, is in hiatus with a following short vowel, the accent shifts in Vulgar Latin to this following vowel, the *i* or *e* afterwards becoming a yod: *muliĕrem > \*muliére; filiŏlum > \*filiŏlu.*

### 4. UNACCENTED WORDS.

With the intensification of stress accent in Vulgar Latin, many unemphatic words lost their accent and became attached as proclitics and enclitics to other larger and more emphatic words. This was particularly true of personal pronouns used as direct and indirect objects of verbs and of verbs used as auxiliaries. The vowels of these words developed regularly as pretonic initial or unaccented final vowels. Dissyllabic words of this sort often became monosyllabic.

### 5. PORTUGUESE ACCENT.

The accent falls on the same syllable in Portuguese as in Vulgar Latin.

## 6. VULGAR LATIN TONIC VOWELS.

It is thought that the variation of a given vowel in Classical Latin was one of quantity (cf. the difference in Modern German between the *a* of *Strasze* and the *a* of *Gasse*), while the corresponding variation in Vulgar Latin was one of quality, with the exception of the vowel *a*, in which no qualitative distinction was made. Thus long *o* (*ō*) and short *o* (*ŏ*) of Classical Latin became close *o* (*ọ*) and open *o* (*ǫ*) respectively in Vulgar Latin. The development of Classical Latin vowels into Vulgar Latin vowels is shown in this table.

| Classical Latin | Vulgar Latin |
|:---:|:---:|
| ă ⎫ ā ⎭ | a |
| ĕ ⎫ ae ⎭ | ę |
| ē ⎫ i oe ⎭ | ẹ |
| ī | i |
| ŏ | ǫ |
| ō ⎫ ŭ ⎭ | ọ |
| ū | ụ |
| au | au |

A. The frequent change of *e* to *i* in Medieval Latin documents (cf. MT, 31–33), which is contrary to the change indicated in the above table, is purely orthographic and probably arose through confusion of the two letters because of an awareness that they both stood for one and the same sound. The change of *o* to *u* arose in the same way.

## 7. VULGAR LATIN ATONIC VOWELS.

The Vulgar Latin vowels listed in § 6 were further simplified in the unaccented position: *a*, *i*, *ụ*, *ẹ*, and *ọ* remained as in the accented position; *ę* became *ẹ*, *ǫ* became *ọ*, and initial *au*, followed by a syllable containing accented *u*, became *a*.

A. Grandgent (GVL, § 228) judges from "subsequent developments" that initial unaccented *ǫ* did not close to *ǫ*. He may have in mind the situation in French where we find two different products of initial unaccented *o*, e.g., *porter* (from *pŏrtāre*) and *journée* (from *\*diŭrnāta*). But Dauzat has attempted to overcome this difficulty by explaining that the *o* of such forms as *porter* is due to regression or the operation of analogy (Dauzat, § 100). But see § 99, 5 A. Cf. M–L, Gram, I, § 353.

## 8. Syncope in Vulgar Latin.

1. The vowel of the penult of proparoxytones and the vowel of the intertonic syllable generally fell in Vulgar Latin in the following cases: a) when followed by *l* or *r*; b) when preceded by *l* or *r* and followed by *d*, *m*, or *p*; c) when preceded by *s* and followed by *t*; d) when preceded by a labial; e) in a few unclassifiable words like *dĭgĭtum* and *frĭgĭdum*. Cf. M–L, Gram, I, § 29; GVL, §§ 231–238.

2. In the Vulgar Latin of the Portuguese territory this vowel fell much less frequently than elsewhere, particularly when followed by *l* or *r*, and when preceded by a labial; it probably did not fall in *dĭgĭtum* and *frĭgĭdum*.

A. The groups *ab* + consonant and *av* + consonant, arising in Vulgar Latin through the fall of the penult of proparoxytones or the vowel of the intertonic syllable (GVL, § 236), were rare in Portuguese territory.

## 9. Classical Latin and Vulgar Latin Yod.

1. Initial unaccented *i* before a vowel and intervocalic unaccented *i* were consonantal in Classical Latin. Whether initial or not, unaccented *i* and *e* before a vowel generally became consonantal in Vulgar Latin.

2. Vulgar Latin yod preceded by a consonant sometimes fell.

**10.** CONSONANTAL *u*.

1. One and the same character, *v*, stood for a consonant [w] and a vowel [u] in Classical Latin.

2. The consonant sound occurred in the following positions: a) initial before a vowel, b) between two vowels, and c) sometimes when preceded by a consonant and followed by a vowel.

Early in the Empire this sound became a bilabial fricative, i.e., [ƀ] in some regions and a dentilabial, i.e., [v] in others (GVL, § 322).

The sound [w] also occurred as the second element of a diphthong, where it generally remained unchanged in Vulgar Latin, except in initial *au*, followed by a syllable containing accented *u*, where it fell.

3. The vowel sound occurred in the following positions: a) initial before a consonant, b) between two consonants, c) final after a consonant, and d) sometimes when preceded by a consonant and followed by a vowel.

In the last of these positions it became a consonant, i.e., [w] toward the end of the Vulgar Latin period (GVL, § 326). This took place too late for the change to [ƀ] or [v] (as in 2 c above), although isolated examples are found in several Romance languages, e.g., *valuisset* > OPtg. *valvesse; paruit* > It. *parve; januarium* > Fr. *janvier*. This late [w] fell when followed by unaccented *o* or *u*, when preceded by a guttural and followed by accented *o* or *u*, and in a few unclassifiable cases (GVL, § 226).

4. As the letter *v*, preceded by a consonant and followed by a vowel, could stand for the vowel sound and the consonant sound in Classical Latin (2 c and 3 d above), it is possible to distinguish the two sounds in a given word only by determining by means of scansion the number of syllables it contains. For example, if *volvit* is found to have two syllables, the second *v* (as well as the first) stands for [w]; if it is found to have three syllables, the second *v*

stands for [u], and the word may be written *voluit* (perf.
of *velle*), as is the practice in the modern orthography of
Classical Latin.

**11. PROSTHETIC *e*.**

Because initial *s* before a consonant was found difficult
to pronounce, an *e* was prefixed to it and came to form
part of the word.

**12. VULGAR LATIN CONSONANTS.**

1. *C* followed by *e* or *i*, by moving forward toward the
teeth, went through the following stages: [k] > [kj] > [tj]
> [ts].

2. *G* followed by *e* or *i* became [gj] and then a simple yod.

3. *C* + yod became [tsj]. A century or two earlier,
*t* + yod also became [tsj] but this sound had changed to
[ts] by the time that *c* + yod became [tsj]. See GVL,
§§ 277–278.  *G* + yod and *d* + yod became a simple yod.

4. Intervocalic surds and surds preceded by a vowel and
followed by *l* or *r* became voiced. Intervocalic *b* and *b*
preceded by a vowel and followed by *l* or *r* became [ƀ].

5. Final *t* and final *d* preceded by a vowel or a consonant
fell.

6. The group *rs* became *ss*; *ps* became *ss*; *pt* became *tt*;
*nct* became *nt* (except in Gaul); *nf* became *f*; *ns* became *s*; *x*
became *s* before a consonant and in the prefix *ex-* sometimes
before a vowel; and the final consonant of a prefix was
usually assimilated to the initial consonant of the word to
which it was attached.

7. Double consonants remained long as in Classical Latin.

8. The following consonants became silent: *h*; final *m*
except in monosyllables, where it became *n*.

9. The sound of *v* changed from [w] to [v].  See § 10, 2.

**13. MORPHOLOGICAL CHANGES IN VULGAR LATIN.**

1. Nouns.  a) The five declensions of Classical Latin
were reduced to three, nouns of the fourth declension

changing to the second and nouns of the fifth declension changing to the third (except a few which changed to the first, e.g., *dies* and *rabies*).

b) The neuter gender disappeared: neuter singulars became masculine and neuter plurals became feminine singulars of the first declension. Feminine nouns of the second declension became masculine and feminine nouns of the fourth declension became masculine or changed to the first declension.

c) All cases finally disappeared except the nominative and an oblique case formed by the fusion of the accusative and ablative (and in some nouns the dative). And in the first declension, the nominative was replaced by the accusative. Some nouns of the third declension, which had a shift of accent from the nominative to the oblique cases, formed a new nominative with the accent on the same syllable as in the oblique cases.

2. Adjectives. a) The declension of adjectives changed in accordance with the declension of nouns. However, the neuter singular was retained to express in the abstract the quality denoted by the adjective.

b) There was a tendency of adjectives of the third declension to change to the type based on the first and second declensions.

c) The endings of the comparative and superlative of adjectives and adverbs began to disappear and to be replaced by periphrastic expressions (§ 14, 3).

3. Pronouns. a) The nominative, dative, and accusative of most pronouns were retained. In a few pronouns the genitive was retained. The neuters of many pronouns were preserved; they were used to refer, not to single words, for neuter nouns had disappeared, but in an indeterminate way to whole previous statements or propositions.

b) Some pronouns developed into two different forms according as they were accented or unaccented.

4. Verbs. a) The four conjugations of Classical Latin

survived in Vulgar Latin but many verbs shifted from one
conjugation to another.

b) The future indicative fell into disuse (for expressions
which replaced it, see § 14, 5). The imperfect subjunctive
was replaced by the pluperfect subjunctive; it fell into
disuse except in the Portuguese territory, where it assumed
a new function (§ 158, 2). The perfect subjunctive and
the future perfect indicative fused into a new tense (§ 14, 6).
The imperative lost most of its forms except the second
singular and plural of the present. The endings of the
passive voice were lost; deponent verbs, accordingly, took
on active endings. The perfect infinitive, the supine, the
future active participle and the gerundive disappeared. A
new form in -tōrius came to be used as a gerundive.

## 14. CHANGES IN SYNTAX IN VULGAR LATIN.

1. It is probable that the phonological changes (chiefly
the loss of final consonants and the loss and weakening of
unaccented vowels), brought about by an increased stress
accent (§ 16, 2), precipitated the breakdown of the morphological system of Classical Latin, which was thus rendered
unfit for the needs of a highly synthetic syntax.[1] Inflection
was replaced by periphrasis. Analysis took the place of
synthesis. And word order came to assume an all-impor-
tant role in syntax.

Thus we find a much greater use of prepositions, auxiliary
verbs and other periphrastic forms of expression in Vulgar
Latin.

2. *Ad* with the accusative replaced the dative. *De* with
the ablative replaced the genitive; and with the fall of final
*m* the accusative and ablative became identical in form
and function.

[1] Vossler (*The Spirit of Language in Civilization*, London, 1932, Chapter IV)
argues, on the contrary, that the synthetic syntax of Classical Latin became
atrophied through disuse as a result of a new mode of thinking, a new *Weltan-
schauung*.

3. New periphrastic comparatives of adjectives and adverbs were formed with *magis* and *plus*.

4. Pronouns were used more commonly than in Classical Latin. *Is* and *idem* fell into disuse and *ille* became the regular pronoun of the third person. At the same time *ille* began to function as definite article while *ūnus* came to be used more widely as an indefinite article.

5. New periphrastic future tenses were formed with the infinitive and the present tense of the following auxiliaries: *dēbēre, habēre, īre, vadĕre, velle* and *venīre*. The tense formed with the infinitive and the present tense of *habēre* came into commonest use. Another tense, formed with the infinitive and the imperfect indicative of *habēre*, appeared along with the future, first probably as a past future tense in indirect discourse (as the infinitive plus accusative construction was being avoided), and later with many of the uses of the conditional in the Romance languages.

6. When used with the past participle, the present indicative and subjunctive of *habēre* formed a new perfect indicative and a new perfect subjunctive respectively, while the old perfect indicative continued in use. The old perfect subjunctive and the future perfect indicative fused into a single tense, which was used as a future indicative or subjunctive (Tempuslehre, §§ 8–11). A new pluperfect indicative was formed with the imperfect indicative of *habēre* plus the past participle, while a new pluperfect subjunctive was formed with the old pluperfect subjunctive of *habēre* plus the past participle, the old pluperfect subjunctive having become the imperfect subjunctive in Vulgar Latin in place of the Classical Latin imperfect subjunctive.

7. The forms of the passive voice were replaced by a new passive formed with *esse* plus the past participle. At the same time, the passive was avoided by using the reflexive construction or *homo* as an indefinite pronoun.

8. The subjunctive had fewer functions; they were more like those of the Romance languages than like those of

Classical Latin. Some of the lost forms of the imperative were replaced by the subjunctive. The infinitive replaced the supine and the subjunctive clause introduced by *ut*. On the other hand, the infinitive plus accusative construction was avoided and replaced by a clause introduced by *quia, quod, quoniam* or *ut*.

**15. WORDS AND WORD FORMATION IN VULGAR LATIN.**

1. There was a large body of common words which were the same in Classical Latin and Vulgar Latin. Many words are found in Vulgar Latin which had developed from Classical Latin according to the regular laws of semasiology, but a surprisingly large number of meanings seem to follow the law of specialization. Many Classical Latin words disappeared entirely. New words of uncertain origin appeared; some of these were probably Classical Latin words which had never been used in texts that are now extant. And many more new words were derived from Greek, Celtic and German.

New verbs were formed from nouns, adjectives, present participles, and past participles while new nouns were formed from verbs.

2. Phonological attrition, due to the increased stress accent of Vulgar Latin, sometimes reduced words to a single syllable. These words and others were reinforced by the use of suffixes and prefixes of all kinds. Thus augmentatives, diminutives and inchoatives were used without their special meaning and with no other effect than to give more body to the original word. Where this could not be done the word often disappeared to make way for a more robust competitor.

## PORTUGUESE

**16. FROM VULGAR LATIN TO PORTUGUESE.**

1. The differentiation of Vulgar Latin from one region to another, which finally resulted in its transformation into

the several Romance languages, is thought to have been due to the following causes: a) the relative geographic isolation of one group from another, b) the development of separate political units, c) the variation of cultural and educational circumstances, d) the period of romanization, e) dialectal differences in the language of the Italic colonists, f) the original linguistic substrata, and g) subsequent linguistic superimposures.

Probably the most important cause of differentiation was the intensified stress accent, superimposed, as it were, upon the Vulgar Latin of Italy, Gaul and the Iberian peninsula in varying degrees by the invading Germanic races.

2. It is believed that Classical Latin always had a stress accent, and that a pitch accent, which never affected popular speech, was introduced toward the middle of the second century B.C. among the highly educated classes by Greek teachers, pronouncing Latin in their own fashion (Kent, § 66, 1). Five or six centuries later the stress accent of popular speech was greatly intensified in the mouths of invading Goths, who accented Latin with the greater stress accent characteristic of their own language. One of the results of this intensified stress accent was the increased syncope of the vowel of the posttonic penult and the intertonic syllable between certain pairs of consonants, which took place in Vulgar Latin (§ 8).

A. The stress accent of popular Latin was sufficiently strong to cause some syncope before the advent of the Goths (CPh, II, 454).

3. Additional Germanic invasions (Franks, Burgundians, Lombards, etc.) brought about further intensification of the stress accent, and with the rise of the Romance languages, syncope of the vowel of the posttonic penult and the intertonic syllable became a general phenomenon no longer limited to the special positions in which it occurred in Vulgar Latin. But these additional Germanic invasions

did not reach the territory where Portuguese was to develop. Aside from Visigoths and Suevi no Germanic tribes ever settled in this territory and Visigoths and Suevi left but slight traces of their stay (BF, II, 108–109). The linguistic result was that there was less stress accent than in other Romance territory and accordingly, less syncope (§ 53 and § 58). The failure of $e$ and $o$ to diphthongize and the slow formation of yod (§ 87, 2) and of Ptg. $u$ (§ 93, 1 A) are further evidence of a weaker stress accent.[1]

The Visigoths and Suevi left only about twenty words in the Portuguese language (RFE, XIX, 234–238). The relatively large number of Germanic place-names in northern Portugal and in Galicia is due to the settlement of the Visigoths in this territory after the year 700, that is, after the transition to Romance and after their complete amalgamation with the earlier Roman and Celtic inhabitants, when they were fleeing from the south and centre of Spain from the Moors and had to protect themselves in fortified towns, contrary to their previous custom elsewhere (RG, I, 361).

The separate Romance which developed in the south among the Mozarabs (RL, XI, 354) was entirely free of Germanic influence; hence the especial fondness of the people of the south even today for proparoxytones (BHi, VII, 194) and the impression they give of singing when they speak (Esquisse, p. 154, n. 1). Thus while certain characteristics of Old Portuguese, such as the fall of intervocalic $l$ and $n$, arose in the north, the resistance to syncope, a far more distinctive characteristic, was stronger in the south (cf. Ent, 278).

A. The remark of Gamillscheg: "No puede hablarse, en lo que se refiere al desarrollo fonético, de una influencia del gótico sobre el ibero-románico" (RFE, XIX, 260) and his reference to Brüch's study (RLiR, II, 66 ss.) have no bearing on the question of

[1] For a similar hypothesis applied to Neapolitan and other Italian dialects, see Vaughan, 11–14. See also Pope, § 223.

accent as Brüch does not discuss it and as far as phonology is concerned deals only with Germanic *h* and *w*.

## 17. OLD AND MODERN PORTUGUESE.

Vulgar Latin along the western coast of the Iberian peninsula, freer from Germanic stress accent than anywhere else, freer especially than in the rest of the peninsula, grew into Portuguese. No one knows exactly when it ceased to be Vulgar Latin and began to be Portuguese.

The earliest documents in Portuguese appeared at the end of the twelfth century and mark the historical beginning of Old Portuguese. For four centuries the language underwent many changes. The most important of these was the marked intensification of stress accent which occurred in the sixteenth century. This is shown by the increased syncope found in verse (§ 54 and § 59) and by the tendency toward greater word individuation (§ 118). Toward the end of the sixteenth century nearly all of the distinctive characteristics of Old Portuguese had disappeared; the language had become in all essentials the same as the language of today.

A. Increased stress accent and increased word individuation developed in Portuguese in practically the same period as decreased stress accent and decreased word individuation (i.e., liaison) in French. Cf. Pope, § 170 and § 223.

B. The history of the Portuguese language has been divided by some into three periods: a) the Old or National Period—from the twelfth to the sixteenth century, b) the Middle or Classical Period—from the sixteenth to the eighteenth century, and c) the French or Arcadian Period—from the eighteenth century to the present day. See LP, I, 192–193.

## 18. LEARNED WORDS, DOUBLETS AND REGRESSIVE WORDS.

1. From the earliest times new Latin words have entered into Portuguese, first through the church and the law, later through the work of scholars and men of letters, and

still later through science. These learned or semi-learned words have not undergone all the changes which popular words have undergone, first, because they have often been taken into the language after certain changes had ceased to take place, and second, because of a conscious effort to preserve their Latin form.  See Meillet, 319

A. Late learned words with popular changes in imitation of popular words are sometimes found in dialects, e.g., *politigo* for *político*, *inorante* for *ignorante*, the suffix *-airo* for *-ario* (Esquisse, § 60 d; RL, XI, 141 and 278; RL, XII, 307).

B. Literary Portuguese probably contains fewer learned words than literary Spanish.

2. Sometimes a learned or semi-learned word already existed as a popular word; the two forms are then called doublets, e.g., *pélago* and *pego; artigo* and *artelho*.  Borrowings from dialects and other languages may also become doublets, e.g., *arena* (from Sp.) and *areia*.

3. Sometimes a popular word was modified or replaced by the Latin word from which it originally came; the new word is called a regressive word.  Thus OPtg. *seenço* was replaced by *silêncio, vesso* by *verso*, the suffix *-ão* by *-ano*, e.g., *romão* by *romano*.  This is a form of contamination.

A. By a conscious or unconscious striving for discrimination, regression often restored a difference between two words which regular phonological development had destroyed, e.g., both *vēnam* and *vēla* regularly became *vea* in Old Portuguese; the regression to *vela* has restored the distinction in form.  In some cases regression did not take place, e.g., both *\*fĭdāre* (for *fĭdĕre*) and *fīlāre* became *fiar,* which survives with the meanings of both originals.  In other cases the resultant form has lost one of its meanings, i.e., one of the two original words has disappeared, e.g., *\*adcalescere* and *\*adcadescere* both became *aquecer* in Old Portuguese, which survives in Modern Portuguese with only the meaning of *\*adcalescere*.  Cf. BSC, X, 814.

4. Contrary to the advice of King Edward (Dom Duarte) in his "Leal Conselheiro" early in the fifteenth century

that the writer "nom ponha pallavras latinadas nem d'outra linguagem," he himself introduced many Latin words, spellings, and constructions in this very work, and the practice became general a century later, not only in translations from Latin but in original works. Devotion to Latin led some poets to write exclusively in that language.

**19. Spanish Influence.**

In the first half of the fifteenth century, Spanish poets such as the Marqués de Santillana gave to the Spanish language the high position in poetry that Alfonso el Sabio had won for it in prose. It was natural, then, that Portuguese poets, who had abandoned the tradition of their early lyric, should turn to Spanish for that contact with the Renaissance which had thus far been denied them. Accordingly, we find them in the second half of the century writing much of their verse in Spanish (in the "Cancioneiro Geral"), and such distinguished poets as Gil Vicente, Sá de Miranda, and Camões continued to do so in the sixteenth century.

Many violent attacks against this practice were made by grammarians such as Fernão de Oliveira and poets such as António Ferreira. In his Elegy on the death of Ferreira, Diogo Bernardes was able to say,

> Pois dando à patria tantos versos raros,
> um só nunca lhe deu em lingua alheia.

In the defense of Portuguese against Spanish, efforts were made to prove that Portuguese was superior to all the other Romance languages because it was more like Latin than any of them, or as some writers put it, because it represented a state of Latin less corrupt than any of the others. This was the argument of the "Dialogo em louvor da nossa linguagem" of João de Barros, published in 1540, and of the "Dialogo em defensam da lingua portuguesa" of Pedro de Magalhães de Gandavo, which appeared in

1574, four years before Henri Estienne's "Dialogue"
against the *italianisants*. The argument was continued
and elaborated in the following century in many books and
treatises, the most notable of which was the "Breves
louvores da lingua portuguesa: com notaveis exemplos da
muita semelhança que tem com a lingua latina" of Alvaro
Ferreira de Vera, published in 1631. That these works
were not without effect is revealed in the efforts of the
Portuguese to make their language as unlike Spanish as
possible, a tendency already noted by Duarte Nunes de
Leão in his "Origem da Lingoa Portuguesa" (N-L, Origem,
126), published in 1606.

## 20. FRENCH INFLUENCE.

The Romance language which had the greatest influence
on Portuguese from the earliest times was French (Rom,
II, 293). The infiltration of French manners and customs
and the introduction of French coins and commercial products into Portugal had begun in the tenth and eleventh
centuries (BSC, VII, 188–190). It was Afonso Henriques,
the son of Count Henry of Burgundy, who by wresting the
title of king from Alfonso VII of Castile and León in 1143
and by taking Lisbon from the Moors in 1147, established
the House of Burgundy, the first dynasty of Portuguese
monarchs, and laid the foundations of a new country in
the lower valley of the Tagus. Frenchmen came as pilgrims
to the shrine of Santiago in Galicia, as soldiers of fortune
to help fight the Moors, and as monks from the Benedictine
Abbey of Cluny. After the Sixty Years of Captivity (1580–
1640), begun under the ominous figure of Philip II of
Spain, France became a friend and ally of Portugal in the
wars of John IV against Spain. And now again Frenchmen came as courtiers, statesmen, scholars, and soldiers.
To the spread of the doctrine of Boileau was added in the
second half of the eighteenth century the influence of the
Encyclopedists and of French scientific thought.

The influence of French in words and expressions has continued steadily until it has become a cause of alarm, and many modern Ferreiras have risen to defend the purity and integrity of their mother tongue. But this influence has been an important force in accentuating the difference between Portuguese and Spanish.

## 21. PORTUGUESE.

To the often asked question, "Why did a separate language develop on the western extremity of the Iberian peninsula?", the answer would seem to be: a) because of geographic isolation by high plateaus and waste land, b) because of less Germanic influence in the critical formative period, c) because of political independence as early as the middle of the twelfth century under a leader of extraordinary prowess and statesmanship, d) because of the ultimate triumph, in spite of literary and political opposition, of the spirit of those sixteenth-century critics who believed that their language was worthy of preservation as a separate tongue, and e) because of the steadily increasing influence of French.

A. Celtic influence has been suggested as the cause of the development of Portuguese as a separate language (Wechssler, 459).

## 22. THE SPREAD OF PORTUGUESE.

As a result of discovery and colonization, Portuguese has been carried to all parts of the world. It is spoken in Brazil, the Azores, the Madeira Islands, the Cape Verde Islands, in parts of West Africa, East Africa, India, and the Malay Peninsula. The number of people speaking it is about fifty-seven million, seven million of whom are in continental Portugal.

That all of Portugal's discoveries were made to the south and east is explained by the fact that they were inspired

by the project of finding an eastern sea route to India.
The plan of Columbus to reach India by sailing west was
rejected by John II, who later challenged the right of
Spain to the lands that Columbus discovered.  The ques-
tion of determining the respective rights of Portugal and
Spain soon became acute.  Pope Alexander VI intervened
in the matter, which was finally settled in 1494 by the
Treaty of Tordesillas between John II and Ferdinand and
Isabella.  It was agreed that Portugal should receive all
lands east of a line running from pole to pole three hundred
and seventy leagues west of the Cape Verde Islands while
Spain should receive all lands west of the line.

Brazil, the only exception in the eastward trend of Portuguese discovery, whether discovered by accident or not,
was at first looked upon by the Portuguese as merely a
way-station on the route to India.  But Manuel I's claim
to possession led to fresh disputes with Spain as to the
exact location of the new country with respect to the line
of demarcation, disputes which continued for almost three
hundred years.

## 23. DIALECTS.

Standard Portuguese is that spoken in the region between Lisbon and Coimbra and imitated by educated people
throughout the country (VPN, § 39).

The continental dialects of Portuguese are found either
in Portugal or in neighboring sections of Spain.  The chief
dialects in Portugal are, in the northwest, Interamnense
with the subdialects of the provinces of Douro and Minho;
in the northeast, Trasmontano; in the centre, Beirão; and
in the south, Meridional with the subdialects Estremenho,
Alentejano and Algarvio (Esquisse, § 7).  Some of these
dialects extend into Spain: Trasmontano at Ermisende in
León (RL, VII, 139–145); Beirão at San Martín de Trevejo
in Extremadura (RL, XXVI, 247–259; Onís, 63–69); and
Alentejano at Olivenza in Extremadura (RL, II, 347–349).

The chief continental dialect outside of Portugal is Galician. Some have classified Galician and Portuguese as co-dialects (RL, II, 345).

Mirandês, which is spoken in a very small region in the extreme east of Tras-os-Montes, is considered by some to be a branch of Leonese (Hanssen, § 3, 15; M-L, Intro, p. 53, note 1 of Castro) but is really a separate language intermediate between Galician-Portuguese and the Asturian-Leonese dialect of Spanish (PhM, II, 76).

The continental dialects never became sufficiently differentiated from the literary language to be able to exert a great influence on it (Rom, II, 290), while the dialects of other parts of the world were too remote to do so. On the complex problem of the regional elements involved in the rise of Portuguese, see ZRPh, LVII, 632.

## PORTUGUESE ORTHOGRAPHY

### 24. PERIODS OF PORTUGUESE ORTHOGRAPHY.

The history of Portuguese orthography is divided into three periods: a) the phonetic period, which coincided with the period of Old Portuguese; b) the etymological period, which lasted from the Renaissance to the twentieth century; and c) the reformed period, which began with the adoption of the Portuguese Government's *nova ortografia* in 1916.

### 25. THE PHONETIC PERIOD.

In the phonetic period scribes tried to represent phonetically the sounds of the words they wrote. As there were many new sounds which did not exist in Latin and for which no tradition had developed, they were obliged to adapt old graphs and invent new ones. And many inconsistencies developed. Scribes would often represent the same sound in different ways and different sounds in the same way (RL, IX, 261). For example, aware that *g* was hard in some words, they assumed that it could be hard in all words, hence the spelling *gisa* for *guisa;* disregarding this conclusion and aware also that *g* was soft in some words, they assumed that it could be soft in all words, hence the spelling *fugo* for *fujo*.   Thus in *gisa* and *guisa*, two graphs, *g* and *gu* represent the same sound, while in *gisa* and *fugo*, two sounds, [g] and [ʒ] are represented by the same letter.

**26. CONFUSION OF GRAPHS.**

1. Use of *qu* for *c*: *cinquo* for *cinco; nunqua* for *nunca*.

A. Because of this confusion, *quo* was sometimes used to represent the sound [kw], e.g., *quoall* (RL, IV, 207, A.D. 1453).   Cf. section 2 A below.

B. The use of *c* for *qu* is found but is rare, e.g., *pecena* for *pequena* and *esceeçidas* for *esqueecidas* (Abraham, § 11).

2. Confusion of *g* and *gu*: *alguo* for *algo; amigua* for *amiga; algem* for *alguem; gerra* for *guerra*.

A. Because of the use of *gu* for *g* [g], scribes began early in the fifteenth century to use *guo* for *gu* [gw], e.g., *linguoa* (Castelo, folio 41 vo); *daguoa* (RL, IV, 202, A.D. 1456), i.e., *de aguoa*.   By the end of the fifteenth century *guo* was replaced by *go*: *agoa* for *agua; goardar* for *guardar*. The use of *o* for *u* [w] was then adopted in other positions, e.g., *continoar, Manoel*. Cf. section 1 A above.

3. Confusion of *g, gi,* and *j*: *agia* for *haja; mangar* for *manjar; sega* for *seja*.

4. Confusion of *i, y,* and *j*: *aya* for *haja; iulgar* for *julgar; oye* for *hoje; ljuro* for *livro; mujto* for *muito; ydade* for *idade*.

5. Confusion of *u* and *v*: *auer* for *haver; vsar* for *usar; ovuir* for *ouvir*.

6. Use of *x* for *is*: *rex* for *reis; ex* for *eis*.

7. Confusion of *m, n,* and til: *āno* and *año* for *anno; camīho* for *caminho; cimco* for *cinco; grāde* for *grande; hõe* (RL, VIII, 256) for *home* or *homem; hūanal* (RL, I, 336) for *humanal; hūildade* (RL, XVI, 103) for *humildade; menesmo* (RL, VIII, 36; RL, XI, 88) for *mēesmo* (old); *põho*

for *ponho; poner* (Cd'A, I, 157, n. 1) for *põer* (old); *saom*
for *são* (from *sanu-*); *senpre* for *sempre; tẽpo* for *tempo;*
*emader* (FM, II, Glossary) for *ēader.*

A. This confusion obviously did not occur in the initial position.

B. The til was used in some cases for intervocalic *m* to save
space in an effort to keep the line from running into the margin
(CA, I, xvii, n. 2).

C. It seems that there was a predilection for *n* before *p* and *b*
(cf. BF, I, 45; Rad, 51).  This consistent use by many scribes
may indicate that the Old Portuguese sound was [n] or a combined [n] and [m]; or perhaps it may simply indicate nasalization
of the preceding vowel (cf. Manual, § 35, 1 c). As late as 1672
Bento Pereira found it necessary in his "Ars Grammaticae" (Pereira, 288) to urge the use of *m* before *p.*

D. Two acute accents on two similar vowels were sometimes
used for the til: *húú* for *hũu* (old); *homéés* for *homẽes* (old).

E. The use of final *m* to indicate the nasalization of the final
vowel arose perhaps in monosyllables in legal prose in imitation
of Latin spelling, e.g., *com, quem, rem* (old), *tam* (RL, XXVIII,
28).  The change from *n* to *m* took place in the course of the
thirteenth century (AHP, IV, 198).

**27.** USE OF *h.*

1. The letter *h* was used to show hiatus between unlike
vowels or between vowels of unlike quality: *poher* for *poer*
(old); *tehudo* for *teudo* (old); *mãho* (AHP, III, 21, A.D.
1331) for *mão*, the spelling *mãho* representing the word with
two syllables before the diphthong *ão* developed; *veher* for
*vẹẹr* (modern *vier*), whereas *vẹẹr* (modern *ver*) was never
written with *h* because both *e*'s were of the same quality.
Cf. SpV, § 75.

A. This *h* survived in some words until it was eliminated by
the *nova ortografia;* one can, for example, distinguish the new or
remodeled theatres in Lisbon by the sign *saida*, which in the
older theatres is spelled *sahida.*

2. The letter *h* was used before initial vowels, perhaps

at first to show hiatus with the final vowel of a preceding
word; later, this purpose being forgotten, it came to be
considered as part of the regular spelling of the word: *ha*
for *a* (article); *hi* for *i* or *y* (old); *hidade* for *idade;* *hir* for *ir;*
*hordenar* for *ordenar;* *honde* for *onde;* *hu* for *u* (old); *hum*
for *um;* *husar* for *usar.*

A. In *he* (for *é*) the *h* was probably used to distinguish the
verb from the conjunction *e.* The spelling *é,* instead of *he,* is
referred to as new in 1574 by Magalhães de Gandavo in his
"Regras que ensinam a maneira de screver a orthographia da
lingua portuguesa." The spelling *he* for the conjunction is rare,
e.g., Rom, XI, 374, line 30; RL, VII, 61.

B. The *h* in *alghũu* was used in imitation of *hũu,* which scribes
realized was a component of *algum.*

3. The letter *h* was used by false regression: *themor* (FM,
II, Glossary) for *temor; theudo* for *teudo* (old).

4. Initial *h* was often omitted in words in which it existed
in Classical Latin: *ouve* for *houve; omẽ* for *homem.*

5. The letter *h* was used after a consonant for consonantal *i: sabha* for *sabia* (old); *servho* for *servio* (old); *termho*
for *termio* (old). This use of *h* has survived only in the
graphs *lh* and *nh.*

6. In early Portuguese *ni, n,* and *nn* were used to represent the sound [ɲ], and *li, l,* and *ll* were used to represent
the sound [ʎ]. The graphs *nn* and *ll* came from Spain via
Galicia and are especially common in the "Cancioneiro da
Ajuda."

Pedro A. d'Azevedo states (RL, IX, 263) that the first
known dated occurrence of *lh* was in a document of the
year 1269 and of *nh* in a document of the year 1273.
However, these dates can be moved back slightly, for in
the "Livro de D. João Portel," which Azevedo published
subsequently, *lh* (in *lha*) appears in a document of 1265
(AHP, IV, 306) and *nh* (in *gaanhar*) in a document of

1267 (AHP, VI, 68).[1]  The theory generally accepted for
the origin of these graphs is that they were borrowed from
Provençal (Grund, I, 922, n. 3; Huber, § 61).  The borrowing may have been brought about in several ways: a)
through the reading of Troubadour poetry (RL, XI, 84),
b) through the work of the secretaries of French prelates,
who occupied many of the principal sees in Portugal in the
twelfth and thirteenth centuries (RL, XXVIII, 25), and
c) through the work of reorganization by French scribes
of the chancery of Afonso III or Dinis between the years
1270 and 1280 (CA, I, xv, n. 4).  The theory of Provençal
borrowing is in a measure confirmed by a document dated
1281 in which [ʎ] is represented in a Provençal proper
noun by the graph *lh*, viz., *Vidalhac*, but in all other words
by the graph *ll*, e.g., *fillado* (RL, VII, 73–74).  See also
RL, VI, 263.

a. The sound [ɲ] did not exist in all words in Old Portuguese
in which it exists today.  This is shown by early spellings, e.g.,
*raina* [rɐĩɐ] and *dieiros* in the same text with *senior* and *tenio*
(RL, VIII, 82, A.D. 1214).  The spellings *-iho* and *-iha* (from
Lat. *-inu* and *-ina*), in which *h* was used simply to indicate
hiatus, at first represented the pronunciations [ĩu] and [ĩɐ].  And
the combination *nh* (or *˜h*) in the word *nenhum* (or *nẽhum*) did
not at first represent the sound [ɲ] but came about through the
union in a new compound of the words *nen* (or *nẽ*) and *hum*.  It
thus happened that when [ĩu] and [ĩɐ] became [iɲu] and [iɲɐ]
and when [nẽũ] became [niɲũ], the combination *nh* (and *˜h*),
which had previously been adopted for [ɲ] in other positions,
was already in the proper place.[2]

However, any supposition that this prior occurrence of *nh*
(and *˜h*) in positions where the sound [ɲ] later developed, was

---

[1] Both *lh* and *nh* appear in a document dated 1262 of the "Livro de D. João
Portel" (AHP, VII, 474) but the repeated use of *nh* in the word *dinheiro*, in which
a palatalized nasal had not developed at the time, indicates that this manuscript
is a copy made considerably later than the year 1262.

[2] Obviously the combination *˜h* was used in many positions where the sound [ɲ]
did not later develop, e.g., *mẽhos* for *mẽos* (modern *menos*), *põher* for *põer* (modern
*pôr*).

the origin of the graph *nh*, and later by imitation, of the graph *lh*, cannot be substantiated, in view of the fact that *nh* and *lh* (as well as *mh*, *bh*, *vh*, etc.) appeared before [īu] and [īɐ] became [iɲu] and [iɲɐ]. This is proved by spellings found in early dated documents, e.g., *vinha* (from *vīněam*) and *uelha* in the same text with *dineyros* (RL, IX, 268–269, A.D. 1273); *quihentos* (from OSp. *quiñentos*) and *lhy* in the same text with *muino* and *muĩo* (from *mŏlīnum*) (RL, VIII, 45, A.D. 1293); and *termhos* (RL, IX, 270, A.D. 1273).

**28.** Intrusive Orthographic *p*.

1. The practice in Vulgar Latin and Medieval Latin of inserting a *p* between *m* and *n* for the purpose of preserving the sound of both nasal consonants (GVL, § 307) was continued in Old Portuguese merely by orthographic tradition, as the group was probably pronounced [n] with nasalization of the preceding vowel; e.g., *dampno; solĕpnemente*. That the *p* had no phonetic value is shown by the fact that it was sometimes entirely misplaced, e.g., *compdenar* (FM, II, Glossary) for *condenar*. Cf. FM, I, xxviii.

2. A *p* was likewise inserted in forms of the verb *escrever*, e.g., *escrepver*, *escprito*, perhaps through reminiscence of the Latin forms *scrīpsī* and *scrīptus*. This *p* sometimes took the place of *c*, e.g., *esprever*, *esprito*. Cf. FM, I, xxix.

**29.** Double Vowels.

1. Double vowels first developed through the fall of an intervocalic consonant, e.g., *cree* (from *crēdit*); *poboo* (from *pŏpŭlum*).

2. They continued to be used by tradition long after they had contracted in pronunciation.

3. Later they were used in place of single vowels to indicate nasalization or perhaps the lengthening of the nasalized vowel, e.g., *coontar* (from *compūtāre*); *seentir* (from *sentīre*). In many of these cases, the nasalizing consonant

(intervocalic *n*) had fallen, e.g., *liōões* (from *leōnes*); *maão* (from *manum*).   Cf. Ent, 289.

4. They were also used in place of single tonic vowels after the fall of other intervocalic consonants, e.g., *ceeos* (from *caelos*); *mandaae* (from *mandāte*); *quaaes* (from *quales*).

5. It is thought that they were also used to indicate stress.  This use probably originated through the fact that in their original occurrence (i.e., after the fall of an inter-vocalic consonant) one of the two vowels was usually stressed (FM, I, xxi).

6. They were used by a sort of orthographic contamination, e.g., *deestro* (from *dextrum*) in imitation of *seestro* (from *sinistrum*).

7. Early in the sixteenth century they came to be used to indicate the open sound of the vowel (*a*, *e*, and *o*), the closed sound being indicated by a single vowel.  This use is mentioned in 1536 by Fernão de Oliveira in his "Grammatica da Lingoagem Portuguesa" (Oliv, 28).

## 30. Double Consonants.

1. All double consonants which existed in Classical Latin may be found in Old Portuguese, where they do not, how-ever, represent long sounds.  Intervocalic *rr* and inter-vocalic *ss* are the only double intervocalic letters which represent sounds different from the single intervocalic letter.  The use of intervocalic *ff* for *f*, e.g., *deffender* for *defender*, may have been adopted in order to indicate un-mistakably the sound of *f*, inasmuch as Latin intervocalic short *f* had become *v* in Portuguese and was probably pronounced *v* in the Latin of the time (RF, XXV, 649). Where the scribe used intervocalic *ss* for *s*, e.g., *ussar* for *usar*, intervocalic *s* for *ss*, e.g., *dise* for *disse*, and inter-vocalic *r* for *rr*, e.g., *corer* for *correr*, he simply failed to recognize the difference in sound.   Such spellings may have resulted from imitation of the indiscriminate use of other single and double intervocalic consonants where there was

no difference in pronunciation, e.g., *pallavra* for *palavra; cavalo* for *cavallo.* However, aside from the intervocalic position, most new cases of doubling seem to have had a phonetic purpose.

A. In Old Galician, *ll* and *nn* were used instead of *lh* and *nh.*

2. These are the cases in which double consonants occurred in other than the intervocalic position:

a) Initial *ff* and *ff* after a consonant: *ffe* for *fe; conffirmar.* This use may have developed in imitation of the use of *ff* in the intervocalic position.

b) Initial *ll*: *llãa* for *lã.* This use may indicate a longer sound than modern initial *l*; it is possible that this long sound saved initial *l* from falling when the word in which it stood was joined in close syntactical union with a preceding word ending in a vowel.

c) Final *ll* and *ll* before a consonant: *mortall* for *mortal; malldade* for *maldade.* This use indicates the velar sound [ł], which *l* still has in these positions today.

d) Initial *rr, rr* before and after *l* and *n*, and *rr* after *s: rreter* for *reter; Carrlos* for *Carlos; honrra* for *honra.* This use indicates the more vibrant sound which *r* still has in these positions today.

e) Initial *ss* and *ss* after a consonant: *ssempre* for *sempre; consselho* for *conselho; converssar* for *conversar.* This use was probably adopted to indicate voiceless *s* because of an awareness that in the intervocalic position *ss* was voiceless while *s* was voiced.


31. THE ETYMOLOGICAL PERIOD.

In the etymological period (sometimes called the pseudo-etymological period), Latin and Greek spellings were introduced with utter disregard for pronunciation. This practice had begun long before the sixteenth century in a small group of words, especially in works translated from Latin (see RL, XIX, 64), e.g., *escripto, feicto, nocte, reigno, sancto*,[1] but it was the writers and particularly the printers of the Renaissance who gave it a vogue that was to last down to our times.

We accordingly find *ch, ph, rh, th*, and *y* in words of Greek or supposed Greek origin, e.g., *chrystallino, eschola, phrase, rhetorico, theatro, estylo, nympha;* and *ct, gm, gn, mn, mpt*, and double consonants in words of Latin origin, e.g., *aucthor, fructo, augmento, digno, magno, damno, somno, prompto, bocca, peccar, cabello, setta*. At the same time, orthographic false regressions abounded, e.g., *th* in *thesoura* and in *ethymologia; y* in *phylosophia;* double *c* in *occeano*. Among these belongs the change of final *s* to *z* in *mez, portuguez, poz*, etc., which arose through imitation of words like *simplez, vez, fez*, etc.

Opinion in favor of the new spelling was far from unanimous. Duarte Nunes de Leão condemned it in his "Orthografia da lingoa portuguesa" (1576) as did Alvaro Ferreira de Vera in his "Ortographia ou arte para escrever certo na lingua portuguesa" (1633). Constructive criticism was not lacking but it was generally disregarded. João Franco Barreto in his "Ortografia da lingua portugueza" (1671) first proposed the modern use of accent marks to indicate open and close vowels and the modern use of the final graphs -*ão* and -*am* to distinguish accented and unaccented third plurals and Bento Pereira in his "Ars Grammaticae" (1672) recommended the modern use of *i* and *j*, and *u* and *v*, and condemned the use of double vowels and initial double consonants (Pereira, 287–318).

The eighteenth century was a period of bitter orthographic polemic; it ended with etymological spelling rampant. One book in particular, the "Orthographia ou arte de escrever e pronunciar com acerto a lingua portugueza" of João de Moraes Madureyra Feyjó, which was first

---

[1] The letter inserted in imitation of the Latin spelling was sometimes misplaced, e.g., *scãtifica* (Abraham, § 19, 1) for *sãctifica; maglino* for *maligno*.

printed in 1734, had tremendous influence in the cause of etymological spelling for more than a century and a half. The author not only urged the Latin spelling of newly borrowed words but also their pronunciation according to this spelling (Moraes, 5–7). The restoration of the sound [g] as well as the letter *g* in words like *digno* and *phleugma* resulted from efforts of this kind on the part of grammarians.

While the Spanish Academy was reforming orthography in the eighteenth century on a rational phonetic basis, the Academy of Lisbon was consolidating the tradition of two centuries by setting up etymology as the supreme principle of orthography. Perhaps it was influenced in this policy by French orthography and by a pedantic desire to devise a new mark of distinction for men of letters and the small reading public (RHi, I, 4).

## 32. The Reformed Period.

The *nova ortografia* represents a return to phonetic spelling but it differs from the phonetic spelling of the Middle Ages in that it has been made uniform by convention. It was formulated by a commission appointed by the Portuguese government in 1911 and was officially adopted by Portugal in 1916. Its original form has been slightly altered by subsequent amendments and by the "Acôrdo Ortográfico Luso-Brasileiro," on the basis of which it was finally adopted by Brazil in 1931. Cf. RL, XIV, 200–226; Romão; VO; R-M, 322–323.

# PHONOLOGY

## TONIC VOWELS

**33. V. L. Tonic *a* (Cl. L. *ă* and *ā*).**

1. V. L. tonic *a* > Ptg. *a: prātum* > *prado; bonitātem* > *bondade; căput* > *cabo; măre* > *mar.*

A. Cl. L. *alăcrem* > V. L. *\*álěcrem* > *\*alěcrem* (GVL, § 195, 1) > *alęgre.*

2. V. L. tonic *a* + *i̯* > *ai* or *ei: andamĭum* (Du Cange) > *andaimo; -ārĭum* > *-airo* > *-eiro,* e.g., *contrārĭum* > *contrairo* (old and popular), *primārĭum* > *primeiro; bāsĭum* > *beijo; \*bassĭum* > *baixo; căvĕam* > *gaiva; \*răbĭam* (for *răbĭem*) > *raiva; săpĭam* > *sabia* > *saiba; lāĭcum* > *leigo.*

A. The consonants with which attraction took place in these examples are *b, p, v, m, r, s* and *ss.* A consonant affected by yod (except *s* and *ss*) prevented attraction: *allĭum* > *alho; facĭo* > *faço; aranĕam* > *aranha.* See § 90.

B. Attraction took place relatively late in words in which *ai* did not become *ei*; for example, the change from *sabia* to *saiba* has been ascribed to the end of the thirteenth century (ZRPh, XIX, 515, n. 1). These words probably came into the language late (Behr, 9–12). For an effort to relate this difference in Castilian to syllabication, see Rom, XLI, 248–249. The difference has been explained also as regional in origin, *ei* coming from the north, *ai* from the south (Meier, 28).

C. If *a* and the yod were in contact in Latin, the result was *ei: amāvī* > *amai* > *amei; lāĭcum* > *leigo.* But if hiatus with *e* developed through the fall in Portuguese of an intervocalic consonant, the change to *ei* did not take place: *amātĭs* > *amades* > *amais; tālēs* > *taes* > *tais.* For the development of *réis* (from *regāles*), see § 99, 3 D.

3. V. L. tonic *a* + *i̯* from the palatal consonant of a following group (*ct, sc, x*) > *ei: fascem* > *feixe; fraxĭnum* >

*freixo; lacte* > *leite; plăcĭtum* > *\*plactum* > *preito; saxum* > *seixo.*

A. The vowel was not affected if the group was *gn* or *cl*: *agnum* > *anho; novācŭlam* > *\*novacla* > *navalha.*

4. V. L. tonic *a* + *u̯* and therefore the diphthong *au* > *ou* [o]: *amāvit* > *amaut* > *amou; causam* > *cousa; sapŭit* > *soube; taurum* > *touro.*

A. The intermediate stage was pronounced [ow], the afterglide of which began to disappear probably in the sixteenth century and now survives only in the north of Portugal (Esquisse, § 56 e).

B. It was the consonantal quality of the second element of the diphthong *au* or of its successor *ou* that sometimes prevented the voicing of a following medial consonant, e.g., *paucum* > *pouco; raucum* > *rouco; cautum* > *couto.*

c. Examples of the change to *ou* are found as early as the first half of the tenth century (BF, II, 186).

D. Cl. L. *paupĕrem* > V. L. *\*poperem* (Manual, § 47, 3 a) > *pǫbre.*

E. If the attraction took place late, *au* remained unchanged: *aquam* > *auga* (old and dialectal); *tabŭlam* > *tabua* > *tauba* (Esquisse, § 43 c).

F. The fall of intervocalic *d* took place early enough for the development of *a* + *o* to *ou: vado* > *vou.*

5. V. L. tonic *a* + *l* followed by a consonant > *ou* [o] or *al: altĕrum* > *outro; falcem* > *fouce; saltum* > *souto;* and *altum* > *alto; falsum* > *falso.* See § 94, 1 A and B.

6. V. L. tonic *a* followed by a nasal > [ẽ] or [ɐ̃]: *agnum* > *anho; amat* > *ama; ambos* > *ambos; aranĕam* > *aranha; manum* > *mão; pannum* > *pano; rānam* > *rã; tantum* > *tanto.*

A. The intermediate stage was [ẽ], which has survived before consonant groups beginning with a nasal (cf. § 95, 1), in the diphthong *ão* (§ 78, 3), and after contraction (§ 78, 2). For the change of final [ẽ] to [ẽw], see § 157, 2.

B. This [ɐ̃] closed one more step to [ɔ] in the word *fome* (from *famem*), a change which was brought about through the influence of *come* in such expressions as *Come quem tem fome* (Nascentes). Although spelled *fame*, it is found in rimes with *come* and *home* in the early Cancioneiros (CD, note to line 2741). See LP, I, 251–254 for proverbs and other expressions containing rimes of *fome*, *come*, and *home*, e.g., *Quem tem fôme*, *côme um hôme* (Beira Alta). The *f* in Fr. *soif* arose through similar influence of *beif* in such expressions as *beif se as seif* (Nyrop, I, § 503, 3). For other explanations of *fome*, see Nascentes.

**34.** V. L. Tonic *ę* (Cl. L. *ĕ* and *ae*).

1. V. L. tonic *ę* > Ptg. *ę*: *dĕcem* > *dęz; pĕdem* > *pé; pĕtram* > *pędra; quaerit* > *quęre; lĕvem* > *lęve.*

A. C. L. *stĕllam* > V. L. *\*stēllam* (GVL, § 163) > *estrêla.*
B. The *ę* of *vęspa* (from *vĕspam*) has been explained as due to the influence of *bêsta* (Grund, I, 926).

2. V. L. tonic *ę* + *i̯* > *ę* or *ei*: *cerĕsi̯am* (Vok, I, 192) > *cereja; ingĕni̯um* > *engęnho; matĕri̯am* > *madeira; nĕrvi̯um* (Ainsworth) > *nęrvo; sĕdĕam* > *sęja; supĕrbi̯am* > *sobęrba; tĕrti̯um* > *têrço; vĕni̯o* > *vęnho.*

A. The development to *ei* is found only where the *ę* and the yod were separated by a short *r*. It occurred with other consonants in Old Portuguese, e.g., *cereija* for *cereja* and in dialects, e.g., *beinho* (Opúsculos, II, 204) for *venho.*
B. Final *i* had the same effect as yod: *hĕri* > *eire* (old).
c. Toward the beginning of the nineteenth century, *ę* followed by *ch, j, lh, nh,* or *x,* became [ɐ] in the pronunciation of Lisbon (VPN, 92; Dunn, 10–11).

3. V. L. tonic *ę* in proparoxytones with *e* or *i* in the penult developed as follows:   a) it became *i* if the penult was *i* (from Cl. L. *ĭ*): *dĕcĭmum* > *dízimo; pĕrtĭcam* > *pirtiga* (Grund, I, 927); b) it became *ę* if the penult was *e* (from Cl. L. *ĭ*): *lĕvĭtum* (REW) > *lêvedo; mĕspĭlam* > *nêspera; pĕrdĭtam* > *\*perdeda* > *pęrda* (§ 114); *pĕrsĭcum* > *pêssego;* c) it remained *ę* if the penult was *e* (from Cl. L. *ĕ*): *nĕpĕtam* > *néveda; vĕspĕram* > *véspera.*

A. The form *tíbio* (which is common to Portuguese and Spanish) has been explained as coming from a V. L. *\*tĭpedo* (for *tĕpĭdum*), in which the close *i* arose through the influence of the semantically related *frīgĭdum*. This explanation is all the more convincing because this close *i* is found only in those regions (Portugal and Spain) where the close *i* of *frīgĭdum* survived (Language, XIII, 145–146).

4. V. L. tonic *ę + i̯* from the palatal consonant of a following group (*ct, x, gr*) > *ei: despĕctum* > *despeito; intĕgrum* (§ 3 a) > *inteiro; lĕctum* > *leito; sĕx* > *seis.*

A. This change did not take place if the group was *cl: veclum* (ApPr) > *vęlho*. The *e* of *velho* is sometimes pronounced [ɐ] in Lisbon through the influence of words in *-elho* in which the *e* was originally close. The form *speclum* (ApPr) (for *spĕcŭlum*) probably had *ę* through the influence of the common ending *-ĭcŭlum* (S-G, § 29) and thus became *espęlho.*

5. V. L. tonic *ę + u̯* > *eu: ĕquam* > *euga* (popular).

6. V. L. tonic *ę* in hiatus with a following *a* > *i: jūdaeam* > *judia; mĕam* > *\*mę̧a* (Manual, § 66, 1) > *mia* > *minha.*

A. This change did not take place in later borrowings, e.g., *rĕam* > *ree* > *ré.*

7. V. L. tonic *ę* in hiatus with a following *o* > *ę: dĕus* > *dęus; ĕgo* > *eo* (GVL, § 385) > *ęu; jūdaeum* > *judęu; mĕum* > *męu.*

A. These words rime in the early Cancioneiros with each other but not with the third singular ending *-eu* of weak preterits; it is, therefore, likely that the *e* had not closed at that time.

B. If the hiatus arose relatively late, that is, in a late borrowing or through the fall in Portuguese of an intervocalic consonant, this change did not take place: *rĕum* > *réu; caelum* > *céu.*

8. V. L. tonic *ę* followed by a syllable ending in *o* > *ę: catĕllum* > *cadęlo; mĕtum* > *mędo.*

9. V. L. tonic *ę* followed by a consonant group beginning with *m* or *n* > [ẽ]: *dentem* > *dente* [dẽntə]; *tempus* > *tempos* [tẽmpuʃ].

A. In some dialects the vowel did not close (Esquisse, § 40 b; RL, II, 111; RL, XI, 270).

10. V. L. tonic ẹ + a final nasal consonant, + an *n* that became final in Portuguese, or + *nes* > [ẽ], then [ẽj] and in the region between Lisbon and Coimbra [ĕj]: *quĕm* > *quem* [kĕj]; *bĕne* > *bem* [bĕj]; *vĕnit* > *vem* [vĕj]; *tĕnes* > *tens* [tĕjʃ].

**35. V. L. Tonic ẹ (Cl. L. ē, ĭ, and *oe*).**

1. V. L. tonic ẹ > Ptg. ẹ: *acētum* > *azẹdo*; *cĭto* > *cẹdo*; *sĭtim* > *sẹde*; *vĭrĭdem* > *vẹrde*.

A. Cl. L. ĭ became *i* in a few learned and semi-learned words: *artĭcŭlum* > *artigoo* > *artigo*; *fĭrmum* > *firme*; *lĭbrum* > *livro*; *mĭssam* > *missa*; *pĭum* > *pio*. It is possible that the *i* of Latin *benignum, malignum* and *dignum* was long (cf. CR, XV, 311–314), although the development of *gn* in OPtg. *benino, malino* and *dino* shows these words to be semi-learned. *Cĭrcum* > *cêrco* and also *circo*. Likewise *cĭppum* > *cẹpo* and *cipo* unless *cipo* came from *\*cīppum*, which may have arisen through the influence of *cīpum* on *cĭppum* (GVL, § 163). The *i* of *siso* (from *sẹso* < *sensum*) and the *i* and the accent of *juiz* (from *jūdĭcem*) were probably due to the influence of *juizo* (cf. RL, XXIII, 86); that this accent was an early development is shown by the rime *juyz : fiz* (CV, No. 1023). *Chrĭstam* > *crista* and *ēscam* (LEW) > *isca* through the closing effect of *s* plus a stop in Vulgar Latin (SM, I, 614).

B. There was a tendency to pronounce ẹ open in learned words, e.g., *complētum* > *complẹto*; *fētĭdum* > *fétido*; *sēdem* > *séde*. Cf. GIt, § 21 and M-L, Gram, I, § 15. This tendency was probably intensified by a following *r*: *vērum* > *vẹro*. Cl. L. *nĭvem* > V. L. *\*nẹve* (cf. Sp. *nieve*), whence Ptg. *nẹve*. The *e* of *sé* (from *sēdem*) may have developed in imitation of the Old Portuguese third singular present indicative *sẹ* (§ 198, 3). There is no apparent reason for the opening of ẹ in *fé* (from *fĭdem*) and *véu* (from *vēlum*).

2. V. L. tonic ẹ + i̯ > *i* or *ei*: *fērĭam* > *feira*; *mystērĭum* > *misteiro* (old); *sēpĭam* > *siba*; *vindēmĭam* > *vindima*.

A. The consonants with which the change took place in these examples are *m*, *p*, and *r*, the change to *ei* appearing only with *r*. *Círio* (from *cērĕum*) is probably a borrowing from Spanish.

B. In late learned and semi-learned words the yod had no effect whatever and the vowel opened to *ę* as in other learned words where there was no yod (§ 35, 1 B): *cērĕum* > *céreo;* *dēvĭum* > *dévio;* *ēbrĭum* > *ébrio;* *mystērĭum* > *mistério;* *nĭtĭdum* > *nédio.*

C. A consonant affected by yod prevented the *ę* from closing: *cĭlĭa* > *cęlha;* *cerevĭsĭam* > *cervęja;* *consĭlĭum* > *consęlho; justĭ-* *tĭam* > *justęza; stamĭnĕam* > *estamęnha; vĭdĕo* > *vęjo; vĭtĭum* > *vêzo.* For the sound of *e* in some of these words in the pronunciation of Lisbon, see § 34, 2 c.

The word *tainha* is not an exception, as it comes, not from *tagēnĭa* (Facciolati) but from *\*tagenia* with the accent of the Greek word ταγηνίαν, thus: *\*tagēnia* > *taêia* > *taiia* (§ 99, 3) > *tainha.* Nor is the word *juizo* an exception as it comes, not from *judĭcĭum* but from *\*judicĭum*, which arose through the influence of the suffix *-ĭcĭum.* The change to *ei* is found in some of these words in Old Portuguese, e.g., *cerveija* for *cerveja* and in dialects, e.g., *beijo* (Opúsculos, II, 204) for *vejo.*

D. In early learned and semi-learned words Cl. L. *ĭ* followed by a consonant affected by yod became *i: ervĭlĭam* > *ervilha; justĭtĭam* > *justiça; mĭlĭum* > *milho; mirabĭlĭa* > *maravilha; tĭ-* *nĕam* > *tinha; vĭtĭum* > *viço.* There is other evidence that some of these words are semi-learned, viz., the development of *t + ĭ* in *justiça, viço*, as compared with *justeza, vêzo* (cf. § 89, 4 A). In purely learned words the yod did not affect either the vowel or the consonant: *cĭlĭum* > *cílio; exĭlĭum* > *exílio; famĭlĭam* > *fa-* *mília; mĭnĭum* > *minio;* although it partially affected a *t: vĭtĭum* > *vício.*

E. If the yod developed through hiatus after the fall in Portuguese of an intervocalic consonant, the result was *ei: habētis* > *havedes* > *haveis.*

3. V. L. tonic *ę + ĭ* from the palatal consonant of a following group (*ct, sc, gr*) > *ei: benedĭctum* > *bēeito* (old); *pĭscem* > *peixe; strĭctum* > *estreito; filĭctum* > *feito* (old); *nĭgram* > *neira* (RL, XXI, 271).

A. The vowel was not affected if the group was *cl, gl,* or *gn:
apicŭlam > abę̄lha; artĭcŭlum > artę̄lho; \*impĭgnus > empę̄nhos;
lĭgnum > lę̄nho; tēgŭlam > tę̄lha.* For the sound of *e* in these
words in the pronunciation of Lisbon, see § 34, 2 c.

B. Forms such as *sortilha* (from *sortĭcŭlam*) and *lentilha* (from
*lentĭcŭlam*) resulted from confusion of the suffixes *-ĭcŭlam* and
*-ĭcŭlam* (GVL, § 42, 2).

4. V. L. tonic *ę* followed by final *ĭ > i: fēcī > fiz; -ĭstī*
(2d sg. perf. ind.) *> -iste* (old); *vigĭntī > viinte > vinte.*

5. V. L. tonic *ę* in proparoxytones with *e* or *i* in the
penult developed as follows: a) it became *i* if the penult
was *i* (from Cl. L. *ĭ*): *dēbĭtam > dívida; lēgĭtĭmum > leĭdimo
> liidimo > lídimo; sērĭcum > \*sirigo > sirgo* (§ 52, 1);
b) it remained *ę* if the penult was *e* (from Cl. L. *ĭ*): *bĭbĭtum >
bêbedo.* Cf. M-L, Gram, I, § 80.

6. V. L. tonic *ę* in hiatus with a following *a > i: \*dĭam*
(for *dĭem*) *> dia; vĭam > via.*

7. V. L. tonic *ę* in hiatus with a following *a* or *o* through
the fall in Portuguese of an intervocalic consonant *> ei:
aliēnum > alhę̄o > alheio; crēdo > crę̄o > creio; foedum >
feio; sĭnum > seio; tēlam > teia; vēnam > veia.*

A. The change to *ei* did not take place until the beginning of
the sixteenth century.

8. V. L. tonic *ę* followed by a syllable ending in *a > ę̄:
apothēcam > bodę̄ga; ĭlla > ę̄la; mētam > mę̄da; monētam
> moę̄da; rēgŭlam > rę̄gra; tēlam > tę̄la; vēla > vę̄la.*

A. Some of these words are learned or semi-learned.

9. V. L. tonic *ę* followed by a syllable ending in *o > i:
ĭpsum > isso.*

10. V. L. tonic *ę* followed by [ŋk] or [ŋg] *> i: domĭnĭcum
> domingo; lĭngŭam > língua; syrĭngam > seringa; pro-
pĭnquum > provinco* (Eluc).

11. V. L. tonic *ę* followed by *l >* Ptg. *ę̄: crūdēlem > cruę̄l;
fĭdēlem > fię̄l.*

A. The following *l* may have caused the *ę* to open in *véu* (section 1 B above) and in *tela* and *vela* (section 8 above).

**36.** V. L. TONIC *į* (CL. L. *ī*).

1. V. L. tonic *į* > Ptg. *i: audīre* > *ouvir; frīgĭdum* > *frio; lītem* > *lide*.

A. The development of *pêga* (from *pĭcam*) and *estêva* (from *stĭvam*) is not clear.

2. V. L. tonic *į* + *į* > *i: dīxī* > *disse; fīlĭum* > *filho; frĭctum* > *frito*.

A. The form *coelho* (from *cŭnīcŭlum*) resulted from confusion of the suffixes *-īcŭlum* and *-ĭcŭlum* (GVL, § 42, 2).

**37.** V. L. TONIC *ǫ* (CL. L. *ŏ* ).

1. V. L. tonic *ǫ* > Ptg. *ǫ: fŏrtem* > *fǫrte; hŏspĭtem* > *hóspede; pŏrtam* > *pǫrta; rŏtam* > *rǫda*.

2. V. L. tonic *ǫ* + *į* > *ǫ* or *oi: cŏrĭum* > *coiro; fŏlĭa* > *fǫlha; fŏrtĭam* (Du Cange) > *fôrça; hŏdĭe* > *hoje;* \**mŏrĭo* (for *mŏrĭor*) > *moiro* (old); *Saxŏnĭam* > *Sansonha* (old); *sŏmnĭum* > *sǫnho*.

A. The change to *oi* is found only where the *ǫ* and the yod were separated by a short *r*. It is also found under the same conditions in learned words in modern popular speech: *histŏrĭam* > *história* > *histoira* (popular); *memŏrĭam* > *memória* > *memoira* (popular). The change to *oi* is found likewise where the *ǫ* and the yod were separated by a single *m* or *n* in words in which the action of the yod was comparatively late, that is, words with Romance yod or semi-learned words: *cŏmĕdo* > *comeo* > *coimo* (old); *daemŏnĭum* > *demónio* > *demoino* (FM, II, Glossary; and popular).

3. V. L. tonic *ǫ* + *į* from the palatal consonant of a following group > *oi: nŏctem* > *noite; ŏcto* > *oito*.

A. The *i* of *oi* was absorbed in Modern Portuguese by a following [ʃ]: *cŏxum* (LEW, s.v. *coxim*) > *coixo* > *coxo; cŏxam* > *coixa* (RL, XXVII, 21) > *coxa*.

B. If the group was *cl*, the vowel simply closed to *ǫ: ŏcŭlum* > *ŏclum* > *ôlho; rŏtŭlam* > \**rŏclam* > *rôlha*.

4. V. L. tonic ǫ + u̯ > ǫ: pŏtŭit > poude > pôde; pŏsŭit > pôs.

A. The intermediate stage was ou, which had become ǫ before the time of the change of au to ou.

5. V. L. tonic ǫ followed by a syllable ending in o > ǫ: fŏcum > fǫgo; pŏpŭlum > pǫvo; pŏsĭtum > pǫsto.

A. The same change took place if the ǫ was in hiatus with final o: tertiŏlum (Du Cange) > terçoo > terçô.

6. V. L. tonic ǫ followed by a nasal consonant > [õ] or [o]: dŏmĭnam > dǫna; bŏnam > bõa > bǫa; pŏntem > ponte [põntə]; lŏnge > lǫnge; sŏnum > sõo > sǫm; bonum > bõo > bǫm.

A. In some dialects the vowel did not close (Esquisse, § 40 b; RL, II, 111; RL, XI, 270).

B. Even after the nasal resonance disappeared, the vowel remained close, e.g., bǫa.

**38.** V. L. Tonic ǫ (Cl. L. ō and ŭ).

1. V. L. tonic ǫ > Ptg. ǫ: amōrem > amǫr; autŭmnum > outǫno; bŭccam > bǫca; cŭrsum > cǫrso; fŭndum > fǫndo (old); lŭmbum > lǫmbo; lŭtum > lôdo; nōmen > nǫme; pŭnctum > pǫnto; trŭncum > trǫnco; tŭrdum > tǫrdo; tŭrpem > tǫrpe; tŭrrim > tôrre; ŭndam > ǫnda; ŭnde > ǫnde; vōta > bǫda.

A. Cl. L. ō became Ptg. ǫ in a group of words most of which are learned or semi-learned: atrōcem > atrǫz; ferōcem > ferǫz; remōtum > remǫto; sacerdōtem > sacerdǫte; sōlem > sǫl; sonōrum > sonǫro; terrae mōtum > terremǫto; velōcem > velǫz; vōcem > vǫz; vōtum > vǫto.

B. Cl. L. ŭ became Ptg. u in a group of words most of which are learned or semi-learned: crŭcem > cruz; cŭlpam > culpa; cŭrtum > curto; cŭrvum > curvo; fŭndum > fundo; fŭrtum > furto; mŭndum > mundo; secŭndum > segundo; sŭlcum > sulco; sŭrdum > surdo; ŭrsum > usso (old) and urso. It is possible that this u was in some words the result of the influence of an initial palatal: *jŭgum* > *jugo; jŭstum* > *justo; plŭmbum* > *chumbo.*

c. The *ǫ* of *jǫvem* (from *jŭvĕnem*) has been explained as due to the dissimilating effect of the *v* (Rad, 14). Cl. L. *nōbĭlem* > semi-learned *nǫbre*, in which the *ǫ* was due to the influence of *pobre.* Cl. L. *nŭcem* > V. L. *\*nŏcem* (cf. Sp. *nuez*) > *nǫz.* Cl. L. *nŭram* (for *nŭrum*), through the influence of *sŏcram* or *sŏrōr,* > V. L. *\*nŏram* (cf. Sp. *nuera,* It. *nuora*) > Ptg. *nǫra* (see REW). For Cl. L. *octōbrem* there was apparently a V. L. *octŭbrem* (Carnoy, 64), whence *outubro.* The *ǫ* of *tǫsse* (from *tŭssim*) may have developed in imitation of the third singular present indicative *tǫsse* (§ 176, 3). There is no apparent reason for the opening of *o* in *nó* (from *nōdum*).

2. V. L. tonic *ǫ* + *i̯* > *ǫ, u, oi,* or *ui: cĭcōnĭam* > *cegǫnha; pŭtĕum* > *pǫço;* *\*risōnĕum* > *risǫnho; verecŭndĭam* > *vergǫnha; cŭnĕum* > *cunho; testĭmōnĭum* > *testemunho; querimōnĭam* > *caramunha; gŭrgŭlĭo* > *gorgulho; nastŭrtĭum* > *mastruço; augŭrĭum* > *agoiro; calŭmnĭam* > *coima; cŭphĭam* (Du Cange) > *coifa; gŭvĭam* (Du Cange) > *goiva; rŭssĕum* > *roixo* (Opúsculos, II, 34) > *rǫxo; sal mŭrĭam* > *salmoira; tonsōrĭa* > *tesoira; plŭvĭam* > *chuiva* > *chuva; rŭbĕum* > *ruivo; intrōĭtum* (LEW, s.v. *intrā*) > *entruido* > *entrudo.*

A. The consonants with which attraction took place in these examples are *b, f, v, m, r,* and *ss.* It also took place in learned words in modern popular speech where the *ǫ* and the yod were separated by a single *r* or *n: glōrĭam* > *gloira* (popular); *Antōnĭum* > *Antoino* (Estremenho). The attracted vowel disappeared in *roxo* and *chuva.*

B. It is not clear why some forms have *o* or *oi* while others have *u* or *ui.* The theory has been advanced that *u* came directly from Cl. L. *ŭ* before the change to *ǫ* (RHi, LXXVII, 8–9; MP, XI, 349).

C. In learned words the yod had no effect whatever and the vowel opened to *ǫ* as in other learned words where there was no yod (§ 38, 1 A): *cerĭmōnĭam* > *cerimónia; glōrĭam* > *glória; testĭmōnĭum* > *testemónio.*

3. V. L. tonic *ǫ* in proparoxytones with an *i* in the

penult > *u: \*dŭbĭtam* > *dúvida*.

4. V. L. *ǫ* + *i* from the palatal consonant of a following
group > *u: lŭctam* > *luita* > *luta; trŭctam* > *truita* > *truta*.

A. Aside from certain dialects, where the intermediate stage
*ui* has survived (Esquisse, § 56 i), the general tendency is for *ui*,
whatever its origin, to contract to *u*, e.g., *commūnes* > *comuũes*
(BF, II, 215 and 220) > *comuns; plŭvĭam* > *chuiva* > *chuva*.

B. If the group was *cl* or *gn* (or *ngl*), the vowel simply closed
to *u: acŭcŭlam* (Du Cange) > *acŭclam* > *agulha; pŭgnum* >
*punho; ungŭlam* > *unha*.

5. V. L. tonic *ǫ* + *lt* > *ut: ausculto* > *ascuito* > *escuto;*
*mŭltum* > *muito; vŭltŭrem* > *abuitre* > *abutre*.

A. The intermediate stage *ui* has been preserved in *muito*
through the influence of the apocopated form *mui*.

6. V. L. tonic *ǫ* followed by final *i* > *u: \*fŭgī* (for *fŭge*)
(2d sg. impv.) > *fuge* (old); *pŏtŭī* > *\*pǫdi* (§ 37, 4) > *pude;*
*fŭī* > *fui*.

7. V. L. tonic *ǫ* followed by a syllable ending in *a* > *ǫ:*
*fōrmam* (LEW) > *fǫrma; hōram* > *hǫra; -ōsam* > *-ǫsa*, e.g.,
*formōsam* > *formǫsa*.

8. V. L. tonic *ǫ* followed by a syllable ending in *o* > *u:*
*tōtum* (neuter) > *tǫdo* > *tudo*.

9. V. L. tonic *ǫ* in hiatus with *a* > *u: dŭas* > *duas; sŭam*
> *sua*.

10. V. L. tonic *ǫ* and final *o* in hiatus > *ou: dŭōs* > *dous;*
*sŭŭm* > *sou* (old).

11. V. L. tonic *ǫ* + *l* > *ǫ: dŭlcem* > *dǫce; insŭlsum* >
*ensǫsso*.

12. V. L. tonic *ǫ* followed by [ŋk] or [ŋg] became *u:*
*jŭncum* > *junco; nŭmquam* > *nunca*.

39. V. L. TONIC *u* (CL. L. *ū*).

1. V. L. tonic *u* > Ptg. *u: acūtum* > *agudo; mūtum* >
*mudo; scūtum* > *escudo*.

2. V. L. tonic *u* + *i* remained unchanged: *addūxit* >

*adusse* (old); *frūctum* > *fruito* > *fruto;* *lūctum* > *luito* > *luto;* *pecŭlium* > *pegulho.*

A. For the contraction of *ui* to *u,* see § 38, 4 A.

## PRETONIC VOWELS

**40. V. L. PRETONIC *a* (CL. L. *ă* AND *ā*).**

1. V. L. pretonic *a* > Ptg. *a* [ɐ]: *ăpertum* > *aberto;* *cătēnam* > *cadeia; sāpōnem* > *sabāo.*

2. V. L. pretonic *a* + *i̯* > *ai* or *ei: ārĕŏlam* > *eiró* (RL, XV, 342); *bāsiāre* > *beijar;* *\*bassiāre* > *baixar; disvăriāre* (Du Cange) > *desvairar; \*gāviottam* > *gaivota; săpiāmos* > *saibamos.*

A. The consonants with which attraction took place in these examples are *p, v, r, s* and *ss.* The same change took place with a Romance yod (the consonant being *m*): *\*exfamināre* > *esfamear* > *esfaimar.* A consonant affected by yod (except *s* and *ss*) prevented attraction: *ăliēnum* > *alheio; \*māneānam* > *manhã; rătiōnem* > *razom* > *razão.* The *e* of such forms as *menhã* and *rezão,* which arose in the late fifteenth or early sixteenth century, developed by dissimilation.

B. This change took place also if the *a* and the yod were in contact in Latin: *mājorīnum* > *meirinho;* and if the yod developed through the fall in Portuguese of an intervocalic consonant: *\*adradīcāre* > *arreigar; trādĭtōrem* > *treidor* (old).

3. V. L. pretonic *a* + *i̯* from the palatal consonant of a following group (*ct, x, gr*) > *ei: factiōnem* > *feição; frāgrāre* > *flagrāre* (GVL, § 292) > *cheirar; jactāre* > *jeitar* (Eluc); *lactūcam* > *leituga; laxāre* > *leixar* (old).

A. In learned words, *a* followed by *ct* (in which *c* did not become a yod) remained unchanged, viz., [a]: *actiōnem* > *acção; activum* > *activo.* If the group was *pt,* the *a* remained [a] whether the *p* fell in pronunciation or not: *aptitudĭnem* > *aptidão* [aptidẽw]; *baptizāre* > *baptizar* [batizar]. In the earlier learned borrowings *praticar* (from *practicāre*) and *tratar* (from *tractāre*), the *a* has become [ɐ].

4. V. L. pretonic *a* + *u̯* and therefore the diphthong

*au* > *ou* [o]: *audīre* > *ouvir; laudāre* > *louvar;* \**săpŭĕram* (for *săpŭĕram*) > *soubera.*

A. In some words *au* had become *o* in Vulgar Latin, e.g., *oriclam* (GVL, § 229, 7) > *orelha.*

B. V. L. *au* followed by a syllable containing accented *u* > *a: augŭrium* > \**agŭrium* (GVL, § 228) > *agoiro; auscultat* > *asculta* (GVL, § 228) > *ascuita* (old). For an analysis of this change, see RHi, LXXVII, 155.

C. If the diphthong *au* arose in Old Portuguese through the fall of an intervocalic consonant, no further change took place: *salūtāre* > *saudar;* \**a + lo* > *au;* although in Old Portuguese these words are occasionally found with *au* changed to *ou: soudar, ou.*

5. In learned words the prefix *ab* followed by *s* > *au: absentem* > *ausente; abstinentiam* > *austinencia* (BF, I, 126); *absolūtum* > *ausoluto* (old).

A. This change was condemned in the eighteenth century (Moraes, 158).

B. In the popular development of this prefix, the *b* fell, e.g., *abstinentiam* > *astēeça* (Rom, XI, 363).

6. V. L. pretonic *a + l* followed by a consonant > *ou* [o] or *al* [ał]: \**alĭqu'ūnum* (GVL, § 71) > *algum; altarĭum* > *outeiro; palpāre* > *poupar* and *palpar.* See § 94, 1 A and B.

7. V. L. pretonic *a* preceded or followed by a labial > *o: quadraginta* > *quarenta* > *corenta* (old and popular); *quam magnum* > *quamanho* > *comanho* (old); Germ. *wardōn* (REW) > *guarir* > *gorir* (old); cf. Rom, X, 341–342; M-L, Gram, I, § 363.

8. V. L. pretonic *a* and tonic *a* in hiatus contracted to *a* [a]: *pălātĭum* > *paaço* > *paço; pānātam* (Du Cange) > *paada* > *pada.*

9. V. L. pretonic *a* and intertonic *a* in hiatus contracted to *a* [a]: \**pānatarĭum* > *paadeiro* > *padeiro; sānātīvum* (Du Cange) > *saadio* > *sadio.*

10. V. L. pretonic *a* and tonic *ę* or *ę* in hiatus > *ę: ānĕllum* > *āello* > *ęlo; săgĭttam* > *saeta* > *sęta.*

A. If the contracted vowel was followed by a group beginning with a nasal, it closed, according to § 34, 9: *călĕntem* > *caente* > *queente* > *quẹnte*.

11. V. L. pretonic *a* and tonic *ọ* in hiatus > *ọ*: *majōrem* > *maor* > *mọọr* > *mór*.

A. If the contracted vowel was followed by a nasal, it closed, according to § 37, 6: *palŭmbum* > *paombo* > *poombo* > *pọmbo*.

12. V. L. pretonic *a* in hiatus with tonic *i* remained: *sălīre* > *sair; cănīnum* > *cainho*.

13. V. L. pretonic *a* in hiatus with tonic *u* remained: *pădŭlēs* (Du Cange; for *pălūdēs*) > *paúis; salūtem* > *saúde*.

41. V. L. PRETONIC *ẹ* (CL. L. *ē*, *ĭ*, *oe*, *ĕ* AND *ae*).

1. V. L. pretonic *ẹ* > Ptg. *e* [ə]: *caepŭllam* > *cebola; foetōrem* > *fedor; pĭcāre* > *pegar; sēcūrum* > *seguro; sermōnem* > *sermom* > *sermão*.

A. Some words in which this change took place were later replaced by regressive words: *fĭgūram* > *fegura* (old), replaced by *figura; lĭcentĭam* > *lecença* (old), replaced by *licença; virtūtem* > *vertude* (old), replaced by *virtude*.

2. When pretonic *e* was at the same time the initial letter of the word, it remained unchanged in spelling but came to be pronounced [i] in Modern Portuguese: *aeternum* > *eterno; ervĭlĭam* > *ervilha*.

A. The *i* of *igreja* (from *eclĕsĭam*) and of *idade* (from *aetātem*), as is shown by the spelling, developed much earlier. But the change of the *cl* of *eclĕsĭam* to *gr* was a semi-learned development (§ 86, 1 d). For an attempt to explain the *i* of these words, see RL, XIII, 433–434. Cf. section 4 A below.

The eighteenth century spellings *egreja* and *edade* were used in imitation of the Latin spellings and of the spelling of other words with initial *e*, now come to be pronounced [i].

3. V. L. pretonic *ẹ* + *i* > *i* or *ei*: *laesiōnem* > *lijom* (old); *prensiōnem* > *\*presionem* > *prijom* (old); *serviāmus* > *sirvamos; vindēmiāre* > *vindimar; fĕriāmus* > *feiramos* (old); *fēriāri* > *feirar*.

A. The change to *ei* took place if the intervening consonant was a short *r*. The change to *i* took place if the intervening consonant was a short *s* and in all other cases except where the yod affected the consonant preceding it. In this case the *e* remained unaffected: *mĕliōrem* > *melhor;* \**mētiāmus* (for *mētiāmur*) > *meçamos; prētiāre* > *prezar; sĕniōrem* > *senhor; videāmus* > *vejamos.* The palatalized consonants [ʒ], [ɲ], and [ʎ], produced by the yod in some of these words, later closed the *e* to [ɪ], a change that is only occasionally shown orthographically: *mĕliōrem* > *milhor* (old); *tĭnĕŏlam* > *tinhó.* The change to [ɪ] took place whether the palatalized consonant was produced by yod or not, e.g., *regendum* > *regendo* > [rɪʒẽndu]; it also took place before palatalized *s* (*s* + consonant), e.g., *vestīre* > *vestir* [vɪʃtir], and after initial *ch*, e.g., *plicāre* > *chegar* [ʃɪgar].

In *história* (for *hestoria* < *hĭstŏrĭam*) and *mistura* (for *mestura* < *mĭstūram*), the change to *i* was a regression to the Latin form and not a result of the later normal development of *e* before palatalized *s*.

The word *humilhar* (from *hŭmĭliāre*) is semi-learned.

4. V. L. pretonic *ę* + *i̯* from the palatal consonant of a following group (*ct, sc, x*) > *ei: fictĭcĭum* > *feitiço; lĕctūram* > *leitura; miscēre* > *meixer* (old).

A. Initial *ei* became *i: exemptum* > *eisento* > *isento;* \**exĭtum* (for *exĭtum*) > *eixido* > *ixido* (old). Learned spellings conceal this change in many words beginning in *ex-*, e.g.: *exactum* > *exacto* [ɐjzatu] or [izatu]. This was the regular development of OPtg. *ei*, no matter what its origin: *eclĕsĭam* > *eigreja* > *igreja; ĭnĭmīcum* > *eimigo* > *imigo* (old). For the prefix *enx-*, see § 111, 3.

B. If the group was *ct* plus yod, the diphthong was formed by the yod which came from [k], while the action of the following yod was limited to its effect on the *t: correctiōnem* > *correição; directiōnem* > *direiçom* (old). The development of *lição* (from *lectiōnem*) is not clear. In learned words, the [k] did not become a yod but fell in pronunciation, and the *e* has become [ɛ]: *directiōnem* > *direcção.*

5. V. L. pretonic *ę* followed by a labial > *o: ĭmāgĭnem* > *imagem* > *omagem* (Rom, X, 336); *sepultūram* > *sepultura*

> *sŏpultura* (RL, XVI, 11); *\*sĭmĭlĭāre* > *semelhar* > *somelhar* (old).

A. This change is common in certain dialects, e.g., Ptg. *beber* > *bober;* Ptg. *semana* > *somana* (RL, XXVII, 103–104). In some dialects the *o* closes to *u*, e.g., Ptg. *beber* > *buber;* Ptg. *semana* > *sumana* (Esquisse, § 69 c; RL, V, 145; RL, XI, 274; RL, XII, 305).

6. V. L. pretonic *ę* followed by *ų* > *i: aequālem* > *igual;* *\*mĭnuāre* (for *mĭnuĕre*) > *minguar.*

7. V. L. pretonic *ę* followed by *l* + a consonant > [ɛ]: *dēlĭcātum* > *delgado; \*bellitātem* > *beldade.*

8. V. L. pretonic *ę* preceded or followed by *r* sometimes fell: *perĭcŭlum* > *perigo* > *prigo* (old); *quĭrĭtāre* > *\*c'rĭtāre* (GVL, § 229) > *gritar; thērĭăcam* > *theriaga* > *triaga* (popular); *bērillum* > Sp. *brillo* > *brilho.*

A. This change took place in Vulgar Latin and in Portuguese.

9. V. L. pretonic *ę* followed by *r* > *a: aerāmen* > *arame; serrāre* (Du Cange, s.v. *serāre*) > *çarrar* (old); *quĕrimōnĭam* > *caramunha; \*verrēre* (for *verrĕre*) > *varrer.*

10. V. L. pretonic *ę* followed by a consonant group beginning with *m* or *n* > [ē]: *mendĭcum* > *mendigo; mĕmŏrāre* > *lembrar.*

A. When pretonic initial *ę*, followed by a consonant group beginning with *m* or *n*, was at the same time the initial letter of the word, it generally became [ī]: *intrāre* > *entrar; implicāre* > *empregar.*

11. V. L. pretonic *ę* followed by [ŋg] > *i: vĭndicāre* > *vingar; \*nec-ūnum* > *nengum* > *ningum* (old).

12. V. L. pretonic *ę* and a following tonic *ę* in hiatus > *ę: vĭdēre* > *vęer* > *vęr; sĭgĭllum* > *sęęllo* > *sêlo.*

13. V. L. pretonic *ę* and a following intertonic *ę* in hiatus > *ę: crēdĭtōrem* > *creedor* > *crędor; mĕdĭcīnam* > *meezinha* > *męzinha; praedĭcāre* > *preegar* > *prègar.*

14. V. L. pretonic *ę* and tonic *į* in hiatus > *i: \*cĭnĭtĭa* > *cęįnza* > *ciinza* > *cinza; \*crēdĭtum* > *cręįdo* > *criido* > *crido; vĕnīre* > *vęįr* > *viir* > *vir.*

15. V. L. pretonic *ę* in hiatus with tonic *a, o, u* or *ę* > *i*

(sometimes *e* pronounced [j]): *crĕātum* > *criado; lĕōnem* > *leom* > *leão; minūtum* > *miudo; vēnĕria* > *veeira* > *vieira.*

**42.** V. L. PRETONIC ĭ (CL. L. *ĭ*).

V. L. pretonic ĭ > Ptg. *i: dīcendum* > *dizendo; prīmārium* > *primeiro.*

**43.** V. L. PRETONIC ọ (Cl. L. *ō*, *ŭ*, AND *ŏ*).

1. V. L. pretonic ọ > Ptg. *o* [u]: *cŭpidĭtĭam* (Du Cange) > *cobiça; dŏrmīre* > *dormir; fŏrmīcam* > *formiga; monstrāre* > *mostrar; plōrāre* > *chorar; pŏtēre* (GVL, § 403, 1) > *poder; sŭperāre* > *sobrar; sŭperbiam* > *soberba.*

A. In some dialects this *o* became *e*, e.g., Ptg. *procurar* > *precurar* (RL, XI, 271); Ptg. *fortuna* > *fertuna* (RL, XXVII, 107).

2. V. L. pretonic ọ + ĭ > *u* or *oi: dŏrmiāmus* > *durmamos;* \**mŏriātis* (for *mŏriāmĭnī*) > *moirades* (old).

A. The change to *oi* took place if the consonant separating the *o* and the yod was a short *r*. The change to *u* took place in all other cases except where the yod affected the consonant preceding it. In this case the *o* remained, although it too came to be pronounced [u], in accordance with § 43, 1: *mŭlĭĕrem* > \**mŭlĭĕrem* > *molher* (old); \**pōneāmus* (for *pōnāmus*) > *ponhamos. Molher* [muʎer] came to be spelled *mulher* in the course of the sixteenth century in imitation of its Latin etymon and of Spanish *mujer.*

3. V. L. pretonic ọ + ĭ from the palatal consonant of a following group > *oi: octāvum* > *oitavo.* See § 92, 7 c.

A. If the group was *gn*, the vowel became *u* or *o* [u]: *cognātum* > *cunhado; cognōsco* > *conheço.*

4. V. L. pretonic ọ (from Cl. L. *ŭ*) + *lt* > *ut: auscultāre* > *ascuitar* > *escutar; cŭltellum* > *cuitello* > *cutelo.*

5. V. L. pretonic ọ + ŭ > *o: pŏtuissem* > *podesse* (old); *pŏsuissem* > *posesse* (old).

6. V. L. pretonic ọ followed by a consonant group beginning with *m* or *n* > [ō]: *rŭmpendum* > *rompendo; compŭtāre* > *contar.*

A. Words in which [ū] appears may be learned or semi-learned: *umbilīcum* > *umbigo; unguentum* > *ungüento*.   Popular forms of these words are *embigo* and *enguento*.   For *cumprir* (from *complīre* for *complēre*), see § 176, 8 B.

7. V. L. pretonic *ǫ* followed by *l* + a consonant > *o* [o]: *\*voltāre* (REW) > *voltar; volvendum* > *volvendo*.

8. V. L. pretonic *ǫ* and tonic *ǫ* in hiatus > *ǫ: cŏlōrem* > *coor* > *côr*.

9. V. L. pretonic *ǫ* and intertonic *ǫ* in hiatus > *ǫ: cŏlō-rātum* > *cǫrado*.

10. V. L. pretonic *ǫ* in hiatus with tonic *a, e,* or *i* > *o* [u] or [w]: *sōlānum* > *soão; vŏlāre* > *voar; dŏlēre* > *doer; mŏnē-tam* > *moeda; pŏlīre* > *poir; mŏlīnum* > *moinho*.

**44.** V. L. PRETONIC *ụ* (CL. L. *ū*).

V. L. pretonic *ụ* > Ptg. *u: dūrāre* > *durar; mūrālĭa* > *muralha*.

## FINAL VOWELS

**45.** V. L. FINAL *a* (CL. L. *ă* AND *ā*).

1. V. L. final *a* > Ptg. *a: causam* > *cousa; mensam* > *mesa; clamat* > *chama; hebdŏmăda* > *domaa* > *doma* (old).

2. V. L. final *a* and tonic *ǫ* in hiatus > *ǫ: mŏlam* > *moo* > *mó; \*telariŏlam* > *\*telariŏlam* > *\*teleirola* > *teeiroo* > *teiró; \*avŭlam* > *\*avŏlam* > *avoo* > *avó*.

A. The vowel change and shift of accent in *\*avŏlam* were due to the influence of V. L. *\*filiŏlam;* cf. Sp. *abuela* and *hijuela*.

B. Nasalization closed tonic *ǫ* to *ǫ* and kept it close (§ 37, 6 B); hence, assimilation did not take place when hiatus was produced by the fall of intervocalic *n: bŏnam* > *bõa* > *bǫa; sŏnat* > *sǫa*.

3. V. L. final *a* followed by a nasal > [ẽ]: *amant* > *amam*.

A. For the change from [ẽ] to [ẽw], see § 157, 2.

**46.** V. L. FINAL *ę* (CL. L. *ē, ĭ, ĕ* AND *ae*).

1. V. L. final *ę* > Ptg. *e: ille* > *êle; veritātem* > *verdade;*

*famem* > *fome; carnem* > *carne; dīxĭt* > *disse; dentem* >
*dente; sĭtim* > *sêde.*

2. If *ę* was the final letter of the word in Vulgar Latin
and was preceded by a short *l, n, r, s* or *c*, or the group
*t + į* preceded by a vowel, it fell: *male* > *mal; sōlem* > *sol;
hŏmĭnem* > *omẽ* (old); *canem* > *cam* (old); *ratiōnem* >
*razom* (old); *vĕnĭt* > *vem; fīnem* > *fim; commūnem* > *comum; amōrem* > *amor;* \**habŭĕrit* (for *habúĕrit*) > *houver;
quaerĭt* > *quer; mensem* > *mês; vĭcem* > *vez; pŏsŭĭt* >
\**poset* > *pôs; facĭt* > *faz; fēcĭt* > *fêz; -ĭtĭem* > *-ez.*

A. If the consonant was long, the *e* did not generally fall:
*ĭlle* > *êle; tŭrrim* > *tôrre; vallem* > *vale.*

B. In proparoxytones, *e* preceded by *r* generally fell in Old
Portuguese, but it has been restored in Modern Portuguese:
*arbŏrem* > *arvor* (TA, Glossary) and *árvore; carcĕrem* > *carcer*
(FM, II, Glossary) and *cárcere.*

In learned proparoxytones, *e* preceded by *n* did not fall:
*canŏnem* > *cânone.*

C. In certain dialects a paragogic *e* is found after *l* and *r:
mare* > *mar* > *mare; sōlem* > *sol* > *sole.*　See § 116, 2.

D. The assibilation of *c* and of *t* plus yod took place before the
fall of final *e.*

E. Final *ę* preceded by *c* plus yod did not fall, e.g., *facĭem* >
*face,* except where *c* plus yod became confused with *t* plus yod:
*acĭem* > *az* (old); *facĭem* > *faz* (old).　Cf. § 89, 2 B; § 98, 3.

3. If *e* was not the final letter, it did not fall, although it
was preceded by *l, n, r, s* or *c*, or the group *t + į;* this is
shown by the plurals of some of the nouns and verbs listed
in section 2 above: *sōlēs* > *sóis; canēs* > *cães; ratiōnēs* >
*razões; hŏmĭnes* > *omẽes* (old); *amōres* > *amores;* \**habŭĕrint*
(for *habúĕrint*) > *houverem;* \**quaerent* (for *quaerunt*) >
*querem; mensēs* > *meses; vĭcēs* > *vezes;* \**facent* (for *facĭunt*)
> *fazem; -ĭtĭes* > *-ezes.*

A. In the change from *omẽes* to *homens* final *e* disappeared by
contraction.

4. V. L. final *ę* and a preceding *ę* in hiatus resulting from

the fall of intervocalic $d > ę$: *fĭdem > fee > fé; mercēdem > mercee > mercê; sēdem > see > sé; crēdit > crê.*

A. This change took place much earlier than the fall of Portuguese *d* (from Latin *t*) in second plural endings.

B. For the *e* of *fé* and *sé*, see § 35, 1 B.

5. V. L. final *ę* and a preceding *e* in hiatus resulting from the fall of intervocalic $n > ē$: *tĕnes > tēes > tens; \*bĕnes > bēes > bens; hŏmĭnes > homēes > homens.*

A. For the sound of final *-ens*, see § 34, 10.

6. V. L. final *ę* in hiatus with a preceding *ę* where the hiatus resulted from the fall of intervocalic *t* (2d pl.) > Ptg. *i: movēte > movede > movei; habētis > havedes > haveis.*

A. Contraction of the two vowels is sometimes found in Old Portuguese, e.g., *stētis > estedes > estes* (CG, facsimile, fôlha 51 vo, col. 3). Cf. Theoria, 33. The commoner change to *-eis* took place probably because the final vowel had already partially closed before the fall of *d* (first quarter of fifteenth century). However, Hanssen referring to the same forms in Spanish, argues that the contracted ending *-es* is regular and that *-eis* developed in imitation of *-ais* (Hanssen, § 26, 3).

7. V. L. final *ę* in hiatus with a preceding *ę* where the hiatus resulted from the fall of intervocalic *l* > Ptg. *i: \*mĕlēs > méis.*

A. The development was the same if the preceding vowel was *ę*, because tonic and intertonic *ę* followed by *l* had become *ę: crūdēlēs > cruéis; fĭdēlēs > fiéis; -ĭbĭlēs > -iveis* (§ 35, 11 and § 60, 7).

8. V. L. final *ę* and a preceding [j] (Cl. L. *g*) > *i: grĕgem > grei; lēgem > lei; rēgem > rei* (RF, XX, 563). See § 73, 4.

9. V. L. final *ę* and tonic *į* in hiatus > *i: cīvīles > civis; audītis > ouvides > ouvis; fĭnēs > fiis > fins.*

10. V. L. final *ę* in hiatus with *a, o* or *u* > *i: vadit > vai; canes > cāes* [kẽjʃ]; *sōlēs > sóis; padūlēs* (Du Cange; for *palūdēs*) *> paúis; \*amabătis* (for *amabātis*) *> amáveis.*

11. V. L. final *ę* + a following nasal consonant > [ẽ],

then [ēj] and in the region between Lisbon and Coimbra
[ĕj]: *dēbent* > *devem.*

**47.** V. L. FINAL *į* (CL. L. *ī*).

1. V. L. final *į* > *e*: *habuī* > *houve; amastī* > *amaste;
servī* (2d sg. impv.) > *serve; illī* > *lhe.*

A. This change was not completed until the beginning of the
fourteenth century (Grund, I, 953).

2. V. L. final *į* preceded by a single *c*, *s* or *l* fell: *fēcī* >
*fiz; pŏsuī* > *\*pŏsį* > *pus; salī* (2d sg. impv.) > *sal* (old).

3. V. L. final *į* in hiatus with a tonic vowel > *į*: *amāvī* >
*amai* > *amei, fuī* > *fui.*

A. If the tonic vowel was *e* and the hiatus arose through the
fall of *n*, the *į* of the resultant *ēi* fell: *vĕnī* (2d sg. impv.) > *\*vĕi*
> *vem.* Cf. the change of *bĕito* to *bento* (§ 92, 7 A). At a later
date final *em* came to be pronounced again with *į*: *vem* > [vĕj]
(§ 34, 10).

4. V. L. final *į* and tonic *į* in hiatus > *i*: *vīdī* > *vii* > *vi.*

A. If the hiatus arose through the fall of *n*, the result was *ī*:
*vēnī* > *vēi* > *vii* (§ 35, 4) > *vim* (§ 78, 2).

**48.** V. L. FINAL *ọ* (CL. L. *ō*, *ŭ*, AND *ŏ*).

1. V. L. final *ọ* > Ptg. *o* [u]: *amō* > *amo; casŭm* > *caso;
cĭtŏ* > *cedo; sŭmŭs* > *somos.*

A. This *o* became [u] as early as the twelfth century (Behr, 15).
Cf. Theoria, 23; RF, XXII, 405–406.

2. V. L. final *ọ* in hiatus with *a* or *ę* > *u* [w]: *caelum* >
*céu; malum* > *mau; dĕus* > *deus; mĕum* > *meu.*

A. The letter *u* appeared first in words in which the hiatus
existed in Latin; it appeared much later in words in which the
hiatus arose through the fall in Portuguese of an intervocalic
consonant. Accordingly, in medieval documents we commonly
find the spellings *deus*, *meu*, etc. alongside the spellings *ceo*, *mao*,
etc. And in the meter of the early Cancioneiros, *eu* in *deus*,
*meu*, etc. is a diphthong while the vowels of *ceo*, *mao*, etc. count

as separate syllables. Neither the sound [w] nor the letter *u* developed in words in which the tonic vowel in hiatus was ę in Vulgar Latin: *crēdo* > *creǫ* > *creio* [krẹju]; *plēnum* > *chẹǫ* > *cheio* [ʃɐju]. The 3d sg. pret. ending *-eu* [ew] is an Old Ptg. development in which the [w] arose in imitation of the endings *-ou* [ow] and *-iu* [iw].

There were four combinations of tonic *e* and final *o* (or *u*) in early Portuguese: [ew], e.g., *meu* (§ 34, 7 A); [eu], e.g., *ceo* (§ 34, 7 B); [eu], e.g., *creo* (§ 35, 7); and [ew], e.g., *defendeu* (§ 166, 3). The sound [ew] must have become [ew] before [ɛu] became [ɛw], else *meu* and *céu* would both have the same diphthong today. And the sound [eu] must have remained dissyllabic, for if it had not, it would be the same today as the third plural preterit ending *-eu* [ew] and the diphthong *ei* would not have developed. In Modern Portuguese these four combinations of tonic *e* and final *o* have become respectively [ew], [ɛw], [ɐju] and [ew].

B. In hiatus with tonic į final *o*, although still spelled *o*, became [w], and in some regions [u] with an intercalated [j] before it: *fīlum* > *fio* [fiw] and [fiju]; *rīvum* > *rio* [riw] and [riju].

3. V. L. final ǫ and tonic *o* in hiatus > ǫ: *avŭlum* > *avǒlum* (cf. § 45, 2 A) > *avoo* (§ 37, 5 A) > *avô*.

A. If the hiatus arose through the fall of *n*, the result was ǫ̃ (§ 78, 2): *dōnum* > *dõo* > *dǫm*; *bŏnum* > *bõo* > *bǫm*.

B. If the hiatus existed in Latin, the result was *ou*: *dŭōs* > *dous* (old); *sŭŭm* > *sou* (old).

4. V. L. final ǫ and posttonic *o* in hiatus > *o* [u]: *oracŭlum* > *oragoo* > *orago*; *pŏpŭlum* > *poboo* > *povo*.

5. V. L. final ǫ and tonic ų in hiatus > *u*: *crūdŭm* > *cru*; *cūlum* > *cu*; *nūdŭm* > *nú*.

A. If the hiatus arose through the fall of *n*, the result was ũ: *ūnum* > *ũu* > *um*. Ptg. *um* is not the result of apocope like Sp. *un* but is the phonological equivalent of Sp. *uno*. See § 78, 2 B.

6. V. L. final ǫ sometimes became *e*: *tostum* > *toste* (old); *quōmŏdŏ* > *come* (old and dialectal); *magĭstrŭm* > *mestre*; *miracŭlŭm* > *milagre*; *lībĕrŭm* > *livre*; *contentŭm* > *contente*; *saecŭlum* > *segre* (old).

A. This change has been attributed to the influence of other adverbs such as *onde* (from *ŭnde*) and *tarde* (from *tarde*) particularly in alliterative expressions such as *tarde ou toste* and to the influence of French or Provençal words.

B. In some words in Modern Galician *o* and *e* alternate, e.g., *milagro* and *milagre* (L-F, 24, footnote).

7. V. L. final *ǫ* sometimes fell: *anellum* > *anel; linteŏlum* > *lençol; lusciniŏlum* > *rouxinol; vascellum* > *baixel.*

A. Perhaps this *o* first became *e*, which then fell according to § 46, 2. It is more likely, however, that these words are borrowings from French or Provençal. A similar change is found in Vulgar Latin: *barbarus non barbar* (ApPr); *figulus non figel* (ApPr); *masculus non mascel* (ApPr).

## 49. Cl. L. Final *ū*.

There are no cases where Classical Latin final unaccented *ū* comes into Portuguese. The accusative singular of neuter nouns and the accusative plural of masculine nouns of the fourth declension have no derivatives in Portuguese, as nouns of this declension joined the second declension in Vulgar Latin (§ 13, 1).

A. Meyer-Lübke (M-L, Intro, § 130) and Grandgent (GIt, § 50) mention the OIt. plural *mano* to prove that Cl. L. *ū* became *o* but Grandgent elsewhere (GIt, § 156) points to the shift in declension and cites the form *manos* in Vulgar Latin (GVL, § 355).

## SECONDARY TONIC

## 50. The Secondary Tonic and its Disappearance.

1. In early Portuguese, where the tonic syllable was apparently less stressed than in Modern Portuguese, all atonic syllables had more vitality than they have today. A secondary accent fell on the second syllable before the tonic, as in Vulgar Latin (GVL, § 153). This is revealed by the fact that the intertonic in hiatus with the vowel of this

syllable was sometimes assimilated to it as the final was
to the tonic (§ 60, 5). It is also revealed by the fact that
a palatalized consonant did not have the same effect on
an *e* in this syllable that it had on pretonic *e* (cf. § 41, 3 A):
*degenerar, jejuar, mexedor, mexicano* (AStNS, CXXV, 374);
in all of these words this *e* is pronounced [ə].

A. In some words the secondary accent fell irregularly on a
syllable which bore the primary accent in a related or root word.

2. The secondary tonic became a pretonic initial vowel
in words in which syncope of the intertonic took place.
And the vowel resulting from contraction or from assimilation and contraction of the secondary tonic and the intertonic likewise became a pretonic initial. Thus the number
of words bearing a secondary accent was greatly reduced in
early Portuguese. With the increased stress on the tonic
vowel that developed in the sixteenth century, the secondary accent continued to disappear, with the result that all
words (except adverbs in -*mente* and augmentatives and
diminutives with an intercalated z) now have but one
accent.

## POSTTONIC PENULT

**51. SYNCOPE OF THE POSTTONIC PENULT IN VULGAR LATIN.**

The posttonic penult (*ă, ĕ, ĭ, ŏ* or *ŭ*) fell when standing
between certain pairs of consonants in the Vulgar Latin
period: *altĕrum > outro; dŏmĭnum > dono; lĕpŏrem > lebre;
ŏcŭlum > ôlho; pŏsĭtum > posto; vĭrĭdem > verde.* Cf. § 8.

**52. SYNCOPE OF THE POSTTONIC IN PORTUGUESE.**

1. If the posttonic penult was *e* or *i* (Cl. L. *ĕ* or *ĭ*), preceded by *l, m, n* or *r*, or preceded by *c* and followed by *t*, it
fell in the late Vulgar Latin or early Portuguese period:
*alĭquod > algo; *pūlĭcam* (for *pūlĭcem*) > pulga; gallĭcum
> galgo; amĭtes > andes > andas* (with shift in declension);
*dŏmĭtum > dondo* (RL, XXVII, 30); *līmĭtes > lindes; anĭmam > alma; manĭcam > manga; ērĭgo > ergo; sērĭcum >*

*sirgo; placĭtum > prazo.*   Cf. Behr, 46–47.

A. This change took place before the time of the fall of intervocalic *l* and *n* but after the time of the voicing of intervocalic [k] and *t*.

B. The posttonic bears the same relation to the tonic as the final in paroxytones does to the tonic.   Compare the fall of final *e* after *l, n* and *r* (§ 46, 2).

C. If metathesis had not taken place in *\*rĕtĭnam*, syncope would probably not have occurred.   The development was accordingly: *\*rĕtĭnam > \*renida > renda*.   In Spanish the order was the reverse; metathesis took place after syncope: *\*rĕtĭnam > riedna > rienda*.

D. Grandgent (GIt, § 68) finds that syncope took place under similar conditions in early Italian.

2. If the *e* was preceded by *m* but followed by a short *n*, it did not fall: *fēmĭnam > fêmea; gĕmĭnum > gémeo; hŏmĭnes > homées > homens*.

A. The nasalization of the penult by the adjacent nasal consonants may have increased its resistance to syncope.

**53.** SURVIVAL OF THE POSTTONIC PENULT.

All posttonic penults which did not fall in Vulgar Latin and in which the conditions of § 52, 1 did not obtain, remained in Portuguese: *angĕlum > angeo > anjo; bĭfĕram > bêbera; cŭbĭtum > covedo* (old); *dēbĭtam > dívida; dĕcĭmum > dízimo; \*dŭbĭtam > dúvida; duracĭnum > durázio; fraxĭnum > freixeo > freixo; jŭvĕnes > jovées > jovens; lēgĭtĭmum > lídimo; persĭcum > pêssego; \*rĕtĭnam > rédea; -abĭlem > -ável; -ibĭlem > -ível; capĭtŭlum > cabidoo > cabido; macŭlam > mágua; nĕbŭlam > névoa; perĭcŭlum > perigoo > perigo; pŏpŭlum > povoo > povo; spatŭlam > espádua; tabŭlam > tábua.*   Cf. Grund, I, 957, § 107.

A. The penult disappeared in some forms through assimilation and contraction, but not because of syncope.

B. *Freixeo* became *freixo* through absorption of the *e* of the penult by [ʃ] and *angeo* became *anjo* through absorption of the *e* of the penult by [ʒ].

c. In most of these words in Spanish the posttonic penult fell: *breva, codo, deuda, diezmo, duda, durazno, fresno, rienda, -able, -ible, cabildo, niebla, peligro, pueblo, espalda, tabla.* For syncope of the posttonic penult in Spanish, see Manual, §§ 25–26.

D. On the preservation of posttonic *-ul-*, see M-L, Intro, § 133; Biblos, VII, 520.

**54. LATER SYNCOPE OF THE POSTTONIC PENULT.**

With the greatly intensified stress accent which developed in the sixteenth century, the penult of proparoxytones began to fall quite generally in colloquial and dialectal Portuguese, whether the vowel was *a, e* or *o.* This change is not commonly revealed in spelling, which had become fairly fixed by printing and was being more and more influenced by Latin. Here are some examples of this change: Ptg. *árvore > arvre;* Ptg. *áspero > aspro;* Ptg. *diálogo > diaglo;* Ptg. *dívida > divda;* Ptg. *hóspede > ospde;* Ptg. *pêssego > pêsgo;* Ptg. *sábado > sabdo;* Ptg. *têmporas > tempras;* Ptg. *cómodo > comdo.* Cf. Grund, I, 957; RL, XI, 272; NS, XXXIV, 457; Opúsculos, II, 190 and 285.

**55. THE VOWEL OF THE POSTTONIC PENULT.**

1. V. L. posttonic *a* > Ptg. [ɐ]: *stŏmăchum > estômago; anătem > adem; hebdŏmăda > doma* (old).

A. Hiatus with another *a* was followed by contraction. If the other *a* was tonic the contracted vowel became [a].

2. Posttonic *a* and final *e* in hiatus through the fall in Portuguese of an intervocalic consonant became *ei: -abātis > -ávades* (§ 154, 1) *> -áveis.*

3. V. L. posttonic *a* and tonic *ę* in hiatus *> ę: pĕlăgum > peago > peego > pęgo.*

4. V. L. posttonic *a* and tonic *ǫ* in hiatus *> ǫ: mŏnăchum > moago > moogo > mǫgo > mǫgo.*

A. The tonic vowel of *mǫgo* was closed by metaphony (§ 100, 7).

5. V. L. posttonic *a* and final *o* in hiatus after the fall of intervocalic *n* (which had nasalized the *a*) *> ão* [ẽw]: *raphănum > rabão.*

6. V. L. posttonic ę (Cl. L. ĭ) > Ptg. *e* [ə] or *i: dĕcĭmum* > *dízimo;* \*dŭbĭtam > *dúvida; bĭbĭtum > bêbedo; persĭcum* > *pêssego.*

7. V. L. posttonic ę (Cl. L. ĕ) > *e* [ə]: *nĕpĕtam > néveda; vĕspĕram > véspera.*

8. V. L. posttonic ę followed by *r > a: aĕrem > aar > ar; aspĕrum > asparo* (old); *passĕrem > pássaro.*

9. V. L. posttonic ǫ in hiatus with final *a* > [w]: *tabŭlam* > *tábua; nĕbŭlam > névoa.*

## INTERTONIC VOWELS

**56. SYNCOPE OF THE INTERTONIC IN VULGAR LATIN.**

The intertonic vowel fell in the Vulgar Latin period under the same conditions as the posttonic penult, although not so extensively: *calĭdarium > caldeiro; compŭtāre* > *contar;* \**consūtūram > costura; honōrāre > honrar; labōrāre* > *lavrar; libĕrāre > livrar.* Cf. § 8.

A. While Classical Latin long vowels cannot be posttonic penults, they can be intertonic.

**57. SYNCOPE OF THE INTERTONIC IN PORTUGUESE.**

1. If the intertonic vowel was *e* (Cl. L. ē, ĕ or ĭ) or *i* (Cl. L. ī), preceded by *l*, *m* or *r*, or preceded by *c* and followed by *t*, it fell in the late Vulgar Latin or early Portuguese period: \**bellĭtātem > beldade; delĭcātum > delgado; follĭcāre > folgar; mĕlĭmēlum > marmelo* (see Nascentes); *molīnarium > molneiro > moleiro; olĭvaria* > *olveira* (old); \**salĭcarium > salgueiro; comĭtātum > condado; semĭtarium > semedeiro > sendeiro; arēnarium > arneiro; verēcundĭam > vergonha; vērĭtātem > verdade;* \**amīcĭtātem* (for *amīcĭtĭam*) > *amizade; rĕcĭtāre > rezar.* Cf. KJ, IV (Part I), 346.

A. With few exceptions this change took place before the time of the fall of intervocalic *l* but after the time of the voicing of intervocalic [k] and *t*. In *solteiro* (from *solĭtarium*) it was obviously very early while in *soidade* (old and dialectal) (from *solĭtātem*) the intertonic remained exceptionally late and was thereby preserved.

B. The intertonic vowel bore the same relation to the secondary tonic as the final did to the tonic; it was sometimes assimilated to the secondary tonic (§ 50, 1) and fell under conditions somewhat similar to those under which final *e* and *i* fell (cf. § 46, 2 and § 47, 2).

c. If metathesis had not taken place in *sĭbĭlāre*, syncope would probably not have occurred. The development was accordingly: *sĭbĭlāre* > *\*silibare* > *silvar*. The intertonic was reintroduced in modern *oliveira* through the influence of the word *oliva*. In its regular development in Portuguese, *judĭcāre* became *juigar* (RL, XXIII, 27, s.v. *desjuigado*), which was replaced at an early date by *judgar*, a borrowing from Old Spanish, which later became *julgar* in Portuguese.

D. In some words syncope of the intertonic was avoided because of the unpronounceable combination of consonants that would have resulted from it, e.g., *aprĭcāre* > *abrigar; neglĕgentĭam* > *negrigença* (old and popular). Words in which such syncope did occur, with the consequent loss of one of the consonants, are extremely exceptional and are probably borrowings from Spanish, French, or Provençal: *aestĭmāre* > *esmar; mastĭcāre* > *mascar; vindĭcāre* > *vingar.*

2. If intertonic *e* was preceded by *m* but followed by a short *n*, it did not fall: *nomĭnāre* > *nomear; rūmĭnāre* > *rumiar; semĭnāre* > *semear.*

3. If intertonic *e* was preceded by *n*, it did not fall as the posttonic penult did: *\*adrepoenĭtēre* > *arrepēeder* > *arrepender; genĕrālem* > *geeral* > *geral; inĭmīcum* > *eimigo* (old); *monĭmentum* > *moimento; vanĭtātem* > *vaidade.*

A. This seems to indicate either that syncope of the intertonic took place later than syncope of the posttonic penult or that intervocalic *n* fell earlier before the intertonic than before the posttonic penult.

B. Two like vowels contracted after the fall of consonantal *n*, e.g., *arrepender;* compare Sp. *arrepentir*, in which the intertonic fell before the time of the voicing of intervocalic *t*, although

Menéndez Pidal (Manual, § 54, 1) attributes the *t* to learned influence.

c. The development of *bondade* (from *bonǐtātem*) was probably influenced by the adjective *bom*.

4. Where there were two vowels between the initial and the tonic vowel, the first was a secondary tonic, the second an intertonic: *caballǐcāre* (Du Cange) > *cavalgar;* \**humilǐ-tōsum* > *humildoso; lēgalǐtātem* > *lealdade;* \**adlumǐnāre* (for *illumǐnāre*) > *alumiar.*

A. In *herēdǐtāre*, intervocalic *d* fell and intervocalic *t* became *d*; then the vowel resulting from contraction of the two *e*'s fell, because it was an intertonic vowel preceded by *r: herēdǐtāre* > \**hereedar* > \**heredar* > *herdar. Comungar* (from *communǐcāre*) developed by analogy with forms in which the *e* was not intertonic but posttonic, e.g., *comungo* (from *commūnǐco*). The form *irman-dade* (from *germanǐtātem*), which replaced an older and regular *irmãidade*, developed through the influence of *irmã;* a similar development took place in *orfandade* through the influence of *órfã.*

## 58. SURVIVAL OF THE INTERTONIC.

All intertonic vowels which did not fall in Vulgar Latin and in which the conditions of § 57 did not obtain, remained in Portuguese: *capǐtālem* > *cabedal; cīvǐtātem* > *ciidade* > *cidade; cupǐdǐtǐam* (Du Cange) > \**cobeíça* > *cobiiça* > *cobiça; medǐcīnam* > *meezinha* > *mezinha; mirābǐlǐa* > *maravilha; nūdǐtātem* > *nuydade* (DC, 362); *praecōnāri* > *pregoar; salūtāre* > *saudar; suspīrāre* > *suspirar; tradǐtōrem* > *treidor* (old); *voluntātem* > *voontade* > *vontade.*

A. In some of these words the intertonic vowel finally disappeared through assimilation and contraction, but not because of syncope.

B. The intertonic did not fall in Portuguese and Spanish in learned or semi-learned words, e.g., *carǐtātem* > Ptg. *caridade* and Sp. *caridad*. It generally fell in Spanish in popular words unless it was *a* (Manual, §§ 23–24): *capĭtālem* > *cabdal* > *caudal; cīvitātem* > *cibdad* > *ciudad; cupĭdĭtĭam* (Du Cange) > *cobdicia* > *codicia.* Ptg. *caudal* was borrowed from Spanish while Ptg. *coudel* (from *capĭtellum*) was probably borrowed from Provençal.

### 59. LATER SYNCOPE OF THE INTERTONIC.

With the greatly intensified stress accent which developed in the sixteenth century, the intertonic, as well as the pretonic initial and the vowel which had previously been the secondary tonic (i.e., all pretonic vowels) began to fall in learned as well as popular words when standing before or after a liquid: Ptg. *cerimónia* > *cermónia;* Ptg. *parecer* > *parcer;* Ptg. *esperar* > *esprar;* Ptg. *poderoso* > *podroso;* Ptg. *coronel* > *cornel* Ptg. *superior* > *suprior;* Ptg. *oferecer* > *ofrecer;* Ptg. *experimentar* > *exprimentar;* Ptg. *corregidor* > *corgidor;* Ptg. *averiguar* > *avriguar;* Ptg. *esterilidade* > *estrelidade;* Ptg. *perigo* > *prigo;* Ptg. *paraíso* > *praíso;* Ptg. *verão* > *vrão;* Ptg. *corôa* > *crôa;* Ptg. *pelo* > *plo;* Ptg. *para* > *pra;* Ptg. *querer* > *qu'rer.* This change is not generally revealed in spelling, which had become fairly fixed by printing and was being more and more influenced by Latin; it is revealed by the rhythm of the verse of Sá de Miranda and Gil Vicente, although it is uncommon in the later, more polished verse of Camões (SaM, pp. cxxii–cxxiii, erroneously numbered cxx and cxxi; ZRPh, IV, 600; RL, XXVII, 126).

For sporadic examples of this change before the sixteenth century, see CD, note to line 299; FM, I, xxiii.

### 60. THE VOWEL OF THE INTERTONIC.

1. V. L. intertonic *a* and secondary tonic *a* in hiatus > *a* [a]: *\*panatarĭum* > *paadeiro* > *padeiro; sanatīvum* (Du Cange) > *saadio* > *sadio.*

2. V. L. intertonic *ę* and secondary tonic *ę* in hiatus > *ę: crēdĭtōrem* > *creedor* > *crędor; mĕdĭcīnam* > *meezinha* > *męzinha; praedĭcāre* > *preegar* > *prègar.*

3. V. L. intertonic *ǫ* and secondary tonic *ǫ* in hiatus > *ǫ: cŏlōrātum* > *coorado* > *cǫrado.*

4. The intertonic vowel was assimilated to the tonic as the pretonic initial was: *adcalescit > acaece > aqueece > aquece; cupĭdĭtĭam (Du Cange) > *cobẹíça > cobiíça > cobiça.

5. The intertonic was assimilated to the secondary tonic as the final was to the tonic: *admĭnacĭāre > ameaçar > amèçar (RL, VI, 339; RL, VII, 107); cīvĭtātem > *ciedade > ciidade > cidade; consĭdĕrāre > *consierar > consiirar > consirar (old); dīvīnĭtātem > *diviedade > diviidade > divindade.

6. V. L. intertonic ẹ preceded or followed by r > a: querimōnĭam > caramunha; sacerdōtem > saçardote (old).

## INITIAL SHORT CONSONANTS

**61. LABIALS.**

1. Cl. L. initial b > Ptg. b: bĕne > bem; bŭccam > boca.

A. There was some confusion between initial b and v; see Comp, 90 and section 4 A below.

2. Cl. L. initial f > Ptg. f: ferrum > ferro; fĭlĭum > filho.

3. Cl. L. initial p > Ptg. p: pacem > paz; persōnam > pessoa.

A. Initial p sometimes became b, perhaps by sandhi: pōlīre > buir.   See Comp, 89–90.

4. Cl. L. initial v [w] > Ptg. v: vallem > vale; vidēre > ver; vīnum > vinho; vītem > vide.

A. Initial v became b in a few words: vagīnam > bainha; vessīcam > bexiga; vīpĕram > bibera (Fab, Glossary); vōtum > bodo.

B. The change of initial v to g has been attributed to Germanic influence (M-L, Gram, I, § 416; Comp, 93): vastāre > gastar; vītĭcŭlam > guedelha; vomitāre > gomitar (popular); vorācem > goraz.

C. Initial v became f in OPtg. femença (from vehementĭam). The change of initial v to f is not altogether unknown in the Romance languages, e.g., Fr. fois (from vĭcem).   Cf. Huber, § 177.   The change to f in ferrolho (from verŭcŭlum) was due to contamination by ferro.

**62. Palatals and Velars.**

1. C. L. initial *c* followed by *a*, *o*, or *u* > Ptg. *c* [k]:
*cantāre* > *cantar; colōrem* > *côr; cūlum* > *cu*.

A. The change of initial velar *c* to *g* has been attributed to
sandhi (GIt, § 87): *camellam* > *gamela; cattum* > *gato; cavĕam* >
*gaiva*. For the same change in dialectal Portuguese, see RL,
XI, 140.
B. The change to *ch* is found in borrowings from French:
*chapéu, chefe, charrua*.

2. Cl. L. initial *c* followed by *e* or *i* (V. L. [ts]) > Ptg. *c*
[s]: *centum* > *cento; cĭrca* > *cêrca; cīvĭtātem* > *cidade*.

A. Ptg. *chinche* (from *cīmĭcem*) was probably borrowed from
It. *cimice* either directly or through Spanish.
B. The assimilation of pretonic *a* to *e* took place too late to
affect the development of initial *c*, e.g., *calentem* > *caente* >
*queente* > *quente*.

3. C. L. initial *g* followed by *a*, *o*, or *u* > Ptg. *g: gallīnam*
> *galinha; gŭbernāre* > *governar*. For *g* followed by *u̯*, see
§ 69, 4.
4. Cl. L. initial *g* followed by *e* or *i* (V. L. [j]) > Ptg. *g*
[ʒ]: *genŭcŭlum* > *geolho* > *joelho; gĭngīvam* > *gengiva; gĕnĕ-
rum* > *genro; gentem* > *gente*.

A. The changes through which this sound passed were the
following: [g] > [gj] > [j] > [dʒ] > [ʒ].
B. The form *germānum* seems to have developed regularly at
first, e.g., *germāo* (AHP, VII, 477, A.D. 1282) and *germaho* (Eluc,
A.D. 1288). The loss of the *g* in *irmāo* has been attributed to its
intervocalic position in the frequent occurrence of *germāo* and
*germāa* with possessive adjectives (Grund, I, 991).

5. Cl. L. initial *j* [j] > Ptg. *j* [ʒ]: *januarĭum* > *janeiro;
jūrāre* > *jurar; jūlĭum* > *julho*.

A. Beginning with Vulgar Latin this sound and the sound
coming from Classical Latin initial *g* followed by *e* or *i* (section 4
above) have been identical.

**63.** Dentals.

1. Cl. L. initial *d* > Ptg. *d: dare* > *dar; dĕcem* > *dez; dolōrem* > *dor.*

2. Cl. L. initial *t* > Ptg. *t: taurum* > *toiro; tenēre* > *ter; tŭrrim* > *tôrre.*

**64.** Liquids.

1. Cl. L. initial *l* > Ptg. *l: latus* > *lados; 'linguam* > *língua; lŭpum* > *lôbo.*

A. That this *l* was longer in Old Portuguese than it is today is indicated by the fact that it was sometimes written *ll* and that it did not fall when it became intervocalic by sandhi (except in unaccented monosyllables).   Cf. § 30, 2 b.

2. Cl. L. initial *r* > Ptg. *r: rīvum* > *rio; rŏsam* > *rosa; rŭbĕum* > *ruivo.*

**65.** Sibilants.

1. Cl. L. initial *s* > Ptg. *s: sal* > *sal; sĭgĭllum* > *sêlo; sŏnum* > *som.*

A. The change of initial *s* to *x*, e.g., *syringam* > *seringa* > *xeringa* (RL, XI, 278; RL, XII, 307), has been attributed to Arabic influence (RA, VII, 117), but as it occurred also in regions that were free of Arabic influence, it is more likely that it was due to the close similarity of dialectal cacuminal *s* [ś] to [ʃ] (Ent, 302).   This similarity accounts for the common use of Arabic *shîn* in Portuguese aljamiado texts to represent Portuguese initial *s* and intervocalic *ss* while *sîn* is used to represent *ç*. On the disappearance of cacuminal *s* in literary Portuguese, see KJ, IV, Part I, 327; on its survival in dialectal Portuguese, see PhM, I, 34, n. 1 and 189; Esquisse, § 59 e.   Cf. G-D, C, § 32, 4, n. 6.

B. The *c* of *cerrar* (from *sērāre*) developed by contamination with some other word, perhaps *cercar* (cf. Nascentes).   The *z* of *zoar* (from *sonāre*) is probably onomatopœic.

2. Cl. L. z (Greek ζ) > Ptg. z or c [s]: zēlum > zeo (old)
and zêlo; zĕphўrum > zéfiro; zēlum > cio (cf. Nascentes);
ζωμόν > çumo.

A. It is thought that in Vulgar Latin, z sometimes became
confused with d plus yod or merely yod (GVL, § 339). This
may have occurred in gengibre (from zingĭber) or the z may have
been assimilated to the g of the following syllable.

**66. Nasals.**

1. Cl. L. initial m > Ptg. m: male > mal; mĕtum > mêdo;
monētam > moeda.

A. The change of initial m to n in nêspera (from mĕspĭlam)
goes back to Vulgar Latin as most Romance languages have forms
with n (REW).

B. Initial m sometimes nasalized the following vowel: matrem
> māi; mĕam > mia > minha; mĭhī > mi > mim; multum >
muito [mũjntu]. This phenomenon is very common in popular
and dialectal Portuguese: mensem > mes > mês (RL, V, 59);
mensam > mesa > menza (RL, V, 58); mĭssam > missa > minsa
(Opúsculos, II, 313); mūlum > muu > mũ (RL, XXVI, 249);
forms of the verb medir (RL, XXVI, 254, s.v. mil). Cf. Esquisse,
§ 40 a.

2. Cl. L. initial n > Ptg. n: natāre > nadar; nŏvum >
nôvo.

A. The change of initial n to m in mastruço (from nasturtĭum)
goes back to Vulgar Latin as several Romance languages have
forms with m (REW).

B. Initial n sometimes nasalized the following vowel: nec > ne
> nem; *ne-quem > nĕguem > nenguem > ninguém; nīdum >
nio > ninho; nūdum > nũu (BF, I, 46).

## INITIAL CONSONANT GROUPS

**67. Consonant + l.**

1. Cl. L. initial bl > Ptg. br: blandum > brando; blĭtum
> bredo; blasphemāre > brasfamar (Fab).

A. The form blasfemar is learned.

2. Cl. L. initial *cl* > Ptg. *ch* or *cr: clavem* > *chave; clamāre* > *chamar; clavum* > *cravo.*

A. The development of *cl* was similar to that of *pl* (see sections 5 A and 5 B below).

B. In learned words *cl* has remained unchanged: *clīma* > *clima; clarum* > *claro; classem* > *classe.*

3. Cl. L. initial *fl* > Ptg. *ch* or *fr: flagrāre* (GVL, § 292) > *cheirar; flammam* > *chama; flaccum* > *fraco; phlegma* > *freima.*

A. The development of *fl* was similar to that of *pl* (see sections 5 A and 5 B below).

B. In learned words *fl* has remained unchanged or has been restored: *flavum* > *flavo; flōrem* > *flor; flŭidum* > *flúido.*

4. Cl. L. initial *gl* > Ptg. *l* or *gr: glandem* > *lande; glarĕam* > *leira; globellum* (Du Cange) > *lovelo* > *novelo; glūten* > *grude; glossam* > *grossa* (old). See section 5A below.

A. In learned words *gl* has remained unchanged: *glōbum* > *globo; glōrĭam* > *glória.*

5. Cl. L. initial *pl* > Ptg. *ch* or *pr: plāgam* > *chaga; plēnum* > *cheio; plus* > *chus* (old); *plăgam* > *praia; placēre* > *prazer.*

A. Words in which *pl, cl, gl,* and *fl* became *pr, cr, gr,* and *fr* respectively correspond in general to Spanish words in which no change took place (Hanssen, § 19, 3); they are less popular and later, and were perhaps used by a different class of people (RL, XXVIII, 23).

B. The development of *pl* to *ch* seems to have been as follows: *pl* > *pll* (lengthening of *l*) > [pʎ] (whence Castilian [ʎ]) > *pi̯* > *ptch* > *tch* > *ch* (Ent, 287–288; RC, XI, 1120–1130; ZRPh, XLII, 228–229; M-L, Gram, I, § 422). The last change, from [tʃ] to [ʃ], took place about 1700 (Grund, I, 972, n. 2) but [tʃ] is still heard in certain dialects (RL, XIX, 173; RL, XXVII, 99).

C. In learned words *pl* remained unchanged or was restored: *plūmam* > *pluma; plantāre* > *plantar.*

D. The word *lhano* (from *planum*) was borrowed from Spanish.

**68.** CONSONANT + *r*.

1. Cl. L. initial *br* > Ptg. *br: bracas* > *bragas; bracchĭum* > *braço.*

2. Cl. L. initial *cr* > Ptg. *cr: crēdo* > *creio; creātum* > *criado.*

A. In some words initial *cr* became *gr: crassum* > *graxo; cratem* > *grade; crētam* > *greda; quirītāre* > *\*c'ritāre* (GVL, § 229) > *gritar.*

3. Cl. L. initial *dr* > Ptg. *dr: dracōnem* > *dragão.*

4. Cl. L. initial *fr* > Ptg. *fr: fraxĭnum* > *freixo; frūctum* > *fruto.*

5. Cl. L. initial *gr* > Ptg. *gr: graecum* > *grego; granum* > *grão.*

6. Cl. L. initial *pr* > Ptg. *pr: pratum* > *prado; prĕtĭum* > *preço.*

7. Cl. L. initial *tr* > Ptg. *tr: tradĭtōrem* > *treidor* (old); *trĕdĕcim* > *treze.*

**69.** VELAR + *u̯*.

1. Cl. L. initial *qu* followed by tonic *a* > Ptg. *qu* [kw]: *quattuor* > *quatro; quando* > *quando; quasi* > *quási.*

A. There is a tendency for *u̯* in this position to fall in dialectal Portuguese (Esquisse, § 48 d).

2. Cl. L. initial *qu* followed by pretonic *a* > Ptg. *c* [k]: *quattuordĕcim* > *catorze; quaternum* > *caderno; quantitātem* > *cantidade* (old); *qualitātem* > *calidade* (old); *quam magnum* > *camanho* (old).

A. The form *quamanho* developed through the influence of tonic *quão;* MPtg. *quantidade* and *qualidade* are regressive words.

3. Cl. L. initial *qu* followed by *e* or *i* > Ptg. *qu* [k]: *quaerendum* > *querendo; quid* > *que; quīntum* > *quinto.*

4. Initial *gu* [gw] occurs only in words of Germanic origin. Where the following vowel is *e* or *i*, the [w] has disappeared: *wardōn* > *guardar; \*werra* (REW) > *guerra; wīsa* > *guisa.*

**70.** DENTAL + i̯.

Cl. L. initial $d + i̯$ > Ptg. $g$ [ʒ] or $j$: *diaria̯* > *geira;*
*deorsum* > *juso* (old).

A. See § 12, 3.   The development is the same as that of initial
$j$ (§ 62, 5).

B. The word *jornal* could be derived directly from *diurnālem*
but is a borrowing from French.

**71.** PROSTHETIC *e*.

1. The *e* which was prefixed in Vulgar Latin to initial
consonant groups consisting of *s* plus one or two consonants
(§11), became *e* [ɪ] in Portuguese: *scūtum* > *escudo; stŭdium*
> *estudo; strĭctum* > *estreito; spērāre* > *esperar; sphaeram*
> *espera* (old) and *esfera; scriptum* > *escrito; smaragdum*
> *esmeralda* (with shift of declension).

A. This *e* has disappeared in many dialects particularly in the
north (Grund, I, 955; Esquisse, § 50 a; RL, II, 19 and 40; RL, IV,
34-35; Opúsculos, II, 189).

2. Lat. initial *scl* > Ptg. *escr: sclavum* > *escravo.*

3. The *u̯* of initial *squ* followed by pretonic *a*, fell: *squa-
māre* > *escamar;* followed by tonic *a*, it remained: *squalum*
> *esqualo.*

4. Prosthetic *e* is found with initial *sc* followed by *e* or *i*:
*scindo* > *escindo.*   But it did not develop in learned words
with initial *sc* followed by *e* or *i*: *scēnam* > *cena; sceptrum*
> *cetro; scientiam* > *ciência; scillam* > *cila; scintillam* >
Sp. *centella* > *centelha.*

## INTERVOCALIC SHORT CONSONANTS

**72.** LABIALS.

1. Cl. L. intervocalic $b$ > Ptg. *v: dēbet* > *deve; fabam* >
*fava; habēre* > *haver; nūbem* > *nuvem.*

A. Some words have *v* in Old Portuguese but *b* in Modern
Portuguese by regression: *bĭbĕre* > *bever* (old) and *beber; sēbum* >

*sevo* (old) and *sebo; tabŭlam* > *távoa* (old) and *tábua*. The intervocalic *b* of *beber* may have developed by assimilation to the initial *b*. Intervocalic *b* has remained in learned and semi-learned words: *diabŏlum* > *diabo; scabellum* > *escabelo*.

2. Cl. L. intervocalic *v* [w] > Ptg. *v: avēnam* > *aveia; lavāre* > *lavar; nŏvem* > *nove*.

A. Intervocalic *v* followed by unaccented *u* regularly fell in Vulgar Latin, sometimes to be restored by analogy with a form of the word in which the *v* was not followed by *u* (GVL, § 324). Such restoration did not take place in Portuguese in the derivative of the ending *-īvum* (Comp, 108): *aestīvum* > *estio; fugitīvum* > *fugidio; rīvum* > *rio; sanatīvum* (Du Cange) > *sadio*. In adjectives ending in *-īvum*, the *v* of the feminine fell by analogy with the masculine. In *vivo* (from *vīvum*) the *v* was preserved or restored through the influence of the verb *viver*. Cl. L. *bŏvem* became V. L. *boe* (Vok, II, 479), whence Ptg. *boi;* perhaps the *v* fell by dissimilation (MP, XI, 349). In *cidade* (from *civĭtātem*) the *v* probably fell because it stood between two *i*'s (cf. Kent, § 181, VII).

3. Cl. L. intervocalic *f* > Ptg. *v: aurĭfĭcem* > *ourives; defensam* > *devesa; profectum* > *proveito; Stĕphănum* > *Estēvão*.

A. The *b* of *bêbera* (from *bĭfĕram*) developed probably by assimilation to the initial *b*. The form *defesa* (from *defensam*) is semi-learned, having been influenced by the learned *defensa* or the French *défense*, with both of which it has meanings in common. Leite finds that as place-names *Defesa* and *Devesa* occur in separate regions (RL, XI, 354). The *b* of *rábão* (from *raphănum*) may have arisen through the Latin pronunciation *p* of Greek *ph* (GVL, § 332).

4. Cl. L. intervocalic *p* (V.L. *b*) > Ptg. *b: apĭcŭlam* > *abelha; lŭpum* > *lôbo; rīpam* > *riba; sapit* > *sabe*.

A. In some words this *p* developed further to *v: nĕpĕtam* > *néveda; pŏpŭlum* > *poboo* > *povo; praesaepem* > *preseve* (old) but modern *pesebre; propinquum* > *provinco* (Eluc); *scōpam* > *escôva*.

This additional step may have been occasioned by dissimilation in some of these words (cf. RL, XXXIV, 306).

### 73. Palatals and Velars.

1. Cl. L. intervocalic *c* followed by *a, o* or *u* (V.L. *g*) > Ptg. *g: amīcum > amigo; caecum > cego; dīco > digo.*

A. In *pouco* (from *paucum*) and *rouco* (from *raucum*) the *c* was prevented from voicing by the *u̯* of the diphthong.

2. Cl. L. intervocalic *c* followed by *e* or *i* (V.L. [ts]) > Ptg. *z: dīcis > dizes; placēre > prazer; vĭces > vezes.*

A. The changes through which this sound passed in Portuguese were the following: [ts] > [dz] > [z]. See Hanssen, § 17, 10.

B. The *c* of *receber* developed as initial *c* because the word was felt to be a compound. The *c* of *racimo* (from *racēmum*) is regressive as the form *razimo* is found in Old Portuguese. The *c* of *recente* (from *recentem*) is learned.

3. Cl. L. intervocalic *g* followed by *a, o* or *u* > Ptg. *g: legūmen > legume; negāre > negar; plagam > chaga.*

A. In some words this sound fell in Vulgar Latin: *ĕgo > eu; legālem > lial; litĭgāre > lidar; strĭgam > estria.* See GVL, § 263. For the theory that this *g* remained after the accent and fell before it, see RHi, LXXVII, 146.

The word *rua* (from *rūgam*) belongs to this list unless it is a borrowing from French.

4. Cl. L. intervocalic *g* followed by *e* or *i* (V.L. [j]) fused with the following *e* or *i: magĭstrum > maestre > mestre; rēgĭnam > rainha; sĭgĭllum > seello > sêlo; vigĭntī > viinte > vinte; cōgĭtāre > cuidar; dĭgĭtum > dedo; frĭgĭdum > frio; grĕgem > grei; lēgem > lei; rēgem > rei.*

A. This change took place in the Vulgar Latin period in most of these words (GVL, § 259).

B. In many of these words there was a further fusion with a preceding *e* or *i*.

C. In learned and semi-learned words Vulgar Latin intervocalic [j] became [ʒ]: *mūgĭlem > mugem; -ūgĭnem > -ugem; -agĭnem >*

*-agem; fŭgĕre* > *fugir* (with shift of conjugation); *mūgīre* > *mugir; regendum* > *regendo; vĭgĭlāre* > *vigiar*. Cornu explains some of these forms as popular by the rule that [j] preceded by *u* became [ʒ] (Grund, I, 991). This would explain *mugem*, if it is a popular word as Behr contends (Behr, 32–33).

D. The verb *velar* (from *vĭgĭlāre*) is a semi-learned word (borrowed from Spanish) in which the regular change occurred, that is, [j] and the following vowel contracted and the resultant vowel again contracted with the preceding vowel.

5. Cl. L. intervocalic *j* > Ptg. *j* [ʒ]: *\*ajat* (for *habĕat*) > *haja; cūjum* > *cujo; jējūnāre* > *jejuar*.

A. This sound fused with a preceding unaccented *e: dējectāre* > *deitar; pējōrem* > *peor* > *pior* (§ 99, 6). The *j* of *majōrem* was probably lost in imitation of *peor: majōrem* > *maor* > *moor* > *mór*. The forms *maior* and *peior* (old) are not popular (Behr, 42). In the development of *majōrinum* to *meirinho, j* ceased to be intervocalic after the fall of intertonic *o* in Vulgar Latin. The development of *Maio* (from *Majum*) is not clear.

### 74. DENTALS.

1. Cl. L. intervocalic *d* (V.L. [đ]) fell in Portuguese: *lampăda* > *lampaa* > *lampa; nīdum* > *nīo* > *ninho; nūdum* > *nuu* > *nú; \*pedūcam* > *peúga*.

2. Cl. L. intervocalic *t* (V.L. *d*) > Ptg. *d* [đ]: *catēnam* > *cadeia; natam* > *nada; vēritātem* > *verdade*.

A. This *d* fell in the second plural of all tenses in which it remained intervocalic, a development which may have been of dialectal origin, that is, may have arisen in some region where intervocalic *d* (from Cl. L. *t*) always fell, as is the case today in San Martín de Trevejo and other parts of Spain (RL, XXVI, 249). The same change took place but at a much earlier date in the development of *\*metĭpsĭmum* to *meesmo*, now *mesmo*.

B. In *couto* (from *cautum*) the *t* was prevented from voicing by the *ų* of the diphthong.

### 75. LIQUIDS.

1. Cl. L. intervocalic *l* fell in Portuguese: *dolōrem* > *door* > *dor; salīre* > *sair; sōles* > *sóis*.

A. Intervocalic *l*, after becoming attached to the preceding vowel, became gutturalized as *l* is today at the end of a syllable; this gutturalized intervocalic *l* fell in the course of the tenth century (ZRPh, XXVIII, 603; Lições, 291; Ent, 288; Sachs, 22).

B. In learned and semi-learned words intervocalic *l* did not fall: \*alĕcrem (for alăcrem) > alegre; calōrem > calor; salarĭum > salário; scŏlam > escola. Along with these there are some regressive words with *l*, which have replaced popular words in which *l* had fallen: dolorōsum > doroso (old) and doloroso; silentĭum > seenço (old) and silêncio; zēlum > zeo (old) and zêlo. It is possible that the *l* of \*alĕcrem lengthened in Vulgar Latin in imitation of words with the prefix ad- plus initial *l*; that is the explanation Grandgent gives of the long *l* of It. allegro (GIt, § 100). Palavra (from parabŏlam) is probably a borrowing from Spanish as the type of metathesis it displays is characteristic of Spanish; the regular Portuguese form of the word was paravoa (old). Contamination also contributed to the preservation of *l*: thus the *l* of pêlo (from pĭlum) is explained by the *l* of cabêlo (from capĭllum), the *l* of melão (from melōnem) by the *l* of mel (from mĕl).

2. Cl. L. intervocalic *r* > Ptg. *r: carum > caro; erat > era.

## 76. Sibilants.

Cl. L. intervocalic *s* > Ptg. *s* [z]: \*ausāre > ousar; causa > coisa; rŏsam > rosa.

A. In Old Portuguese and in certain dialects of the north of Portugal, intervocalic *s* became [ʒ] (FM, I, xxiv; Esquisse, § 59 e; RL, XI, 277; RL, XII, 307; RL, XXVII, 101). This change is found in Spanish (JdeV, 74). It was due to the close similarity of dialectal cacuminal z [ż] to [ʒ] (Ent, 302).

## 77. Intervocalic *m*.

Cl. L. intervocalic *m* > Ptg. *m: fūmāre > fumar; sŭmŭs > somos.

A. Intervocalic *m* nasalized the preceding vowel (CA, I, xxii, n. 4) but this nasalization soon disappeared, except in dialects (cf. Opúsculos, II, 313).

B. Intervocalic *m* sometimes nasalized the following vowel as an initial *m* did: *vīmen* > *vime* > *vimem* (old); *amiddŭlam* (ApPr) > *amêndoa*.

## 78. INTERVOCALIC *n*.

1. In the course of the tenth century, intervocalic *n* nasalized the preceding vowel and fell. The nasal resonance of the vowel persisted and spread to the following vowel. From this point there were several different developments depending on the nature of the vowel combination, the position of the accent, and the consonant following the second vowel. For previous studies of this problem, see Behr, 44–49; RC, XI, 84–93; MLN, L, 16–17; ZRPh, XLI, 555–565; NS, XI, 129–153; Ent, 289; RPh, I, 35–39.

2. If both vowels were like vowels and the first was tonic, the second final, the nasal resonance remained and the vowels contracted; *bŏnum* > *bǫo* (§37, 6) > *bom; lanam* > *lãa* > *lã; tĕnes* > *tẽes* > *tens*.

A. The nasal resonance has fallen in some of these words in southern Galician and certain other dialects (Fab, Glossary, s.v. *boo*).

B. Because unaccented final *e* became *i* and contracted with tonic *i* (§ 46, 9), words like *fīnes* belong to this category: *fīnes* > *fiis* > *fins*. And because unaccented final *o* became *u* and contracted with tonic *u* (§ 48, 5), words like *ūnum* belong to this category: *ūnum* > *uno* > *ũu* > *um; tribūnum* > *tribum* (BF, II, 222).

C. If the first vowel was a posttonic penult and the second vowel final, the nasal resonance fell, unless both vowels were *e*'s: *sabănam* (Du Cange) > *savaa* (FM, II, Glossary) and *diacŏnum* > *diagoo* (old); but *hŏmĭnes* > *homẽes* > *homens; ordĭnes* > *ordẽes* > *ordens*. Even if they were *e*'s the nasal resonance fell in certain dialects, e.g., *home* (RL, III, 59; RL, XI, 277; RL, XII, 308; RL, XXVII, 127; RL, XXVIII, 224). The nasal resonance remained in *órfã* (from *orphănam*) through the influence of *órfão* and perhaps also of *irmã*.

3. If the first vowel was tonic in any of the pairs *a–o*, *o–e*, and *a–e*, the nasal resonance remained and these combinations later became nasal diphthongs: *germānum* > *irmão; manum* > *mão; lectiōnes* > *lições; pōnes* > *pões; canes* > *cāes*.

A. The nasal resonance fell in these words in southern Galician.

B. Instead of *-ão* the suffix *-ano* is found in learned and regressive words: *humānum* > *humano; castellānum* > Sp. *castellano* > OPtg. *castelhão* > MPtg. *castelhano*.

C. The diphthong *ão* developed also with the pair *a–o* when both vowels came after the accented syllable: *orgănum* > *órgão; orphănum* > *órfão; Stĕphănum* > *Estêvão*. In some dialects this unaccented *ão* became *o*, e.g., *orgo, orpho* (Esquisse, § 56 j; RL, XI, 275; RL, XII, 307). An early stage of these forms, before contraction of the vowels and before the loss of the nasal resonance, is occasionally found in Old Portuguese documents, e.g., *orfõos* (RL, I, 334) and *orgoons* (RL, III, 116).

D. The pair *o–e* with both vowels after the accented syllable is found both with and without the nasal resonance in the plural of *demo: daemŏnes* > *démões* (FM, II, Glossary) and *demoes* (FM, II, Glossary, s.v. *demões;* Rom, XI, 376).

4. If the first vowel was tonic *i̯* and the second vowel *a* or *o*, a palatalized nasal developed between them and the nasal resonance disappeared: *gallīnam* > *gallīa* > *galinha; vicīnam* > *vizīa* > *vizinha; vīnum* > *vīo* > *vinho*.

A. The date of this development has not been determined. In the early Cancioneiros (CA, CB and CV), some of the poems of which were written as late as the first quarter of the fourteenth century, derivatives of Lat. -*ī num* and -*ī nam* did not rime with words in which the sound [ɲ] came from Lat. *n* plus yod. Only one exception has been pointed out, namely, *camho : mihō : uihō: myhō*, i.e., *camīo : Minho : vīo : Minho* (CV, No. 912), where the poor rime or assonance arose through the necessity of using a proper noun (RF, XXIII, 341–342). It must be remembered that assonance is fairly common in this early verse (cf. CD, cxxv).

We now know that the use of the graph *nh* in derivatives
of Lat. -*ínum* and -*ínam* in the critical edition (CA) of the "Cancioneiro da Ajuda" is not in conformity with the manuscript (CA-
Carter, xiv); its use in the Italian apographs (CB and CV) is of
no significance for pronunciation at the time the poems were
written, because these manuscripts are of the late fifteenth or early
sixteenth century.

B. If the first vowel was pretonic and the second vowel was
tonic *i* in hiatus with a following *a* or *o*, the nasal resonance
spread to all three vowels. Later a palatalized nasal developed
between the last two vowels in the regular way: *litaniam* >
*lidaia* > *ladainha; venibam* > *venia* > *vẹia* > *viia* > *viinha* >
*vinha*.

C. A palatalized nasal developed with the accent reversed,
that is, between *i* (or *e*, which in hiatus became *i*) and a following
tonic *a* or *u: dīvīnāre* > *adivinhar* (with prosthetic *a*); *ordīnāre* >
*ordinhar* (Crest, Glossary); *\*daemoniātos* > *demōiados* (RL, I,
338) > *demoinhados* (RL, I, 345); *\*ne* (for *nec*)-*ūnum* > *nē*
*hum* > *nenhum*. In certain dialects of the north of Portugal and in
Galician, a palatalized nasal developed between *ẹ* and a following
tonic *ẹ: \*vēnĕram* (for *vénĕram*) > *vinhera* (Esquisse, § 75 r).
Perhaps this was due to the complete dissimilation of *ẹẹ* to [je]
in the regions in question before the disappearance of the nasal
resonance. The word *dinheiro* had the same development:
*denarium* > *dieiro* > *dinheiro*, and is therefore probably a borrowing from a dialect. Compare with this the regular development of *vieiro* (from *venarium*).

D. Just as a palatalized nasal developed between tonic *i* and
final *a*, a labialized nasal [m] developed between tonic *u* and
final *a: ūnam* > *hūa* > *uma* (Lições, 60). But this happened
only in *uma* (and its derivatives). It was brought about by the
intensification and preservation of the nasal resonance in the
earlier form *ūa* through the influence of the masculine form *um*
[ū]. The form *ūa* was preferred by the grammarian João de
Moraes Madureyra Feijó (Moraes, 71–72) in the early eighteenth
century, is still popular in all parts of Portugal, and is used in
verse before a noun beginning with *m* (Opúsculos, II, 139–140).
Between tonic *u* and final *a*, *m* did not generally develop nor
did the nasal resonance remain: *\*commūna* > *comũa* > *comua;*

*lūnam* > *lūa* > *lua*.   The form *luma* (for *lua*) is found in certain dialects (Comp, 216, n. 1; RL, VIII, 167; RL, XXVIII, 29).

5. If the first vowel was pretonic and the second vowel was followed by a dental, a consonantal *n* sometimes developed between the second vowel and the dental, the nasal resonance remaining on the second vowel: *\*anēthŭlum* > *endro; \*cĭnĭtĭa* > *cę̄ı̨za* > *ciinza* > *cinza; dīvĭnĭtātem* > *diviidade* > *divindade; \*manūtĭa* > *māuça* > *maunça; mĭnūtĭas* > *mĭuças* > *miunças; tĕnētis* > *tēedes* > *tendes; poenĭtentĭam* > *pendença* (old); vĕnītĭs* > *vę̄ı̨des* > *viides* > *vindes*.

A. This change always took place if both vowels were alike or became alike by assimilation.   In other cases the presence of a dental after the second vowel did not always assure the production of a consonantal *n: \*admĭnacĭam* > *ameaça; monētam* > *moeda; vanĭtātem* > *vaidade; vēnātum* > *veado.*

B. After the dental element of *ç* [ts] and *z* [dz] disappeared, the [n] also disappeared but the nasal resonance remained: *cinza* [sĩdzɐ] > *cinza* [sĩzɐ].

6. If both vowels were alike and the second was followed by a velar, a velar *n* [ŋ] developed: *enecāre* > *engar; benedicāmus* > *bēeigamos* > *bengamos* (old).

7. If a final contracted nasal vowel, a nasal diphthong, or a consonantal nasal of some kind did not develop, the nasal resonance disappeared in the course of the fifteenth century: *arēnam* > *arēa* > *area* > *areia; bŏnam* > *bõa* > *boa; corōnam* > *corõa* > *corôa; mŏnăchum* > *moago* > *mogo; tenēre* > *tēer* > *teer* > *ter; anellum* > *ãello* > *eelo* > *elo.*

A. The nasal resonance has remained in some of these words in certain dialects, e.g., *bõa* (RL, XI, 274; RL, XII, 308).

B. Intervocalic *n* remained unchanged in learned words, e.g., *fortūnam* > *fortuna; unīre* > *unir;* and in borrowings, e.g., *poenam* > Sp. *pena* > Ptg. *pena; septimānam* > Sp. *semana* > Ptg. *semana.*   The words *menos* (from *mĭnus*), *menor* (from *minōrem*) and *feno* (from *fēnum*) are regressive words and replace OPtg. *meos, meor* and *feo* respectively; they are probably borrowings from Spanish, adopted in order to avoid confusion with other words that had identical forms, e.g., *meos* (from *mĕōs* and *mĕdĭōs*), *feo* (from *foedum*).    Cf. BSC, X, 814.

## INTERVOCALIC LONG CONSONANTS

**79. LABIALS.**

1. Cl. L. intervocalic *bb* > Ptg. *b*: *abbātem* > *abade*.

2. Cl. L. intervocalic *ff* > Ptg. *f*: *offendo* > *ofendo*.

3. Cl. L. intervocalic *pp* > Ptg. *p*: *cĭppum* > *cepo*; *stŭppam* > *estôpa*.

**80. PALATALS AND VELARS.**

1. Cl. L. intervocalic *cc* followed by *a*, *o*, or *u* > Ptg. *c* [k]: *bŭccam* > *boca*; *peccāre* > *pecar*; *sĭccum* > *sêco*.

2. Cl. L. intervocalic *cc* followed by *e* or *i* > Ptg. *c* [s]: *acceptāre* > *aceitar*; *accentum* > *acento*.

A. In the development of *occidentem* to *ouciente* (BF, I, 47; Eluc), the first *c* [k] probably changed to *p* and vocalized (cf. § 92, 7 c).    Cf. PhM. I, 241.

3. Cl. L. intervocalic *gg* followed by *e* or *i* > Ptg. *g* [ʒ]: *exaggerāre* > *exagerar*; *suggerĕre* > *sugerir* (with shift of conjugation).

**81. DENTALS.**

1. Cl. L. intervocalic *dd* > Ptg. *d*: *addĕre* > *adir* (with shift of conjugation): *addūco* > *adugo* (old).

2. Cl. L. intervocalic *tt* > Ptg. *t*: *mĭttit* > *mete*; *sagĭttam* > *seta*.

**82. LIQUIDS.**

1. Cl. L. intervocalic *ll* > Ptg. *l*: *caballum* > *cavalo*; *gallīnam* > *galinha*.

A. Words in which *ll* became *lh* are borrowings from Spanish: *bēryllum* > *brilho*; *grillum* > *grilho* (old).    The word *caballarĭum* became *cavaleiro* and *cavalheiro*; and *castellānum* became *castelão* and *castelhano* (OPtg. *castelhão*); the forms with *lh* are borrowings from Spanish.

2. Cl. L. intervocalic *rr* > Ptg. *rr*: *ferrum* > *ferro*; *tŭrrim* > *tôrre*.

**83. SIBILANTS.**

1. Cl. L. intervocalic *ss* > Ptg. *ss* [s]: *ŏssum* > *ôsso; passum* > *passo.*

A. In a few words *ss* became *x* [ʃ]: *vessicam* > *bexiga* (cf. It. *vescica*, GIt, § 109, 6); *Messĭas* > *Mexias* (old). This palatalization of *ss* has been attributed to the following *i̯* (Comp, 118–119; RL, XXXIV, 307), but is probably the result of confusion of dialectal [ś] with [ʃ] (cf. § 65, 1 A).

**84. NASALS.**

1. Cl. L. intervocalic *mm* > Ptg. *m: commūnem* > *comum; flammam* > *chama.*

A. The nasalization of the preceding vowel has disappeared except in certain dialects.

2. Cl. L. intervocalic *nn* > Ptg. *n: annum* > *ano; pannum* > *pano.*

A. Words in which Cl. L. *nn* became Ptg. *nh* are borrowings from Spanish: *\*ante-annum* > Sp. *antaño* > *antanho; pĭnnam* > Sp. *peña* > *penha; stannum* > Sp. *estaño* > *estanho.*

B. The preceding vowel was nasalized but this nasalization has disappeared except in certain dialects.

## MEDIAL CONSONANT GROUPS

**85. CHANGES TO GROUPS IN VULGAR LATIN.**

1. Most of the changes undergone by medial consonant groups had their inception in Vulgar Latin and it is generally difficult to determine how far they had progressed by the beginning of the Portuguese period. There are a few, however, which took place clearly in Vulgar Latin (see §12, 6).

2. Cl. L. medial *rs* > V.L. and Ptg. *ss: persĭcum* > *pêssego; persōnam* > *pessoa; ursum* > *usso* (old); *versum* > *vesso* (old).

A. MPtg. *urso* and *verso* are regressive words.

3. Cl. L. medial *ps* > V.L. and Ptg. *ss: ipse > êsse; gypsum > gêsso.*

A. It has been maintained that *ps* became [ks] (M-L, Gram, I, § 458); this assumption would very conveniently explain *caixa* (from *capsam*) and *queixo* (from *capsum*). It should be pointed out, however, that if this is correct, *caixa* would be the only word in which *a* followed by *x* did not become *ei* (cf. § 33, 3). Cf. HR, V, 349.

4. Cl. L. medial *pt* > V.L. *tt* and Ptg. *t: aptāre > atar; captāre > catar; inceptāre > encetar; ruptum > rôto; scrīptum > escrito; septem > sete.* Cf. Carnoy, 158.

A. There are many words in which the *p* was preserved and had a different subsequent development (§ 92, 7 c).

5. Cl. L. medial *nct* > V.L. and Ptg. *nt: junctum > junto; sanctum > santo.*

A. It is difficult to determine the time of this change (Carnoy, 165–166). It did not take place in the Vulgar Latin of Gaul and certain other regions (GVL, § 267).

6. Cl. L. medial *ns* > V.L. and Ptg. *s: mensem > mês; pensāre > pesar; sponsum > espôso.*

A. A similar change took place in the group *nstr*, which became *str: instrumentum > estormento* (old); *monstrāre > mostrar.*

7. Cl. L. medial *nf* > V.L. and OPtg. *f: confortāre > cofortar* (old); *infantem > ifante* (old); *infernum > iferno* (old).

A. This *n* was restored by regression at an early date, perhaps through the influence of the common prefixes *in-* and *con-* (cf. M-L, Gram, I, § 403, 3).

8. Cl. L. *x* followed by a consonant > V.L. and Ptg. *s: expertum > esperto; sextum > sesto* (now spelled *sexto*).

9. The final consonant of a prefix was assimilated to the initial consonant of the word to which it was attached: *adversum > avêsso; advenīre > avir; obviāre > oviar* (old); *subterrāre* (Du Cange) *> soterrar; subtīlem > sutil.*

A. The final consonant of the prefix was often restored by regression: *adventum* > *avento* (old) and *advento; advocātum* > *avogado* (old) and *advogado*.

## 86. MUTE + LIQUID.

1. A mute followed by *l* or *r* (except in the groups *cl, gl, gr,* and *bl*) had the same development in Portuguese as a single intervocalic mute; if the liquid was *l*, it became *r: colŭbram* > *coovra* (RL, XXVII, 24); *laborāre* > *lavrar; fĕbrem* > *fevre* (old and popular); *aprīlem* > *abril; duplāre* > *dobrar; lĕpŏrem* > *lebre; lacrĭmam* > *lágrima; sŏcrum* > *sogro;* \**anēthŭlum* > \**anedlo* > *āedro* > *endro; pĕtram* > *pedra; quadraginta* > *quarenta; hĕdĕram* > *edra* > *hera.*

A. A long consonant followed by *l* or *r* had the same development as an intervocalic long consonant: *approbāre* > *aprovar; lĭttĕram* > *lêtra; supplicāre* > *supricar* (old).

B. There are some semi-learned words in which *b* did not change, e.g., *nōbĭlem* > *nobre; octūbrem* > *outubro;* and some regressive words in which *b* was restored, e.g., *cobra* (for *coovra*); *febre* (for *fevre*).

C. These groups were sometimes broken up by metathesis of the *r: pigrĭtĭam* > \**pegriça* > *preguiça; tenĕbras* > *teevras* > *trevas.*

D. Words in which *gr* survived unchanged and words in which *cl* and *gl* became *gr* are semi-learned words or borrowings from other languages: *nĭgrum* > *negro; eclĕsĭam* > *igreja; rēgŭlam* > Sp. *regla* > *regra; miracŭlum* > *milagre; saecŭlum* > *segre* (old). See ZRPh, XLII, 227–230. Cf. Biblos, VII, 518. For the popular development of *cl* and *gl,* see § 92, 8; for that of *gr,* see § 92, 4.

E. The words *māi* (from *matrem*) and *pai* (from *patrem*) present a special problem. Intermediate forms *made* and *pade* have been explained as having arisen in the pronunciation of children because of their trouble in pronouncing *r* (RL, XXIII, 50 and 64). These intermediate forms have also been explained as having developed by analogy with *frade* (from *fratrem*), in which the *r* fell by dissimilation (Nascentes, s.v. *māe*). The form *pai* is found in rime with *vai* (CA, line 8380) in a poem written in the first half of the thirteenth century (CA, II, 297); *mãe* is not found in the early Cancioneiros (RL, XXIII, 50).

F. For the development of *cadeira* (from *cathedram*), see RFE, VII, 58.

2. In the regular development of the group *bl* the *b* was assimilated to the *l*: *fabŭlāre* > *fablar* > *fallar* > *falar*: *\*tabularia* > *\*tablaria* > *taleira; ŭbī illum* > *\*ublo* > *ullo* (Esquisse, § 72 a; Opúsculos, II, 19), i.e., *ulo; sŭb illum* > *\*sublo* > *solo* (CV, No. 507).

A. There are no words in which *bl* became *vr*. Words in which it became *br* are semi-learned words or borrowings from Spanish: *oblĭgāre* > *obrigar; oblītāre* (REW) > *obridar* (old); *diabŏlum* > Sp. *diablo* > *diabro* (FM, II, Glossary, s.v. *diaboo*).

B. The development of *bl* in *falar* has been explained as due to the influence of *calar* (Grund, I, 975) and also as due to dissimilation of the *v* in an intermediate form *\*favlar* (MP, XI, 349). But neither of these explanations would account for the same development in *taleira, ullo,* and *solo.* Cf. Nascentes, s.v. *falar.*

## 87. Groups Ending in Yod.

1. These groups consist of one or two consonants followed by unaccented *e* or *i* in hiatus with a following vowel. The yod may be of Vulgar Latin or Portuguese origin. Vulgar Latin yod arose through hiatus originally existing in Classical Latin; Portuguese yod through hiatus brought about by the fall in Portuguese of intervocalic *d, g, l,* or *n,* or through original Classical Latin hiatus in later borrowings from Latin, i.e., in semi-learned words. Groups in which yod developed from a palatal consonant are treated separately(§ 92).

2. That yod was relatively slow in forming in the Portuguese territory is shown by the voicing of *p* and *b* in forms like *saiba* and *raiva* (§ 88 A), the lack of attraction in early forms like *sabia* (RL, XXIII, 79), and the long retention of syllabic value by the *e* in hiatus in forms like *fêmea* (§ 91, 1 B).

**88. GROUPS UNAFFECTED BY VULGAR LATIN YOD.**

Vulgar Latin yod did not affect a preceding medial *b*, *p*, *f*, *v*, *m* or *r*, or a preceding group ending in *b*, *v*, *m* or *r*: *\*rabĭam* (for *rabĭem*) > *raiva; rŭbĕum* > *ruivo; sēpĭam* > *siba; sapĭat* > *saiba; cuphĭam* (Du Cange) > *coifa; cavĕam* > *gaiva; vindēmĭam* > *vindima; cŏrĭum* > *coiro; superbĭam* > *soberba; nervĭum* (Ainsworth) > *nervo; dormĭāmus* > *durmamos; atrĭum* > *adro.*

A. It is evident that yod did not prevent the voicing of a preceding medial *b* or *p*. It has been suggested that yod lengthened *p* to *pp* after a Classical Latin short vowel but not after a long vowel (M-L, Gram, I, § 506): *ăpĭum* > *\*appiu* > *aipo*, but *sēpĭam* > *siba;* and accordingly, the *b* of *caibo* (from *căpĭo*), etc. and the *b* of *saiba* (from *săpĭat*), etc. have been explained as analogical with other forms of these verbs in which there was no yod (Grund, I, 959).    But the form *aipo* is probably semi-learned; cf. Sp. *apio*.

B. Preceding groups ending in *p*, *f*, *l*, or *n* (except *mn*), if there were any, were not affected by yod.    For *mn* plus yod see § 89, 9 B.

**89. GROUPS AFFECTED BY VULGAR LATIN YOD.**

1. Vulgar Latin yod affected a preceding medial *c*, *t*, *d*, *g*, *l*, *ll*, *n*, *s*, and *ss* and a preceding group ending in *c*, *t*, *d*, and *g*.

2. Lat. *c* + *i̯* preceded by a vowel or a consonant > Ptg. *ç* or *c* [s]: *bracchĭum* > *braço; facĭo* > *faço; \*incalcĭāre* > *encalçar; lanceāre* > *lançar; facĭem* > *face.*

A. The intermediate stage was [ts], from which the dental element disappeared in the course of the sixteenth century (cf. KJ, IV, Part I, 327).

B. Lat. *c* plus yod, preceded by a vowel, sometimes became *z:* *fidūcĭam* > *fiuza* (old); *Gallaecĭam* > *Galiza; judĭcĭum* > *juizo.* This is the regular development of *t* plus yod.    The confusion in these words arose as a result of the common use in Vulgar Latin of *c* plus yod for *t* plus yod (see section 4 A below).

c. Lat. *ct* plus yod became *iç*: *destructiōnem* > *destruição;*
*electiōnem* > *eleição.* As a result of the use of *ct* for *pt* (§ 92,
7 c), *pt* plus yod likewise became *iç*: *conceptiōnem* > *conceição.*

3. Lat. *t* + *i̯* preceded by a consonant > *ç* or *c* [s]:
*fŏrtĭam* (Du Cange) > *fôrça; lentĕum* > *lenço; tertiarĭum* >
*terceiro; silentĭum* > *seenço* (old).

4. Lat. *t* + *i̯* preceded by a vowel > *z: pretiāre* > *prezar;*
*ratiōnem* > *razão; satiōnem* > *sazão; vĭtĭum* > *vêzo; -ĭtĭam*
> *-eza.*

A. Lat. *t* plus yod preceded by a vowel did not develop regularly in most cases but became *ç*: \**mētĭo* (for *mētĭor*) > *meço;*
*oratiōnem* > *oração; palatĭum* > *paço; platĕam* > *praça; plŭtĕa*
> *choça; pŭtĕum* > *poço; -itĭam* > *-iça; -ĭtĭem* > *-ice.* This de-
velopment arose in Vulgar Latin through a semi-learned mistaken
use of *c* plus yod for *t* plus yod in an effort to avoid the popular
and long established assibilated pronunciation of *t* plus yod;
that is, [kj] came to be used as the result of an effort to say [tj]
instead of [tsj] (TAPA, XLVII, 147). Cf. GVL, § 276; Hanssen
§ 19, 14. It has been pointed out that *t* plus yod had become
assibilated somewhat earlier than *c* plus yod (§ 12, 3).

B. Words in which *st* plus yod became *ch* are borrowings from
Galician: *bĕstĭam* > *bicha; comestiōnem* > *comichão.*

5. Lat. *d* + *i̯* preceded by a vowel > Ptg. *j* [ʒ]: *adiutāre*
> *ajudar; hŏdĭe* > *hoje; pŏdĭum* > *pôjo; vĭdĕo* > *vejo.*

A. In a few words *d* plus yod became *i* [j]: *mĕdĭum* > *meio;*
*mŏdĭum* > *moio; pŏdĭum* > *poio; radĭum* > *raio.* Some of these
words are semi-learned words, some are borrowings from Spanish
(Behr, 37–38). Cf. TAPA, XLVII, 150–151. *Fastio* (from
*fastīdĭum*) is a borrowing from Spanish (cf. Manual, § 53, 3).

6. Lat. *d* + *i̯* preceded by a consonant or a diphthong >
Ptg. *ç: ardĕo* > *arço* (old); \**perdĕo* (for *perdo*) > *perço*
(old); *verecundĭam* > *vergonça* (old); *audĭo* > *ouço.*

A. It seems that in certain regions *d* between *n* and yod fell;
hence the variant *vergonha* of OPtg. *vergonça* and OPtg. *rigonha*
(from *iracundĭam*). Cf. OFr. *graignor* (from *grandiōrem*). See
Carnoy, 156.

B. The word *gôzo* (from *gaudĭum*) is a borrowing from Spanish.

7. Lat. *g* + *i̯* preceded by a vowel or a consonant >
Ptg. *j* [ʒ]: *fŭgĭo* > *fujo; pulēgĭum* > *poejo; spongĭam* >
*esponja.*

A. The words *correia* (from *corrĭgĭam*) and *ensaio* (from
*exagĭum*) are probably borrowings from Spanish. *Navio* (from
*navigĭum*) may be a borrowing from a dialect of Italy (MP, XII,
194). For the different development of the tonic vowel of *correia*
and *navio*, see RHi, LXXVII, 132.

8. Lat. *l* or *ll* + *i̯* preceded by a vowel > Ptg. *lh*:
*alĭēnum* > *alheio; fīlĭum* > *filho; mulĭĕrem* > *\*mulĭĕrem* >
*mulher; allĭum* > *alho; malleāre* > *malhar.*

A. This change has taken place in learned words in certain
dialects, e.g., *familĭam* > *família* > *familha* (Alentejano).
B. In some words, yod did not prevent the fall of *l*: *salĭo* >
*saio; dolĕo* > *doyo* (old); *Julĭānum* > *Juião* (old). This has been
explained as a development peculiar to Old Galician (Huber,
§ 44, 1). It has been explained in the verb forms as due to
analogy with the other persons in which there was no yod (RL,
XXXIII, 198).

9. Lat. *n* + *i̯* preceded by a vowel > Ptg. *nh*: *senĭōrem*
> *senhor; tĕnĕo* > *tenho; vīnĕam* > *vinha.*

A. This change has taken place in learned words in popular
speech: *Antōnĭum* > *António* > *Antonho* (popular); *daemŏnĭum*
> *demónio* > *demonho* (popular).
B. There are two examples with *mn* plus yod: *sŏmnĭum* >
*sonho; calumnĭam* > *caomia* > *coima*. This double development
is found only in Portuguese (cf. Sp. *sueño* and *caloña*, Fr. *songe*
and OFr. *chalonge*, It. *sogno* and OIt. *calogna*). The form *calonha*
(Eluc) is probably a borrowing from Spanish. The *m* of *coima*
is probably due to contamination by Arabic *quîma* (Dozy, 257).
For this and other attempts to explain the development of *coima*,
see Nascentes; MP, XI, 349. The derivation of *conha* from
*calumnĭam* (RL, III, 265) was a mistake which Nunes did not
repeat in his "Compêndio."
c. The group *ln* followed by *e* or *i* in hiatus must have lost
the *l* as soon as yod developed (ALLG, I, 248): *balnĕum* >
*\*banĭum* > *banho.*

10. Lat. *s* + *i̯* preceded by a vowel > Ptg. *j* [ʒ]: *basi̯um* > *beijo; casĕum* > *queijo; eclēsĭam* > *igreja.*

11. Lat. *ss* + *i̯* and *sc* + *i̯* > Ptg. *x* [ʃ]: *\*bassi̯um* > *baixo; passiōnem* > *paixão; russĕum* > *roxo; ascĭŏlam* (Du Cange) > *enxó; fasci̯am* > *faixa* and *faxa.*

## 90. Effect of Vulgar Latin Yod on Vowel and Consonant.

It might be said that in general Vulgar Latin yod spent its force either on the preceding vowel or the preceding consonant. If it affected the preceding consonant, it had no effect on the preceding vowel. The only exceptions are the closing of tonic *ę*, *ǫ* and *o̦* with consonants affected by yod: *tĕrti̯um* > *têrço; hŏdĭe* > *hoje; cŭnĕum* > *cunho;* and the attraction of yod with *s*, *ss* and *sc: casĕum* > *queijo; passiōnem* > *paixão; fasci̯am* > *faixa.* The apparent effect of yod on pretonic *ę* was rather the subsequent effect of the palatalized consonant (see § 41, 3 A).

A. Yod affected both vowel and consonant at the same time more frequently in dialectal Portuguese: *veinho* for *venho; fuijo* for *fujo* (Opúsculos, II, 204).

B. The yod which came from the palatal consonant of a consonant group likewise had in general no effect on the preceding vowel if it affected another consonant of the consonant group, e.g., *agnum* > *anho.*

## 91. Groups Ending in Portuguese Yod.

1. The Portuguese yod which arose through the fall of intervocalic *d*, *g*, *l* or *n:* a) did not affect the preceding consonant: *aci̯num* > *azeo* (old); *būci̯num* > *búzio; \*cŭti̯nam* > *côdea; lītĭgāre* > *lidiar* > *lidar; \*rĕtĭnam* > *rédea;* b) if it developed early, it was attracted to the preceding vowel: *cŏmĕdo* > *\*comio* > *coimo* (old); *\*exfamĭnāre* > *esfaimar;* or it closed the preceding vowel and fell: *lĭmpĭdum* > *limpo; tŭrbĭdum* > *turvo; tĕrmĭnum* > *termio* > *têrmo;* c) if it developed late, it did not affect the preceding vowel

and remained: *cŭtĭnam > côdea; fēmĭnam > fêmea; gĕmĭnum > gémeo; *rĕtĭnam > rédea; sĭmĭlam > sêmea.

A. In the hypothetical development of the word *sujo* a Portuguese yod affects the preceding consonant: sūcĭdum > *çusio
(by metathesis) > çujo, now spelled *sujo* (RHi, V, 421).

B. The *e* of *côdea, fêmea*, etc. counted as a separate syllable
as late as the verse of the "Cancioneiro Geral" (A.D. 1516) but
became a yod soon after this time (Grund, I, 1001, § 265).

2. The yod of later borrowings from Latin (semi-learned
words) did not affect the preceding consonant but affected
the preceding vowel and fell: bĕstĭam > bêsta; christĭānum
> cristão; confessĭōnem > confissão; relĭquĭas > religas
(Bausteine, 582); stŭdĭum > estudo; vīsĭōnem > visão; in-
sĭdĭas > inssidas (RL, XX, 197).

A. In learned words the vowel did not close, e.g., *sessão* (from
*sessiōnem*) and the yod did not generally fall, e.g., *família* (from
*familĭam*), *grémio* (from *grĕmĭum*). Cf. § 35, 2 B.

B. In dialectal and popular Portuguese this yod was sometimes attracted to the preceding vowel regardless of the nature
of the preceding consonant: daemŏnium > demónio > demoino
(popular); Tīmŏthĕum > Timóteo > Temóito (Algarvio).

## 92. Groups Containing a Palatal Consonant.

1. Lat. *c* preceded by a consonant and followed by *e* or
*i* > Ptg. *c* [s]: mancĭpĭum > mancebo; mercēdem > mercê;
vincendum > vencendo.

A. In *urze* (from *ulĭcem*) and *catorze* (from *quattuordĕcim*) the *c*
developed in the intervocalic position before the fall of the posttonic penult.

2. Lat. *sc* followed by *e* or *i* > Ptg. *x* [ʃ]: fascem > feixe;
miscēre > mexer; pĭscem > peixe; vascellum > baixel. .

A. The position of the accent does not seem to have anything
to do with the development (cf. M-L, Gram, I, § 473). In
semi-learned words *sc* followed by *e* or *i* became *c*: discĭpŭlum >
decipolo (cf. FM, I, xxiv); *-escēre > -ecer.

3. Lat. *g* preceded by a consonant and followed by *e* or *i*
> Ptg. *g* [ʒ]: *algentem* > *algente; angĕlum* > *angeo* > *anjo;
argillam* > *argila; longe* > *longe; spargēre* > *espargir* (with
shift of conjugation); *virgĭnem* > *virgem.*

A. Old and popular forms such as *arzila, esparzir,* etc. are
probably the result of a semi-learned confusion of *c* and *g* in this
position in Vulgar Latin (Carnoy, 157).

B. The group *ng* followed by *e* or *i* became *nh* in a few words
borrowed from Spanish: *quīngentos* > OSp. *quiñentos* > *quinhentos; *ringĭre* (for *ringi*) > Sp. *reñir* > *renhir.* The word
*inhenho* (from *ingĕnŭum*) presents a special problem: *ingĕnŭum*
first became *engeo* (Eluc) or *engēo,* which later became *engenho*
(Eluc), perhaps by contamination of *engenho* (from *ingĕnĭum*);
by assimilation of *ng* to *nh, engenho* then became *inhenho* (cf.
Comp, 134).

4. Lat. *gr* > Ptg. *ir: fragrāre* > *flagrāre* (GVL, § 292) >
*cheirar; intĕgrum* > *inteiro.*

5. Lat. *gn* > Ptg. *nh: agnum* > *anho; cognātum* > *cunhado; cognoscendum* > *conhecendo; insignem* > *insinhe* (old);
*lĭgnum* > *lenho; pŭgnum* > *punho.*

A. The changes through which this sound passed were the
following: [gn] > [jn] > [jɲ] > [ɲ]. *Reino* (from *regnum*) was
prevented from going beyond the second stage through the
influence of *rei.*

B. The *g* of *gn* fell in semi-learned words: *dignum* > *dino*
(old); *insignāre* (Du Cange) > *ensinar; benignum* > *benino* (old);
*malignum* > *malino* (old); *signum* > *sino.* This *g* was restored
in spelling and pronunciation in *digno, benigno* and *maligno.*

6. Lat. *ngl* > Ptg. *nh: singŭlos* > *senhos* (Flor, Glossary);
*singularĭum* > *senlheiro* > *senheiro* (old); *ungŭlam* > *unha.*

A. The intermediate stage was *nlh,* shown in the form *senlheiro*
(Cd'A, III, Glossary).

7. Lat. *ct* > Ptg. *it: factum* > *feito; lĕctum* > *leito; nŏctem* > *noite.*

A. If the $i$ of $it$ became nasalized, a consonantal $n$ developed (§ 78, 5) and the $i$ fell: *benedĭctum* > *beēeito* > *bēito* > *bento; hac nŏcte* > *\*a nocte* > *aōite* > *oonte* (RL, XXVII, 55) > *ontem; pĕctĭnem* > *peitē* > *pēitē* > *pentem* > *pente*. The same change occurred where the $i$ was of a different origin: Ptg. *muito* > *munto* (popular, RL, IV, 231; HR, VI, 264).

B. The $i$ of $it$ generally fell when preceded by $u$: *trŭctam* > *truita* > *truta; frŭctum* > *fruito* > *fruto*. It contracted with a preceding $i$ (§ 36, 2): *\*dīctum* > *dito*.

C. Lat. *ct* and *pt* were sometimes interchanged in Portuguese territory. The regular development of *pt* in Vulgar Latin was to *tt* (§ 85, 4). A different development took place later, viz., *pt* > *\*ft* > *ṵt: aptum* > *auto* (old); *praeceptum* > *preceuto* (old); *raptum* > *rauto* (RL, XVI, 10); *adoptāre* > *adoutar* (Eluc); *baptizāre* > *boutiçar* (Eluc). It was this *pt* (or its derivative *\*ft*) which was interchanged with *ct* (or its derivative *\*[χt]*). Cf. Traité, 204; BF, III, 96–97.

This use of one group for the other was determined by the nature of the preceding vowel.

When preceded by $e$, *pt* had the same development as *ct: accĕptum* > *aceito; concĕptum* > *conceito; praecĕptum* > *preceito; recĕptam* > *receita; sĕptĭmum* > *seitimo* (old); *septuaginta* > *seitenta* (old). This development of *pt* to *[χt]*, followed by vocalization of the palatal was characteristic of Celtic (Dottin, 100).

When preceded by $a$ or $o$, particularly pretonic $o$, *ct* had the same development as *pt: actīvum* > *autivo* (Eluc); *actum* > *auto; contractum* > *contrauto* (Eluc); *tractātum* > *trautado* (Fab, Glossary); *doctum* > *douto; doctōrem* > *doutor; octāvum* > *outavo* (FM, II, Glossary); *octŭbrem* (Carnoy, 64) > *outubro*.

The development of *-oct-* in some regions to *-oit-* and in others to *-out-*, followed by inter-dialectal influence, may have been the origin of the confusion of *ou* and *oi*, which existed much earlier than has generally been believed, e.g., *noute* (AHP, IV, 190, A.D. 1385; BF, IV, 347, 1450?; Abraham, §28). As a consequence of this early confusion, the use of *oi* spread in the sixteenth century to words which originally had *ou*, e.g., *coisa* (for *cousa* < *causam*) and the use of *ou* spread to words which originally had *oi* not coming from *oc(t)*, e.g., *couro* (for *coiro* < *cŏrium*), with the result that *ou* and *oi* have become generally interchangeable, although *ou* is more literary, *oi* more colloquial. It is significant that such spellings as *noute* are found earlier than such spellings as *couro* and *coisa.*

Before the beginning of the seventeenth century, *ou* had lost its diphthongal character, which is still preserved, however, in the north of Portugal. For dialectal differences, see Esquisse, § 56 e; Fink, 98. The change from *ou* to *oi* has been explained as due to dissimilation of the two elements of *ou* (RL, XXXII, 288).

Cf. Grund, I, 936; Bourciez, § 332 b; PhM, I, 75; AStNS, LXV, 47; BHi, XXXIX, 398.

D. The Romance group *c't* became [dzd], then [dz] by dissimilation, and finally z [z]: *\*amīcĭtātem* (for *amīcĭtĭam*) > *amizade; placĭtum* > *prazo; recĭtāre* > *rezar.*

E. In learned words the *c* of *ct* generally fell: *actum* > *acto* [atu]; *victĭmam* > *vítima;* but *factum* > *facto* [faktu].

8. V.L. *cl* and *gl* > Ptg. *lh: apĭcŭlam* > *abelha; novacŭlam* > *navalha; ŏcŭlum* > *ôlho; vermĭcŭlum* > *vermelho; rŏtŭlam* > *\*roclam* > *rôlha; sĭtŭlam* > *\*seclam* > *selha; vĕtŭlum* > *veclum* (ApPr) > *velho; rēgŭlam* > *relha; tēgŭlam* > *telha.*

A. The combination *tl* regularly became *cl* in Vulgar Latin (GVL, § 284).

B. In the group *bl, b* was assimilated to *l* (§ 86, 2). The same assimilation took place in some words in Spanish (Manual, § 57, 1). But in *ralhar* (from *rabulāre*) and *trilho* (from *trībŭlum*), *bl* became *cl,* unless these words were borrowed from Spanish (which does not seem possible in the case of *ralhar* as Sp. *rallar* has a different meaning and comes from *\*radulāre*).

C. The group *pl* in *\*scoplum* (from *scŏpŭlum*) seems to have become *cl: scŏpŭlum* > *\*scoclum* > *escôlho.* Sp. *escollo* was borrowed from Portuguese and perhaps from French either directly or through It. *scoglio* (AGI, XIII, 374–375). Gröber adopts the same Vulgar Latin form *\*scoclum* for French, Provençal, and Italian but needlessly assumes the assimilation of *p* to *l* for Sp. *escollo* (ALLG, V, 461–462). Meyer-Lübke borrows the French, Spanish, and Portuguese forms from It. *scoglio,* which he believes to be Neapolitan in origin (M-L, Gram, I, § 491).

D. There are many words in Portuguese in which the group *cl* did not develop because of lack of syncope: *diabŏlum* > *diaboo* > *diabo; oracŭlum* > *oragoo* > *orago; perĭcŭlum* > *perigoo* > *perigo.*   Cf. M-L, Intro, § 133.

E. The group *cl* preceded by a consonant became *ch: astŭlam* > *acha; conchŭlam* > *concha; mascŭlum* > *macho; sarcŭlum* > *sacho.*   The preceding consonant was lost in some of these words (RL, XIII, 273).

9. Lat. medial *x* > Ptg. *x* [ʃ] or *ss: buxum* > *buxo; coxam* > *coxa; fraxĭnum* > *freixo; dīxit* > *disse; \*traxŭit* > *trouxe* [trosə].

A. The change of *x* to [ʃ] may have been caused in some words by final *i̯*, thus *dīxī* > *dixe* but *dīxĭt* > *disse,* e.g., "E aa cima dixe-lhes eu . . . e o abade me disse . . ." (Flor, 71); see also Carter, 30; RL, XXIII, 30.   See RL, XXXIV, 307.

B. In learned words *x* is pronounced [s]: *auxílio, máximo, próximo, sintaxe.*   In the prefix *ex-* plus a vowel, *x* is pronounced [z]: *exame, exercício.*

C. Followed by a voiceless stop, *x* is pronounced [ʃ]: *extranĕum* > *extranho; sĕxtum* > *sexto.*   The [k] of *x* in this position disappeared in Vulgar Latin (§ 12, 6).

10. Arabic *kha* and *ḥa* preceded by the *l* of the Arabic article > *f: al-khass* > *alface; al-khaiyât* > *alfaiate; al-khomra* > *alfombra; al-khilél* > *alfinete; al-ḥeire* > *alfeire; al-ḥelâwa* > *alféloa; al-ḥofre* > *alfobre.*   Intervocalic *kha* and *ḥa* sometimes have the same change: *al-mokhadda* > *almofada; at-taḥôna* > *atafona.*   Cf. Deux, 9–10.

A. This change took place because the sound of *f* was the closest acoustical equivalent of these sounds in Portuguese.   In learned words *kha* became [k] while *ḥa* became *h* (mute) or was entirely lost.

**93. GROUPS CONTAINING A *u̯*.**

1. In many combinations *u̯* disappeared in Vulgar Latin: *aestuarĭum* > *esteiro; battualĭa* > *batalha; februarĭum* > *fevereiro; mortŭum* > *morto; quattuor* > *quattor* (Seelmann,

218) > *quatro; septuaginta* > *setaenta* > *setenta.*   See § 10, 3.

A. A u̯ of Portuguese origin was slow in forming (cf. Grund, I, 1001, § 265); it has fallen in a few dialectal forms: *consonantem* > *consoante* > *consante* (Esquisse, § 48 d); Ptg. *Manuel* > *Nel.*

B. When preceded by medial *b, p, c, t, s,* or *x,* u̯ was attracted to a preceding *a* or *o: habŭit* > *houve; sapŭit* > *soube; placŭit* > *prougue; pŏtŭit* > *pôde* (cf. § 33, 4; § 37, 4; § 40, 4; § 43, 5).   The form *prougue* shows that attraction took place after the time of the palatalization of *g* followed by *e* or *i.* And that u̯ was relatively slow in forming in the Portuguese territory is shown by the voicing of the medial consonant. Compare Ptg. *soube* and Sp. *supe.* When preceded by medial *g,* u̯ was attracted to a preceding *e* in dialectal Portuguese: *ĕquam* > *égua* > *euga* (dialectal); *regŭlam* > *régua* > *reuga* (dialectal).

C. The u̯ of the diphthong *au* was attracted to the final syllable in certain dialectal forms of learned words: *causam* > *causa* > *cásua; flautam* (REW) > *flauta* > *flátua* (RL, VII, 39).

2. Lat. *qu* preceded by a vowel and followed by *a* > Ptg. *gu* [gw]: *aquam* > *água; aequālem* > *igual; ĕquam* > *égua.*

A. Preceded by a consonant the *q* did not voice: *quīnquaginta* > *cinquaenta* > *cinqüenta* (§ 99, 3), the u̯ remaining because the following *a* survived sufficiently late.   It is not clear why the u̯ fell in *nunca* (from *numquam*).

3. Lat. *qu* preceded by a vowel and followed by *e, i, o* or *u* > Ptg. *g* [g] or *gu* [g]: *alĭquem* > *alguém; aquĭlam* > *águila; *sĕqŭo* (for *sĕqŭor*) > *sigo; antĭquum* > *antigo.*

A. If *q* was long it did not voice: *accu̯-(h)īc* > *aqui.*   The words *freqüente* (from *frequentem*) and *tranqüilo* (from *tranquillum*) are learned.

B. In a few words, u̯ fell early enough in Vulgar Latin for [k] to be assibilated: *cŏquĕre* > *cŏcēre* > *cozer; laquĕum* > *lacĕum* > *laço; torquĕre* > *torcēre* > *torcer.*   GVL, § 254; Grund, I, 962; Manual, § 52, 3.

C. Lat. *cu* (unaccented) preceded by a vowel and followed by *o* had the same development: *vacŭum* > *vago.*

4. Lat. *gu* preceded by a consonant and followed by *a* >

Ptg. *gu* [gw]: *lingŭam* > *língua*.

5. Lat. *gu* preceded by a consonant and followed by *e* or *o* > Ptg. *g* [g] or *gu* [g]: *distingŭo* > *distingo; sanguen* > *sangue*.

A. The word *ungüento* (from *unguentum*) is learned.

6. Lat. *lŭ* > Ptg. *lv: valuĭsset* > *valvesse* (CV, No. 963); *\*doluĕrunt* (for *doluērunt*) > *dolveron* (CSM, I, No. 241, p. 336, col. 2).

7. Lat. *dŭ* > Ptg. *v: \*crēduit* (M-L, Intro, § 191) > *creve* (old); *\*sēduit* (GVL, § 428) > *seve* (old).

A. The development of this group was probably as follows: *dŭ* > *dv* > *vv* > *v*.

8. Lat. *nŭ* followed by *a* > Ptg. *ngŭ: manuāle* > *mangual; \*minuāre* (for *minuĕre*) > *minguar*.   M-L, Gram, I, § 503.

9. Lat. *nŭ* followed by *e* or by *a* which became *e* > Ptg. *n: januarĭum* > *janeiro; januellam* > *janela; manuarĭa* > *maneira*.   M-L, Gram, I, § 503.

10. A Romance *ŭ* developed from bilabial *v* followed by *g fabrĭcam* > *fravega* > *\*fravga* > *\*frauga* > *frágua; -ĭficāre* > *-evegar* > *\*-evgar* > *\*-eugar* > *-iguar* (Manual, § 18, 2).

A. These forms are borrowings from Spanish, as the posttonic penult of *fravega* and the intertonic of *-evegar* would not have fallen in Portuguese.   The ending *-evegar* (or *-ivigar*) was fairly common in Old Portuguese and although it has been replaced by *-iguar*, the latter is not used as much in Portuguese as in Spanish.   Cf. AStNS, CXXIV, 336, s.v. *\*ădvērĭfĭco*.

## 94. GROUPS BEGINNING WITH *l*.

1. Lat. *l* preceded by *a* and followed by *t, p* or *c* [s] > OPtg. *ŭ* in the diphthong *ou*, now pronounced [o]: *altarĭum* > *outeiro; altĕrum* > *outro; saltum* > *souto; palpāre* > *poupar; \*talparĭa* > *toupeira; calcem* > *couce; falcem* > *fouce*.

A. That vocalization of *l* was an early change is proved by

a) the fact that it occurred in all Romance territory, except
Rumania and Italy (literary Italian), b) the fact that it did
not occur in Arabic borrowings (notably initial *al* plus a consonant), c) the fact that it did not occur in Germanic borrowings
(names of people and place names), and d) the fact that it did
not occur in Romance groups. See Biblos, VIII, 96–97; GVL,
§ 288; Grund, I, 976.

B. There are many forms in which this change did not take
place: *altum > alto; palpāre > palpar; calceāre > calçar*. Me-
méndez Pidal thinks that these forms were due to the strong
learned reaction of the twelfth century, which allowed only a
few popular forms with *o* (Ptg. *ou*) to survive (M-P, Orig, 122).
But Piel thinks that both types, e.g., both *poupar* and *palpar*,
are popular and show the instability of *l* in this position (Biblos,
VIII, 100–101). See also ZRPh, LVII, 630–631.

2. Lat. *lt* preceded by *ŭ* > OPtg. *ịt* > MPtg. *t: auscultāre
> ascuitar > escuitar* (with change of prefix) > *escutar;
cultellum > cuitello > cutelo; vultŭrem > abuitre > abutre.*
See BHi, XXXIX, 397–399.

A. The *i* of *muito* was perhaps prevented from falling through
the influence of the apocopated form *mui*. There is a popular
form *munto*, which developed according to § 92, 7 A.

**95.** GROUPS BEGINNING WITH A NASAL CONSONANT.

1. If *m* or *n* was the first consonant of a group, it nasalized
the preceding vowel. This nasal resonance has survived in
Modern Portuguese but *n* has lost its consonantal value
before *l, r, s, ç, c* [s], *j, g* [ʒ], *f* or *v*, e.g., *enviar* [ivjar]. Before *d* or *t, n* has preserved its consonantal value, e.g., *antes*
[ẽntɪʃ], and before *c* [k] or *g* [g] its velar value, e.g., *encantar*
[iŋkẽntar]. In these groups, *m* before *b* or *p* has not lost
its consonantal value, e.g., *ambos* [ẽmbuʃ]. For *n* plus
yod, see § 89, 9.

For groups beginning with an *n* which arose from a
nasalized vowel, see § 78, 5 and 6; § 92, 7 A.

2. Lat. *mn* > Ptg. *n: autumnum > outono; columnam >*

*coona* (Eluc); *damnum* > *dano; dŏmĭnum* > *dono; scamnum* > *escano; sŏmnum* > *sono.*

A. Because of lack of syncope the Romance group *mn*, which became *mbr* in Spanish, did not develop in Portuguese (§ 52, 2; § 57, 2): *fēmĭnam* > Sp. *hembra* but Ptg. *fêmea.* Portuguese words in which Romance *mn* became *mbr* are borrowings from Spanish, e.g., *deslumbrar* (from Sp. *des* + *lumbrar* < *lūmĭnāre*).

3. In the Romance group *md*, which arose through the fall of posttonic or intertonic *e* after the voicing of inter-vocalic *t*, *m* changed to *n* by assimilation to the dental: *cŏmĭtem* > *conde; līmĭtes* > *lindes; semitarĭum* > *sendeiro.* The subsequent development was the same as that of original Classical Latin *nd* (section 1 above).

4. After the fall of *p* in the Classical Latin or Vulgar Latin group *mpt*, *m* became *n* by assimilation to the dental: *exemptum* > *isento; promptum* > *pronto; computāre* > *contar.* The subsequent development was the same as that of original Classical Latin *nt* (section 1 above).

5. Lat. *mpl* > Ptg. *nch* or *mpr: amplum* > *ancho; im-plēre* > *encher; complēre* > *cumprir* (with shift of con-jugation); *implicāre* > *empregar; simplĭcem* > *simprez* (old).

A. The change to *nch* was much earlier than the change to *mpr.* The group *nfl* also became *nch* in *inchar* (from *inflāre*).

6. The Romance group *mbl* (§ 113, 1) > Ptg. *mbr: cŭmŭ-lum* > *combro; similāre* > *sembrar.*

**96. MISCELLANEOUS GROUPS.**

1. Lat. *lb* and *rb* > Ptg. *lv* and *rv* respectively: *albam* > *alva; arbĭtrum* > *álvidro* (old); *arbŏrem* > *árvore; carbōnem* > *carvão; herbam* > *erva; sībilāre* > *silvar; turbĭdum* > *turvo.*

A. This was perhaps a Vulgar Latin change (cf. Carnoy, 141).

B. Yod did not interfere with this development: *superbĭam* > *soberva* (Crest, Glossary).   See § 88.

C. The original Latin *b* was restored in regressive words: *barbam* > *barva* (old) and *barba; superbum* > *sobervo* (old) and *soberbo.*

2. A nasal consonant ending a group sometimes nasalized the following vowel as an initial consonant did: *vermem* > *verme* > *vermem* (old); *\*remussicāre* (for *re-mussitāre*) > *remusgar* > *resmugar* > *resmungar* (cf. Nascentes).

## FINAL CONSONANTS

**97. CLASSICAL LATIN FINAL CONSONANTS.**

1. Cl. L. final *b* fell in early Portuguese: *sŭb* > *so* (old).

A. This word seems to be the only example and the *b* was later restored in it: MPtg. *sob* [sobə].

2. Cl. L. final *c* fell in late Vulgar Latin or early Portuguese: *dīc* > *di* (old); *nec* > *nem; sīc* > *si* > *sim* (§ 112, 1).

3. Cl. L. final *d* fell in Vulgar Latin: *ad* > *a; quid* > *que*.

4. Cl. L. final *m* fell in Vulgar Latin and final *n* in early Portuguese (GVL, § 310): *amōrem* > *amor; nōmen* > *nome*. Because of proclisis, both *m* and *n* remained as *n* in monosyllables in Vulgar Latin. In Portuguese they nasalized the preceding vowel but lost their consonantal value: *cum* > *com; in* > *em; nōn* > *nom* > *não; quem* > *quem; rem* > *rem* (old).

A. In *ja* the *m* of Lat. *jam* was lost by wrong division of the word *jamais*.

B. Ptg. *tão* and *quão* do not come from *tam* and *quam* but are rather apocopated forms of *tanto* and *quanto* (PhM, I, 251; Comp, 362, n. 2; Hanssen, § 12, 5), in which consonantal *n* was lost because it became final and in which the diphthong *ão* developed in the general fusion of *-ã*, *-õ*, and *-ão* (§ 157).

C. For the sound of final *-em*, see § 34, 10 and § 46, 11.

5. Cl. L. final *r*, by metathesis with a preceding unaccented vowel, became the last element of a medial group: *inter* > *entre; quattuor* > *quattor* > *quattro* > *quatro; semper* > *sempre; sŭper* > *sôbre*.

A. This change probably took place in Vulgar Latin (GVL, § 245).

B. In *sŭper-lo, in which the r of super was not final, this change did not take place: *super-lo > sobello (old and dialectal), e.g., sobellos bēes (RL, V, 136). For sobolo, see Rom, X, 339. The word cadáver (from cadāver) is learned.

c. The preposition pro became *por in Vulgar Latin (GVL, § 14). The r of *por and the r of per were really never final in Vulgar Latin or Portuguese because of the regular proclitic position of these words. Both per and por existed in early Portuguese with separate meanings (RF, XXIII, 351; RF, XXV, 667) but soon came to be interchanged as a result of phonological confusion in which per came to be pronounced por (Rom, XI, 91–95), per surviving in combinations with the definite article, e.g., pelo, por surviving when not combined. The combinations polo, pola, etc. have survived in dialects of the north and in Galician.

6. Cl. L. final s remained in Portuguese: hŏmĭnes > homens; vīvis > vives.

A. Final s (of a word or a syllable) began to palatalize in the thirteenth century (CA, I, xxiii). But see Bourciez, § 341 a.

B. The [k] of final x became a yod and s remained: sex > seis (§ 34, 4).

7. Cl. L. final t fell in Vulgar Latin: bĭbit > bebe; cantant > cantam; post > pois.

## 98. Consonants Becoming Final in Portuguese.

1. Lat. l, r and s, followed by final e or i, became final in Portuguese through the fall of this e or i: amōrem > amor; male > mal; mensem > mês; salī (2d sg. impv.) > sal (old).

A. Final l is pronounced [ł] in Portuguese.

2. Lat. c followed by final e or i became Ptg. z, which became final through the fall of this e or i: facit > faze > faz; vĭcem > vez; fēcī > fiz.

A. Pronounced [dz] this z did not rime with final s in the early Cancioneiros (CA, I, xxii, n. 6).

B. This z is spelled s in Modern Portuguese if the preceding vowel is not accented: pomĭcem (GVL, § 207, 3) > pomes; simplĭcem > simples.

3. Lat. *t* + *i̯* followed by final *e* became Ptg. *z*, which became final through the fall of this *e*: *-ĭtĭem* > *-ez*.

A. The final *z* in *az* (old) (from *acĭem*) and *faz* (old) (from *facĭem*) is a result of the confusion in Vulgar Latin of *c* plus yod and *t* plus yod. Cf. § 89, 2 B.

4. Lat. *n*, followed by final *e* (chiefly acc. sg. 3d declension and 3d sg. of verbs) or final *t* (3d pl. of verbs), became final through the fall of this *e* or *t*. Later it nasalized the preceding vowel but lost its consonantal value (ZRPh, XLI, 558): *vĕnit* > *vem; amant* > *amam; dēbent* > *devem; bĕne* > *bem; fīnem* > *fim; amārunt* > *amarom* (old); *commūnem* > *comum*. Final *-im* and *-um* had no further change but final *-em* became [ẽj] (§ 34, 10; § 46, 11) and final *-am* and *-om* both became [ẽw] (§ 157, 2).

A. The *n* of *tanto* and *quanto* became final through apocope of the final syllable (§ 97, 4 B).

B. The nasal resonance of a final vowel occasionally produced a consonantal *n* in a sort of liaison between the final vowel and the initial vowel of a following word, e.g., *tam nasynha* (for *tam asynha*) (CG, facsimile ed., fôlha CCXI vo, col. 3).

## GENERAL PHONOLOGICAL PHENOMENA

**99.** ASSIMILATION, DISSIMILATION, AND CONTRACTION OF VOWELS IN HIATUS.

1. The changes undergone by vowels in hiatus were not sporadic but took place with great regularity.

Original Latin hiatus sometimes persisted until the word came into Old Portuguese, e.g., *leōnem* > *leom* (old) (cf. Sp. *león*). But hiatus was generally eliminated in Vulgar Latin by reduction of the unaccented vowel to a semivowel, by the total disappearance of the unaccented vowel, or by contraction (GVL, §§ 222–227). Therefore, most of the cases of hiatus in Old Portuguese were due to the fall of an intervocalic consonant, e.g., *dolēre* > *doer*. But this new hiatus of Old Portuguese was in turn eliminated in the same way, namely, by reduction of the unaccented vowel to a semivowel

(5 and 6 below), by the total disappearance of the unaccented vowel (7 below), by contraction (2 below), or by assimilation and contraction (3 below), and in the case where none of these developments could take place (4 below), by the insertion of a [j] or a [w], which is not shown in spelling, e.g., *lua* [luwɐ]. The only case where this [j] is shown in spelling is between tonic ę and a following *a* or *o* (§35, 7).

2. If the two vowels in hiatus were the same and of the same quality, they were contracted: *vĭdēre* > *\*vędęr* > *vęęr* > *ver;  palatĭum* > *paaço* > *paço;  oracŭlum* > *oragoo* > *orago.*

A. This contraction, which had begun to take place toward the end of the thirteenth century, was completed by the end of the fifteenth century (Lições, 157–159; Cd'A, I, 358). An examination of the rhythm of early verse shows that it took place earlier between two unaccented vowels than it did between two vowels of which one was accented (RPh, I, 36–37).

B. Two pretonic *a*'s in hiatus were contracted to [a]: *panatarĭum* > *padeiro;* two pretonic *e*'s in hiatus were contracted to [ɛ]: *crēdĭtōrem* > *crędor;* and two pretonic *o*'s in hiatus were contracted to [ɔ]: *cŏlōrātum* > *cǫrado.*

3. An unaccented vowel in hiatus with an accented vowel was assimilated and contracted, if it was one or two steps more open (in the series *a, ę, ę, i* or the series *a, ǫ, ǫ, u*) than the accented vowel (RR, XXII, 43): *anĕllum* > *āello* > *ęęlo* > *ęlo;  \*cadētam* > *caeda* (RL, XXVII, 18; FM, II, Glossary) > *quęda;  calentem* > *caente* > *queente* > *quęnte;  canalĭcŭlam* > *caelha* > *quęlha;  pĕlăgum* > *peago* > *pęęgo* > *pęgo;  portugalense* (Nascentes, s.v. *português*) > *portugalęs* > *portugaes* > *portuguęęs* > *português;  sagĭttam* > *saeta* > *sęęta* > *sęta;  venīre* > *vęir* > *viir* > *vir;  cīvīlēs* > *civiis* > *civis;  mŏlam* > *moa* > *mǫǫ* > *mó;  mŏnăchum* > *moago* > *mǫǫgo* > *mǫgo;  sōlam* > *soa* > *sǫǫ* > *só;  palŭmbum* > *paombo* > *poombo* > *pǫmbo;  nūdum* > *nuo* > *nuu* > *nú;  \*mŏlūtum* (for mŏlĭtum) > *muudo* > *mudo* (BF, I, 203).

A. If the unaccented vowel was two steps more open than the

accented vowel, both vowels were affected, the unaccented vowel
closing one step, the accented vowel opening one step, e.g.,
*saęta* > *sęęta; sǫa* > *sǫǫ; majōrem* > *maor* (§ 73, 5 A) > *mǫǫr* >
*mór*. This change did not take place between tonic *ę* and a following *a,* where a different solution was adopted (see § 35, 7).

B. The *e* of *quęnte* and the *o* of *pǫmbo* were closed by the following nasal. The *o* of *mǫgo* was closed by metaphony. The *e* of
*português* was closed through the influence of *francês, inglês,* etc.
The *e* of *quęlha* was closed through the influence of other words
ending in *-ęlha* (from *-ĭcŭlam*). All these vowels must have
closed after contraction had taken place.

C. Because of some disturbing outside influence, dissimilation
instead of assimilation took place in the development of the
word *rainha* (from *rēgĭnam*). The words *rei* and *reino,* although
not accented on the *i,* may have had some influence on the Old
Portuguese form *reīa,* as suggested by D'Ovidio (ZRPh, VIII,
85). At any rate dissimilation was favored in this word by the
effect of *r* on unaccented *e*. Assimilation was prevented in *boa*
(from *bŏnam*), by the nasal resonance, which was later lost
(§ 45, 2 B).

D. In the development of *réis* the accent apparently shifted
for some unknown reason to the vowel of the root; then assimilation and contraction took place: *rēgāles* > *reais* > *\*réais* > *reeis*
> *réis*.

4. An unaccented vowel in hiatus with an accented
vowel remained unchanged, if it was three steps more open
(in the series *a, ę, ẹ, i* or the series *a, ǫ, ọ, u*) than the
accented vowel: *salīre* > *sair; padūlem* (for *palūdem*) >
*paúl; mūlam* > *mua*.

5. An unaccented vowel in hiatus with an accented vowel
was dissimilated, if it was more close (in the series *a, ę, ẹ,
i* or the series *a, ǫ, ọ, u*) than the accented vowel (RR,
XXII, 43): *gĕnĕstam* > *gęęsta* > *giesta; vĕnĕrĭa* > *vęeira* >
*vieira; vēnarĭum* > *vęeiro* > *vieiro; vēnātum* > *veado* [vjadu];
*vadit* > *vai; malum* > *mao* > *mau; vŏlāre* > *voar* [vuar];
*fĭdēlem* > *\*fęęl* (§ 35, 11) > *fiel*.

A. Lat. *cŏlŭbram* became *\*cŏlŏbram* (D'Ovidio, 16, n. 1), whence
OPtg. *coovra* (RL, XXVII, 24). If both *o*'s of this form were

open, as the modern form *cǫbra* indicates, Grandgent's opinion
that pretonic *ŏ* did not become *ǫ* in Vulgar Latin seems to be
confirmed (see § 7 A). For if the pretonic *o* was close, the modern
form would be *\*cuǫvra*.

B. Further closing of the unaccented vowel of *sūdōrem* was
not possible, hence the opening of the accented vowel: *sūdōrem
> suór.*

C. Dissimilation did not take place in the development of
*crēděntĭam*, because tonic *e* had been closed by the following yod
(§ 34, 2): *crēděntĭam > \*crẹẹnça > crença.*

D. Dissimilation did not take place in the development of
*avolum* because tonic *o* was first closed by metaphony: *avŏlum*
(Du Cange) *> avǫo > avǫo > avô.* See § 123, 6 B.

6. An unaccented vowel in hiatus with an accented
vowel became more close, if it was not in the same series as
the accented vowel: *caelum > céu; pĕdōnem > peom >
peão* [pjẽw]; *\*vĕnūtum > vĩudo* (old); *sōlēs > sóis; dŏlēre >
doer* [duer]; *mŏlīnum > moinho* [mwiɲu].

A. Between tonic *ẹ* and *o* an *i* [j] was inserted (see § 35, 7).

7. An unaccented *e* in hiatus with an unaccented *a* or *o*
often disappeared: *monisterium > moesteiro > mosteiro;
\*mē-lo > mo; \*dē-lo > do.*

## 100. METAPHONY.

1. Metaphony (umlaut) is the assimilating influence
exerted by a final vowel upon a tonic vowel. Besides being
found in Portuguese, it is found in Leonese (RA, XIV,
151–152), in some Italian dialects (M-L, It, 348–351), and
in Rumanian.

In Portuguese, metaphony is not an independent phonological phenomenon; it is indissolubly associated with inflection.[1] It seems to have occurred chiefly where discrimination or increased inflectional differentiation was felt

---

[1] Inflection is understood to include difference in declension such as the difference
between *capelo* and *capela*.

to be necessary. See RL, XXVIII, 19. There was no metaphony in uninflected words, e.g., *lǫgo* (from *lŏco*, REW). And there was often no metaphony where there was no risk of ambiguity, e.g., *dó* (from *dŏlum*, GVL, § 21), but *avô* (from *avŏlum*) because of *avó*. Because of this function of supplementing already existing inflection, metaphony is the least consistent phonological change in Portuguese and the one most easily interfered with by other forces, particularly by analogy. And because the interference of analogy continued long after the action of metaphony had ceased, the situation in Modern Portuguese is considerably different from that described by the grammarians of the sixteenth century. At the present time there is still some uncertainty in the use of metaphonic forms and great variation from one dialect to another. See Cavacas, 149, 162, and 163; Grund, I, 931, n. 4, and 1013, n. 2.

2. Evidence of the action of metaphony appears as early as the thirteenth century. Such forms as *isto* and *tudo* are found in the early Cancioneiros (cf. Cd'A, I, 370, n. 1; RL, XXIII, 45, s.v. *isto*, and 88, s.v. *todo*). The form *isto* occurs in only one rime, *disto : oantre tristo* (i.e., *o Antecristo*) (CV, No. 1041) although there are several examples in CSM (pp. 111, 141, 315, 474). Cf. BF, I, 348, n. 3. The form *tudo* does not occur in rime except in an obscure line of CV, No. 371 as emended by Nobiling (RF, XXV, 695). The rime *medo : cedo* is found repeatedly (CV, Nos. 241, 413, 421, 522, 865, 917) but the rime *essa : abbadessa* (CV, Nos. 944, 1137) seems to indicate that the *e* of *essa* had not yet opened. In the "Cancioneiro Geral," vowel changes which are evident in spelling, viz., from *e* to *i* and from *o* to *u*, have become much more numerous (cf. Cavacas, 184–185). It is therefore probable that the vowel changes which are not evident in spelling, viz., from *ẹ* to *ę*, *ẹ* to *ę̣*, *ǫ* to *ọ*, and *ọ* to *ǫ*, have

likewise become more numerous. Although this conclusion is not borne out by a study of the rimes (Cavacas, 167–172), the increasing number of unquestionably bad rimes seems to invalidate the testimony of rimes in this verse and in that of the following century. Perhaps printing and a consequent greater awareness of the written or printed word led poets to rime more for the eye alone than in the earlier period. Cf. Lições, 143, n. 1.

3. Metaphony took place in Portuguese through the action of final *a* and *o* upon tonic *e* and *o*, final *e* being neutral. The range of variation of an *e* was the series: *ę, ẹ, i*, while the range of variation of an *o* was the series: *ǫ, ọ, u*.

4. Final *a* opened tonic *ẹ* to *ę: ĭstam > ẹsta > ęsta* (§ 35, 8).

5. Final *a* opened tonic *ọ* to *ǫ: formōsam > formọsa > formǫsa* (§ 38, 7).

6. Final *o* closed tonic *ę* to *ẹ: mĕtum > mędo > mẹdo* (§ 34, 8); and it closed tonic *ẹ* to *i: ĭpsum > ẹsso > isso* (§ 35, 9).

7. Final *o* closed tonic *ǫ* to *ọ: fŏcum > fǫgo > fọgo* (§ 37, 5); and it closed tonic *ọ* to *u: tōtum > tọdo > tudo* (§ 38, 8).

## 101. NASALIZATION.

1. The nasalization of vowels has been attributed to Celtic influence (cf. M-L, Intro, § 238). It was produced by nasal consonants in any position, initial, medial or final. Whether some form of nasal remained in the end and what that form was depended chiefly on the combination of sounds with which the nasal resonance was associated rather than on the original position of the nasal consonant. This is demonstrated by the following examples.

| Intervocalic *n* | Initial or Final Nasal | Resulting Nasal Sound |
|---|---|---|

| | | |
|---|---|---|
| *těnes* > *tens* (§ 78, 2) | *nec* > *ne* > *nem* (§ 66, 2 в) | *ē* |
| | *in* > *em* (§ 97, 4) | |
| *fīnes* > *fins* (§ 78, 2 в) | *mihī* > *mi* > *mim* (§ 66, 1 в) | *ī* |
| *canes* > *cāes* (§ 78, 3) | *matres* > *māes* (§ 66, 1 в) | *āe* |
| *pōnes* > *pōes* (§ 78, 3) | \*-*ŭdĭnem* > \*-*oen* (§ 46, 2) > | *ōe* |
| | -*ōe* (old) | |
| *manum* > *mão* (§ 78, 3) | *vadunt* > *vão* | *ão* |
| *vīnum* > *vinho* (§ 78, 4) | *nīdum* > *ninho* (§ 66, 2 в) | [ɲ] |
| *venītis* > *vindes* (§ 78, 5) | *multum* > *muito* [mũjntu] | [n] |
| | (§ 66, 1 в) | |
| *benedīcāmus* > *bengamos* | \**nec-ūnum* > *ningum* (old) | [ŋ] |
| (old) (§ 78, 6) | (§ 66, 2 в) | |

2. The nasal resonance generally closed an open tonic vowel: *canto* > *canto* [kẽntu]; *těmpus* > *tempos* [tẽmpuʃ]; *pŏntem* > *ponte* [põntə]; but it prevented pretonic *e* and *o* from closing further: *sentīre* > *sentir* [sẽntir]; *voluntātem* > *vontade* [võntadə]. And it diphthongized final *e*, accented or unaccented, to [ẽj]: *bene* > *bem* [bẽj]; *dēbent* > *devem* [dɛvẽj].

**102. ASSIBILATION.**

1. The sound [s] in Modern Portuguese comes from:

a) Lat. initial *c* followed by *e* or *i*: *centum* > *cento; cīvitātem* > *cidade* (§ 62, 2).

b) Lat. *c* preceded by a consonant and followed by *e* or *i*: *mancĭpĭum* > *mancebo* (§ 92, 1).

c) Lat. *c* + *i̯* preceded by a vowel or a consonant: *facĭo* > *faço; lanceāre* > *lançar* (§ 89, 2).

d) Lat. *t* + *i̯* preceded by a consonant: *fŏrtĭam* (Du Cange) > *fôrça* (§ 89, 3).

e) Lat. initial *s: sal* > *sal* (§ 65, 1).

f) Lat. medial *ss: ŏssum* > *ôsso* (§ 83).

g) Lat. medial *x: dīxit* > *disse; \*traxŭit* > *trouxe* (§ 92, 9).

2. The sound [z] in Modern Portuguese comes from:

a) Lat. *c* preceded by a vowel and followed by *e* or *i*: *dīces* > *dizes* (§ 73, 2).

b) Lat. intervocalic *s: causam* > *coisa* (§ 76).

c) Lat. *t* + *i̯* preceded by a vowel: *vĭtĭum* > *vêzo* (§ 89, 4).

d) Lat. intervocalic *x* in the prefix *ex-: exāmen* > *exame* (§ 92, 9 в).

e) Greek initial ζ: *zĕphȳrum* > *zéfiro* (§ 65, 2).

3. The sound [ʃ] in Modern Portuguese comes from:

a) Lat. *sc* preceded by a vowel and followed by *e* or *i: pĭscem* > *peixe* (§ 92, 2).

b) Lat. *ss* + *i̯* and *sc* + *i̯*: *\*bassĭum* > *baixo; fascĭam* > *faixa* (§ 89, 11).

c) Lat. medial *x: fraxĭnum* > *freixo* (§ 92, 9).

d) Lat. initial *cl, fl*, and *pl: clavem* > *chave; flammam* > *chama; plagam* > *chaga* (§ 67, 2, 3, and 5).

e) Fr. *ch*: Old Fr. *chapel* (Nascentes) > *chapéu;* Fr. *chef* > *chefe* (§ 62, 1 в).

f) Lat. *s* followed by a surd: *vestīre* > *vestir* (§ 97, 6 а).

g) Lat. final *s*, and Lat. intervocalic *s* and *c* followed by a final *e* or *i: dŭos* > *dois; mensem* > *mês; vĭcem* > *vez; fēci* > *fiz* (§ 97, 6 а; § 98, 1 and 2).

4. The sound [ʒ] in Modern Portuguese comes from:

a) Lat. initial *g* followed by *e* or *i: gentem* > *gente* (§ 62, 4).

b) Lat. *g* preceded by a consonant and followed by *e* or *i: longe* > *longe* (§ 92, 3).

c) Lat. *g* preceded by a vowel and followed by *e* or *i: vigilāre* > *vigiar* (§ 73, 4 c).

d) Lat. initial *j: januarĭum* > *janeiro* (§ 62, 5).

e) Lat. intervocalic *j: cūjum* > *cujo* (§ 73, 5).

f) Lat. initial *d* + *i̯: diarĭa* > *geira* (§ 70).

g) Lat. medial *d* + *i̯: hŏdĭe* > *hoje* (§ 89, 5).

h) Fr. *j*: Fr. *jardin* > *jardim;* Fr. *forge* > *forja.*

i) Lat. *s* followed by a sonant: *eleemosȳnam* > *esmola.*

A. The combination of *s* and a sonant did not exist in Classical Latin but came about in Vulgar Latin and early Portuguese through syncope or metathesis. Portuguese final *s* and *z* also have this sound when standing before a word beginning with a sonant.

## SPORADIC CHANGES

### 103. ABBREVIATION.

Nicknames are sometimes made by omitting all that precedes the accented syllable: *Manel* (for *Manuel*) > *Nel*; *José* > *Zé*; *Joaquim* > *Quim*; *Madalena* > *Lena*; *Maneca* > *Neca*; *Ricardo* > *Cardinho* (with suffix *-inho*); *Fernando* > *Nandinho*; *Francisco* > *Xico*.

In the language of children the tonic syllable sometimes alone survives but doubled: *Helena* > *Lele*; *Herminia* or *Emilia* > *Mimi*; *António* > *Toto*.

### 104. ANALOGY.

Analogy, as frequently understood, may be defined as the process whereby a new form is invented in imitation of one or more other forms of the same paradigm or in imitation of the corresponding form of another paradigm. But analogy thus defined is really contamination, for true analogy involves at least four forms, viz., the form invented, another form of the same paradigm, and two forms of another paradigm which provide the model relationship on which the invention is based.

### 105. ANAPTYXIS.

1. A parasitic vowel was sometimes inserted between the elements of a consonant group if one of these elements was *l* or *r*. This was brought about by the vocalic nature of *l* and the strongly vibrant nature of *r*: *chrŏnĭcam* > *caronica* (old); *clavĭcŭlam* > *cravelha* > *caravelha*; *sepulcrum* > *sapulcoro* (FM, II, Glossary, s.v. *sapulcro*); *februarĭum* > *fevereiro*; *fĭbram* > *fêvera*; *flōrem* > *flor* > *felor* (dialectal); *glōrĭam* > *glória* > *gueloria* (dialectal); *plantāre* > *plantar* > *pelantar* (dialectal); *tertiarĭum* > *terceiro* > *tereceiro* (FM, II, Glossary). See Esquisse, § 62; Opúsculos, II, 33.

2. A parasitic [ə] is generally inserted in the pronunciation of learned words after the prefixes *ab-*, *ad-*, *ob-*

and *sob-* (*sub-*) in order to avoid the juxtaposition of the final consonant of the prefix with the following initial consonant: Ptg. *advertir* > [ɐdəvərtir]; Ptg. *observar* > [obəsərvar].  See AStNS, CXXV, 379; and Rom, XII, 32, n. 1.

A. If the [ə] is not inserted, partial assimilation of the consonants takes place: *obsequĭum* > *obséquio* [obzɛkju].

## 106. Apheresis.

1. The loss of the initial vowel of a word is a very common phenomenon but it did not take place with any regularity: *acūmen* > *gume;* Ptg. *aliança* > *liança* (popular, Barbosa, 23); *apothēcam* > *bodega; adultĕrĭum* > *dulterio* (Eluc); *\*adlumināre* > *alumiar* > *lomear* (FM, II, Glossary); *hebdŏmăda* > *doma* (old); *eclīpsem* > *cris* (old); *epistŏlam* > *pistola* (RL, XVI, 10); *imagināre* > *maginar* (old and dialectal); *\*inŏdĭum* (REW) > *enojo* > *nojo; \*inamorāre* > *namorar; hominatĭcum* (Md'Ar) > *homenagem* > *menagem; hōrŏlŏgĭum* > *relógio; horrōrem* > *rôr* (RL, VII, 41); *occasiōnem* > *ocajom* > *cajom; iracundĭam* > *\*arigonha* > *rigonha* (Rom, XI, 95; Ineditos, I, Glossary; Eluc).

A. The loss of initial *a* and *o* in nouns may have been occasioned by confusion of these vowels with the definite article. That this confusion existed is shown by the change to the masculine gender of OPtg. *cajom.*

B. It has been argued that *namorar* is a borrowing from Spanish, as initial *in-* would have become *ẽ* in Portuguese (Lições, 274–277).  But it is probable that apheresis took place in this word before the time of the fall of intervocalic *n;* apheresis took place in *nojo,* which does not appear to be a borrowing.  It is possible too that the *n* of *\*inamōrāre* first lengthened as in Italian (GIt, § 100).

2. In some words, not only the initial vowel but sometimes the whole initial syllable was lost: *insanĭam* > *sanha; spasmum* > *pasmo;* Ptg. *absolutamente* > *solutamente* (RL, V, 164).  Ptg. *resurreição* > *surreição* (RL, V, 164); Ptg.

*destruir* > *struir* (RL, II, 101); Ptg. *sistema* > *stema* (RL, XI, 278).

A. The development of *sanha* from *insaniam* may have been influenced by *saniem* (RF, XX, 579).

**107. APOCOPE.**

1. The loss of the last syllable of a word used as a proclitic is uncommon in Portuguese because of the comparative strength of unaccented syllables. The few cases that are found are mostly of Spanish origin or due to Spanish influence: *centum* > *cento* > *cem*; *dŏmĭnum* > *donno* > *dom*; *grandem* > *grande* > *grão* (used only in compound nouns); *quantum* > *quanto* > *quão*; *tantum* > *tanto* > *tão*; *sanctum* > *santo* > *são*; *ille* > *ele* > *el* (old); *mille* > *mil*; *inde* > *em* (old); *multum* > *muito* > *mui*.

2. Some apocopated forms are found only in stereotyped expressions, some only in place names: *bellum* > *bel*, e.g., *a bel prazer*; *casam* > *cas*, e.g., *em cas de*; *malum* > *mal*, e.g., *mal tempo*; *montem* > *mon*, e.g., *Monsanto*; *castellum* > *castel*, e.g., *Castel-Branco*; *vallem* > *val*, e.g., *Valverde*.

**108. ASSIMILATION AND DISSIMILATION.**

Assimilation and dissimilation took place between vowels and between consonants, sometimes when they were adjacent and sometimes when they were remote, i.e., separated from each other by other sounds. For assimilation and dissimilation of adjacent vowels, see § 99. There was no dissimilation of adjacent consonants.

It does not seem possible to formulate very definite rules for the assimilation and dissimilation of vowels and consonants that are remote from each other. The consonants involved are chiefly *l*, *r*, *m*, and *n*.

A. Assimilation took place also between a vowel and a consonant, e.g., the opening effect of *r* on an adjacent pretonic *e* (see § 41, 9).

B. Most of the changes in medial consonant groups (§§ 85–96) are examples of total or partial assimilation.

**109. Assimilation.**

1. Assimilation of remote vowels: *novacŭlam* > *navalha;* Ptg. *riqueza* > *requeza* (old); Ptg. *pedir* > *pidir* (old and dialectal); Ptg. *cordura* > *curdura* (CV, No. 690).

2. Assimilation of remote consonants: *parabŏlam* > *paravra* (old); *animalĭa* > *alimalia* (old); *morbum* > *mormo; glōrĭam* > *groria* (old).

3. Assimilation of adjacent consonants: *molīnarĭum* > *molneiro* > *moleiro; eleemosȳnam* > *esmolna* (RL, XXV, 246; RL, XXVII, 36; DC, 285) > *esmola; lūnŭlam* > *lula; *manēre-aịo* > *manrei* > *marrei* (old); *sal nĭtrum* > *salitre; *amāre-lo* > *amarlo* > *amá-lo; *tōtōs-los* > *todollos* (old); *dēben-lo* > *devem-no;* Ptg. *fīz-lo* > *fi-lo.*

A. In these examples, the consonants were brought together by the fall of an intertonic vowel or a posttonic penult, or by new juxtapositions of closely related words.

B. The assimilation was progressive in *moleiro, esmola,* etc. (see RL, III, 175; AStNS, CXXIV, 337), unless metathesis of *ln* took place before the assimilation (see RL, II, 180–181); cf. *monleiro* (Eluc, s.v. *conducteiro*). The assimilation was progressive in *devem-no,* etc. also; this was due to the necessity of preserving the characteristic *n* of the ending of the third plural.

4. Assimilation of the nasal resonance: *hāc nŏcte* > *onte* (popular) > *ontem; pĕctĭnem* > *peitem* > *pēitem* > *pentem* (old and dialectal); *nūbem* > *nuve* > *nūve* > *nūvem* > *nuvem; mūgĭlem* > *mugee* > *mūge* > *mugem.* See Language, VII, 142.

**110. Dissimilation.**

1. Dissimilation of remote vowels: *lōcustam* > *lagosta; sexaginta* > *sessenta* > *sassenta* (old); *dīcēbat* > *dizia* > *dezia* (old) and *dizia* [dəziɐ]; *vīcīnum* > *vezinho* (old) and *vizinho* [vəziɲu]; *dīvīnum* > *devino* (old) and *divino* [dəvinu]; *rotatōrem* > *redor; rotundum* > *redondo.*

A. The dissimilation in *vezinho, devino* and *redondo* originated in
Vulgar Latin (GVL, § 229, 4 and 6). The pretonic *i* of modern
*vizinho* and *divino* is merely orthographic. For dissimilation of
remote vowels in Modern Portuguese, see ZRPh, XIX, 578, n. 1;
AStNS, CXXV, 378–379.

2. Dissimilation of remote consonants: *locāle* > *lugar;
anĭmam* > *alma; memorāre* > *nembrar* > *lembrar; priōrem*
> *priol* (old); *globellum* (Du Cange) > *lovelo* > *novelo;
*ligacŭlum* > *legalho* > *negalho; arbĭtrum* > *álvidro* (old).

A. Although the two consonants in Lat. *anĭma* and in OPtg.
*nembrar* were not the same, they were both nasals; the dissimilation was away from a nasal to an *l*.

B. Sometimes the force of dissimilation was so intense that
it caused the disappearance of one of the like consonants: *crĭbrum*
> *crivo; rostrum* > *rosto; arātrum* > *arado; proprĭum* > *propio*
(old and dialectal).

C. In the sixteenth century two *b*'s or two *v*'s in the same
word were dissimilated so that the first one was *b*, the second
one *v: bĭbĕre* > *bever* (with shift of conjugation); *vīvum* > *bivo*.
See SaM, Glossary, sub *b*.

3. Dissimilation of the nasal resonance: *campānam* >
*campāa* > *campa; *ventānam* > *ventāa* > *venta; quintānam*
> *quintāa* > *quinta;* OPtg. *pentem* (Gil Vi, III, Glossary)
> *pente.*

**111.** Confusion of Prefixes and of Initial Syllables.

1. Because of its common occurrence, initial *es-* (from
Lat. *ex-* and from prosthetic *e* plus *s* followed by a consonant) sometimes took the place of initial *as-* (from Lat.
*abs, as-* and *aus-*) and initial *os-* (from Lat. *obs-*): *abscondit*
> *asconde* > *esconde; abstinentĭam* > *estença* (old); *aspa-
răgum* > *espargo; auscultāre* > *ascuitar* > *escutar; obscū-
rum* > *escuro.*

A. The opposite exchange took place in OPtg. *asperar* (for
*esperar* < *spērāre*), which may have developed in imitation of
*asconder, ascuitar,* etc. (Cd'A, I, 366) or under the influence of

Lat. *aspectāre* (PhM, II, 163) or of Ptg. *aspirar* (Huber, § 119, 1 c).

2. The confusion between pretonic *an-* (or *am-*) and *en-* (or *em-*) arose probably as a result of the similarity in the pronunciation of these nasal sounds before the time when *en-* closed to [i̯]: *anguīlam* (Sommer, 205) > *anguia* (old) and *enguia; ampullam* > *empôla;* *\*ancorāre* > *ancorar* and *emcorar* (see *emcorou,* Crest, 110); *\*imparāre* > *emparar* (old) and *amparar; imperātōrem* > *emperador* (old) and *amperador* (old); *\*resplendescentem* > *resplendecente* and *resplandecente; inter* (in proclisis) > *entre* and *antre* (old); *\*in-tum* > *então* and *antam* (old).

A. This confusion is very common in certain dialects (see Esquisse, § 49 b and § 50 d; RL, VII, 37; RL, XI, 271; RL, XIX, 172); sometimes even in the tonic position (Esquisse, § 44 m; RL, XII, 307).

B. The change of *entre* to *antre* has been explained as due to the influence of *ante* (RL, VIII, 70).

3. A sort of fusion or contamination took place between initial *eix-* (from Lat. *ex-* and *ax-* followed by a vowel and Lat. *asc + i̯*) and initial *ens-* (from Lat. *ins-*), resulting in the new prefix *enx-* [iʃ]: *exemplum* > *eixempro* > *enxempro* (old); *exheredāre* > *enxerdar* (Crest, Glossary); *exsūgĕre* > *enxugar* (with shift of conjugation); *exāmen* > *enxame;* *\*exŭviālem* (RL, VII, 120–121) > *enxoval;* *\*exaltiāre* > *enxalçar;* *\*exaquāre* > *enxaguar; axungiam* > *enxúndia* (for *di,* see Grund, I, 991); *asciŏlam* > *enxó;* *\*asciātam* > *enxada;* *\*insapidum* > *enxabido; insertāre* > *enxertar;* *\*insulfurāre* > *enxofrar.*

A. For the loss of *i̯* in *eix-,* cf. § 92, 7 A.

B. Similar confusion has occurred in Old Portuguese and in modern dialects between initial *e-* and *in-: eligĕre* > OPtg. *enleger* (with shift of conjugation); *aeternum* > *eterno* > *interno* (Esquisse, § 50 a); *edūcāre* > *educar* > *inducar* (RL, XI, 274); *electiōnem* > *eleição* > *inleição* (RL, XI, 140).

C. The change of *eix-* to *enx-* has been attributed to the ease with which the vowel *i* became nasalized without any external influence (Grund, I, 981).

D. The word *ensaio* (from *exagĭum*) is a borrowing from Spanish.

E. The *x* and the prefix of *enxôfre* (from *sulfŭrem*) developed in imitation of the verb *enxofrar*.

## 112. CONTAMINATION.

1. Contamination is the process whereby the development of a word is influenced by another word of similar sound or by another word of similar or related meaning or use; in some cases the other word is both of similar sound and of similar or related meaning or use: *castellum* > *castrello* (Eluc) with the *r* of *castro* (from *castrum*); *\*stēllam* (GVL, § 163) > *estrêla* with the *r* of *astro* (from *astrum*); *astrŏlŏgum* > *estrollogo* (old) with the *e* of *estrêla; caelestem* > *celestre* (old) with the *r* of *terrestre* (from *terrestrem*); *\*admanescēre* > *amanhecer* with the *nh* of *manhã* (from *\*maneānam*); vīnētum > *vinhedo* with the *nh* of *vinho* (from vīnum); *reposĭtam* > *resposta* with the *s* of *responder* (from *respondēre*); sīc > *sim* with the nasalization of *nom* or *não* (from nōn); *pŭppem* > *pôpa* with final *a* from *prôa* (from prōram) through the expression *de pôpa a prôa;* Fr. *camion* > *camião* > *caminhão* with the *nh* of *caminho* or *caminhar*.

A. A form *terreste* in rime with *celeste* (Lusíadas, canto VII, stanza 6) arose either through the influence of *celeste* or by dissimilation of the *r*'s.

B. The nasalization in *sim* has also been explained as due to the presence of the sibilant and the vowel *i* (Grund, I, 981).

C. The word *asa* has been explained (RL, XIII, 258–261) as having developed by contamination: *alas* > *aas* > *asas* with medial *s* from the *z* of *azes* (from *acĭes*); but see PhM, II, 153 and Grund, I, 970. The word *sarar* has been explained (RL, XIII, 389–392) as having developed by contamination: *sanāre* > *sāar* > *sar* > *sarar* with the additional syllable from *çarrar;* but see Rom, XI, 95–96.

D. Endings have sometimes developed by contamination: *devo-*

*tiōnem* > *devoçom* > *devaçom* > *devação* with the *a* of the common ending *-açom* or *-ação* (from *-atiōnem*); *institutiōnem* > *instituição* with the *i* of the ending *-uição* (from *-uctiōnem*); *libertātem* > *liberdade* with *-dade* from nouns in which both *t*'s were intervocalic, e.g., *caridade* (from *caritātem*).

2. Popular etymology is a form of contamination: *aquaeductum* > *aqueduto* > *arqueduto* through the influence of *arco* (from *arcum*) (RL, XXXII, 283); *sacristānum* (Du Cange) > *sacristão* > *sachristão* through the influence of *christão* (from *christiānum*), and *sancristão* through the influence of *sam* (from *sanctum*), and *sanchristão* through the influence of both these words; Fr. *canapé* > *camapé* through the influence of Ptg. *cama*; *Satănas* > *Satanás* > *Santanás* through the influence of *sam* (from *sanctum*) (Opúsculos, I, 344); *lītaniam* > *ladainha* through the influence of OPtg. *ladino* (from *latīnum*); *ecclesiastĭcum* > *eccresiastico* (RL, V, 134) > *crelegiastico* through the influence of OPtg. *creligo* (from *clērĭcum*) (see RL, XXVI, 142); Ptg. *tintura d'iodo* > *tintura d'ódio* through the influence of *ódio* (Esquisse, § 78 b); *dilŭvĭum* > *dinuvio* (dialectal) through the influence of *nuvem* in the expression *nuvem de água* (RL, XII, 306).

3. False regression is a form of contamination, which was often only orthographic: *innocentem* > *innocente* > *ignoçente* (Fab, Glossary; BF, III, 64); *hymnos* > *innos* > *jgnos* (Abraham, § 19, 2) with *g* from other words in which *gn* was etymologically correct although the *g* was silent; cf. *inorancia* (PMH, Scriptores, 77); *spĭssum* > *espesso* > *esperso* (RL, XVI, 6) with *r* from other words in which *rs* was correct.

113. EPENTHESIS.

1. A *b* was inserted between *m* and *r*, and between *m* and *l*: *hŭmĕrum* > *\*omro* > *ombro*; *memorāre* > *\*memrar* > *nembrar* > *lembrar*; *cŭmŭlum* > *\*comlo* > *combro*; *similāre* > *semblar* > *sembrar*; *cŭcŭmĕrem* > *cogombro* (with shift of declension); Arabic *alkhomra* > *alfombra*.

2. A *d* was inserted between *n* and *r: honōrāre > ondrar* (old); *ingenerāre > engendrar.*

A. This was not a Portuguese change but occurred only in words borrowed from Spanish (Comp, 144).

3. A *v* was inserted between the diphthong *ou* and a following vowel: *audit > ouve; laudat > louva; claudĕre > chouvir* (old) (with shift of conjugation); *gaudēbat > gouuja* (AHP, III, 95), i.e., *gouvia; caulem > couve.* Cf. Fr. *pouvoir.*

A. This *v* was produced by the labial element of the diphthong *ou.* At first it did not appear in verb forms accented on the ending; its later spread to these forms was due to analogy (RF, XXV, 664).

4. In some words an *r* was inserted: *tonāre > troar.*

A. The *r* of OPtg. *celestre* (from *caelestem*) is thought to be an epenthetic *r* (AStNS, LXV, 40). But see § 112, 1.

5. A phenomenon much like epenthesis is the exchange of one consonant for another: *mēdĭcam > melga; magĭdam > \*madiga > malga; pallĭdum > pardo; papȳrum > papel; ulĭcem > urze; judicāre > julgar; portatĭcum* (Du Cange) *> portadego > portalgo* (old).

A. The change from *d* to *l* is found in Vulgar Latin, e.g., *adipes non alipes* (ApPr). The change from *l* to *r* is common in the development of consonant groups in Portuguese (see § 86, 1 and § 95, 5).

B. In the Old Portuguese forms *juigar* and *portadego,* in which *l* did not develop, the intertonic vowel and the posttonic penult did not fall (see § 53 and § 58).

6. The development of a consonantal *n* from a preceding nasalized vowel should not be confused with epenthesis, e.g., *minūtĭas > miuças > miunças.* See § 78, 5.

### 114. HAPLOLOGY.

An unaccented group of sounds sometimes fell when the preceding or following group was identical or nearly so, or began or ended with the same consonant: *perdĭtam* > *\*per-deda* > *perda; vendĭtam* > *vendida* > *venda; simplĭces* > *simprezes* > *simprez* and *simples* (pl.); *aurĭfĭces* > *ourivezes* > *ourives* (pl.); *sŏror* > *sór; rotatōrem* > *\*redador* > *redor; jejunāre* > *jejuar* > *juar* (RL, VII, 245); *\*-tatōsum* > *-dadoso* > *-doso*, e.g., *\*aetatōsum* > *\*idadoso* > *idoso.*

A. The adjective suffix *\*-tatōsum* was formed by adding *-ōsum* to the noun ending *-tāt(em)*. Other examples are *bondoso, maldoso,* and *cuidoso*. But see Traité, 336.

B. Haplology occurred also in popular and dialectal Portuguese in combinations of two or more words: *duas vezes* > *duas bês* (Esquisse, § 70 a); *Madre de Deus* > *Madre Deus* (popular); *pelo amor de Deus* > *pelo amor Deus* (popular). Perhaps the expressions, *en nom Deus,* found in a document of 1271 (RL, VIII, 40) and *fillo deus* (Crest, 8) are examples of haplology.

## 115. METATHESIS.

1. Two adjacent sounds were sometimes reversed. These sounds could be two vowels: *genŭcŭlum* (Du Cange) > *geolho* > *joelho; dehonestāre* > *deostar* > *doestar;* two consonants: *mĕrŭlum* > *melro* > *merlo* (dialectal, RL, IV, 220); *sibilāre* > *silvar;* a vowel and a consonant: *\*inŏdĭum* > *enojo* > *enjôo; instrumentum* > *estormento* (old).

2. Sometimes a consonant (usually *r*) was shifted from one syllable to another: *fenestram* > *feestra* > *fresta; pigrĭtĭam* > *pegriça* > *preguiça; tĕnĕbras* > *teevras* > *trevas; fabrĭcam* > *fravega* (RL, XXV, 247); *capistrum* > *cabresto; praesaepem* > *pesebre; satisfacĕre* > *satisfazer* (with shift of conjugation) > *sastifazer* (popular).

A. Learned *fábrica* had the same change in dialectal *fráveca* (RL, XXVIII, 230).

B. A similar shift of the nasal resonance is also found: *anătem* > *ánade* > *\*āade* (RL, XXVI, 112) > *adem* (NS, XI, 144). For criticism and a different explanation, see BF, I, 164.

3. Sometimes two consonants in different syllables ex-

changed positions: *eleemosynam* > *esmolna* > *esmola; plantāre* > *chantar* > *tanchar; machĭnam* > *máquina* > *mánica*
(popular); *catalŏgum* > *catálogo* > *catágolo* (popular); Ptg.
*bicarbonato* > *bicabornato* > *bitabornaco* (RL, XXVII, 112);
Ptg. *Ilhavo* > *Ivalho.*

A. This type of metathesis took place as a regular change
between the *l* of an initial group and the *r* of a following syllable:
*clystērem* > *cristel; clērĭcum* > *creligo* (old); *flōrem* > *frol* (old).
Perhaps the *l* first changed to *r* according to § 67, with subsequent
dissimilation of the *r* of the following syllable. See AStNS,
LXV, 44, s.v. *frol;* and H-MP, I, 608, footnote.

### 116. PARAGOGE.

1. An *s* was often added to adverbs ending in a vowel:
*ante* > *antes;* \**extunce* (cf. GVL, § 47) > *estonce* > *estonces*
(old); *numquam* > *nunca* > *nuncas* (old); *-mente* (GVL,
§ 41) > *-mente* > *-mentes* (Esquisse, § 77 a).

A. This change arose perhaps through the influence of adverbs
ending in *s* such as *mais* (from *magis*), OPtg. *pos* (from *post*), etc.

2. A paragogic vowel (usually *e*) was added commonly
in dialectal Portuguese to words ending chiefly in *l* and
*r: animal* > *animale; mare* > *mar* > *mare.*   See Esquisse,
§ 59 d and f, § 66 c; RL, XXVII, 122; Cd'A, I, 367; S-A,
20–21.   But see Meier, 44.

3. An *e* is added in Modern Portuguese to borrowings
ending in a consonant which does not occur as a final in
native words: Fr. *chic* > *chique;* Fr. *bric-à-brac* > *brica-
braque;* Fr. *kiosk* > *quiosque;* Eng. *beef* > *bife;* Eng. *club* >
*clube;* Eng. *film* > *filme;* Arabic *al-khaiyât* > *alfaiate.*

### 117. PROSTHETIC *a.*

In early Portuguese an *a* was prefixed to words beginning
in *r: remittĕre* > *remeter* (with shift of conjugation) > *arre-
meter; ranam* > *rãa* > *arrã* (old and popular).   See Rom,
XI, 75–79; Mus, III, 216–217; Abraham, § 32, 2.

A. The *r* was lengthened in order to preserve the sound it had in the initial position. Prosthetic *a* before *r* is a different phenomenon from OPtg. *er* (and *ar*), which was a separable particle arising from the Latin prefix *re-* (see Rom, IX, 580–589).

B. In some words, initial *a* came from the Latin prefix *ad-*: *adplicāre* (AStNS, CXXIV, 339) > *achegar; *adoculāre* (Rom, XI, 90–91) > *aolhar* > *olhar; advenīre* > *avir*. In others, it is thought to have arisen through agglutination of the definite article: *mōra* (pl.) > *mora* > *amora; nanam* > *anã; medietātem* > *metade* > *ametade*. See Comp, 266–267.

c. Through the influence of words with initial *a* from the Latin prefix *ad-* and from the agglutinated article, prosthetic *a* soon spread to other words which did not begin in *r: memōrare* > *lembrar* > *alembrar* (old); *monstrāre* > *mostrar* > *amostrar; *minatiāre* > *meaçar* > *ameaçar* (AStNS, CXXIV, 335). See Comp, 58–59. This was particularly common in dialectal Portuguese (see Esquisse, § 66 a; RL, XI, 142 and 272; RL, XII, 307). The use of the Arabic article *al* as a prefix may have also been a contributing factor (M-L, Gram, I, § 383).

D. OPtg. *atal* (from *talem*) and *atanto* (from *tantum*) may have developed through the spread of prosthetic *a*. They have been explained as having arisen in Vulgar Latin through the influence of words like *aqui* and *aquel* (Huber, § 108, 1).

## 118. SANDHI.

The initial or final sound of a word often developed as in the medial position because of the juxtaposition of the word with the preceding or following word. This is a common phenomenon in old and dialectal Portuguese, but with the tendency toward word individuation of the modern literary language, it has largely disappeared except between words which were closely related syntactically, where it may be called syntactical phonology, e.g., combinations of conjunctive pronouns with verbs and of prepositions with articles and pronouns.

a) Tonic *ī* followed by *a* or *o:* Ptg. *vim aqui* > *vī nh aqui* (Esquisse, § 159); Ptg. *dá me a mim o pau* > *dá m'a mim nho pau* (Opúsculos, I, 342). See § 78, 4.

b) Assimilation of vowels in hiatus: Ptg. *até agora* >
*ateegora* > *ategora* (old); Ptg. *outra hora* > *outrora;* Ptg. *é*
*uma hora* > *é um hora* [ɛumɔrɐ] (colloquial).   See § 99, 3.

c) Assimilation of adjacent consonants: *não na tinha* (RL,
XI, 140–141) for *não a tinha; chamem no conde* (RL, VI,
151) for *chamem o conde; se fezer mha senholo que tem no*
*coraçõ* (CB, No. 223) for *se fezer mha senhor o que tem no*
*coraçõ.*   See § 109, 3.

**119. WRONG DIVISION.**

Two words standing in frequent juxtaposition were sometimes wrongly divided, with the result that a vowel, a
consonant, or a whole syllable was permanently attached
to or detached from the beginning of the second of them.

a) The word *maluta* arose from the addition of a syllable
of the indefinite article *uma* to *luta* (RHi, V, 423).

b) The word *zorate* arose from the addition of the *s* of
the masculine plural of the definite article *os* to the plural
form *orates* (RHi, V, 425; see also RR, III, 310–312).

c) The word *dil* (dialectal for *ir*) arose from the addition
of the *d* of the preposition *de* to *il* in the expression *hei-d'il*
(for *hei de ir*) (RL, XXXI, 199).

d) The word *Thiago* arose from the addition of the *t* of
*Sant'* (for *Santo*) to *Iago.*   The graph *th* was used for *t* by
false regression.

e) The word *ume* arose from the separation of the initial
*a* of *aume*, which had contracted with the final *a* of *pedra*
in the compound *pedra-ume* (from *petra alūmen*). See RL, V,
59–60.

f) The word *ameixa* arose from the separation of the
initial *d* of *\*damascĕa* in the expression *prūna \*damascĕa*
(for *prūna damascēna*).

g) The word *aleijão* arose from the addition of the definite
article *a* to *leijão* (from *laesiōnem*).   Later, the final *a* of
the feminine indefinite article, perhaps in its earlier form
*ūa*, was contracted with this initial *a* and the contracted

vowel was detached from the article, thus changing the gender of the noun: *ūa aleijão* > *ūaleijão* > *ū aleijão*, i.e., *um aleijão* (RL, III, 131).

h) The word *léste* arose from the addition of the French definite article to the word *éste*.

A. When the article is attached to the following word, as in the last two examples, the phenomenon is really one of agglutination and not of wrong division.

# MORPHOLOGY

## NOUNS

**120. DECLENSIONS.**

There was little left of the Classical Latin declensions in Vulgar Latin. The fourth and fifth declensions, the neuter gender, and all cases except the nominative and accusative disappeared. With the disappearance of the nominative in Portuguese, case distinction came to an end. Inflection for number alone remained.

The form derived from the Latin accusative now has to function as subject, as object of a verb, and as object of a preposition.

**121. NOMINATIVE SINGULAR.**

There are a few exceptional nouns which have survived in the nominative instead of the accusative. The most important of these are: *būbo* > *bufo; cancer* > *câncer; daemon* > *demo; dĕus* > *deus; draco* > *drago; index* > *êndes; gŭrgŭlĭo* > *gorgulho; magister* > *mestre; homo* > *ome* (old indef. pron.); *sŏror* > *sór; Carŏlus* > *Carlos; Marcus* > *Marcos.*

A. An analogical plural of these nouns was formed by the addition of *s* or *es*, e.g., *deuses, gorgulhos. Deuses* replaced an older plural *deus* (from *deōs*), e.g., *todos os Deus* (Ineditos, II, 117). An analogical feminine *deusa* was formed from *deus*. OPtg. *deessa* was probably borrowed from French *déesse,* which came from a Latin form with the Greek ending *-issa.*

B. The accusative of learned *câncer* survived with a different meaning: *cancrum* > *cancro.* The form *drago* has generally been supplanted by *dragão* (from the accusative *dracōnem*). Both *drago* and *dragom* were used interchangeably in Old Portuguese, e.g., Rom, XI, 382.

C. The nominative *\*serpes* (from *serpens*) was apparently taken for an accusative plural, with the result that a new singular, *serpe* was formed by dropping the final *s.*

117

D. In *mestre* metathesis of the last syllable took place according to § 97, 5. For a different explanation of the final *e* of *mestre*, see § 48, 6.

E. The genitive survived in the names of the days of the week: *Martis* > *martes* (old); *Jŏvis* > *joves* (old); *Vĕnĕris* > *vernes* (RL, VII, 194). The *s* of OPtg. *lūes* (from *lunae*) and of OGal. *mercores* (from *Mercŭrĭi*) developed by analogy with *martes*, *joves* and *vernes*. These names did not survive except in Galician, where only *lus* and *martes* have survived today. See ZRPh, XIX, 614. Being based on the heathen names of gods and planets they were proscribed in the year 316 by Pope Sylvester, who ordained that they should henceforth be replaced by *ferĭa secunda*, etc. See Hampson, I, 137–138, s.v. *feria*.

Vestiges of the ablative are found in a few adverbs: *hāc hōrā* > *agora; hāc nŏcte* > *ontem; hōc annō* > *ogano* (old); and perhaps *mĕlĭōre* > *melhor* and *pĕjōre* > *pior*.

On the survival of the nominative and other cases than the accusative, see RHi, II, 117–119; Rom, XI, 79–81; Mus, III, 217; Lições, 39–47; H-MP, I, 607–609.

## 122. First Declension.

1. The endings of the accusative singular and plural of nouns of the Classical Latin first declension and the endings derived from them in Portuguese are:

|      | Classical Latin | Portuguese |
|------|-----------------|------------|
| Sg.  | *-am*           | *-a* (§ 12, 8) |
| Pl.  | *-as*           | *-as*      |

2. These endings and a preceding tonic *o* in hiatus were assimilated and contracted: *mŏlam* > *mó*. See § 99, 3.

3. These endings and a preceding tonic *ā* in hiatus became *-ā* and *-ās: lanam* > *lāa* > *lã; germānas* > *irmāas* > *irmās*. See § 78, 2.

A. In certain dialects the plural ending *-ās* became *-āes* by analogy with nouns of the third declension in *-āes* (from *-ānes*): *mattiānas* (REW) > *maçãs* > *maçães* (RL, XI, 142; RL, XII, 309; Esquisse, § 70 a).

B. In a few words the nasal resonance was lost by dissimilation and the accent shifted from the ending probably by analogy with other nouns ending in unaccented *a: campānam* > *campā* > *campa; *ventānam* > *ventā* > *venta; quintānam* > *quintā* > *quinta.* Rodrigues Lapa does not consider this explanation satisfactory (BF, I, 163–164). However, it is noteworthy that those words in which the accent did not shift, viz., *avelã, irmã, manhã, maçã,* etc. are words in which the nasal resonance remained on the ending and most of them words without a nasal in the preceding syllable.

**123. SECOND AND FOURTH DECLENSIONS.**

1. The endings of the accusative singular and plural of masculine and neuter nouns of the Classical Latin second and fourth declensions and the endings in Portuguese resulting from their fusion are:

|  | Cl. L. 2d Decl. Masc. | Cl. L. 4th Decl. Masc. | Cl. L. 2d Decl. Neut. | Cl. L. 4th Decl. Neut. | Portuguese |
|----|----|----|----|----|----|
| Sg. | -ŭm | -ŭm | -ŭm | -ū | -o (§ 12, 8; § 48, 1) |
| Pl. | -ōs | -ūs | -a | -ŭa | -os |

The fusion consisted in the adoption in Vulgar Latin of the endings of masculine nouns of the second declension by masculine nouns of the fourth declension and neuter nouns of the second and fourth declensions: *passūs* > *passos; castella* > *castelos; cornū* > *corno; cornŭa* > *cornos.* See GVL, § 347 and § 355, 1.

2. These endings in hiatus with a preceding tonic *a* or *ę* became -*u* and -*us: caelum* > *céu; palos* > *paus.* See § 48, 2. They contracted to -*u* and -*us* with a tonic *ų* with which they were in hiatus: *cūlum* > *cu.* See § 48, 5.

3. These endings and a preceding *ā* in hiatus became -*ão* and -*ãos: granum* > *grão; orphănos* > *orfãos.* See § 78, 3 and 3 c.

A. In many nouns of late Latin formation or adoption the ending derived from -*ānum* was replaced by the ending derived from -*ānem: sacristānum* (Du Cange) > *sacristam* (old); *cap-pellānum* (Du Cange) > *capelam* (old); *castellānum* > *castelam* (old); *alemannum* > *alemam* (old).  The plurals accordingly end in -*āes: sacristães; capelães; castelães; alemães*.  See Manual, § 83, 4; and D'Ovidio, 22, n. 2.  On Sp. *alemán*, see Hanssen, § 15, 1. The singular ending -*ão* of all these nouns in Modern Portuguese developed according to § 157, 2.

B. In dialectal Portuguese the plural ending -*āos* became -*ões* and -*āes* by analogy with nouns which in Latin belonged to the third declension and ended in -*ōnes* and -*ānes: germānos* > *irmões* and *irmães* (RL, XI, 142 and 280; RL, XII, 309; Esquisse, § 70 a; Grund, I, 1013).

4. These endings and a preceding tonic -*ō* in hiatus became -*om* and -*ons: dōnum* > *dom; sŏnos* > *sons*.  See § 78, 2.

A. The form *dões*, the OPtg. plural of *dom*, was formed on the analogy of nouns which in Latin belonged to the third declension and ended in -*ones*.  The form which has survived in Modern Portuguese is *dons*.

B. OPtg. *padrom* (from *patrōnum*) became *padrão* by analogy with nouns which in Latin belonged to the third declension and ended in -*ōnem*.  Later *padrão* became *patrão* through the influence of learned *patrono*.

5. These endings and a preceding tonic *ū* in hiatus became -*um* and -*uns: jejūnum* > *jejum* (see Estudos, II, 73–74).  See § 48, 5 A; § 78, 2 B.

6. In nouns with Classical Latin radical *ŏ* metaphony generally took place in the singular (§ 100, 7): *pŏpŭlum* > *pǫvo; hŏrtum* > *hǫrto;* but not in the plural: *pŏpŭlōs* > *pǫvos; hŏrtōs* > *hǫrtos*.

The pronunciation of final *o* became [u] at an early date (see § 48, 1 A).  This extreme closeness of the final vowel increased its assimilating effect on the tonic vowel.  It must be assumed that the *o* of final -*os* did not acquire this close pronunciation until after the time of the action of metaphony; therefore, final -*os* did not have any effect on the tonic vowel at all. This is what Almeida Cavacas means when he says that the ending of the plural must have had "um som diferente menos surdo" than the ending of the singular (Cavacas, 145). It is interesting to note that unaccented initial *o*, followed by *s*, is still pronounced [o] in some words, e.g., *hospedagem*, *hospital*.

A. Attempts have been made to account for the supposed difference between Old Portuguese final *-o* and *-os* by tracing it to the difference between Classical Latin *ŭ* and *ō* in *-ŭm* and *-ōs* (see Grund, I, 464; M-L, Gram, I, § 641; Huber, § 93,2; M-P, Orig., § 35, 3). The Classical Latin difference has apparently survived in Asturian, Central Italian and the dialect of Logudoro in northern Sardinia (see M-L, Gram, I, § 308). However, metaphony was caused in Portuguese not only by final *o* from Cl. L. *ŭ* but also by final *o* from Cl. L. *ō*, e.g., *vŏlvō* > *vǫlvo* (§ 176, 2).

In an effort to explain the lack of metaphony in the plural, Gonçalves Viana likewise goes back to an early distinction between singular and plural endings. He suggests that the radical vowel of the plural remained open in neuter nouns because of the ending *-a*, that it continued open even after this ending was replaced by the masculine ending *-os*, and that the open radical vowel of originally masculine nouns remained open by analogy with originally neuter nouns (see Rom, XII, 74 and 80). But this theory is untenable as it is certain that *-os* had replaced *-a* long before the action of metaphony had ceased (cf. ZRPh, IX, 143).

B. Metaphony is found also in nouns in which the ending and radical *ǫ* contracted: *avolum* (Du Cange) > *avô; tertiŏlum* (Du Cange) > *terçô*. See § 37, 5 A.

C. There are many learned and semi-learned nouns in which metaphony did not take place: *glŏbum* > *glǫbo; mŏdum* > *mǫdo*.

D. Some nouns with Classical Latin *ō* (*ŭ*) adopted a radical *ǫ* in the plural by analogy with nouns in which metaphony had taken place in the singular: *fŭrnos* > *fǫrnos; tŭrdos* > *tǫrdos*. But there are many nouns with Classical Latin *ō* (*ŭ*) in which neither the action of metaphony in the singular nor of analogy in the plural took place: *lŭpum* > *lôbo* and *lŭpos* > *lǫbos; lŭtum* > *lôdo* and *lŭtos* > *lǫdos*.

E. The *ǫ* of *ôlho* was due to the palatal (see § 37, 3 B). And the ǫ of the plural ǫlhos developed by analogy with nouns in which metaphony had taken place in the singular.

F. Neither metaphony nor the analogical simulation of metaphony took place if radical o was followed by a nasal consonant, because a nasal consonant closed an open o and kept a close o unchanged: dŏmĭnum > dǫno and dŏminos > dǫnos; lŭmbum > lǫmbo and lŭmbos > lǫmbos.  See § 37, 6.

G. Nouns with the suffix -ŏttum (GVL, § 37) have ǫ in the plural by analogy with the singular: -ŏttum > -ǫto and -ŏttos > -ǫtos.

H. In dialectal Portuguese metaphony is sometimes found in both the singular and the plural and sometimes in the plural and not in the singular.   And in a given dialect there is generally much inconsistency from one word to another.   See RL, IV, 328; RL, VII, 45; RL, XI, 142 and 270; RL, XII, 309; RL, XIV, 83; RL, XIX, 172; RL, XXVII, 131; Grund, I, 931.   This wide variation between dialects and between words in the same dialect is doubtless due to a variation in the relative force of metaphony and analogy.

I. Lat. ōvum developed as follows: ōvum > ǫum (GVL, § 324) > ǫum (GVL, § 167) > ǫvum (GVL, § 167) > ǫvo (cf. Sp. huevo) > ǫvo.   The last step was brought about by metaphony.

7. In nouns with Classical Latin radical ĕ metaphony took place in both the singular and plural: catĕllum > cadẹlo and catĕllos > cadẹlos; cappĕllum (REW) > capẹlo; cappĕllos > capẹlos.

A. While final -os did not affect radical ǫ it was probably sufficiently close to affect radical ẹ.   Or perhaps the ẹ of the plural of these nouns developed by analogy with the singular.

8. Some feminine nouns of the second and fourth declensions adopted the endings derived from the first declension: amethystum > ametista; sapphīrum > safira; fagum > faia; sŏcrum (f.) > sogra; while others did not change their form but became masculine: fraxĭnum > freixo; pīnum > pinho (old); alaternum > aderno.   One noun, mão (from manum), did not adopt the endings derived from the first declension or change its gender.

9. Some neuter plurals retained the ending *-a* and became feminine singulars: *arma* > *arma; vōta* > *boda; dōna* > *doa* (Crest, Glossary); *lĭgna* > *lenha; fŏlĭa* > *folha; cornŭa* > *corna*. These nouns formed a new plural by the addition of *s* and their forms correspond accordingly to those derived from feminine nouns of the first declension. Some of them still retain the collective force which they all probably acquired in the period of transition from plural to singular, e.g., *lenha*—"firewood."

**124. THIRD AND FIFTH DECLENSIONS.**

1. The endings of the accusative singular and plural of masculine, feminine, and neuter nouns of the Classical Latin third declension and of nouns of the Classical Latin fifth declension and the endings in Portuguese resulting from their fusion are:

|  | Cl. L. 3d Decl. Masc. | Cl. L. 3d Decl. Fem. Neut. | Cl. L. 5th Decl. | Portuguese |
|---|---|---|---|---|
| Sg. | *-em* | *-(e)* | *-em* | *-(e)* (§ 12, 8) |
| Pl. | *-es* | *-(i)a* | *-es* | *-(e)s* or *-is* |

The accusative singular and plural of nouns of the fifth declension are identical with the accusative singular and plural of masculine and feminine nouns of the third declension. The fusion consisted in the adaptation of the stems and endings of neuter nouns to correspond with masculine nouns (see sections 5, 6 and 7 below). The nasal resonance survived in OPtg. *rem* (from *rem*) as the word was a monosyllable (see § 97, 4).

2. The ending of the singular fell when preceded by a short *l, n, r, s,* or *c,* or by the group *t* + *i̯* (§ 46, 2): *sōlem* > *sol; canem* > *cam* (old); *seniōrem* > *senhor; mare* > *mar; mensem* > *mês; vĭcem* > *vez; dūrĭtĭem* > *durez.* But the *e* of the ending of the plural of these nouns did not fall (§ 46, 3): *sōles* > *sóis; canes* > *cães; seniōres* > *senhores; menses* > *meses; vĭces* > *vezes.*

3. Nouns with stems ending in a short *l* lost this *l* in the plural because it was intervocalic; and the ending generally became *-ịs* because of the hiatus (see § 46, 10): *sōles* > *sóis;* \**animāles* > *animais*.

A. This *l* was not lost in dialectal Portuguese if the plural was formed by adding *s* to singular forms which had a paragogic *e: animal* > *animale* (see § 116, 2) and *animale* + *s* > *animales*. See Esquisse, § 70 a. See also M-L, Gram, II, § 53.

B. The form *soles* is found in Old Portuguese (see Fab, 106). The noun *mal* came from the adverb *male*. There was a plural *maes* in Old Portuguese (see RL, XVI, 104 and 107; Abraham, Glossary) and Old Galician (Crest, Glossary). But *males* was much commoner and is the form which has survived. The plural *cônsules* (from *consŭles*) is learned.

C. Final *e* did not fall when preceded by long *l: vallem* > *vale; pellem* > *pele*. In dialectal Portuguese, however, it sometimes fell with consequent shortening of the consonant (Esquisse, § 67). Analogical plural forms were then made by adding *-es* to the new singulars and the *l* now short and intervocalic fell: *vallem* > *valle* > *val* and *val* + *es* > *vaes; pellem* > *pelle* > *pel* and *pel* + *es* > *peis*. See Esquisse, § 70 a; RL, II, 27; RL, XI, 280; RL, XXVII, 128.

4. Nouns whose stem ended in short *n* lost this *n* after it had nasalized the preceding vowel (see § 98, 4): *canem* > *cam* (old); *dracōnem* > *dragom* (old); *fīnem* > *fim; hŏmĭnem* > *omen* > *homem*. In the plural the nasal resonance spread to the ending and the two vowels either formed a nasal diphthong or contracted: *canes* > *cães* (§ 78, 3); *dracōnes* > *dragões* (§ 78, 3); *fīnes* > *fins* (§ 78, 2 B); *hŏmĭnes* > *omēes* > *homens* (§ 78, 2 c).

A. For the later development of *cam* to *cão* and *dragom* to *dragão*, see § 157, 2. For the loss of the final nasal resonance in the noun *pente* (from *pĕctĭnem*), see § 110, 3.

B. It is evident that in Old Portuguese the singular of nouns ending in unaccented *-en* or *-em* (from *-ĭnem*) was correctly spelled with one *e*, the plural with two *e*'s; for example, in the

"Vida de S. Nicalau" (Bausteine, 581–586), all the singular forms
of *homem* (three) have one *e*, all the plural forms (four) have two
*e*'s.   The singular forms with two *e*'s, found in some manuscripts,
are merely orthographic imitations of the plural.   See RC, XI,
85; Carter, 23.

c. The ending *-ŭdĭnem* (for -ūdĭnem) developed as follows:
*-ŭdĭnem* > *-oen* > *-oē* or *ōe;* its plural developed as follows:
*-ŭdĭnes* > *-oēes* > *-ōes*.   The singular *-oē* then became *-om*
(and later *-āo*) by analogy with the ending coming from Lat.
*-ōnem* (see *dragom* above), as both types were the same in the
plural.

5. Many Classical Latin neuter accusatives did not end
in *e* but in the stem-ending *l* or *r*; they adopted in Vulgar
Latin the masculine ending *-e(m)*: *mĕl* > *\*mĕlem* > *mel;*
*ūber* > *\*ubĕrem* > *úbere; marmor* > *marmŏrem* > *mármore;*
*sulfur* > *sulfŭrem* > *enxufere* (old and popular) and *enxôfre*.
See GVL, § 347.

A. That *\*mĕlem* had the short *l* of the original Classical Latin
accusative and not the long *l* of the other oblique cases is shown
by the plural *méis* (from *\*mĕles*).

B. For the final *e* of *úbere*, etc., see § 46, 2 B.

c. Cl. L. *rōbur* became V. L. *rōbŏrem* (GVL, § 347) but Ptg.
*roble* is doubtless a late borrowing from Spanish.   The medial
group *bl* never survived in Portuguese words; even in borrowings
from Spanish it generally changed to *br* (§ 86, 2 A).

6. Neuter accusatives ending in *-en* did not adopt the
ending of the masculine accusative, because *-en* was
taken to be the equivalent of *-em*.   Then final *n* fell, just
as final *m* had fallen at an earlier date: *nōmen* > *nome;*
*lūmen* > *lume; culmen* > *cume; legūmen* > *legume; sanguen*
> *sangue; acūmen* > *gume; aerāmen* > *arame* (§ 97, 4).
New plurals were accordingly formed by adding *s* to the
singular as in masculine nouns, e.g., *nomes*. See GVL, § 369.

A. These nouns generally adopted the masculine ending in
the Vulgar Latin of the Spanish territory: *nōmen* > *\*nōmĭnem*
> Sp. *nombre*.   Inasmuch as the ending *-ĭnem* did not spread
in the Vulgar Latin of the Portuguese territory, it is not likely

that OPtg. *vermem* came from a V. L. *\*verminem* nor that OPtg. *vimem* came from a V. L. *\*viminem*. The spelling *vimee* (FM, II, Glossary) is of no significance as unaccented single vowels were often written double in this document (FM, I, xxv). Nor is it likely that Ptg. *sangue* came from the Latin masculine form *sanguinem* through an OPtg. *\*sangue*. See Comp, 116. For *vermem*, see § 96, 2 and for *vimem*, see § 77 B.

B. The suffix *-umen* belongs to this group. It became *-ume* in Portuguese and through a V. L. *\*-uminem*, *-umbre* in Spanish. In many words it replaced the suffix *-udinem*, e.g., *consuetudinem* > Ptg. *costume* and Sp. *costumbre* (Manual, § 83, 4). Cf. D'Ovidio, 25, n. 3.

7. A few neuter accusative singulars ending in *-us* were taken for masculine accusative plurals of the second declension and a new singular was formed by dropping the *s*: *tempus* > *tempos; stercus* > *estercos; corpus* > *corpos; pectus* > *peitos; latus* > *lados; pignus* > *empenhos* (with prefix *em-*). The new singulars are *tempo, estêrco, corpo*, etc.

A. Metaphony took place in the new singular *corpo*.

B. The neuter *caput* became *cabo* and adopted the plural ending of nouns coming from the Classical Latin second declension.

8. The Latin accusative *-icem* of proparoxytonic nouns and adjectives became *-ez*, which is now spelled *-es: aurificem* > *ourivez* > *ourives; simplicem* > *simprez* > *simples*. See § 98, 2 B. The plural of these words was shortened by haplology (§ 114): *aurifices* > *ourivezes* > *ourives*.

A. Haplology occurred in paroxytonic plurals in dialectal Portuguese: *vices* > *vezes* > *bês* (§ 114 B); *felices* > *felizes* > *feliz* (RL, IV, 220).

B. A new popular singular *ourive* has been formed by dropping the final *s* of the shortened plural *ourives*. Some plurals, erroneously taken for singulars, have been pluralized again in popular Portuguese by the addition of *-es: pedes* > *pés* > *péses* (Esquisse, § 70 a; RL, VII, 45; and RL, XII, 309). Such plurals are common in Modern Galician: *reges* > *reis* > *reises; leges* > *leis* > *leises*.

9. A few nouns of the fifth declension adopted in Vulgar Latin the endings derived from the Classical Latin first declension: *rabĭem* > *raiva; dĭes* > *dias.*

A. Some nouns belonged to both declensions in Classical Latin, e.g., *matĕrĭam* and *matĕrĭem.*

10. Some nouns of the third (and fifth) declension adopted the endings derived from the first declension or those derived from the second declension: *axem* > *eixo; acĭem* > *aço; cŭcŭmĕrem* > *cogombro; passĕrem* > *pássaro; grŭem* > \**grŭam* > *grua* (§ 38, 9); *grŭem* > \**grŭum* > *grou* (§ 38, 10); *ŏs* > *ŏssum* (GVL, § 356, 3) > *ôsso; vas* > *vasum* (GVL, § 356, 3) > *vaso; gramen* > *grama; inguen* > *ingua; septembrem* > *setembro; octŭbrem* (Carnoy, 64) > *outubro; novembrem* > *novembro; decembrem* > *dezembro.*

A. The shift of declension in *setembro, outubro,* etc. was occasioned by analogy with the names of most of the other months, *janeiro, fevereiro,* etc.

B. The plural *daemŏnes* became *démões* in Old Portuguese but this form later adopted the plural ending of nouns derived from the second declension and became *demos.* This shift was facilitated by the fact that the singular was *demo* (from the nominative *daemon*) (§ 121).

11. Some masculine nouns and some nouns of common gender formed a distinguishing feminine modeled on nouns of the Classical Latin first declension: *leōnem* > *leom* > *leão,* fem. *leôa; pavōnem* > *pavom* > *pavão,* fem. *pavôa; seniōrem* > *senhor,* fem. *senhora; infantem* > *infante,* fem. *infanta; parentem* > *parente,* fem. *parenta; hŏspĭtem* > *hóspede,* fem. *hóspeda.*

A. The formation of these feminines began sporadically very early: *senhora* (Cd'A, I, 368–369; RL, XXIII, 85; FM, I, xxx); *parenta* (RL, XXIII, 64); *ospeda* (AHP, III, 18, A.D. 1325). But it did not become general until the sixteenth century. The feminines *chorona* and *ladrona* were obviously formed much later than *leôa* and *pavôa.*

## ADJECTIVES

**125. Declensions.**

The declensions of adjectives had the same fate in Portuguese as the declensions of nouns. All cases except the accusative disappeared and as there were no longer any neuter nouns to modify, the neuter endings fell into disuse. The neuter singular, identical with the masculine singular, has survived with the force of an abstract noun.

**126. First and Second Declensions.**

1. The endings of the masculine and feminine accusative singular and plural of adjectives of the Classical Latin first and second declensions and the endings derived from them in Portuguese are:

|          | Classical Latin | Portuguese     |
|----------|-----------------|----------------|
| Masc. Sg.| -ŭm             | -o (§ 12, 8)   |
| Masc. Pl.| -ōs             | -os            |
| Fem. Sg. | -am             | -a (§ 12, 8)   |
| Fem. Pl. | -as             | -as            |

2. These endings and a preceding ã in hiatus became -ão, -ãos, -ã, and -ãs: sanum > são; sanōs > sãos; vanam > vã; vanas > vãs (§ 78, 2 and 3).

3. In hiatus with a preceding tonic a or ę the masculine endings became -u and -us (§ 48, 2): malum > mau; malōs > maus; rĕum > réu (§ 34, 7 в); rĕos > réus; they contracted with tonic u and became -ú and -ús (§ 48, 5): nūdum > nú; nūdos > nús; they contracted with tonic ō and became -om and -ons (§ 78, 2): bŏnum > bom; bŏnōs > bons.

4. In hiatus with a preceding tonic a the feminine endings contracted and became -á and -ás: malam > má; malas > más; with tonic ę and o assimilation took place: rĕam > ree > ré (§ 34, 6 a); sōlam > soa > só (§ 99, 3 a).

A. The masculine forms of *só* had close *o* at first (see rime: *soo : negô-o* in CA, No. 416). But the masculine plural became *sós* by analogy with adjectives of the *novo* type and the masculine singular became *só*, perhaps in order to avoid confusion with the verb form *sou*. The early feminine forms *soa* and *soas* still survive in certain dialects (RL, III, 60 and 325).

B. Assimilation was prevented in *boa* (from *bŏnam*) by the nasal resonance (§ 45, 2 B).

5. In some adjectives an analogical feminine has replaced the phonological form, e.g., *parva* has replaced *parvoa* (from *parvŭlam*) as the feminine of *parvo* (from *parvŭlum*); *antiga* has replaced *\*antigua* (from *antīquam*, § 93, 2) as the feminine of *antigo* (from *antīquum*, § 93, 3); *sadia* has replaced *\*sadiva* (from *sanatīvam*) as the feminine of *sadio* (from *sanatīvum*, § 72, 2 A).

6. A few adjectives of the first and second declension adopted the endings derived from the third declension: *lībĕrum* > *livre; contentum* > *contente; firmum* > *firme.*

7. In adjectives with Classical Latin radical *ŏ* metaphony generally took place in the masculine singular (§ 100, 7): *nŏvum* > *nǫvo; grŏssum* > *grǫsso;* but not in any of the other forms: *nǫvos, nǫva, nǫvas; grǫssos, grǫssa, grǫssas.* See § 123, 6.

A. For dialectal variations, see references in § 123, 6 H.

B. The *v* of *nŏvum* fell in Vulgar Latin, but it was soon restored by analogy with the feminine forms and the masculine plural (GVL, § 324).

8. Metaphony or the analogical simulation of metaphony did not generally take place in any of the forms of adjectives with Classical Latin *ō* (*ŭ*): *rŭptum* > *rôto;* and *rôtos, rôta, rôtas; tōtum* > *tǫdo;* and *tǫdos, tǫda, tǫdas; fŭscum* > *fǫsco;* and *fǫscos, fǫsca, fǫscas.*

A. Metaphony took place in the noun *rǫta* (from *rŭptam*, Nascentes), which was not affected by analogy with forms of the adjective. It likewise took place in the indefinite pronoun *tudo* (from the neuter *tōtum*), which was not affected by analogy with forms of the adjective.

B. Metaphony took place in the feminine singular and plural of the adjective ending *-oso*, e.g., *formōsam* > *formǫsa; formōsas* > *formǫsas.* The masculine singular, instead of becoming *-\*uso*, remained unchanged by analogy with adjectives of the *novo* type and the masculine plural remained unchanged also, as final *-os* was neutral with respect to the radical vowel (see § 123, 6). Thus the inflection of *formoso* toward the end of the sixteenth century was *formǫso, formǫsos, formǫsa, formǫsas.* These forms are given by Nunes de Lião in 1576 (N–L, Orth, 17 ro). But there is evidence that *formǫsos* had become *formǫsos* even earlier (Oliv, Chapters 8 and 18). And thus analogy with the *novo* type became complete.

9. In some adjectives with Classical Latin radical *ĕ* metaphony took place in the masculine singular and plural, as in masculine nouns with radical *ĕ* (§ 123, 7): *adversum* > *avêsso; adversos* > *avêssos; graecum* > *grego; graecos* > *gregos; laetum* > *ledo; laetos* > *ledos;* and the *e* of the feminine singular and plural became close by analogy with the masculine singular and plural: *adversam* > *avêssa; adversas* > *avêssas; graecam* > *grega; graecas* > *gregas; laetam* > *leda; laetas* > *ledas.*

In other adjectives with Classical Latin radical *ĕ*, metaphony took place in the feminine singular and plural, that is, final *a* kept the radical vowel open: *bellam* > *bęla; bellas* > *bęlas; caecam* > *cęga; caecas* > *cęgas; fĕram* > *fęra; fĕras* > *fęras;* and the *e* of the masculine singular and plural remained open by analogy with the feminine singular and plural: *bellum* > *bęlo; bellos* > *bęlos; caecum* > *cęgo; caecos* > *cęgos; fĕrum* > *fęro; fĕros* > *fęros.*

A. When any of these forms occurred as other parts of speech they were not affected by analogy, e.g., *avęssas* (fem. pl. noun); *\*mure(m)-caecum* > *morcęgo.*

10. Adjectives with radical *ē* (*ĭ*) were not affected by metaphony; their feminine forms developed by analogy with their masculine forms. They, therefore, have *ę*

throughout like the *avẹsso* type: *quiētum* > *quẹdo* and *quẹ-dos, quẹda, quẹdas; secrētum* > *segrẹdo* and *segrẹdos, segrẹda, segrẹdas; sĭccum* > *sêco* and *sẹcos, sêca, sêcas.*

A. From this section and the above section it is clear that there is no alternation in the radical *e* of any adjectives.

**127. THIRD DECLENSION.**

1. The endings of the accusative singular and plural (masculine and feminine) of adjectives of the Classical Latin third declension and the endings derived from them in Portuguese are:

|      | Classical Latin | Portuguese |
|------|-----------------|------------|
| Sg.  | *-em*           | *-(e)* (§ 12, 8) |
| Pl.  | *-es*           | *-es* or *-is* |

2. The singular ending preceded by a short *l, n, r, s* or *c* fell: *\*hispaniōnem* (Manual, § 66, 2) > *espanhol; commūnem* > *comum; meliōrem* > *melhor; \*cortensem* (GVL, § 39) > *cortês; simplĭcem* > *simprez* (old).

A. For the development of *comuns*, the plural of *comum*, see § 38, 4 A.

3. Adjectives with stems ending in a short *l* lost this *l* in the plural because it was intervocalic and the ending generally became *-is* because of hiatus (see § 46, 10): *persōnāles* > *pessoais; possĭbĭles* > *possíveis.*

A. The plurals of the learned adjectives *fácil* and *útil* have popular endings: *fáceis* and *úteis.*

4. Some adjectives of the third declension adopted the endings derived from the Classical Latin first and second declension: *acrem* > *acrum* (ApPr) > *agro* and *agra; vĕtĕrem* > *vedro* and *vedra* (old); *rŭdem* > *rudo* and *ruda* (old and dialectal); *latro* (nom. sg.) > *ladro* and from this, *ladra* was formed.

A. In the fusion of the endings *-ão, -am* and *-om, grã,* the apocopated form of *grande,* became *grão* (§ 157, 1 A). This form was taken to be a masculine adjective derived from the Classical

Latin first and second declension and formed in the manner of *são* and *vão* (§ 126, 2) while *grã*, the original apocopated form, was taken to be its feminine and formed in the manner of *sã* and *vã* (§ 126, 2). These two forms have survived in compound nouns, e.g., *grão-mestre* and *grã-cruz*.

5. Some adjectives of the third declension, chiefly adjectives of nationality and adjectives ending in *-or* (from *-ōrem*), formed a distinguishing feminine modeled on the feminine of adjectives of the Classical Latin first and second declension: *\*hispaniōnem* (Manual, § 66, 2) > *espanhol*, fem. *espanhola; incantatōrem* > *encantador*, fem. *encantadora; \*anglensem* > *inglês* (Nascentes), fem. *inglêsa.*

A. These forms are first found in Vulgar Latin, e.g., *-ensam* as the feminine of *-ensem* (M-L, Gram, II, § 60; Carnoy, 243). But many were formed very late, e.g., *espanhola*, which was formed after the period in which intervocalic *l* fell; cf. the masculine plural *espanhóis*. See Comp, 232, n. 2.

B. The only adjectives ending in *-or* which did not form a separate feminine by the addition of *a* were comparatives: *meliōrem* > *melhor* (masc. and fem.).

C. The adjective *comum* formed a feminine *comua*, which was used as late as the eighteenth century but has survived today only as a noun.

### 128. COMPARISON.

1. The substitution of comparative and superlative forms by an analytical method of comparison, which had begun in Vulgar Latin (see § 13, 2 c), was completely accomplished in Portuguese. The only forms that have survived are the following irregular comparatives:

| M. & F. | Classical Latin | Portuguese |
|---|---|---|
| Acc. | *meliōrem* | *melhor* |
| | *pejōrem* | *peior* (old) and *pior* (§ 73, 5 A) |
| | *majōrem* | *maor* (old), *mór*, and *maior* (§ 73, 5A) |
| | *minōrem* | *meor* (old) and *menor* (§ 78, 7 B) |
| Neut. Acc. | *minus* | *meos* (old) and *menos* (§ 78, 7 B) |
| | *plūs* | *chus* (old) |

The tonic *o* of these adjectives was close in Old Portuguese, cf. the rime *maor : amor* in CV, No. 697 and see RF, XXV, 650. It became open first in *mór* (§ 99, 3 A) and through the influence of *mór* spread to *melhọr, piọr, maiọr* and *menọr*. But it did not spread to the learned forms *superiọr, inferiọr,* etc.

A. It is thought that modern dialectal *maor* is not a survival from Old Portuguese but rather a new development from *maior* (Opúsculos, II, 195).

B. The adverbs *melhor* and *pior* probably came from neuter ablative forms (§ 121 E).

C. The comparative *seniōrem* has survived only in the forms of the noun *senhor*. And *júnior* has survived only as a learned word.

D. There is a form *maire* in Old Portuguese which may come from the nominative *major* (see Rom, XI, 81).

2. The superlatives *óptimo, máximo,* etc. and those ending in *-íssimo* are learned and derived directly from Latin forms. But semi-learned forms are found in dialectal Portuguese, e.g., *-íssemo* and *-essíssemo* (RL, XXVII, 132) and *-ismo* (Gal). Sometimes a superlative is made by attaching the learned suffix to a popular form, e.g., *docíssimo* for the learned *dulcíssimo*.

## NUMERALS

**129. ONE TO THREE.**

1. The first three cardinal numerals were declined in Classical Latin but only the first two are declined in Portuguese.

2. *Ūnum > ūu > um* (§ 48, 5 A; § 78, 2 B); *ūnam > ūa > uma* (§ 78, 4 D).

3. *Dŭos > dous* (§ 38, 10) and *dois* (*oi* for *ou*, § 92, 7 c); *dŭas > duas* (§ 38, 9).

4. *Trēs > três*. Neuter *tria* disappeared.

**130.** FOUR TO TEN.

1. *Quattuor* > *quattor* (§ 93, 1) > *quatro* (§ 69, 1; § 97, 5).
2. *Quīnque* > *cinque* (Carnoy, 214) > *cinco*.

There were two *u̯*'s in this word in Classical Latin; the first of them fell by dissimilation in Vulgar Latin (GVL, § 379); cf. *cerquinho* (from *\*querquīnum*). Final *o* developed through the influence of *quatro;* but see Lexique, 93–94.

3. *Sex* > *seis* (§ 97, 6 в).
4. *Sĕptem* > *sẹte* (§ 85, 4).
5. *Octō* > *ọito* (§ 37, 3).
6. *Nŏvem* > *nọve*.
7. *Dĕcem* > *dẹz* (§ 46, 2; § 98, 2).

**131.** ELEVEN TO SIXTEEN.

1. The posttonic penult seems to have fallen in these six numerals, contrary to § 53. This probably took place in the following manner: *trēdĕcim* and *sēdĕcim* became dissyllabic through contraction after the fall of intervocalic *d*; then the remaining numerals of the group shortened in imitation of *treze* and *seze* and through the influence of the Spanish forms, which must have been considerable in view of the importance of numerals in commerce.

Final *e* was preserved in *doze, treze* and *seze*, contrary to § 46, 2. This was due to the influence of *onze, catorze* and *quinze*, in which *z* after syncope was preceded by a consonant. The *e* may have been preserved also in order to avoid confusion with *dous, tres* and *seis* respectively, somewhat similarly pronounced, inasmuch as the slightest cause of confusion in numerals is always carefully avoided because of their importance in exchange.

2. *Ūndĕcim* > *\*ŭndece* (GVL, § 166) > *onze*.
3. *Duŏdĕcim* > *dōdece* (GVL, § 225) > *doze*.
4. *Trĕdĕcim* > *tredece* > *\*trẹeze* (§ 74, 1) > *trẹze*.

Tonic *ę* became *ẹ* through the influence of *trẹs*.

5. *Quattuordĕcim* > *\*quattordece* (§ 93, 1) > *catorze* (§ 69, 2; 92, 1 A).

6. *Quīndĕcim* > *quindece* > *quinze*.

7. *Sēdĕcim* > *sedece* > *\*seeze* (§ 74, 1) > *seze* (old). For the modern form of this numeral, see § 132.

**132. Sixteen to Nineteen.**

1. This group of numerals as formed in Classical Latin disappeared and was replaced in Vulgar Latin by a group formed analytically with *et* or *ac* (GVL, § 379).

The Modern Portuguese forms, which made their appearance toward the middle of the fifteenth century, resulted from the substitution of the conjunction *e* by the preposition *a* with additive force (Comp, 217; S-D, Gram, § 48, n. 2). This change was not so great as it appears, as the conjunction *e* was not yet pronounced [i] (Estudos, II, 100–101).

A. The forms with *a* may have always existed in the spoken language alongside the forms with *e* and may therefore have come from Vulgar Latin forms with *ac* (KJ, IV, Part I, 333).

B. For other uses of *a* for *e*, see Esquisse, § 77 c; RL, XXVII, 156. See also Cortesão, s.v. *dezeseis*.

2. *Sēdĕcim* was replaced by *\*dece et sex*, which became *dez e seis* (old) and later *dezasseis*.

3. *Septendĕcim* was replaced by *decem et septem*, which became *dez e sete* (old) and later *dezassete*.

4. *Duodēvigintī* was replaced by *\*dece et octo*, which became *dez e oito* (old) and later *dezaǫito*, which then developed as follows: *dezaǫito* > *dezǫǫito* (e.g., *dez ooyto*, Graal, 12) > *dezóito* (§ 99, 3 A).

A. The close *o* of popular *dezôito* developed through the influence of *ǫito*.

5. *Undēvigintī* was replaced by *\*dece et nove*, which became *dez e nove* (old) and later *dezanove*.

**133. THE TENS.**

1. Intervocalic *g* fell in all these cardinals, according to § 73, 4. Then, in all those above *trīginta*, *a* was assimilated to the following tonic *e*, according to § 99, 3. The resultant *e* became close because of the nasal (cf. *quente*, § 99, 3 в). The accent did not shift to the penult in these numerals in Portuguese and Spanish as it did perhaps in other Romance languages (ZRPh, VIII, 83–88; Carnoy, 256; Manual, § 89, 3). Cf. RHi, LXXVII, 138.

2. The addition of the tens to the cardinals from one to nine is shown in Portuguese by the conjunction *e*, e.g., *vigintī ūnum* > *vinte e um*. As in the group from sixteen to nineteen in standard Portuguese (§ 132, 1), the preposition *a* is used instead of the conjunction *e* in the cardinals from twenty-one to twenty-nine in dialectal Portuguese, e.g., *vinta um* (Esquisse, § 71 a). This *a* and the *o* of *oito* were assimilated and contracted as in *dezóito* (§ 132, 4): *vinta oito* > *vintǫito* (RL, VII, 45). These dialectal forms are found in Gil Vicente.

3. *Vīgintī* > *viịntị* (§ 35, 4; Jud, 259 and 263) > *vinte* (§ 47, 1).

4. *Trīgĭnta* > *triịnta* > *trinta*.

The tonic *ĭ* of *trīgĭnta* became *ị* through the influence of *viịnte* (ZRPh, VIII, 86; Jud, 264).

A. If the accent shifted to the antepenult of *trīginta* in Portuguese territory, the development must have been as follows: *trīgĭnta* > *tríginta* (GVL, § 142) > *\*trienta* > *triinta* (§ 99, 3) > *trinta*. See Manual, § 89, 3 for Leonese *trinta*.

5. *Quadrāginta* > *quaraenta* (§ 86, 1) > *quarenta*.

The *u̯* of *qu̯* has remained, contrary to § 69, 2 but due to the influence of *quatro*. For the form *corenta*, see § 40, 7.

6. *Quīnquāginta* > *cinquaenta* > *cinqüenta* (§ 93, 2 A).

The fall of the first *u̯* was due to the influence of *cinco*.

7. *Sexāginta* > *sessaenta* (§ 92, 9) > *sessenta*.

It has been suggested that *x* became *ss* through the influence of *seis* (Hanssen, § 57, 1).

8. *Septuaginta* > *setaenta* (§ 85, 4; § 93, 1) > *setenta*.

9. *Octōginta* > *\*octaginta* > *oitaenta* (§ 43, 3) > *oitenta*.

The change to *\*octaginta* was due to the influence of most of the other numerals of this group.

10. *Nōnaginta* > *\*novaginta* > *novaenta* > *noventa*.

The change to *\*novaginta* was due to the influence of *nove*.

## 134. THE HUNDREDS.

1. These numerals, except *centum*, were declined in Classical Latin like the plural of *bonus*. Only the form derived from *centum* and the forms derived from the masculine and feminine accusative of *ducentī*, *trecentī* and *quīngentī* have survived in Portuguese. The remaining ones were replaced in Vulgar Latin by numerals formed analytically with *\*quattro*, etc. and the newly formed accusative plural *\*centos*. Because this accusative was felt to be a separate word, its *c* developed as an initial *c* and not as intervocalic *c*.

The two elements are still separate, that is, each has its own accent, although they are written together as one word.

A. In popular speech, *duzentos*, *trezentos* and *quinhentos* were replaced by *dois centos*, *tres centos* and *cinco centos* respectively.

2. *Centum* > *cento* > *cem* (§ 107, 1).

3. *Ducentōs* > *duzentos* (§ 73, 2).

4. *Trecentōs* > *trezentos* (§ 73, 2).

5. *Quadringentōs* was replaced by *\*quattro centōs*, which became *quatrocentos*.

6. *Quīngentōs* > *quinhentos* (§ 92, 3 B).

7. *Sexcentōs* was replaced by *\*sex centōs*, which became *seiscentos*.

8. *Septingentōs* was replaced by *\*sette centōs*, which became *setecentos*.

9. *Octingentōs* was replaced by *\*octō centōs*, which became *oitocentos*.

10. *Nōngentōs* was replaced by *\*nŏve centōs*, which became *novecentos*.

**135.** THE THOUSANDS.

1. *Mīlle* > *mil* (§ 107, 1).

A. The Classical Latin plural *mīlĭa* survived only as a feminine singular noun, *milha*. It was replaced as a numeral by the singular form *mil*.

2. *Mīliarĭum* > *milheiro*.

A. The form *milhento* was formed from the first syllable of *milheiro* with an ending in imitation of *cento*.

3. The form *milhão* comes either from It. *milione* or Fr. *million*.

**136.** ORDINAL NUMERALS.

1. Some of the first ten ordinal numerals do not come from Classical Latin ordinals but from Classical Latin derivatives of them.

2. *Prīmarĭum* > *primeiro* (§ 33, 2).

A. *Primo* (from *prīmum*) has survived in other uses.

3. *Secundum* > *segundo* (§ 38, 1 в; § 73, 1).

4. *Tertiarĭum* > *terceiro* (§ 33, 2; § 89, 3).

A. *Têrço* (from *tertĭum*) has survived as an ordinal only in the word *têrça-feira*.

5. *Quartum* > *quarto* (§ 69, 1).

A. In Old Portuguese there was a *quarteiro* (from *quartarĭum*).

6. *Quīntum* > *quinto* (§ 69, 3).

A. In Old Portuguese there was a *quinteiro* (from *quintarĭum*).

7. *Sextum* > *sexto* (§ 92, 9 c).

A. *Sexto* became OPtg. *seisto* through the influence of *seis* and *seisto* became OPtg. *seistimo* through the influence of *seitimo*. A V. L. *sĕxĭmum*, which developed through the influence of *sĕptĭmum*, became OPtg. *seismo* and *sesmo*.

8. *Sĕptĭmum* > *sétimo* (§ 85, 4).

A. A parallel development of *sĕptĭmum* was to *seitimo* (old; § 92, 7 c). The form *sétimo* has been explained as due to the influence of *sete* (RL, XXXIV, 306).

9. *Octāvum* > *oitavo* (§ 43, 3).

A. A parallel development of *octāvum* was to *outavo* (old; § 92, 7 c).

10. *Nōnum* > *nono.*

A. This word is obviously learned. The popular form of the feminine has survived in the noun *nôa.* The distributive form *novēnum* became OPtg. *noveo,* which was used as an ordinal (see GVL, § 382).

11. *Dĕcĭmum* > *décimo.*

A. This word is learned. The popular form of the masculine has survived in the noun *dízimo.*

12. All the ordinals above "tenth" are learned in Modern Portuguese. In Old Portuguese, some ordinals were formed by attaching to the cardinals the learned ending *-eno* (from the Latin distributive ending *-ēnum*), e.g., *onzeno, dozeno.* See GVL, § 382.

A. The noun *quaresma* (from *quadragēsĭmam*) must be an early borrowing from Spanish. In Portuguese the posttonic penult would not have fallen.

## ARTICLES

**137. Definite Article.**[1]

1. *Ille* was used as a definite article in Vulgar Latin. The Portuguese forms are derived from the Latin accusative.

| Classical Latin | Vulgar Latin | Portuguese | | |
|---|---|---|---|---|
| *illum* | *\*lo* | *o* | *lo* | *no* |
| *illam* | *\*la* | *a* | *la* | *na* |
| *illos* | *\*los* | *os* | *los* | *nos* |
| *illas* | *\*las* | *as* | *las* | *nas* |

[1] The development of the definite article was very similar to that of the pronouns *o, a, os* and *as.* As they are considered separately, some duplication is unavoidable.

These words were unaccented and lost their first syllable
in Vulgar Latin, becoming *lo, *la, *los and *las with short
l.   And this short l became medial in Portuguese in combination with preceding words; its subsequent development
depended on the final with which it came in contact, which
could be: a) a vowel,  b) r or s,  c) consonantal n.

The fact that the primitive form of the Portuguese
article, while apparently proclitic to the noun it modified,
could be so closely attached to a preceding word ending in
a vowel that the l of the article fell, or to a preceding word
ending in a consonant that this consonant was assimilated
to the l of the article, seems to indicate that the article developed most commonly in the intertonic position, that is,
between two accented syllables, e.g., amei o filho (– ́– – ́–),
but not necessarily adjacent to either of them, e.g., todo o
amor (– ́– – – ́).

2. When preceded by verb forms ending in a vowel, by the
prepositions a, de and para, and by the singular forms of the
adjective todo, l, being short and intervocalic, fell, according
to § 75, 1: *vejo-los livros > vejo os livros; *a-lo > ao; *de-lo
> deo > do; *toda-la casa > toda a casa.   Hence the forms
o, a, os and as, which spread to other positions.  The development and spread of the pronoun o, a, os and as doubtless contributed to the spread of these forms of the article.
For a different explanation of the fall of l, see Rad, 32;
BSLi, XXII, 88.

A. The combination ao became ó in old and popular Portuguese
(AStNS, LXV, 47).

3. Final r and s of a preceding word were assimilated to
the l of lo, etc. (§ 109, 3) and the resultant long l remained
as a short l (§ 82, 1).   This occurred with infinitives, with
prepositions ending in r (§ 97, 5 B and c), with second
singular and first and second plural verb forms, with plural
forms of the past participle, with ambos, ambas and the
plural forms of todo, with the words des, mais, tras, pois, etc.,

e.g., *tomalla paz e a comunhom* (RL, XXI, 138); *pelo; vistelas iuras* (CV, No. 269); *passadallas tres partes* (Crest, 173); *todolos dias.* See also *Apostilas*, II, 79. The combinations with *per* are still used. The rest, although used regularly in the early *Cancioneiros* (RF, XXV, 670), have disappeared from the modern language except in certain dialects, where their use is generally optional (*Esquisse*, § 72 c; RL, XIX, 173; RL, XXVIII, 233, s.v. *lo*; L-F, 8; S-A, § 126).

A. The forms *lo, la*, etc. after imperatives arose from the use of the indicative for the imperative, e.g., *Vedela frol do pinho* (CV, No. 173); *Vede-los Alemães* (Lusíadas, canto VII, stanza 4). But see RL, X, 340.

B. Final *b* of *\*ub* (from *ubi*) was also assimilated to the *l* of *lo*, etc. (§ 86, 2): *\*ublo > ullo > ulo*, e.g., *hulas provas* (CV, No. 1099).

4. The *l* of *lo*, etc. was assimilated to the final *n* of the preposition *en* (from *ĭn*) and the resultant long *n* remained as a short *n* (§ 84, 2): *\*en-lo > enno > ēno.* That this *n* nasalized the *e* is shown by the Old Portuguese spellings *em no* and *ē no.* The assimilation was progressive because the *n* of the preposition was more essential to the meaning than the *l* of the article, which had begun to disappear in other positions. The *ē* of *ēno* was first denasalized (RL, I, 179), then *eno* being unaccented lost its first syllable and became *no.* For new juxtapositions of *em* and the definite article in Modern Portuguese, see Dunn, § 64 e and f.

A. The *l* of *lo*, etc. was likewise assimilated to the final *n* of verb forms (chiefly third plural) in old and dialectal Portuguese (RL, XI, 140–141; RL, XXVIII, 235, s.v. *no*).

B. The *l* of *lo*, etc. was assimilated to the final *n* of V. L. *con* (from *cŭm*) and the resultant long *n* remained as a short *n* (§ 84, 2), which nasalized the *o* of the preposition: *\*con-lo > conno > cō no* (AHP, IV, 303, A.D. 1265). These forms did not last long but were replaced by new juxtapositions of *com* and *o, a*, etc., which because of the loss of *l* developed as if they had originally had intervocalic short *n: com a*, i.e., *cõ a* > *coa* (cf. *boa*, § 78, 7), and *com o*, i.e., *cõ o* > *cõ* (cf. *bom*, § 78, 2) > *co*, in which the nasal resonance fell by analogy with *coa*. These forms have survived only in certain dialects. The juxtapositions from which they sprang and in which the two elements have not combined are now used in their stead: *com o, com a*, etc.

5. A form *el*, which came from the nominative *ille* either directly or through Spanish is now used only with the noun *rei* although in Old Portuguese its use was slightly more extended (see Comp, 261). In Old Portuguese the preposition *a* and this form of the article sometimes contracted to *al* (RL, XXXIII, 212). For an attempt to derive *el* from the accusative, see H-MP, I, 609–610.

6. The first syllable of *illum*, etc. was preserved and therefore the long *l*, when the initial vowel contracted with the final *e* of *sobre* (from *sŭper*) in new juxtapositions of the two words in Vulgar Latin: *sŭper* > *sobre* (§ 97, 5), and \**sobre + ello* > *sobrelo*, e.g., *sobrela alma* (RL, XXV, 141). For additional examples, see RL, V, 126; RL, VII, 64; RL, XXV, 142 et seqq.; RL, XXV, 235; AHP, VI, 232; Est Tr, 110.

A. The explanation that these forms came from \**sobres + lo*, etc. (Rad, 55) is not tenable as the form *sobres* is not found. In Modern Portuguese they have been entirely replaced by new juxtapositions of *sôbre* and *o, a*, etc.

7. The forms *ele, ela*, etc. which came from the nominative and corresponded to the accented forms of the personal pronouns of the third person, were often used before the adjectives *dito* and *mesmo*, particularly in the fifteenth century, e.g., *per eles ditos juizes e meestres* (RL, V, 53, A.D. 1463). In one and the same document we find *a dita Guiomar Gonçallvez* and *ella dita Guiomar Gonçallvez* (AHP, III, 86, A.D. 1445). See FM, I, Introdução L.

8. The primitive forms *lo, la*, etc. are occasionally found in the early Cancioneiros (Cd'A, I, 369–370). Their occurrence in stereotyped expressions in sixteenth century verse

has been attributed to the influence of Spanish (Comp, 266). See also SaM, Glossary, s.v. *a la fé*. For their use in archaic and popular expressions, see AStNS, LXV, 45, s.v. *lo*.

**138.** INDEFINITE ARTICLE.

1. The first cardinal number was used as an indefinite article in Classical Latin. This use spread in Vulgar Latin and Portuguese. For the development of the forms, see § 129, 2.

2. The modern forms *num* and *numa* (from *em um* and *em uma*) developed in imitation of *no, naquele, neste,* etc.

## PRONOUNS

**139.** PERSONAL PRONOUNS.

While only the accusative case of nouns and adjectives has survived in Portuguese, the nominative and accusative and sometimes also the dative case of personal pronouns have survived.

These cases are not always restricted to their original function, as some accusative forms are used as datives and some nominative and dative forms are used as objects of prepositions.

Some forms developed in the accented position, some in the unaccented position.

**140.** ACCENTED FORMS OF THE PERSONAL PRONOUN.

1. The subject pronouns, which generally developed under the tonic accent, and the Classical Latin forms from which they are derived, are:

| Classical Latin | Portuguese |
|---|---|
| *ĕgo* | *eu* (§ 34, 7; § 73, 3 A) |
| *tū* | *tu* |
| *ĭlle* | *êle* (§ 82, 1; § 100, 3) |
| | *el* (old and popular) |

| Classical Latin | Portuguese |
|---|---|
| *illa* | *ẹla* (§ 82, 1; § 100, 4) |
| *nōs* (nom.) | *nós* |
| *vōs* (nom.) | *vós* |
| | *êles* |
| | *eis* (old and popular) |
| | *ẹlas* |

3d sg.: Contrary to § 46, 2 A, *elle* became *el*. This was
due to proclisis. 1st and 2d pl.: The *o* of *nós* and *vós* developed through the influence of *nosso* and *vosso* (Language,
XII, 134–135). 3d pl.: *êles*, *eis* and *elas* did not come
directly from Latin but were formed analogically by the
addition of the plural ending to *êle*, *el* and *ela*, the nominative singular forms. For a different explanation of *eis*, see
Esquisse, § 72 a. The corresponding forms in Spanish,
*ellos* and *ellas*, have come directly from the Latin accusative
plural forms.

2. The pronouns used as objects of prepositions developed under the tonic accent. They are given below
with the Classical Latin and Vulgar Latin forms from which
they are derived.

| Classical Latin | Vulgar Latin | Portuguese |
|---|---|---|
| *mī* (for *mihī*) | | *mi* (old) |
| | | *mim* (§ 66, 1 B) |
| *tibi* | *tī* (GVL, § 385) | *ti* |
| *sibi* | *sī* (GVL, § 385) | *si* |
| *ĭlle* | | *êle* (§ 82, 1; § 100, 3) |
| | | *el* (old and popular) |
| *ĭlla* | | *ẹla* (§ 82, 1; § 100, 4) |
| *ĭllud* (neut.) | | *ello* (old) |
| *nōs* | | *nós* |
| *vōs* | | *vós* |
| | | *êles* |
| | | *eis* (old and popular) |
| | | *ẹlas* |

1st sg.: At first *mi* was used solely as a dative but in the
early Cancioneiros we find *me* gradually taking its place

as a conjunctive dative and accusative (RL, XXIII, 53; RF, XXIII, 344; RF, XXV, 663). 3d sg.: *si* has become *sim* in certain dialects through the influence of *mim* (Esquisse, § 72 a). For the formation of *el*, see section 1 above. *El*, *êle* and perhaps *ela* are nominatives which came to be used as objects of prepositions. If *ello* had survived it would doubtless have become *ilo* (cf. *aquilo*, *isso* and *isto*). 1st and 2d pl.: For the *o* of *nós* and *vós*, see section 1 above. 3d pl.: For the formation of *êles*, *eis* and *elas*, see section 1 above.

A. All these pronouns were used as direct objects of the verb in Old Portuguese and are still so used in Brazil (RF, XXV, 669, 671 and 707; RL, IX, 119; Abraham, § 63, 2).

3. The preposition *cum* was joined as an enclitic to the ablative of personal and reflexive pronouns. All of these combinations have survived in Modern Portuguese.

| Classical Latin | Old Portuguese | Modern Portuguese |
|---|---|---|
| *mēcum* | *mego, comego, migo, comigo* | *comigo* |
| *tēcum* | *tego, contego, tigo, contigo* | *contigo* |
| *sēcum* | *sego, consego, sigo, consigo* | *consigo* |

| Classical Latin | Vulgar Latin | Old Portuguese | Modern Portuguese |
|---|---|---|---|
| *nōbīscum* | *noscum* (ApPr) | *nosco* | *connosco* |
| *vōbīscum* | *voscum* (ApPr) | *vosco* | *convosco* |

For fall of final *m*, see § 97, 4. And for intervocalic *c* in the singular forms, see § 73, 1.

As the meaning of the syllables -*go* and -*co* was lost, the preposition was again attached to these forms, this time as a proclitic. The new combinations conformed to the regular order of pronoun and preposition in Portuguese.

The forms with tonic *i* arose very early (perhaps in Vulgar Latin; see *micum* in Du Cange) through the influence of the forms of these pronouns used with other prepositions and they have survived in Modern Portuguese through the same influence. All four Old Portuguese variants of the singular forms are found in the early Cancioneiros.

In *comigo* the nasal resonance of pretonic *o* disappeared (§ 77 A) and the *o* became [u] (§ 43, 1). But in some dialects the sound [õ] has been preserved through the influence of *contigo*, etc. and of *com* as a separate word. And in standard Portuguese the [õ] of *connosco* [kõnoʃku] has been preserved through the same influence. The open *o* of *nós* and *vós* did not influence the tonic *o* of *connọsco* and *convọsco*.

4. The preposition *en* or *em* was joined as a proclitic to the prepositional forms of the personal pronoun of the third person (section 2 above) and to the forms of the demonstrative pronouns and adjectives *êste* and *êsse*. These combinations developed at first in a regular phonological fashion but finally appeared with an initial *n* (*nêle*, *neste*, *nesse*), which must have been due to some non-phonological influence.

Whether we look upon *en* and *ele* [1] as first combining in early Portuguese or consider them to have combined in Vulgar Latin, the early Portuguese form and pronunciation would have been the same, namely, *ē ele*, inasmuch as both intervocalic *n* and final *n* in monosyllables nasalized the preceding vowel and lost their consonantal value (§ 78, 1; § 97, 4). The nasal resonance spread to the second vowel and then disappeared, as conditions necessary for its preservation did not exist (cf. *eelo*, § 78, 7). Accordingly, the early development of *ē ele* was: *ē ele* > *ēēle* > *eele*. Forms showing these changes are found in great abundance toward the end of the thirteenth century.[2]

---

[1] In this discussion *ele* is used as illustrative of the group, which includes *êste*, *êsse* and the feminine, neuter, and plural forms.

[2] Forms are also found in which the vowels contracted. In some of these the nasal resonance remained: *enle* (RL, VIII, 43, A.D. 1276; Eluc, A.D. 1291); in some it disappeared: *el* (RL, IX, 267, A.D. 1266); *ela* (RL, IX, 268, A.D. 1272). We have seen *cum* lose its meaning in its transformation to *-go* in *migo*, etc. (section 3 above); in the forms *el* and *ela* we see *em* lose its very existence.

Examples of *em* plus forms of *ele*

First change —*eenla* (AHP, VII, 472, A.D. 1277); *eenlla* (AHP, VII, 471, A.D. 1277)

Second change—*eeles* (RL, XI, 89, A.D. 1278); *eelas* (AHP, VI, 71, A.D. 1280); *eele* (RL, VIII, 44, A.D. 1292); *eel* (RL, XXI, 252, A.D. 1303).

Examples of *em* plus forms of *este*

First change —*eensta* (AHP, VII, 471, A.D. 1277); *éésta*, i.e., *ēēsta* (Bausteine, 679, A.D. 1293)

Second change—*eesto* (AHP, IV, 177, A.D. 1297)

Examples of *em* plus forms of *esse*

First change —*eensa* (AHP, VII, 469, A.D. 1275); *eensse* (RL, XXI, 248, A.D. 1289); *eenses* (RL, VIII, 43, A.D. 1292)

Second change—*eesse* (RL, V, 130, A.D. 1294); *eessa* (RL, IX, 275, A.D. 1298)

With the disappearance of the nasal resonance it became necessary to reintroduce the preposition *ẽ* in order to preserve the meaning of the expression. This new *ẽ* is found as early as 1297, viz., *en eeles* (AHP, IV, 177). It might have had the same fate as its predecessor if some outside influence had not become operative. This influence was exerted by the forms of *eno* with denasalized *e* (§ 137, 4). In imitation of *eno* in the effort to preserve some form of nasal, a consonantal *n* was inserted between the new *ẽ* and *eele*, *ẽ* then becoming denasalized.[1] Thus arose the form *eneele*, which is found early in the fourteenth century, e.g., *eneela* (Bausteine, 585); *eneesta* (Bausteine, 584). Then through the influence of the forms of *no* (apocopated *eno*) and the forms of *naquel*, which had developed much earlier (see § 145, 2), *eneele* became *neele*. A dated example of the

---

[1] If forms with both nasalized *e* and consonantal *n*, like *em neste*, exist, as claimed by Leite (Opúsculos, IV, 981), they must be extremely rare. It is evident, therefore, that *ẽ* became denasalized almost immediately after the insertion of consonantal *n*.

latter form is *neeles* (DC, 359, A.D. 1429) and examples are found in the "Livro de Linhagens," e.g., *neesto* (PMH, Scriptores, 279) and in Fernão Lopes, e.g., *neele* (FL, 129). Finally, with contraction of the *e*'s the modern form *nêle* came into existence.

A. The theory that the forms *nêle*, *neste*, etc. arose through the use of *no* for *em* (Comp, 265) does not take into account the intermediate forms cited above.

**141. UNACCENTED FORMS OF THE PERSONAL PRONOUN.**

These forms developed as enclitics and proclitics to the verb or to some other word bearing the accent. As they never occurred in Old Portuguese as the first word of a sentence and rarely as the last word, they seem to have developed most commonly in the intertonic position, that is, between two accented syllables, but not necessarily adjacent to either of them; one of the accented syllables could be the secondary tonic. This is their position when used as infixes in the future indicative and conditional. See Abraham, § 65.

The variety of position of conjunctive pronouns in early Portuguese is proof of a weak stress accent. The general enclisis found in Portuguese today (G-V, Port, 91) is the result of stronger stress accent and is therefore a purely modern development. Yet the freedom and variety of enclisis, that is, the fact that the pronoun does not always have to be enclitic to the verb, is an inheritance from the older language. The failure of the vowels of these pronouns to fall by syncope as in Old Spanish (Manual, § 94, 4) and in Old French is further proof of a weak stress accent.

A. Meyer-Lübke argues that these forms were always enclitic (ZRPh, XXI, 318). In his presentation of the unsolved features of this problem (PMLA, XX, 88–89) Chenery does not take into account the vast difference between Old and Modern Portuguese in the matter of stress accent.

142. UNACCENTED FORMS UNAFFECTED BY ADJACENT
　　　SOUNDS.

The forms of some unaccented pronouns in Portuguese
were unaffected in their development by the sounds of
adjacent words.

| Classical Latin | Portuguese |
|---|---|
| mē | me |
| tē | te |
| sē | se |
| nōs | nos [nuʃ] |
| vōs | vos [vuʃ] |

A. These forms, as given, are unaffected by adjacent sounds.
For their variants when in contact with adjacent sounds, see
§ 143, 3, 6 and 7.

B. While it is a mistake to suppose that the verb and the
pronoun developed separately for a time and then were suddenly
juxtaposed in early Portuguese, it is evident that new juxtapositions of severed elements occurred from time to time. These
are pointed out in § 143.

C. These forms were accusatives in Classical Latin but came
to be used as datives and accusatives in Portuguese. The *o* of
*nos* and *vos*, being unaccented, became [u] (§ 43, 1; § 48, 1).

D. The *m* of dialectal *mos* (for *nos*) (RL, II, 241; RL, XI, 282;
RL, XXXI, 190; Esquisse, § 72 a) developed probably through
the influence of the verb ending -*mos* (PhM, I, 354); it has also
been explained as due to the influence of *me* (ZRPh, V, 255;
Manual, § 94, 1).

E. The final *s* of the first plural of all tenses fell before the *n*
of enclitic *nos*, e.g., *lavāmus nos* > *lavamo-nos*. Cf. popular *mai'
nada*.

143. UNACCENTED FORMS AFFECTED BY ADJACENT SOUNDS.

1. The forms of some unaccented pronouns in Portuguese
were affected in their development by the sounds of adjacent
verbs, other pronouns or other parts of speech.

| Classical Latin | Vulgar Latin | Portuguese | | |
|---|---|---|---|---|
| *ĭllum* (acc.) | *lo | o | -lo | -no |
| *ĭllud* (acc.) | *lo | o | -lo | -no |
| *ĭllam* (acc.) | *la | a | -la | -na |
| *ĭllōs* (acc.) | *los | os | -los | -nos |
| *ĭllās* (acc.) | *las | as | -las | -nas |
| *ĭllī* (dat.) | *li | li (old) and *lhe* | | |
| *ĭllīs* (dat.) | *lis | lis (old) and *lhes* | | |
| *tē* | | che (old) | | |
| *sē* | | xe (old) | | |

The Vulgar Latin forms *lo, *la, *los, *las, *li and *lis
with short *l* probably arose through the wrong division of
such combinations as *mello (from *mē* + *ĭllum*) and *dĭcĕllĭ
(from *dīcĭ(t)* + *ĭllī*).   Cf. GVL, § 392.   They then became
generalized, being used also in the proclitic position.   In
new combinations in the enclitic position the short *l* became
medial; its subsequent development in the accusative forms
depended on the final with which it came in contact.   This
final could be: a) a vowel, b) *r*, *s* or *z*, c) consonantal *n*.

2. When the Vulgar Latin accusative forms of *ille* were
attached to verb forms ending in a vowel (first and third
singular of all tenses, second singular preterits, second
singular and plural imperatives) and to pronouns ending
in a vowel (*me*, *te*, *lhe*), *l*, being short and intervocalic, fell,
according to § 75, 1: *vejo-lo > vejo-o; *me-lo > meo > mo
(§ 99, 7).   Hence the forms *o*, *a*, *os* and *as*, which spread to
other positions.

A. After the fall of intervocalic *l*, like vowels contracted in
Old Portuguese (§ 99, 2).   Thus the pronouns *o*, *a*, *os* and *as*
often contracted with the ending of the verb, e.g., *vejo-o >
vejo*.   See FM, I, xxxiv; Abraham, § 39, 1 g and h.   And
continued contraction of these forms may be the origin of the
idiomatic affirmative answer in the modern colloquial language,
which consists in the repetition of the verb of the question without
a pronoun object (Language, XIV, 205).   However, in the literary
language contraction was successfully resisted in order to preserve the identity of pronoun and verb ending, e.g., *vejo-o* [vɐʒuu].

This resistance found support in those combinations where contraction could not take place, viz., where the verb ending was *-ei*, *-i*, etc. and where the pronoun was masculine and the verb ending *-a* or vice versa, e.g., *da-o; vejo-a.*

B. There is a limited region in the north of Tras-os-Montes where the intervocalic *l* of these forms has not fallen (Esquisse, § 72 a).

C. Imperatives followed by the forms *lo, la,* etc. arose from the use of the indicative for the imperative: *\*deixas-lo* (for *\*deixa-lo*) > *deixa-lo* (Grund, I, 1016); *\*fazedes-lo* (for *\*fazede-lo*) > *fazedello* (RL, VII, 64). On the use of *vês* and *vêdes* as imperatives in the early Cancioneiros, see RF, XXV, 666.

D. Second singular preterits followed by the forms *lo, la,* etc. arose from the addition of *s* to this form of the verb: *tu \*lestes-lo* (for *tu \*leste-lo*) > *tu lêste-lo* (RL, XXVIII, 233, s.v. *lo*).

3. When the Vulgar Latin accusative forms of *ille* were attached to verb forms ending in *r* (infinitives), *s* (first and second plural of all tenses, second singular of all tenses except the preterit, first and third singular of some preterits), and *z* (third singular present indicative of two or three verbs, first and third singular of some preterits) and to pronouns ending in *s* (*nos, vos* and *lhes*), the *r, s* and *z* became *l* by assimilation (§ 109, 3) and the resultant long *l* remained as a short *l* (§ 82, 1): *\*ver-lo* > *vel-lo* > *vê-lo; \*cremos-lo* > *cremol-lo* > *cremo-lo;* and *faz-lo* > *fal-lo* > *fa-lo; \*diga-nos-lo* > *diga-no-lo.* Hence the forms *-lo, -la,* etc.

A. The infinitive form to which *lo, la,* etc. were attached in Vulgar Latin had probably not lost its final *e*, e.g., *\*amáre-lo.* This *e* fell because it was a posttonic penult preceded by *r* (§ 52, 1).

B. Early forms in which assimilation had not yet taken place, like *defender* (in *defender-lo-iades*) in rime with *fazer* (CB, No. 392), are extremely rare.

C. While *i* and *e* preceded by *s* or *c* fell in Old Portuguese when they were final (§ 47, 2; § 46, 2), they did not fall when they were posttonic penults (see § 53). Accordingly, first and third singular preterits ending in *i* or *e* preceded by *s* or *c* developed differently according as they were or were not followed by the accusative forms *lo, la*, etc.: *\*fece* (for *fēcit*) > *fêz* but *\*fece-lo* > *feze-o* (see section 2 above). Only in new juxtapositions did combinations arise without the posttonic penult: *\*fez-lo* > *fê-lo*. These are not found in the early written language. Among the earliest examples of them are *poss-llo* (RL, XIX, 71) and *pô-la* (Fab, 19). The older forms such as *feze-o* are still found in dialectal Portuguese, where forms like *disse-o* and *trouxe-o* may have contributed to their preservation. Forms like *feze* without the pronoun are back-formations.

D. When the accusative forms were attached to almost any preceding word ending in *r* or *s* in Old Portuguese, e.g., *macar, melhor, senhor, por (per), Deus, des, mais, pois, todos, todas*, etc., the same changes took place, e.g., *melho-la fezestes* (CB, No. 185); *pola veer* (CB, No. 177); *pello fazer cavalleiro* (Graal, 40); *Deu-lo sabe poi-la vi* (CB, No. 177); *a toda-lo el diria* (Cd'A, II, 178); *o bon rei en seu podê'-la ten* (CA, No. 460). These combinations have been replaced by new juxtapositions containing the forms *o, a*, etc. but a few of them have survived in the dialects of the north, where their use is optional, e.g., *pola ver* (RL, XXVII, 182); *Deu-lo queira* (RL, XIX, 173; L-F, 8).

E. The accusatives *o, a, os* and *as* came to be attached in new juxtapositions in dialectal Portuguese to verb forms ending in *s*, e.g., *cremos-o*, sometimes with an intercalated *i*, e.g., *cremos-i-o* (Esquisse, § 72 a; RL, XXVII, 143). See also RL, IV, 36–37.

F. In Old Portuguese, particularly in the early Cancioneiros, the *s* of *nós* and *vós* used as prepositional and as subject pronouns was sometimes assimilated to the *l* of the accusative forms, e.g., *a vo'-lo devo muit' a gradecer* (CA, No. 263); *volla averees* (Castelo, folio 83 ro). Cf. RF, XXIII, 343.

G. Final *b* of *\*ub* (from *ubi*) was assimilated to the *l* of the accusative forms (§ 86, 2): *ubi illum* > *ullo* > *ulo*. These forms are still used in the north (Esquisse, § 72 a; Opúsculos, II, 19).

4. When the Vulgar Latin accusative forms of *ille* were attached to verb forms ending in *n* (chiefly third plural), before the time when this *n* was reduced to a nasal resonance on the preceding vowel (§ 98, 4), *l* became *n* by assimilation and the resultant long *n* remained as a short *n* (§ 84, 2).

The assimilation was progressive because the *n* of the verb ending was more essential to the meaning than the *l* of the pronoun, which had begun to disappear in other positions (§ 109, 3 B). And the nasal resonance remained on the vowel (contrary to § 84, 2 B) through the influence of the simple verb ending, that is, the ending without the pronoun, e.g., *dēbent illum* > *\*dēben-lo* > *deven-no* > *devem-no* [dɛvẽjnu]. Hence the forms *-no, na,* etc.

A. Examples in which the nasal resonance did not remain on the ending of the verb are extremely rare, e.g., *denos* (RL, VIII, 84, A.D. 1214) for *dem-nos; falto-me* (RL, II, 20) for *faltom-me.*

B. When the accusative forms were attached to a few other words ending in *n*, the same change took place, e.g., *ben-no* (CA, No. 29); *nõ na* (Crest, 30); *que'-no* (CA, No. 256); *sena* (CV, No. 37). These combinations have generally been replaced by new juxtapositions made with the forms *o, a,* etc., e.g., *bem o, não a, quem o, sem a,* but they have survived in certain dialects (RL, XI, 140–141; RL, XXVIII, 235, s.v. *no*). In a new juxtaposition the *õ* of *nom* and the pronoun *o* sometimes contracted, e.g., *nõ o pode achar* > *nõ pode achar* (Abraham, § 39, 1 f).

The form *quẽ lo* (Crest, 11), in which the til probably represents a consonantal *n*, shows one of these combinations before assimilation took place.

C. The development of the forms *no, na,* etc., after words which end in a nasalized vowel but which did not end in *n* in Latin arose either through imitation of words which ended in *n* in Latin or according to § 98, 4 B, e.g., *nen-no* (CA, No. 11). The article developed similarly after *nem*, e.g., *nem no* (RL, XXXIII, 201).

D. What is known as an epenthetic *n* in Galician after verb forms ending in a diphthong may be rather the result of the spread of the forms *no, na,* etc., e.g., *sei-n-o* for *sei-o* (S-A, § 117; L-F, 7).

5. The dative singular and plural of *ille* became *li* and *lis* in early Portuguese. At the same time a different singular form developed in combination with dissyllabic forms of the accusative, which had continued to coexist

with the monosyllabic forms: *ĭllī-ĭllum* > *\*lĭ-ello* > *\*lhello* (§ 89, 8; § 82, 1), and in combination with any following word beginning with a vowel (RF, XX, 587), e.g., *\*lĭ-aliqu'ūnum* > *lh'algun* (CA, No. 30). Then *lhe*, detached from these combinations, came to be used as the regular dative form, replacing *li*. And *lhi*, a variant of *lhe*, arose through the influence of *li*, and of *mi* and *ti*, which at this time were still used as conjunctive pronouns. In the meantime, *lis* continued unchanged, e.g., *lhi* but *lis* (AHP, I, 379, A.D. 1294). Soon, however, *lis* became *lhis* in imitation of *lhi*, and *lhes* in imitation of *lhe*.

The combination *\*lhello* became *\*lhelo* with short *l* through the influence of *\*lo*, as in OSp. *gelo* (Manual, § 94, 3) and It. *glielo;* and *\*lhelo* became *lhe-o* and later *lho* (section 2 above). The accusatives *lo*, *la*, etc. continued to survive alongside *o*, *a*, etc. and *lhes* combined in new juxtapositions with these forms, thus: *\*lhes-lo* > *lhello* (section 3 above), i.e., *lhe-lo* (CA, No. 81; RL, XXV, 131), a form which has survived in Modern Galician (S-A, 58, footnote). See Huber, § 329. A plural *lhe* became detached from this new *lhe-lo* and combined in new juxtapositions with the accusatives *o*, *a*, etc. to form *lho*, *lha*, etc. The form *lhes* has survived in Modern Portuguese; and in some dialects it is found combined in new juxtapositions with *o*, *a*, etc., e.g., *lhes a* (RL, XIX, 173). Cf. HR, VI, 350.

A. The palatalized *l* of these forms has been explained as having arisen from the combination of *li* and *o*, *a*, etc.: *\*li-o* > *\*lịo* > *lho*, the second element being sometimes the article instead of the accusative pronoun (RL, IV, 36, n. 1; RL, IX, 185). But this explanation fails to account for the development of the Portuguese forms at an earlier period, when *gelo* developed in Spanish and *glielo* in Italian, a period early enough for palatalization of the *l* of *li* to save it from falling when intervocalic.

B. The accusative form in the combination *ĭllī-ĭllum* was sometimes the article, e.g., *que lha donzella fez* (Graal, 10).

6. Lat. *tē* became Portuguese *te*. In combination with
*lo* it became *te-o* and later *to* (§ 99, 7). However, in
Galician, in combination with the final *s* of verb forms
(second singular and first plural), *te-o,* that is *\*țo,* became *cho* (§ 89, 4 в), from which *che* (for *te*) is a back-
formation. The forms *che, cho, cha,* etc. are found occasionally in Old Portuguese; for examples, see RL, IX, 185
and RL, XXVII, 19.

A. The group *ț*, when not preceded by *s*, did not become *ch*
in Galician or Portuguese, as has been assumed in connection
with these forms (JREL, VI, 218–220; AStNS, LXV, 40, s.v. *che*).

7. Lat. *sē* became Portuguese *se*. In combination with
*\*lo* it developed as follows: *\*se-lo > \*se-o > \*șo > xo*
(§ 89, 11), from which *xe* is a back-formation (RL, XXIII,
95, s.v. *x'a*).

A. The *s* of *se* was voiceless in any position; therefore, the
development of *ș* in this case was the same as that of medial *sș*.

**144. Possessive Adjectives and Pronouns.**

A few forms of possessive adjectives developed as proclitics, viz., *mha, ma, ta,* and *sa*. Except for these, which
have not survived, the forms of possessive adjectives have
developed under the tonic accent and are the same as the
forms of possessive pronouns. Plural forms are not given
below; they are derived from Latin accusatives and may
be formed from the singular forms by the addition of *s*.

| Latin | Portuguese |
|---|---|
| *mĕum* | *męu* (§ 34, 7) and *mou* (old) |
| *mĕam* | *minha* (§ 34, 6; § 66, 1 в) |
| *tŭum* | *tou* (old) (§ 38, 10) and *tęu* |
| *tŭam* | *tua* (§ 38, 9) |
| *sŭum* | *sou* (old) (§ 38, 10) and *sęu* |
| *sŭam* | *sua* (§ 38, 9) |
| *nŏstrum* | *nostro* (old) |
| *\*nŏssum* | *nǫsso* |
| *\*vŏssum* | *vǫsso* |

Singular forms: While *teu* and *seu* developed through the influence of *meu*, perhaps in Vulgar Latin (GVL, § 387), *mou* developed through the influence of *tou* and *sou*. The *i* of OPtg. *mia* became a yod in *mha* when the word stood in the proclitic position. This yod was lost in OPtg. *ma* while the *u*, which likewise developed in the proclitic position, was lost in OPtg. *ta* and *sa* (§ 93, 1). The dialectal forms *me'* (for *meu*), *te'* (for *teu*) and *'nha* (for *minha*, Esquisse, § 72 f; RL, VII, 45) resulted from late proclitic use of forms which had developed under the tonic accent. 1st pl.: *nostro* was used in Old Portuguese only in the expression *nostro Senhor* referring to the deity (Comp, 253). The form \**nossum* must have existed in the Vulgar Latin of certain regions (Bourciez, § 372 c; Lexique, 81–85). It developed in the relation *nos* : \**nossum* by analogy with the relation *me* : *meum*, the *s* becoming long to preserve the voiceless sound it had in *nōs*. That this took place in Vulgar Latin is indicated by the existence of OSp. *nuesso*. The *o* of \**nossum* (cf. Ptg. *nosso* and Sp. *nuesso*) developed through the influence of the coexisting form *nostrum*. See Language, XII, 134–135. Efforts have been made to explain the *ss* of *nosso* as a regular phonological development of *str* (RL, IV, 275–276; Hanssen, § 19, 8; Huber, § 188, 3, Anm.). Metaphony did not take place in *nosso*. 2d pl.: The development of *vosso* was the same as that of *nosso*. The *o* of \**vossum* developed through the influence of the coexisting form *vostrum*, which universally took the place of *vestrum* in Vulgar Latin (GVL, § 387).

## 145. DEMONSTRATIVE ADJECTIVES AND PRONOUNS.

1. Demonstrative adjectives and demonstrative pronouns are the same except that the former do not have a neuter form.

| Latin | Portuguese |
|---|---|
| masc. *ipse* | êsse (§ 85, 3; § 100, 3) |
| fem. *ipsa* | ęssa (§ 85, 3; § 100, 4) |
| neut. *ipsum* | esso (old) and isso (§ 85, 3; § 100, 6) |
| | êsses |
| | ęssas |
| masc. *iste* | êste (§ 100, 3) |
| fem. *ista* | ęsta (§ 100, 4) |
| neut. *istud* | esto (old) and isto (§ 100, 6) |
| | êstes |
| | ęstas |
| masc. *\*accu̧-ille* | aquęle (§ 100, 3) |
| | aquel (old and popular) |
| fem. *\*accu̧-illa* | aquęla (§ 100, 4) |
| neut. *\*accu̧-illud* | aquelo (old) and aquilo (§ 100, 6) |
| | aquęles |
| | aqueis (old and popular) |
| | aquęlas |
| masc. *\*accu̧-iste* | aquęste (old) (§ 100, 3) |
| fem. *\*accu̧-ista* | aquęsta (old) (§ 100, 4) |
| neut. *\*accu̧-istud* | aquesto (old) and aquisto (CA, No. 210) (§ 100, 6) |
| | aquęstes (old) |
| | aquęstas (old) |

The word *eccum*, which was used in Vulgar Latin to rein-force demonstratives (GVL, § 24), became *\*accu* through the influence of *atque* or *ac* (GVL, § 65; Bourciez, § 103 and § 127). Cf. *áque* (RL, VIII, 183) for *\*acco* (from *eccum*). For the development of long *c* + *u̧*, see § 93, 3 A.

The plural forms of these adjectives and pronouns are not derived directly from Latin but are analogical forms made by adding the plural ending to the nominative singu-lar forms. *Aqueis* (from *aquel* + *es*) was formed early enough for the short intervocalic *l* to fall.

*\*Accu* also combined with the forms of *ipse*: *\*accu̧-ipsa* > *aquessa* (old and dialectal), but very few examples have been noted (Lições, 55, n. 4 and 56, n. 1).

A. Cornu supports the metaphonic theory for the variation of the tonic vowel of these forms (Grund, I, 929). Meyer-Lübke explains the *i* of the neuter forms as due to the following *ų*, which developed by syntactical phonology in such phrases as *istu es vero* (M-L, Gram, I, § 82). Rodrigues Lapa argues that *aquesto* became *aquisto* through the influence of *aqui* and that *isto*, *isso* and *aquilo* then developed through the influence of *aquisto* (RL, XXXIV, 304). This *i* has also been explained as due to learned influence (Cavacas, 139). The forms *isto* and *isso* appeared much earlier than *aquilo*.

B. Metaphony did not take place in the feminine forms in some regions of northern Portugal (RL, XI, 270; RL, XIV, 83; Esquisse, § 72 b), although there are regions where it took place in *aquela* but not in the other feminine forms (RL, XXVII, 132–133).

C. In proclisis, *aquelle* lost its last syllable and became *aquel*, contrary to § 46, 2 A.

2. The preposition *en* was joined as a proclitic to the forms of *aquele* in late Vulgar Latin or early Portuguese, e.g., *\*inaccų-ille* > *\*enaquelle*. The initial *e* of this form was then lost by apheresis (cf. *namorar*, § 106, 1 B): *\*enaquelle* > *naquele*.

The combinations of the preposition *en* with the forms of *êste* and *êsse* have already been discussed along with the combinations of *en* with the forms of *êle* (§ 140, 4). They did not reach their final stage until the fifteenth century. The combinations of *en* with the forms of *aquele* reached their final stage much earlier, e.g., *naquel*, *naquela* (RL, XXI, 248, A.D. 1282; Bausteine, 679, A.D. 1293; AHP, IV, 176, A.D. 1297; AHP, III, 14, A.D. 1312). See RB, 40; RL, VIII, 255; RL, XI, 92; RL, XX, 193; RL, XXV, 145; Abraham, § 46; and Carter, § 40, for other early examples of *naquele*, *naquela*, etc. in documents which do not contain examples of such forms as *neste*, *nesse*, *nelle*, etc.

3. The masculine forms *êste*, *êsse* and *aquele* combined with *outro*, becoming *estoutro*, *essoutro* and *aqueloutro* respectively (§ 99, 7). Only the second element is inflected to

form the feminines and plurals, e.g., *estoutra*, *essoutros*. Other combinations are *elesso* (RL, XXVI, 145) (from *ĭlle-ĭpse*) (see M-P, Orig., § 68, 2) and *medês* (old) (from \**metĭpse*, GVL, § 24). For the stress and quality of the final vowel of *medes,* see rime *medes : pes* (CD, lines 529 and 531).

4. Forms of the demonstrative *hĭc* survived only in a few adverbs: *hāc horā* > *agora; hāc nocte* > *ontem; hōc annō* > *ogano* (old); *per hōc* > *pero* (old).

**146. RELATIVE AND INTERROGATIVE ADJECTIVES AND PRONOUNS.**

Many forms of relatives and interrogatives were lost in Vulgar Latin and many were interchanged (Bourciez, § 104). The few forms which survived were generally accusatives.

| Classical Latin | Portuguese |
|---|---|
| *quid* | *que* |
| *quem* | *quem* (§ 97, 4) |
| *cūjum* | *cujo* (§ 73, 5) |
| *quālem* | *qual* (§ 69, 1; § 46, 2) |
| *quāles* | *quais* (§ 75, 1; § 46, 10) |

A. The neuter *que* and the masculine *quem* became masculine and feminine singular and plural in Portuguese.

B. The element *o*, *a*, etc. of the relative pronominal expression *o que, a que*, etc. came from the accusative forms of *ille* (§ 143, 2). And in Old Portuguese its form was sometimes *lo que* (§ 143, 3 D); for examples of *lo que*, see RL, XXIII, 49. The combinations of the preposition *en* with the accusatives of *ille* in this use are the same and had the same development as the combinations of *en* with the accusatives of *ille* used as definite article (§ 137, 4): *no que, na que*, etc.

**147. INDEFINITE ADJECTIVES AND PRONOUNS.**

Many Classical Latin indefinite adjectives and pronouns survived in Portuguese and some new ones arose either through the special use of other parts of speech or through new combinations.

| Latin | Portuguese |
|---|---|
| *alid* (GVL, § 71) | *al* (old) (§ 46, 2) |
| *altĕrum* | *outro* (§ 51; § 94, 1) |
| *alĭquod* | *algo* (§ 52, 1; § 93, 3) |
| *alĭquem* | *alguém* (§ 52, 1; § 93, 3) |
| *\*aliqu'ūnum* | *algum* (§ 52, 1; § 93, 3; § 78, 2 B) |
| *cata* (GVL, § 71) | *cada* |
| *hŏmō* | *ome* (old) |
| *hŏmĭnem* | *homem* (old as indef. pron.) (§ 124, 4) |
| *nĕc ūnum* (GVL, § 71) | *nengum* (old) and *ningum* (old) (§ 41, 11; § 66, 2 B; § 73, 1; § 78, 2 B) |
| *\*ne* (for *nĕc*)-*ūnum* | *nē hum* (old); *nium* (dialectal, RL, III, 73; RL, IV, 220); and *nenhum* (§ 78, 4 C; § 66, 2 B; § 41, 3 A; § 78, 2 B) |
| *\*ne* (for *nĕc*)-*quem* | *nenguem* (old and popular) and *ninguém* (§ 41, 11; § 66, 2 B; § 93, 3) |
| *nūllum* | *nulho* (old) |
| *(re)nata* (Rönsch, 345) | *nada* |
| *rem* | *rem* (old) (§ 97, 4) |
| *tālem* | *tal* (§ 46, 2) |
| *tāles* | *tais* (§ 75, 1; § 46, 10) |
| *tōtum* | *todo* (§ 126, 8) |
| *tōtum* | *tudo* (§ 100, 7; § 126, 8 A) |
| *ūnos* | *uns* (§ 78, 2 B) |
| *ūnas* | *umas* (§ 78, 4 D) |

The accent of *alguém* and *ninguém* and the survival of the nasal resonance on their final vowel are due to the influence of *quem*. OPtg. *nulho* was doubtless borrowed from Spanish, where long *l* became [ʎ].

A. Instead of taking *\*ne-quem* as the etymon of *ninguém*, Nobiling has explained the form as having developed in the relation *ningum : ninguém* by analogy with the relation *algum : alguém* (AStNS, CXXVII, 182, s.v. *nĕc* + *ūnus*).

B. *Ningum* was replaced by *nenhum*, which came from a new combination that arose in late Vulgar Latin or early Portuguese.

C. For the development of the feminine forms *alguma*, *ninguma* (old) and *nenhuma*, see § 78, 4 D.

## GENERAL PHENOMENA OF VERBAL INFLEXION

**148. CONJUGATIONS.**

1. Of the four conjugations of Classical Latin, only three remain in Portuguese, because the second and third fused into a single new conjugation. This fusion consisted chiefly in the following five changes:

a) The loss of yod (from Cl. L. *-ĕo* and *-ĕam*, etc.) in the first singular present indicative and the whole present subjunctive of verbs of the Classical Latin second conjugation by analogy with regular verbs of the third conjugation, e.g., *respondĕo > respondo; tĭmĕo > temo.*

b) The shift of accent from the antepenult to the penult in the infinitive, the whole singular and the third plural of the imperfect subjunctive (personal infinitive), the first and second plural present indicative and the second plural present imperative of verbs of the Classical Latin third conjugation, by analogy with the second conjugation, e.g., *vendĕre > vender; dīcĭmus > dizemos.* See SpV, §§ 128, 129, 137, and 475. Furthermore, the *ę* of the infinitive (and personal infinitive) closed to *ę*.

c) The replacement of *-unt* (and *-ĭunt*) by *-ent* (which became Ptg. *-em*) in the third plural present indicative of verbs of the Classical Latin third conjugation, by analogy with the second conjugation, e.g., *perdunt > perdem; capĭunt > cabem.* See GVL, § 449; SpV, § 127.

d) The adoption of a common set of characteristic endings with *ę* in the preterit and the tenses derived from the preterit.

e) The adoption by verbs of both conjugations of the past participle ending *-udo* in Old Portuguese and *-ido* in Modern Portuguese.

Because the Classical Latin future indicative and passive voice disappeared in Vulgar Latin, no other differences remained between the second and third conjugations and the fusion was thus complete.

A. The yod of the first singular present indicative and the whole subjunctive did not fall in all verbs, e.g., *vĭdĕo* > *vejo; tĕnĕo* > *tenho; ardĕo* > *arço* (RL, XIX, 174); *foetĕo* > *feço* (old). And *pōno, pōnam*, etc. of the third conjugation even acquired a yod, becoming Ptg. *ponho, ponha*, etc. (but see MP, XII, 196). The yod of these forms sometimes spread to the whole conjugation, e.g., *tolher* (RL, IV, 134); Gal. *poñer;* Sp. *muñir.*

B. The only forms in which the accent did not shift from the antepenult to the penult are the Old Portuguese second plurals *treides* (from *trahĭtis*) and *treide* (from *trahĭte*) (RL, III, 188–189). For the development of *ei*, see § 33, 2 c.

C. The ending *-unt* survived in only one form, viz., *vadunt*, which became *vão* (§ 157, 2).

D. Some verbs did not share in the fusion to the extent of adopting weak preterit endings. These retained their strong preterits for which a separate set of endings with *ę* developed.

E. The preterit and derived tenses of verbs of the first conjugation shifted to the second conjugation in certain dialects of the north (Esquisse, § 74 a; Comp, 319, n. 1; PhM, I, 390).

2. In addition to the fusion of the second and third conjugations, there were many shifts from one conjugation to another, e.g., *exsūgĕre* > *enxugar; mējĕre* > *mijar; torrēre* > *torrar; lūcēre* > *luzir; cingĕre* > *cingir; -dūcĕre* > *-duzir; -ŭĕre* > *-uir.* These shifts took place in Vulgar Latin but additional shifts took place in some verbs in Portuguese, e.g., *corrigĕre* > OPtg. *correger* > MPtg. *corrigir; cadĕre* > OPtg. *caer* > MPtg. *cair.*

**149.** PERSONAL ENDINGS.

1. The distinction in person provided in Classical Latin by the personal endings has been preserved in Portuguese except in those tenses where the first and third singular have become identical through the fall of final *m* and *t.*

|        | Classical Latin | Portuguese    |
|--------|-----------------|---------------|
| 1st sg. | *-m*           | (§ 97, 4)     |
| 1st sg. | *-ō*           | *-o* (§ 48, 1) |
| 2d sg.  | *-s*           | *-s*          |

|          | Classical Latin | Portuguese |
|----------|-----------------|------------|
| 3d sg.   | -t              | (§ 97, 7) |
| 1st pl.  | -mŭs            | -mos (§ 48, 1) |
| 2d pl.   | -tĭs            | -des and -is (§ 155) |
| 3d pl.   | -nt             | -~ (§ 97, 7; § 98, 4) |

2. The ending of the second plural imperative is different from the ending of the second plural of other tenses.

| Classical Latin | Portuguese |
|-----------------|------------|
| -te             | -de and -i (§ 155) |

3. The preterit has several personal endings that are different from those of other tenses.

|         | Classical Latin | Portuguese |
|---------|-----------------|------------|
| 1st sg. | -ī | -(e) (§47, 1 and 2)<br>-i (§ 47, 3)<br>-i (§ 47, 4) |
| 2d sg.  | -stī | -ste (§ 47, 1) |
| 2d pl.  | -stĭs | -stes (§ 46, 1) |
| 3d pl.  | -rŭnt | -ram (§ 97, 7; § 98, 4; § 157, 2) |

A. The endings of all first singular preterits in Galician, except those of the first conjugation, are nasalized: *debin, fuxin, tiven, dixen, quixen*. This nasalization probably developed first in weak forms, that is, forms ending in tonic *i*, by analogy with the form *vin* (from *vēnī*) and then spread to strong forms. Accordingly, *vi*, the first singular preterit of *ver*, became *vin*. The first singular preterit of *vir* and that of *ver* now being identical, a new first singular of *vir* developed, viz., *viñen*, by analogy with the second singular *viñeche* and the whole plural *viñemos*, etc. and with the characteristic ending *-en* of the first singular preterit of strong verbs.

In some dialects of central and southern Portugal the ending of the first singular of weak preterits and the radical vowel of the first singular of strong preterits were similarly nasalized, e.g., *ouvī, fīz, tīve* (RL, IV, 221; Esquisse, § 74 a and § 76 b). And similar forms are sometimes found in Old Portuguese, e.g., *dormī* (Rom, XI, 360) and *comsentin* (FM, I, 62).

B. In dialectal Portuguese the ending of the second singular preterit is commonly *-stes*, the final *s* having been added by analogy with the second singular of all other tenses (except the imperative).

The Galician second singular ending *-che* is a back-formation from *-cho*, which developed as follows: *-sti-\*lo* > *\*sti̯o* > *-cho* (§ 89, 4 B; BF, I, 342, n. 1).

c. The *-o* of the third singular of strong preterits in Galician may have developed in imitation of the *-o* of the third singular of weak preterits or may have spread from a few strong preterits ending in *-ŭĭt* (cf. Hanssen, § 31, 8). There is only one of these forms in Portuguese, viz., *veio*.

D. In certain regions of the north the ending of the second plural preterit is *-steis* (Esquisse, § 74 e), in which the diphthong developed by analogy with the second plural of other tenses, most of which contain a diphthong of regular phonological origin.

The Galician second plural ending *-stedes* developed by analogy with the second plural of tenses with an intervocalic *d*. And the Galician second plural ending *-chedes* developed through the influence of the second singular *-che* on *-stedes*.

## 150. Loss of ṷ of Stem Ending.

Although *ŭ* was tonic in the infinitive, first and second plural present indicative and second plural present imperative of *attribuĕre*, *battuĕre*, *conspuĕre*, *consuĕre*, *despuĕre*, and *exspuĕre* in Classical Latin, it lost its accent and became *ṷ* in Vulgar Latin when these verbs shifted to other conjugations in which the forms in question were paroxytones. In other forms of these verbs, where it was never tonic, it became *ṷ* also. This *ṷ* fell, perhaps at first when followed by *o* (§ 10, 3), that is, in the first singular present indicative, and then throughout the paradigm (§ 93, 1): *attribuĕre* > *\*attribṷēre* > *atrever*; *battuĕre* > *\*battṷēre* > *bater*; *conspuĕre* > *\*conspṷīre* > *cuspir*; *consuĕre* > *consṷēre* (Seelmann, 54) > *coser*; *despuĕre* > *\*despṷīre* > *despir*; *exspuĕre* (or *spuĕre*) > *\*espṷīre* > *espir* (old). The assumption of a recession of the accent (e.g., *battŭére* to *\*báttuere*, GVL, § 137), while perhaps necessary for Italian and French, is meaningless in the Iberian territory.

**151. Analogical Stem Endings.**

1. The stem endings *g* (from Lat. *g* or *c*) and *c* (from Lat. *cc*) of verbs of the first conjugation have remained [g] and [k] respectively in the present subjunctive in spite of the following *e*, by analogy with the rest of the verb. This is shown orthographically by the insertion of *u* after *g* and the change of *c* to *qu: něgem* > *negue; plǐcem* > *chegue; sǐccem* > *seque.*

A. The sounds [g] and [k] have remained also in the first singular preterit, where the ending *-ei* did not develop until after the period of palatalization of *g* and *c*.

2. The stem ending *g* (from Lat. *g*) of verbs of other conjugations than the first became [ʒ] in the first singular present indicative and the whole present subjunctive, in spite of the following *o* or *a*, by analogy with the rest of the verb. This is shown orthographically by the change of *g* to *j: cingo* > OPtg. *cingo* (see rime *Domingo : çingo*, CV, No. 1030; and Comp, 305, n. 1) > *cinjo.*

3. The stem ending *c*, preceded by a consonant, of verbs of other conjugations than the first became [s] in the first singular present indicative and the whole present subjunctive in spite of the following *o* or *a*, by analogy with the rest of the verb. This is shown orthographically by the change of *c* to *ç: vinco* > *venço.*

A. This change took place in the first singular present indicative and the whole present subjunctive of the verb *torcer* (from *torquēre*), in whose other forms the development of [s] had become possible through the early fall of *ṷ* (§ 93, 3 B): *\*torco* (GVL, § 226) > *torço.*

4. The stem ending *c*, preceded by a vowel, of verbs of other conjugations than the first became [z] in the first singular present indicative and the whole present subjunctive in spite of the following *o* or *a*, by analogy with the rest of the verb. This is shown orthographically by the change of *c* to *z: condūco* > *conduzo.*

A. The stem endings of these forms of some verbs were not affected by analogy: *dīco > digo; *tɩaco > trago*. And a few sporadic regular phonological forms are found in Old Portuguese, e.g., *addūcat > aduga* (Crest, Glossary).

B. This change took place in the first singular present indicative and the whole present subjunctive of the verb *cozer* (from *cŏquĕre*), in whose other forms the development of [z] had become possible through the early fall of *u̯* (§ 93, 3 B): *cŏco* (GVL, § 226) > *cozo*.

C. This change took place in the first singular present indicative and the whole present subjunctive of *luzir* (from *lūcēre*, with shift of conjugation): *lūcĕo > luzo; lūcĕam > luza;* etc. The regular phonological forms would have been *\*luço, *luça,* etc. (§ 89, 2).

5. The stem ending *sc* followed by *e* of verbs of the second conjugation became *c* [s] (§ 92, 2 A): *\*parescit* (REW, s.v. *parēscĕre*) > *parece*. Followed by *o* or *a*, that is, in the first singular present indicative and the whole present subjunctive, *sc* at first remained unchanged: *\*paresco > paresco* (CV, No. 614); but later became [s] by analogy with the rest of the verb. This is shown orthographically by the change of *sc* to *ç: paresco > pareço*.

A. The same analogical development took place in the first singular present indicative and the whole present subjunctive of the verb *conhecer;* and at the same time the radical *o* of all forms became *e* (with the alternations of radical-changing verbs of the second conjugation) in imitation of other inchoatives ending in *-ecer* (RL, XXIII, 20, s.v. *conhocer;* RF, XX, 569): *cognosco > conhosco* (CV, No. 251) > *conheço*. But see Fab, Glossary, s.v. *conhocer*.

B. Forms with the stem ending *sc*, followed by *e*, found in the early Cancioneiros, e.g., *paresces, paresce,* etc., are probably merely orthographic imitations of the old regular phonological forms of the first singular present indicative and the whole present subjunctive, *paresco, paresca,* etc. (RF, XXV, 672).

C. The development of *tecer* (from *texĕre*) was due to the influence of inchoatives ending in *-ecer.* See Grund, I, 994.

6. The stem ending *gu* (from Lat. *qu* or *gu*) of verbs of other conjugations than the first has lost the sound *u̯* in the whole present subjunctive in spite of the following *a* (§ 93, 2 and 4) by analogy with the rest of the verb: *sĕquam* (for *sĕquar*) > *sigua* > *siga; distinguam* > *distinga.*

A. The spelling *sigua*, common in Old Portuguese, is a result of the orthographic confusion between *g* and *gu* and does not faithfully represent the pronunciation (§ 26, 2).

7. The stem ending became [g] in the whole conjugation of the verb *erguer* (from *ĕrĭgĕre* for *ērĭgĕre*) by analogy with the first singular present indicative *ergo* (from *ērĭgo*) and the whole present subjunctive.

A. This change is found in other verbs in dialectal Portuguese, e.g., *tragues, traguido*, etc., by analogy with *trago* (RL, II, 242).

**152. LOSS OF ENDING.**

1. Verb forms which ended in Vulgar Latin in unaccented *e* preceded by a single *l, n, r, s,* or *c* or in unaccented *i* preceded by a single *s* or *c* generally lost this final vowel in Portuguese (according to § 46, 2 and § 47, 2). The forms so affected are: a) the infinitive of all verbs: *servīre* > *servir;* b) the first and third singular personal infinitive of all verbs: *servīrem* > *servir;* c) the first and third singular future subjunctive of all verbs: *amārit* > *amar;* d) the third singular present indicative of a few verbs: *quaerit* > *quer; facit* > *faz;* e) the second singular imperative of a few verbs: *vale* > *val* (old); f) the first and third singular preterit of a few verbs: *fēcī* > *fiz; fēcit* > *fêz;* g) the third singular present subjunctive of a few verbs in certain exclamatory expressions in Old Portuguese: *perdōnet* (Du Cange) > *perdon* (RL, XXIII, 67).

2. In the third singular present indicative and the second singular imperative, the *e* has sometimes been restored by

analogy with most verbs of the second conjugation: *quaerit* > *quer* > *quere; valet* > *val* > *vale; valē* > *val* > *vale*. The *e* of certain first and third singular preterits, which is not a restored *e*, has been explained in § 143, 3 c.

**153.** SHIFT OF ACCENT IN PROPAROXYTONIC VERB FORMS OF THE FIRST CONJUGATION.

The forms of the whole singular and of the third plural present indicative and present subjunctive of many verbs in Classical Latin are proparoxytones. The number of such proparoxytones was considerably reduced in Vulgar Latin by the shift of accent in compound verbs to the root of the verb (GVL, § 139) and by syncope of the posttonic penult between certain pairs of consonants (§ 8). The number of those that remained was obviously reduced to zero in those Romance languages in which the posttonic penult disappeared entirely, viz., French (S-B, § 76) and Spanish (Manual, § 25).[1] No popular proparoxytones remaining, all newly acquired learned proparoxytones underwent a shift of accent by analogy with popular forms, e.g., *vīsĭtat* > Fr. *visite* and Sp. *visita; contĭnŭat* > Fr. *continue* and Sp. *continúa*.

But in Portuguese and Italian, the posttonic penult fell in certain special cases only (§ 52 and GIt, § 68). While this further reduced the number of these proparoxytonic verb forms, e.g., *follĭcat* > Ptg. *folga*, many of them still remain in Italian, e.g., *dúbita, illúmina, incárica, intítola, náviga, nómina, pópola*.[2] And one would expect to find them in Portuguese also. However, in all parts of speech

---

[1] The few exceptions that are found in Spanish (Manual, § 26) do not affect the problem of the verb forms in question.

[2] These verbs are all of the first conjugation and chiefly denominatives. In other conjugations the first syllable was either a prefix or taken to be a prefix, with consequent shift of accent in Vulgar Latin according to GVL, § 139, e.g., *diríge, diríme, divíde, esíge*. The opposite shift was very rare: *ēvitat* > *évita; irrĭtat* > *írrita*.

in Portuguese there are far less proparoxytones than in Italian, not because there was more syncope than in Italian but because of the disappearance of intervocalic consonants with consequent increase in contraction. Thus *pŏpŭlum* became *povo*, not because of syncope but because of contraction: *pŏpŭlum* > *poboo* > *povo*. In verbs such contraction was resisted, as it would have destroyed the uniformity of the paradigm. But because of the rapid trend toward paroxytones occasioned by contraction in other parts of speech, the verb forms in question became paroxytones by a shift of the accent, e.g., \**ad-lūmĭnat* > *alumía; dŭbĭtat* > *duvída;* \**incarrĭcat* > *encarréga;* \**in-nebŭlat* > *ennevôa; nōmĭnat* > *nomẹa* > *nomeia* (§ 35, 7); *pŏpŭlat* > *povôa*.[1] And, of course, the same shift occurred in learned words, as it had in learned words in French and Spanish, e.g., Ptg. *visita, continúa.* See RR, XXVI, 139.

A. This change was pointed out by Caetano de Lima in 1736 (C-L, 35 ss.).

B. For popular vestiges of proparoxytonic forms, see Grund, I, 1022, n. 2. Such forms as *versífico, signífica* and *sacrífica* are found in Old Spanish (Hanssen, § 25, 1).

C. OPtg. *alumea*, which has survived in popular speech, became *alumía* by analogy with forms like *confía* (from \**confĭdat*), as the endings of the weak forms of both types had the same sound, e.g., *alumeamos* and *confiamos.* More verbs were affected by this analogy in Portuguese than in Spanish, e.g., *pronuntío* > Ptg. *pronuncío* and Sp. *pronúncio* (RHi, I, 20–21).

D. Some forms seem to have had the opposite shift, that is, a shift from the penult to the antepenult, e.g., *honōro* > *honro; labōro* > *lavro;* \**adradĭco* > *arreigo.* But this shift is only ap-

---

[1] Compare the corresponding French and Spanish forms, which are paroxytones because of syncope of the posttonic penult: Fr. *doute, charge, nomme, peuple;* Sp. *alumbra, duda, encarga, nombra, puebla.* And compare the corresponding nouns in Portuguese, in which no shift of stress took place: *lume, dúvida, encargo, névoa, nome, povo.*

parent as these forms developed by analogy with the weak forms, in which the intertonic fell in Vulgar Latin (§ 56): *honōrāmus* > *honramos; labōrāmus* > *lavramos;* or in which it became a yod through the fall of an intervocalic consonant (§ 40, 2 в): *\*adra-dīcāmus* > *arreigamos.*

**154.** SHIFT OF ACCENT IN FIRST AND SECOND PLURAL ENDINGS.

1. While the Classical Latin prototypes of the first and second plural endings of the conditional, imperfect indicative, pluperfect indicative, imperfect subjunctive and personal infinitive were paroxytones, they became proparoxytones in Portuguese through the influence of the whole singular and the third plural, in which the accent falls on the syllable immediately following the verb stem, e.g., *amabāmus* > *amávamos.* The future subjunctive comes from a form that was originally a proparoxytone.

A. In some regions of the north this shift did not always take place (Esquisse, § 74 d).
B. This shift is found also in the present subjunctive in dialects throughout the country (RL, I, 200; RL, II, 242; RL, VII, 46; RL, XI, 284; RL, XIV, 85; RL, XXVII, 139; RL, XXVIII, 222; Esquisse, § 74 d; PhM, I, 382).

2. The posttonic penult of the first and second plural of the conditional, imperfect indicative, pluperfect indicative, and imperfect subjunctive has remained. But the posttonic penult of the first and second plural of the future subjunctive and personal infinitive fell (according to § 52, 1), e.g., *fēcĕrĭmus* > *fizermos; facerēmus* > *\*facéremus* > *fazermos.*

**155.** INTERVOCALIC *d* IN THE SECOND PLURAL.

1. There was an intervocalic *t* in the ending of the second plural of all Classical Latin tenses of the active voice except the perfect. This *t* became and remained *d* for several

centuries in Old Portuguese, e.g., *amābātis* > *amávades*. In the future subjunctive and personal infinitive it ceased to be intervocalic because of the fall of the posttonic penult and continued to survive, e.g., *fēcĕrĭtis* > *fizerdes; facerētis* > *\*facéretis* > *\*fazeredes* > *fazerdes*. In the other eight tenses it fell, e.g., OPtg. *amávades* > *amáveis*. See § 74, 2 A.

A. This *d* has survived in certain dialects, particularly Galician.

2. Tonic *a* plus a Romance yod became *ai* (§ 33, 2 c). But posttonic penultimate *a* (which had closed to [ɐ]) plus a Romance yod became *ei* (§ 55, 2), a change which took place in the conditional, imperfect indicative and pluperfect indicative. Thus the stages through which, for example, the ending of the imperfect indicative of the first conjugation passed were: OPtg. *-ávades* > *\*-ávaes* [avɐjs] > *-áveis*. It is curious that no such form as *-ávaes* or *-avais* is found, although it is a necessary step in the development and corresponds to the Spanish form. There can be only one explanation of this, namely, that *d* became silent long before it was dropped in spelling and that scribes became conscious of the discrepancy between pronunciation and orthography with regard to both phenomena (i.e., the fall of *d* and the consequent change of *a* to *e*) at the same time.

The "Chronica do Condestabre de Portugal Dom Nuno Alvarez Pereira" (early fifteenth century) contains over one hundred second plural forms, of which about twenty are spelled with *d*. Old and new forms stand side by side, the words of the same speaker, as *percebiees, erees, auiades* (Cr Cond, 68), and *amarades, derees* (Cr Cond, 171). But the intermediate stage is missing. As the chronicler (Fernão Lopes?) was probably an intimate of the hero and as all the examples are found in quotations, it is likely that he actually heard the words he reports or heard them quoted soon after they were uttered. At times he remembered their very form (i.e., with *d*) while at other times he modernized them completely (i.e., dropped the *d* and changed the *a* to *e*).

A. In the eighteenth century Monte Carmelo mentioned a form *ensináveis* (M-C, 57), which was probably of Spanish origin. The forms *desembargariedes* (DC, 285, A.D. 1260) and *aviedes* (Est Tr, 104) are unusual and hard to explain.

B. In these forms in Spanish, unaccented *a* remained unchanged because in the proparoxytonic forms *d* fell much later than in the paroxytonic forms and in all forms much later than in Portuguese (Rom, XXII, 74 ss.).

3. The dated examples available make it possible to determine fairly closely the critical period during which the *d* of second plural endings disappeared.

| Year | Examples | Source |
|---|---|---|
| 1405 | *fazernosedes, creades, sabedes, dessedes* | Fig, 65 to 68 |
| 1411 | *busquedes, dedes, guardade* | AHP, IV, 45 |
| 1416 | *trabalhades, stades* | RL, I, 336 and 338 |
| 1418 | *leixedes* | cited in RF, XXIII, 177 |
| | | |
| 1434 | *dees, consentaaes* | AHP, III, 86 |
| 1436 | *dizeis, leixaseis* | DC, 319 |

Disregarding forms with *d* in stereotyped expressions such as *comprades e façades comprir, sabede,* and *e hũs e outros al nõ façade,* found commonly as late as the end of the fifteenth century, it would seem that *d* fell in the sixteen years between 1418 and 1434. That this critical period cannot be delimited so precisely is indicated by the form *tenhaes* of the year 1410, cited by Leite (RF, XXIII, 177). Consideration of additional dated documents may show the problem to be much more complicated. See Theoria, 25–34; RF, XXIII, 175–178; RR, XXI, 144–145.

A. Contrary to the opinion of Adolpho Coelho (Theoria, 29–30) and Reinhardstoettner (RPS, 212) that the existence of forms of the second plural with *d* and of others without *d* in the "Leal Conselheiro" of King Edward (Dom Duarte) indicated the simultaneous use of these forms at the time this work was written, namely, between 1428 and 1438 (Studies, 44), Leite de Vasconcellos argues that this apparent simultaneity was due to the fact that King Edward retained the *d* only in passages quoted from older texts, either through fondness of these texts for their quaintness or through disinclination to take the trouble to adapt their orthography (RF, XXIII, 176). He supports his contention by the identification of quoted passages and the observation that in official royal documents King Edward (reign: 1433–1438) always used forms without *d*.

4. There are a few second plural present indicatives and imperatives and one second plural present subjunctive in which the *d* did not fall.

| Latin | Old Portuguese | Modern Portuguese |
|---|---|---|
| *tenētis* | *tēedes* | *tendes* |
| *tenēte* | *tēede* | *tende* |
| *venītis* | *vīides* (§ 99, 3) | *vindes* |
| *venīte* | *vīide* (§ 99, 3) | *vinde* |
| *\*pōnētis* (for *pōnĭtis*) | *põedes* | *pondes* |
| *\*pōnēte* (for *pōnĭte*) | *põede* | *ponde* |
| *\*crēdētis* (for *crēdĭtis*) | *creedes* | *credes* |
| *\*crēdēte* (for *crēdĭte*) | *creede* | *crede* |
| *\*lĕgētis* (for *lĕgĭtis*) | *leedes* | *ledes* |
| *\*lĕgēte* (for *lĕgĭte*) | *leede* | *lede* |
| *\*rīdītis* (for *rīdētis*) | *riides* | *rides* |
| *\*rīdīte* (for *rīdēte*) | *riide* | *ride* |
| *vĭdētis* | *veedes* | *vêdes* |
| *vĭdēte* | *veede* | *vêde* |
| *sĕdēte* | *seede* | *sêde* |
| *vadātis* | *vaades* | *vades* |
| *ītis* | *ides* | *ides* |
| *īte* | *ide* | *ide* |

In the fifteenth century, when hiatus was being rapidly reduced by contraction (§ 99, 2 A), the juxtaposition of three vowels seems to have been resisted. And it was probably this resistance which strengthened the *d* of all these forms (except *ides* and *ide*) long enough to save it permanently.   Where hiatus of three vowels did not exist, the *d* fell, in spite of the risk of confusion with the second singular form, e.g., *dētis* > *dedes* > *deis*.

The development of consonantal *n* (§ 78, 5) saved the *d* in some of these forms.   This was the case with the form *sondes* (from *\*sŭtis*), the *n* of which is explained in § 198, 3. In *ides* and *ide* the *d* was retained in order to save these words from virtual extinction (D'Ovidio, 48, n. 4).

A. It has been suggested that the *d* was retained in many of these forms in order to preserve a more marked distinction between them and the second singular forms (Theoria, 32–33; Comp, 291).   Such second singular imperatives as OPtg. *crei, lei, sei,* and *vei* lend support to this theory for with the fall of *d* the second plural imperatives would have become identical with the second singular forms.   Perhaps reminiscence of the final *d* of the Latin stem may have contributed to the preservation of the *d* of the ending (RR, XXI, 143).   Or was the *d* lengthened in compensation for the contraction (shortening) of the two preceding vowels?

5. The second plural endings *-aides, -aide, -eides* and *-eide* (Esquisse, § 74 e and g) arose in some of the dialects of the north through the influence of the old endings *-ades, -ade, -edes* and *-ede* upon the new endings *-ais, -ai, -eis* and *-ei* respectively (Opúsculos, II, 215; RL, XXVII, 140). The second plural endings of the second conjugation *-endes* and *-ende* developed by analogy with *tendes* and *tende* (Esquisse, § 74 e and g) and this ending even spread to the present subjunctive of the first conjugation in Galician (ZRPh, XIX, 516, n. 4).   The imperatives *-ande* and *-inde* (Esquisse, § 74 g) developed by analogy with *-ende*.

After the fall of *d*, second plural endings sometimes became nasalized, e.g., *sejaães* (Cr Cond, 69), *trouuereēs* (Cr Cond, 132).   This nasalization is found in dialectal Portuguese but only in unaccented *-eis*, e.g., *-avēis, -assēis, -arēis, -iēis* (Esquisse, § 74 e).   It arose perhaps through the influence of third plurals (RL, XXVII, 141–142).

**156.** Hiatus in Verb Forms.

1. There is a group of third plural present indicatives and one third plural present subjunctive in which two vowels are found in hiatus in spite of the general tendency to contraction (§ 99,2).

| Latin | Portuguese |
|---|---|
| *crēdent (for crēdunt) | crêem |
| *lĕgent (for lĕgunt) | lêem |
| vĭdent | vêem |
| tĕnent | têem |
| *vĕnent (for vĕnĭunt) | vêem |
| dent | dêem |
| rīdent | riem |
| *pōnent (for pōnunt) | põem |

In these forms contraction was avoided in order to preserve separately the characteristic vowel *e* of the root and the characteristic vowel *ē* of the third plural ending. The need for separate vowels in root and ending was apparently so great that OPtg. *dem* acquired a radical *e*, made close by analogy with the second singular and the first and second plural. Resistance to contraction was not so strong in *têem* and *vêem* because both vowels in these forms were nasal from the earliest period of nasalization (both being followed by *n* in Latin), with the result that the contracted forms *tem* and *vem*, identical with the third singular forms, developed in the popular and colloquial language. Assimilation and contraction took place in the development of the third plural of *rir: rīdent > riem > riim* (§ 99, 3) *> rim* (old), but the hiatus form, *riem*, is the form which has survived. Lat. *pōnent* (for *pōnunt*) has developed regularly to *põe* but the hiatus form [põjẽj], represented by the spelling *põem*, has also been preserved. See Lições, 94; NS, XI, 139 and 141; Language XI, 243–244.

2. Accented radical *o* and the *o* of the ending of the first singular present indicative of verbs of the first conjugation in hiatus were not contracted but retained their full syllabic

value (contrary to § 99, 2): *corōno* > *corôo; sŏno* > *sôo*.
And accented radical *o* and the *e* of present subjunctive
endings of verbs of the first conjugation in hiatus were not
dissimilated but retained their full syllabic value (contrary
to § 99, 6): *sŏnes* > *sôes; vŏlet* > *vôe*.

A. Forms are occasionally found in Old Portuguese in which
assimilation of the *e* of present subjunctive endings of verbs of
the first conjugation took place (according to § 99, 3): *\*fīdem*
(for *fīdam*) > *fie* > *fii* (PMH, Scriptores, 276); but the analogical form, viz., *fie* with two syllables, is the one which has
survived.

B. In those forms in which hiatus arose through the fall of
intervocalic *n*, the nasal resonance disappeared (contrary to § 78,
2 and 3) by analogy with forms ending in *-a*, in which the nasal
resonance regularly disappeared (according to § 78, 7), e.g., *corōno*
> *corôo*, instead of *corōo*, by analogy with *corôas* (from *corōnas*);
*perdōnes* (Du Cange) > *perdōes* > *perdoes* by analogy with *per-
doas* (from *perdōnas*).

C. Dissimilation took place in the second and third singular
present indicative of *cair* and *soer: cadis* > *cais; sŏlet* > *sói;* and
also in the third plural present indicative of *cair* in Old Portuguese: *\*cadent* (for *cadunt*) > *caim*, e.g., *caãy* (RL, I, 336).

## 157. THE FINAL *-ão*.

1. The origin of the Old Portuguese finals *-am, -om* and
*-ão* is shown in the following table.

| Classical Latin | Old Portuguese |
|---|---|
| -ant (3d pl.)<br>-anem (acc. sg.) | -am |
| -ŭnt (3d pl.)<br>-ōnem (acc. sg.)<br>*-ŭdĭnem (acc. sg.) | -om |
| -anum (acc. sg.)<br>-adŭnt (in vadŭnt) | -ão |

That these finals had all become identical by the second
half of the fifteenth century is proved by the fact that they

rime with each other in the "Cancioneiro Geral" (Lições, 142).  See also NS, XI, 151.

While it is difficult to determine how long before this time the fusion was completed, there is evidence that it began in the thirteenth century.  In the early Cancioneiros, rimes with *foam* (from Arabic *folan*) show that at least *-am* had become *-ão*.  For the rime *foã : en vaõ* (CV, No. 1055) shows that the *ã* of *foã* was pronounced *ão*, and other rimes with *foam* (CV, No. 904 and No. 1149; CB, No. 390 and No. 411) show that the *am* of *am* (from *\*hant*), *prã* (from *plane*), *dam* (from *dant*) and the future ending *-am* (from *\*hant*) was pronounced *ão*.

But there is no evidence that *-om* had begun to share in the fusion.  The last line of CV, No. 208 was thought by Lang to stand alone (HR, I, 14); therefore, *diram* does not rime with *semrazom*.

A. Lat. *\*in-tum* and *non* became OPtg. *entom* and *nom*.  And Lat. *grandem, sanctum, quantum* and *tantum* became OPtg. *gram, sam, quam* and *tam*, the *n* having developed as a final (according to § 98, 4) after apocope of the last syllable.  All these forms shared in the fusion: *não, então, grão, são, quão* and *tão*.

2. The constant use of the spelling *vaão* in medieval documents (RB, 59; Graal, 26, 103, 110; RL, XX, 193; RL, XXI, 118, 119; Abraham, § 53; DC, 315; AHP, I, 348; PM-LA, LV, 360), as contrasted with the constant use of the spellings *dam, estam, ham, vaam* (subj.) and *som* is conclusive evidence that *vão* came from *vadunt,* an exceptional form because the ending *-unt* regularly disappeared in the Iberian peninsula. The spelling *vaão* is used even in documents in which *dam* and *estam* are sometimes spelled *dom* and *estom* (Carter, 27).  It is very probable that it was on the analogy of *vaão* that *-ão* became the ending of all third plurals that originally ended in *-am* and *-om*.  This change in verbs established an analogical trend which was soon to spread to nouns ending in *-am* and *-om*, a development which received great impetus from the small but important group of nouns in which *-ão*

had developed phonologically, that is, had come from Lat.
-*anum*. As common as *ir* among verbs are *mão*, *irmão*
and *cristão* among nouns. And thus, for example, *cam*
and *visom* became *cão* and *visão*. That the original analogical impulse did not come from this group of nouns is
shown by the fact that in their plurals analogy did not
generally operate, e.g., *mãos*, *cães*, *visões*, and by the fact
that in the few forms in which it did, it was not with the
ending -*ãos*, e.g., *verões* (from *\*verãnos*); see § 123, 3 B.
See Language, IX, 203–205.

A. The only verb form spelled with -*ão* beside *vaão* (ind.) in
all of the documents cited above is the subjunctive *vaão*, which
occasionally replaces *vaam* (from *vadant*). Thus we find both
*vaam* (RB, 53; RL, XXI, 108, 126, 141, 142) and *vaão* (RB, 56,
61; RL, XXI, 116) as subjunctives. And the indicative form
was occasionally spelled *vaam* (RL, XXI, 98, 106; Fab, 52).
This interchange of spellings was doubtless due to the complete
identity in sound of *vaão* and *vaam*, -*am* being pronounced *ão* at
the time these documents were written. For other early examples of the spelling *vaão* for the subjunctive, see RL, IV, 138;
AHP, III, 41, 376, 382; AHP, IV, 48; BF, III, 356.

B. Several attempts have been made to explain the change from
-*am* to -*ão* and from -*om* to -*ão* on a phonological basis. Leite
de Vasconcellos (Lições, 141–145, particularly 145, n. 2) supposes
that because of an inexplicable dislike for -*ã* and -*õ*, an *o* [u] was
affixed to them making them -*ão* and -*õo* respectively and that
-*õo* later became -*ão* by dissimilation. He then asks why *bõo*
(from *bŏnum*) did not become *bão* instead of *bom* and answers
that *bõo* still had two *o*'s at the time that -*õ* became -*ão*. But
according to the theory, it had been necessary for -*õ* to appro-
priate another *o* in order to became -*ão*. Leite thus completely
disproves his own argument. Nunes' explanation (Comp, 233–
235) is the same as Leite's and open to the same objection,
although he admits that the change of -*ã* to -*ão* may have been
due to the analogy of original -*ão*. See also Bourciez, § 333 e.
Nobiling (NS, XI, 150–152) finds in Brazilian Portuguese, which
represents an earlier stage of development than the language of
Lisbon, a tendency of, for instance, *lã* to become *lãu̯* and of *bõ*

to become *bõu̯*.   He assumes that the finals -*ã* and -*õ* became -*ão*
by following this tendency to a complete dissimilation, pointing
out that the change from -*õu* to -*ão* was similar to the change
from [ẽj] to [ɐ̃j] in the final -*em*.   He explains that such words as
*lã* and *bom*, even after they had become monosyllabic, were
prevented from further change by the "quantity" of their
vowels, that is, by the fact that the vowels were contractions.
What this difference between an originally single *õ* and a contracted *õ* was, he fails to explain.   The existence in Modern
Portuguese of words like *bom* (from *bŏnum*), *dom* (from *dōnum*);
*lã* (from *lanam*), *irmã* (from *germānam*), *vã* (from *vanam*) along
with their plurals renders untenable a phonological explanation
based on dissimilation.   The later analogical change of contracted *ã* and *õ* to *ão* in certain dialects (RL, III, 65; RL, XIX,
172; Opúsculos, II, 16, 99, 127) has no bearing on the problem.
For a comparison of -*ão* with the Italian third plural ending -*ano*,
see Theoria, 46 and D'Ovidio, 37.

c. Huber's explanation of *vam* as having developed by analogy
with *ham*, *dam* and *estam* (Huber, § 380, 5) has no meaning
inasmuch as he does not tell us what sound the graph -*am* stands
for (BF, V, 198).

D. That *vão* came from *vadunt* has been suggested by Nobiling
(NS, XI, 139), by Leite (Lições, 142) and by Dona Carolina
(RL, XXVIII, 33).

3. For almost two centuries the spelling of these finals
did not change.   But in the fourteenth century we begin
to find accented -*om* in nouns replaced by -*am*, e.g., *doaçam*
(AHP, III, 118, A.D. 1387), and unaccented -*am* in verbs
and less commonly accented -*am* in verbs replaced by -*om*,
e.g., *morõ* (RL, XXI, 270, A.D. 1329) and *estom* (AHP,
IV, 44, A.D. 1411).   Examples of these spellings can be
found in almost any document of the fifteenth century.
As it is likely that these finals had fused at an early date,
these changes in spelling probably do not reflect changes
in pronunciation but rather betray the confusion of scribes
in their effort to use purposively three familiar spellings
to represent one and the same sound.   Thus it would

seem that while -ão continued to be used wherever it had developed phonologically, that is, wherever it was derived from Lat. -anum or -adunt, -am came to be used to represent accented analogical -ão and -om to represent unaccented analogical -ão, and that since the unaccented sound occurred almost exclusively in verbs, -om came to be used also to represent accented analogical -ão in the few verb forms accented on the ending, viz., the present indicative of dar, estar, and haver (and, therefore, the future indicative of all verbs).

In the "Cancioneiro Geral" -om has disappeared (except in bom, com, etc.) but utter confusion between -am and -ão prevails (see RL, XXVIII, 33–34). Even today in the nova ortografia, -am is used for -ão in the unaccented position in verbs.

A. This interchange of the graphs -om and -am in the fifteenth century has been thought to reveal a vacillation in pronunciation rather than mere orthographic confusion (RL, II, 25). And the theory has been advanced that before the final triumph of the analogical influence of vaão, the three forms hã (from *hant), sõ (from sunt) and vaão (from vadunt) vied in exerting an analogical influence on each other and on other third plural forms ending in -om and -am (Carter, 27).

## TENSE ENDINGS

**158. INFINITIVE.**

1. The endings of the infinitive in Classical Latin and Portuguese are:

|  | Classical Latin | Portuguese |
|---|---|---|
| 1st Conjugation | -āre | -ar (§ 46, 2) |
| 2d Conjugation | -ēre ⎫ | -er (§ 46, 2; § 148, 1 b) |
| 3d Conjugation | -ĕre ⎭ | |
| 4th Conjugation | -īre | -ir (§ 46, 2) |

A. Some irregular Classical Latin infinitives disappeared in Vulgar Latin because the verb was replaced entirely or in part by some other verb; thus ferre was replaced by trahĕre and levāre;

*velle* was replaced by *quaerĕre; esse* was replaced in part by *sedēre.* And some irregular Classical Latin infinitives were re-formed on the analogy of regular infinitives of other conjugations than the first: *posse > potēre* (GVL, § 403) > *poder;* and the compounds of *ferre: conferre > conferir; praeferre > preferir; offerre > oferir* (old) and *oferecer; sufferre > sofrer.*

2. The personal infinitive is derived from the Classical Latin imperfect subjunctive.   The endings of the Classical Latin imperfect subjunctive and of the Portuguese personal infinitive of all conjugations are given below.

| Classical Latin Imperf. Subj. 1st Conjugation | Portuguese Personal Inf. 1st Conjugation |
|---|---|
| *-ārem* | *-ar* (§ 46, 2) |
| *-āres* | *-ares* |
| *-āret* | *-ar* (§ 46, 2) |
| *-ārēmus* | *-armos* (§ 154, 1 and 2) |
| *-ārētis* | *-ardes* (§ 154, 1 and 2; § 155, 1) |
| *-arent* | *-arem* (§ 46, 11) |

| Classical Latin Imperf. Subj. 2d Conjugation | Classical Latin Imperf. Subj. 3d Conjugation | Portuguese Personal Inf. 2d Conj. (§ 148, 1 b) |
|---|---|---|
| *-ērem* | *-ĕrem* | *-ẹr* (§ 46, 2) |
| *-ēres* | *-ĕres* | *-ẹres* |
| *-ēret* | *-ĕret* | *-ẹr* (§ 46, 2) |
| *-ērēmus* | *-ĕrēmus* | *-ẹrmos* (§ 154, 1 and 2) |
| *-ērētis* | *-ĕrētis* | *-ẹrdes* (§ 154, 1 & 2; § 155, 1) |
| *-ērent* | *-ĕrent* | *-ẹrem* (§ 46, 11) |

| Classical Latin Imperf. Subj. 4th Conjugation | Portuguese Personal Inf. 3d Conjugation |
|---|---|
| *-īrem* | *-ir* (§ 46, 2) |
| *-īres* | *-ires* |
| *-īret* | *-ir* (§ 46, 2) |
| *-īrēmus* | *-irmos* (§ 154, 1 and 2) |
| *-īrētis* | *-irdes* (§ 154, 1 and 2; § 155, 1) |
| *-īrent* | *-irem* (§ 46, 11) |

As the pluperfect subjunctive had begun to usurp the function of the imperfect subjunctive in Vulgar Latin we find both tenses used as imperfect subjunctives in parallel constructions in medieval Latin documents of the Portuguese territory and later in Portuguese documents, e.g., ". . . seis capellaaens, que *cantassem* por el e lhe *dissessem* cada dia huuma missa oficiada e *sahirem* sobrel com cruz e augua beemta," Fernão Lopes. And the tense derived from the Classical Latin imperfect subjunctive continued to be used sporadically in Portuguese as an imperfect subjunctive as late as the middle of the sixteenth century, e.g., "Determinou el rey dom Manuel . . . de mandar fazer hũa fortaleza na ilha de sam Lourenço . . . pera que as naos da carga da especiaria indo pera a India *fazerē* ali agoada & *irē* por fora da ilha," Fernão Lopes de Castanheda. With complete usurpation by the pluperfect subjunctive of the finite function of the imperfect subjunctive the latter continued to survive as an infinitive in such expressions as *que fazer, tenho que fazer, não sei que fazer* and as a personal infinitive through omission of subordinating conjunctions or through the substitution of prepositions for subordinating conjunctions, such substitution having begun in Medieval Latin, e.g., *plaguit nobis . . . in* (for *ut*) *fazeremus*. This is the theory of José Maria Rodrigues and these are a few of the examples he has gathered in support of his theory (BSC, VIII, 72–93). For additional examples, see RL, XXIII, 83, s.v. *\*seer*'. See also DL, 203–208. See also the following example of the parallel use of the imperfect subjunctive and the pluperfect subjunctive: "ffoy asi deuisado o preyto . . . que *uyesse* ũu uosso frade . . . E *yr* Eu e meus irmaos . . . e *presentarmos* . . . e *irmos* nos cõ elle . . ." (RL, XI, 92–93). Maria Rodrigues points out further in a later study that the shift of accent to the antepenult of the first and second plural imperfect subjunctive along with the shift of accent to the penult of the infinitive of verbs of the Classical Latin third conjugation, that is, the change from, e.g., *placuit facĕre* and *placuit facerēmus* to *placuit \*facēre* and *placuit \*facērĕmus*, contributed to the use of the inflected forms as an infinitive (BF, I, 3).

The theory of Gamillscheg (Tempuslehre, §§ 264–281), which is supported by examples of the imperfect subjunctive as an inflected infinitive in Medieval Latin of the Portuguese territory and of the personal infinitive as a jussive subjunctive in early Portuguese, is essentially the same as that of Maria Rodrigues: With the decrease in the use of subordinating conjunctions in Vulgar Latin and the consequent increase in coordination, the infinitive after verbs of command (which was interchangeable with the subjunctive and, after secondary tenses, with the imperfect subjunctive) was felt to be identical with the imperfect subjunctive, especially because of the influence of the use of the imperfect subjunctive with similar force in jussive clauses. In this new role the imperfect subjunctive then spread to other infinitive constructions, regardless of what the tense of the principal verb was. In the meantime, in purely subjunctive functions (old and new), the imperfect subjunctive was being replaced by the pluperfect subjunctive. To illustrate with hypothetical sentences: With the decrease in the use of *ut* and through the influence of *facere* (for *facerem* 'let me do' or *faceret* 'let him do') in jussive clauses, *mandavit (ut) facere* (for *facerem* or *faceret*) and *mandavit facere* became identical, and *facere* was felt to be an inflected form which could become *faceremus*, etc. as required by the meaning and could be used like the uninflected infinitive after primary tenses, e.g., *mandat facere, mandat faceremus,* etc. For further argument in support of this theory, see Miscelânea, II, 129–130.

A. The theory that the personal infinitive was derived from the Classical Latin imperfect subjunctive had been suggested by Wernekke (Wern) and Mohl (Chron, 248) a number of years before Gamillscheg and Maria Rodrigues elaborated it.

In addition to this development theory there was a theory that might be called the creative theory. According to it, the dialectal pronoun *mos* (§ 142 D), used with the infinitive, was taken to be an ending, after which the other endings were added in imitation of the first plural. This theory, first suggested by Otto (RF, VI, 299–398), was elaborated by Carolina Michaëlis de Vasconcellos (RF, VII, 49–122). Schuchardt then explained the adoption of *mos* as the result of a sort of syntactical contamination by the future subjunctive, which took place at first in verbs with weak preterits (LBl, XIII, 197–206). A variation of the creative theory is that of Leite (PhM, I, 374) and Coelho (see KJ, IV, Part I, 336), according to which the endings were added to the infinitive spontaneously in order to show morphologically the personal distinctions that it already expressed. Inflection of the gerund in dialectal Portuguese, e.g., *em tu estandos* (RL, VII, 51), *ganhando-mos* (RL, XXVII, 159), may have developed in this way unless these forms arose in imitation of the personal infinitive. The point of view of Leite and Coelho is held by Theodoro Henrique Maurer Jr., who argues that what makes the "infinito flexionado" personal is not that it is inflected with personal endings but that it takes a subject (expressed or understood) in the nominative (Dois Problemas, 34–39 and 47–48). See also R-M, 327.

Carolina Michaëlis de Vasconcellos later rejected her own theory to accept that of Maria Rodrigues (BSC, XII, 312–331).

B. A few traces of the personal infinitive are found in Old Spanish (Tempuslehre, § 280) but the personal endings were not retained. An uninflected personal infinitive still exists in Modern Spanish, e.g., "Acabó la porfía por encerrarse el padre y el hijo en la habitación de éste"; and "Pudiste, sin yo saberlo, ver a mi hijo." (Spaulding, § 122).

C. In Galician the third singular of the personal infinitive is sometimes distinguished from the first singular by a paragogic *e.*

## 159. PAST PARTICIPLE.

1. Latin past participles may be divided into three

groups: a) weak, b) proparoxytonic strong, c) paroxytonic strong.

2. The Classical Latin weak and proparoxytonic strong past participle endings and the Vulgar Latin and Portuguese endings which came from them or replaced them are:

|  | Cl. L. | V. L. | OPtg. | MPtg. |
|---|---|---|---|---|
| 1st Conjugation | -ātum | -ātum | -ado | -ado |
| 2d Conjugation | -ētum ⎱ | -ūtum | -udo | -ido |
| 3d Conjugation | -ĭtum ⎰ |  |  |  |
| 4th Conjugation | -ītum | -ītum | -ido | -ido |

Both -ētum and -ĭtum were replaced in Vulgar Latin by -ūtum, which spread at first to a small number of verbs with perfects in -ui and then to all verbs of the second and third conjugations except a small number which have retained their paroxytonic strong past participles (GVL, § 438 and § 440). By the sixteenth century, -ido (from -ĭtum of the Classical Latin fourth conjugation) had entirely replaced -udo.　See M-L, Gram, II, § 331; RF, XXII, 421.

A. The ending -ētum, which was never very common in Latin, has survived in the noun queda (from *cadētam, § 99, 3); -ĭtum has survived in the adjectives bêbedo (from bĭbĭtum) and lêvedo (from *levĭtum, REW) and in the noun dívida (from dēbĭtam); and -ūtum has survived in the noun conteúdo.

B. One verb of the fourth conjugation formed its past participle in -udo in Old Portuguese, viz., vĭudo.

C. For the development of the nasal in vindo (from *venītum) and in OPtg. findo (from fīnītum), see § 78, 5.

3. Many paroxytonic strong past participles have survived in Portuguese.

| Latin | Portuguese |
|---|---|
| apertum | aberto |
| copertum | coberto |
| *dīctum | dito |
| factum | feito |
| mŏrtum (for mortŭum, GVL, § 226) | morto |
| pŏstum (for posĭtum, GVL, § 238) | posto |

*scrīptum*        *escrito*
*\*vīstum* (GVL, § 441; M-L, Intro, § 195)    *visto*

The forms of many more strong past participles have survived, e.g., *accensum > aceso; acceptum > aceito; benedictum > bento; exsūtum > enxuto; impressum > impresso; junctum > junto; natum > nado; prehensum > preso; rŭptum > rôto; tinctum > tinto.* See LP, I, 69–72; Dunn, § 545; Said, 162–170. It is difficult to determine whether many of the surviving strong forms are still really participles because the distinction between the verbal use and the adjectival use of the past participle is extremely elusive in Portuguese and has not yet been defined.

A. The close tonic *o* of *morto* and of *posto* developed by metaphony but the masculine plural and the feminine singular and plural were not affected (cf. § 126, 7).

B. The form *lectum* survived in the compounds *eleito* (from *electum*) and *colheito* (old) (from *collectum*), the feminine of which, *colheita*, exists in Modern Portuguese as a noun; *-eito* was taken to be an ending and spread to other verbs, viz., *tolheito* (old); *escolheito* (old); *coseito* (old).

C. The form *repêso* (from *repensum*) has become a past participle of *arrepender* through the erroneous derivation of OPtg. *repender* (from *\*repoenitēre*) from Lat. *rependĕre*.

D. The form *comestum* became *comesto* (Opúsculos, II, 102) and *bebesto* (Opúsculos, II, 98) developed by analogy with *comesto.*

4. The truncated past participles *côrto, ganho, gasto, baptizo* and *pago* probably arose in Vulgar Latin (or early Portuguese) alongside the weak forms in *-ātum* by analogy with such pairs as *acceptum – acceptātum, ausum – \*ausātum, ūsum – ūsātum,* etc. (cf. GIt, § 199).

A. The forms ending in *e, aceite, assente, encarregue, entregue,* and *fixe* (popular), which developed alongside weak forms in *-ado,* are thought to be the result of analogy with such pairs as *firme – firmado, livre – livrado* (RL, IV, 133–134).

**160.** GERUND.

The endings of the gerund in Classical Latin and Portuguese are:

| | Classical Latin | Portuguese |
|---|---|---|
| 1st Conjugation | -andum | -ando |
| 2d Conjugation | -endum | -endo |
| 3d Conjugation | -endum ⎫<br>-iendum ⎭ | -endo |
| 4th Conjugation | -iendum | -indo |

Cl. L. -*iendum* of the few irregular verbs of the third conjugation (verbs in -*ĭo*) was replaced by -*endum*. And Cl. L. -*iendum* of the fourth conjugation was replaced in Portuguese by -*indo*, a new form, made with the characteristic *i* of the conjugation (cf. RF, XX, 564).

**161.** PRESENT PARTICIPLE.

The endings of the present participle in Classical Latin and Portuguese are:

| | Classical Latin | Portuguese |
|---|---|---|
| 1st Conjugation | -antem | -ante |
| 2d Conjugation | -entem | -ente |
| 3d Conjugation | -entem ⎫<br>-ientem ⎭ | -ente |
| 4th Conjugation | -ientem | -inte |

The development of the tonic vowel of the ending of the present participle was the same as that of the gerund (§ 160). As late as the sixteenth century the present participle had verbal force, but in Modern Portuguese it has survived as an adjective, occasionally as a noun, and in a few cases as a preposition, e.g., *salvante, tirante*.

A. The ending -*iente* has been preserved in learned forms, e.g., *proveniente, suficiente, oriente*. Forms like *dormente* and *servente* are probably survivals of a period before the rise of the ending -*inte*.

**162. PRESENT INDICATIVE.**

1. The endings of the present indicative of verbs of the
first conjugation in Classical Latin and Portuguese are:

| Classical Latin | Portuguese |
|---|---|
| *-o* | *-o* |
| *-as* | *-as* |
| *-at* | *-a* |
| *-āmŭs* | *-amos* [ɐmuʃ] (§ 33, 6) |
| *-ātĭs* | *-ades* > *-ais* (§ 155, 1) |
| *-ant* | *-am* [ẽ̆] > [ẽ̆w] (§ 157, 2) |

A. In dialects of the north *-amos* is pronounced [amuʃ] (RL,
I, 195 and 199; Rom, XII, 69; Esquisse, § 74 d). This sound of
*a* developed by analogy with the *a* of the second plural.

2. The endings of the present indicative of verbs of the
second and third conjugations in Classical Latin and of the
conjugation resulting from their fusion in Portuguese are:

| Classical Latin 2d Conjugation | Classical Latin 3d Conjugation | Portuguese 2d Conjugation |
|---|---|---|
| *-ĕo* | *-o* (*-ĭo*) | *-o* (§ 148, 1 a) |
| *-es* | *-ĭs* | *-es* |
| *-et* | *-ĭt* | *-e* |
| *-ēmŭs* | *-ĭmŭs* | *-ẹmos* (§ 148, 1 b) |
| *-ētĭs* | *-ĭtĭs* | *-ẹdes* (§ 148, 1 b) > *-eis* (§ 46, 6; § 155, 1) |
| *-ent* | *-unt* (*-ĭunt*) | *-em* (§ 148, 1 c; § 46, 11) |

1st sg.: The yod (from *-ĭo*) of the first singular of the
few irregular verbs of the Classical Latin third conjugation
did not generally fall, e.g., *capio* > *caibo; facĭo* > *faço*. In
other Romance languages this yod may have been the
analogical factor which occasioned the shift of some of these
verbs to the fourth conjugation, e.g., It. *capire* (from *capĕre*),
Fr. *mourir* (from *mŏrĕre*, Rönsch, 298), Sp. *recibir* (from
*recĭpĕre*). 3d sg.: This ending fell when preceded by certain
consonants (§ 152, 1), e.g., *facit* > *faz*.

3. The endings of the present indicative of verbs of the fourth conjugation in Classical Latin and Portuguese are:

| Classical Latin | Portuguese |
|---|---|
| -ĭo | -o |
| -īs | -es |
| -ĭt | -e |
| -īmŭs | -imos |
| -ītĭs | -ides > -is (§ 46, 9; § 155, 1) |
| -ĭunt | -em (§ 46, 11) |

1st sg.: In most verbs the yod was lost in Vulgar Latin (GVL, § 416), perhaps by analogy with verbs of the third conjugation. In some, however, it exerted an influence on the radical vowel and disappeared (see § 176). 2d sg.: Final -īs would have regularly become -es (§ 47, 1), but because radical e and o show no evidence of having been affected by this ī, it has been assumed that the -īs of these forms became -es in Vulgar Latin by analogy with verbs of the second and third conjugations (Rom, XIII, 296). 3d sg.: This ending fell when preceded by certain consonants (§ 152, 1), e.g., lūcet > luz. 3d pl.: The ending -em developed by analogy with verbs of the new conjugation resulting from the fusion of the second and third conjugations.

163. PRESENT SUBJUNCTIVE.

1. The endings of the present subjunctive of verbs of the first conjugation in Classical Latin and Portuguese are:

| Classical Latin | Portuguese |
|---|---|
| -em | -e |
| -es | -es |
| -et | -e |
| -ēmŭs | -ẹmos |
| -ētĭs | -ẹdes > eis (§ 46, 6; § 155, 1) |
| -ent | -em (§ 46, 11) |

2. The endings of the present subjunctive of verbs of the second and third conjugations in Classical Latin and of the conjugation resulting from their fusion in Portuguese are:

| Classical Latin 2d Conjugation | Classical Latin 3d Conjugation | Portuguese 2d Conjugation |
|---|---|---|
| -ĕam | -am (-ĭam) | -a |
| -ĕas | -as (-ĭas) | -as |
| -ĕat | -at (-ĭat) | -a |
| -ĕāmŭs | -āmŭs (-ĭāmŭs) | -amos [ɐmuʃ] (§ 33, 6) |
| -ĕātĭs | -ātĭs (-ĭātĭs) | -ades > ais (§ 155, 1) |
| -ĕant | -ant (-ĭant) | -am [ɐ̃] > [ɐ̃w] (§ 157, 2) |

The forms with yod (-ĕam, etc.) of the second conjugation lost the yod in the fusion with the third conjugation (§ 148, 1 a). The yod (from -ĭam, etc.) of the few irregular verbs of the Classical Latin third conjugation did not generally fall, e.g., *capĭam* > *caiba*; *sapĭam* > *saiba* (cf. § 162, 2).

3. The endings of the present subjunctive of verbs of the fourth conjugation in Classical Latin and Portuguese are:

| Classical Latin | Portuguese |
|---|---|
| -ĭam | -a |
| -ĭas | -as |
| -ĭat | -a |
| -ĭāmŭs | -amos [ɐmuʃ] (§ 33, 6) |
| -ĭātĭs | -ades > -ais (§ 155, 1) |
| -ĭant | -am [ɐ̃] > [ɐ̃w] (§ 157, 2) |

In most verbs the yod was lost in Vulgar Latin by analogy with verbs of the third conjugation. In some, however, it fell as a regular phonological change but not before it had exerted an influence on the radical vowel (see § 176).

**164. IMPERFECT INDICATIVE.**

1. The endings of the imperfect indicative of verbs of the first conjugation in Classical Latin and Portuguese are:

| Classical Latin | Portuguese |
|---|---|
| -ābam | -ava |
| -ābas | -avas |
| -ābat | -ava |
| -ābāmŭs | -ávamos (§ 154, 1) |
| -ābātĭs | -ávades (§ 154, 1) > -áveis (§ 155, 1 and 2) |
| -ābant | -avam [avẽ] > [avẽw] (§ 157, 2) |

For the change of *b* to *v*, see § 72, 1.

2. The endings of the imperfect indicative of verbs of the combined second and third conjugation in Classical Latin and Portuguese are.

| Classical Latin | Portuguese |
|---|---|
| -ēbam (-iēbam) | -ia |
| -ēbas (-iēbas) | -ias |
| -ēbat (-iēbat) | -ia |
| -ēbāmŭs (-iēbāmŭs) | -íamos (§ 154, 1) |
| -ēbātis (-iēbātĭs) | -íades (§ 154, 1) > -íeis (§ 155, 1 and 2) |
| -ēbant (-iēbant) | -iam [iẽ] > [iẽw] (§ 157, 2) |

The *b* of the Latin endings fell by dissimilation in *habē-bam*, etc. and *debēbam*, etc. and from these two very common verbs the endings without *b* spread to all verbs of the conjugation (Thurneysen, 30–32). Later the endings -*ęa*, -*ęas*, etc. changed to -*ia*, -*ias*, etc., according to § 35, 6. The endings -*iēbam*, etc. of the few irregular verbs of the Classical Latin third conjugation changed to -*ēbam* in Vulgar Latin (GVL, § 420; M-L, Intro, § 129).

A. Lindsay suggests that the existence of futures in the Latin third and fourth conjugations in -*ēbo* and -*ībo* alongside those in -*am* may have led to the coinage in Vulgar Latin of imperfects without *b*, thus providing the forms for the Romance imperfects (Lindsay, 493). Cf. Bourciez, § 90. Gröber supposes the existence, alongside the forms with *b*, of Old Latin forms without·*b*, first in verbs with stems in *e* and *i*, then by analogy in verbs with consonant stems; he points to *eram* as an imperfect without *b* (ALLG, I, 229–230). For a discussion of the whole problem, see M-L, Gram, II, § 254. See also section 3 A below.

B. The dialectal endings *-eba* and *-iba* do not come directly from the Latin endings but developed at a comparatively late date by analogy with the endings of the first conjugation (see Manual, § 117, 1, n. 1).

C. In Portuguese the accent never shifted from the *i* to the *a* of these endings as in Old Spanish (cf. Hanssen, § 28, 3).

3. The endings of the imperfect indicative of verbs of the fourth conjugation in Latin and Portuguese are:

| Latin | Portuguese |
|---|---|
| *-ībam* | *-ia* |
| *-ības* | *-ias* |
| *-ībat* | *-ia* |
| *-ībāmŭs* | *-íamos* (§ 154, 1) |
| *-ībātĭs* | *-iades* (§ 154, 1) > *-ieis* (§ 155, 1 and 2) |
| *-ībant* | *-iam* [iɐ̃] > [iɐ̃w] (§ 157, 2) |

For the Vulgar Latin endings, see GVL, § 420. The *b* fell as these endings developed by analogy with the endings of the imperfect indicative of verbs of the combined second and third conjugation.

A. The fall of *b* in these endings has been explained as a regular development after *ī*; and according to this explanation, *-ēbam* of the second conjugation became *-ia* by analogy with the endings of the imperfect of verbs of the fourth conjugation (RF, XX, 582–583; RF, XXII, 415).

**165.** THE *v* OF WEAK PERFECTS AND DERIVED TENSES.

Most of the long weak endings (with *v*) of the perfect and derived tenses of the first and fourth conjugations need not be considered in connection with the development of the endings of these tenses in Portuguese, as the short weak endings (without *v*), from which the Portuguese endings were derived, existed concurrently in Classical Latin and were probably not derived from the long endings (REL, IV, 115–119, 212–217).

Although short endings of the fourth conjugation with contracted *ie* before *r* are not attested, assumption of their existence in Vulgar Latin is justified on the basis of forms in Portuguese and other Romance languages, e.g., Ptg. *ouviram*, It. *udirono*, Fr. *ouirent* (from *\*audįrunt*).

## 166. WEAK PRETERIT.

1. The endings of the Classical Latin and Vulgar Latin perfect indicative and the Portuguese preterit of verbs of the first conjugation are:

| Classical Latin | Vulgar Latin | Portuguese |
|---|---|---|
| -āvī | -ái | -ei (§ 33, 2 c) |
| -āstī | -ásti | -aste (§ 47, 1) |
| -āvit | -áut (GVL, § 325) | -ou (§ 33, 4) |
| -āvĭmŭs | -ámus | -amos [amuʃ] |
| -āstĭs | -ástes | -astes |
| -ārunt | -árunt | -arom > -aram (§ 157, 2) |

For the Classical Latin and Vulgar Latin endings, see § 165 and GVL, §§ 424–425. 1st pl.: The *a* of *-amos* is pronounced [a], contrary to § 33, 6; this pronunciation developed by analogy with the *a* of the second singular and the second and third plural. However, in some dialects it is pronounced [ɐ] (RL, I, 33, n. 1; RL, XIV, 85; Rom, XII, 69; M-L, Gram, II, § 276).

2. The endings of the Classical Latin and Vulgar Latin perfect indicative and the Portuguese preterit of verbs of the fourth conjugation are:

| Classical Latin | Vulgar Latin | Portuguese |
|---|---|---|
| -īvī | -íį | -i |
| -īstī | -ístį | -iste (§ 47, 1) |
| -īvit | *-įut | -iu |
| -īvĭmŭs | -ímus | -imos |
| -īstĭs | -ístes | -istes |
| -iērunt | *-įrunt | -irom > iram (§ 157, 2) |

For the Classical Latin and Vulgar Latin endings, see § 165 and GVL, § 423 and § 425. 1st sg.: See RHi,

LXXVII, 122. 3d sg.: The *u* of Ptg. *-iu* sometimes fell, e.g., *servî* (RL, VI, 346).

3. The Classical Latin forms of the *-dĭdī* component of the perfect indicative of compounds of *dare*, their Vulgar Latin derivatives and the endings which developed from them in Portuguese and became the weak preterit endings of the conjugation resulting from the fusion of the Classical Latin second and third conjugations, are given below.

| Classical Latin | Vulgar Latin | Portuguese |
|---|---|---|
| *-dĭdī* | *\*-dẹ́(d)į̇* | *-i* |
| *-dĭdĭstī* | *\*-(de)dẹ́stį̇* | *-iste* (§ 35, 4; § 47, 1; old and dial.) and *-ẹste* |
| *-dĭdĭt* | *\*-dẹ́(de)t* | *-e* (old) and *-ẹu* |
| *-dĭdĭmŭs* | *\*-dẹ́(de)mus* | *-ẹmos* |
| *-dĭdĭstĭs* | *\*-(de)dẹ́stes* | *-ẹstes* |
| *-dĭdērunt* | *\*-dẹ́(de)runt* | *-ẹrom > ẹram* (§ 157, 2) |

These forms spread as endings in Vulgar Latin to many other verbs of the second and third conjugations with stems in *d* or *t* (GVL, § 426; M-L, Intro, § 192) and in Portuguese to all verbs of the combined second and third conjugation except those few which retained their strong perfects from Classical Latin (§ 167). The Portuguese endings are, accordingly, given above with the *d* of the stem detached.

The accent of the first and third singular of perfects in *-dĭdi* reverted in Vulgar Latin to the *-dĭdi* element perhaps by analogy with the accent of the third plural, but the vowel of the simple verb, namely *ẹ*, was not restored (see § 3 b). That *ẹ* was not restored is deduced from the Portuguese endings themselves, particularly as contrasted with the forms of the preterit of Portuguese *dar*. By haplology and in accordance with the Vulgar Latin tendency to reduce all reduplicative forms (M-L, Intro, § 193), the unaccented *-de-* of each form fell. This syllable is indicated above by inclusion in parentheses.

While there is no way of determining the quality of the *e* of the attested Vulgar Latin forms, it has generally been assumed, on the basis of such Romance forms as OIt. *vendiè* and OFr. *perdiet*, that the vowel of the simple verb *dĕdī* was restored (GVL, § 139 and § 426; Bourciez, § 91 b; GIt, § 209). But the explanation that the *-i* of the first singular in French developed through an intermediate \**iei* (S-B, § 342, 2; Pope, § 1006) would not account for the *-i* of the first singular in Portuguese because tonic *ę* did not diphthongize in Portuguese. And as the ending of the second singular was *-iste* in Old Portuguese, there would have been only one ending with *ę*, the second plural, on which to base the analogical development of *ę* in the other endings. It is true that for Italian Grandgent has based the analogical development on the first plural also (GIt, § 140, § 201, § 209) but he did this by assuming the existence of first plural forms with radical *ę* (Cl. L. *ĭ*), viz., \**credĭdmus*, \**perdĭdmus*, in contradiction to his general assumption that radical *ę* was restored. Grandgent's examples imply a difference between the accented radical vowel of the first and third singular and the third plural on the one hand and the first plural on the other. And from the Vulgar Latin forms noted by Sepulcri (SM, I, 214) it might be argued that *ę* was restored in the first singular but not in the third plural, where he still finds the spelling *i*. If such differences actually existed and if they were not consistent from one territory to another, it is conceivable that in some territories *ę* was restored throughout the tense and in other territories it was not restored at all. That it was not restored at all is what we have assumed for the Portuguese territory. See RHi, LXXVII, 54–56.

If haplology is not assumed, these forms can be explained by syncope of the posttonic penult or the intertonic vowel, e.g., \**-dęderunt* > \**-dędrunt* > *-d-ęrom* or by the fall of intervocalic *d*, e.g., \**-dędemus* > \**-dęemos* > *-d-ęmos*.

1st sg.: The second *d* of this ending fell in Vulgar Latin by dissimilation (cf. GIt, § 140). Tonic *ę* became *i* (according to § 35, 4), which contracted with the vowel of the ending.   2d sg.: The *i* of *-iste* developed according to § 35, 4 and the *ę* of *-ęste,* which replaced *-iste,* developed by analogy with all three plural endings.   3d sg.: The ending *e* is found in Old Portuguese and in dialectal Portuguese in forms that are followed by a pronoun enclitic or other closely related word (RL, VI, 334, n. 2); it has been explained as an apocopated *-eu* (Grund, I, 1023; Esquisse, § 56 b). The *u* of *-eu* developed by analogy with the corresponding weak endings of other conjugations, namely, *-iu* and *-ou,* the latter being a diphthong in Old Portuguese. The ending *-eu* is found as early as the year 1066, in the form *cadeu* (Cortesão, s.v. *eu*). See § 48, 2 A. 3d pl.: For the vowel of the penult and the accent of *\*-dęderunt,* see Lindsay, 532.

A. The perfect of a few verbs of the Classical Latin second conjugation ended in *-ēvī,* and although some additional verbs acquired this ending in Vulgar Latin, it does not seem to have spread sufficiently to become the source of the endings of the weak preterit of the combined second and third conjugation in Portuguese (M-L, Intro, § 191).   It has been suggested that endings with the characteristic *ę* of this combined conjugation developed in imitation of the other weak preterits with characteristic *a* and *i* (Hanssen, § 31, 4; RF, XXII, 417).   For a criticism of these theories, see RHi, LXXVII, 51–53.

**167. STRONG PRETERIT.**[1]

1. The endings of the Classical Latin and Vulgar Latin strong perfect and the Portuguese strong preterit are given below.

| Classical Latin | Vulgar Latin | Portuguese |
|---|---|---|
| *-ī* | *\*-į* | *-(e)* |
| *-ĭstī* | *\*-ęstį* | *-iste* (§ 35, 4; § 47, 1; old and dial.) and *-ęste* |
| *-ĭt* | *\*-et* | *-(e)* |
| *-ĭmŭs* | *\*-ęmus* | *-ęmos* |
| *-ĭstĭs* | *\*-ęstęs* | *-ęstes* |
| *-ērunt* | *-ĕrunt > \*-ęrunt* | *-ęrom > ęram* (§ 157, 2) |

[1] So called because two forms, the first and third singular, are accented on the radical vowel.

In Vulgar Latin, -*ĕrunt* was used instead of -*ērunt* (Lindsay, 532; Bauer, § 58). With the loss of the second -*de*- in the third plural of perfects of the -*didi* type (§ 166, 3), the only perfects which still had proparoxytonic third plurals were strong perfects. In Italian the accent falls on the same syllable in all these forms as in Vulgar Latin, e.g., *amarono*, *crederono*, *partirono*, and *fecero*. However, in the Iberian territory the accent shifted to the penult [1] of the third plural of strong perfects by analogy with the third plural of weak perfects, with the result that all third plural preterits in Portuguese and Spanish are paroxytones.[2] And thus arose the *ę* of this ending (*ie* in Spanish), in contrast to the *ę* of the third plural of weak preterits (cf. RHi, LXXVII, 58). Later, the *ę* of -*ęste*, -*ęmos*, and -*ęstes* developed by analogy with the *ę* of -*ęrom* and of all forms of the pluperfect indicative and future subjunctive. The preterit of *dar* is thought to have exerted an analogical influence also (M-L, Gram, II, § 265; RF, XXII, 418; Cavacas, 130–131).

1st sg.: Unaccented final *ī* became *e* (§ 47, 1) and this *e* fell when preceded by *s* or *c* (§ 47, 2). For the preservation of this final *e* when the form was followed by a pronoun, see § 143, 3 c. 2d sg.: For the *i* of -*iste*, see § 35, 4. 3d sg.: Unaccented final *e* fell when preceded by *s* or *c* (§ 46, 2). 1st pl.: The accent shifted to the penult by analogy with the first plural of weak preterits. This shift took place most likely at the same time as the shift in the third plural.

A. Meyer-Lübke suggests that the *ę* of strong preterits was due to the influence of the following *r* of the third plural ending (ZRPh, IX, 253) but he does not explain why *r* did not have the same opening effect on the *e* of weak preterits.

[1] The same shift is found in some forms in Provençal (GPr, § 177, 3).

[2] This difference between Italian on the one hand and Portuguese and Spanish on the other may be accounted for in part by the loss in Italian of all of the tenses derived from the perfect except the pluperfect subjunctive (Italian imperfect subjunctive); this loss diminished considerably the number of forms capable of exerting an analogical influence.

2. The Classical Latin strong perfects which survived in Portuguese may be divided into four groups: a) those in *-ui*, b) those in *-si*, c) a miscellaneous group consisting of the perfects of *facĕre*, *quaerĕre* and *venīre*, and d) a miscellaneous group which is distinguished from the other three groups by the fact that the third plural forms became paroxytones in Portuguese by syncope of the penult and not by a shift of the accent.

3. The *u* of all forms of perfects in *-ui* and of all forms of the derived tenses became *ụ* in Vulgar Latin. This change took place in the first and third plural after the shift of accent to the penult (section 1 above). If the preceding consonant was *d* or *l*, *ụ* became *v* (§ 93, 6 and 7), e.g., *\*sēduī* (GVL, § 428) > *sevi* > *sive* (old). If the preceding consonant was *b*, *p*, *c*, *t*, *s* or *x*, *ụ* was attracted to radical *a* or *o* (§ 93, 1 в). With radical *a* the diphthong *au* was formed, which became *ou* in Portuguese in both tonic and pretonic positions (§ 33, 4; § 40, 4), e.g., *habuit* > *\*haubet* > *houve; habuistis* > *\*haubestes* > *houvestes;* this diphthong was not affected by final *ị*, e.g., *habuī* > *\*haubị* > *houve*. With radical *ŏ* the diphthong *\*ọụ* was formed, which in the tonic position became *ọ* in Portuguese (§ 37, 4), e.g., *pŏtuit* > *pôde;* this *o* was closed to *u* by final *ị* (§ 38, 6), e.g., *pŏtuī* > *\*pọdị* > *pude*. In the pretonic position also, *\*ọụ* became *o* in Portuguese (§ 43, 5), e.g., *pŏtuistis* > *podestes* (old), but as pretonic *o* in general came to be pronounced [u] (§ 43, 1), the *o* of these forms was changed to *u* in imitation of the spelling of the first singular. See ZRPh, III, 506; ZRPh, IX, 260. A preceding intervocalic *c* became *g* (§ 73, 1) before attraction of *ụ* took place but after cessation of the change of *g* followed by *e* or *i* to [ʒ], e.g., *placuit* > *plaguit* (Comp, 343, n. 1) > *\*plauget* > *prougue* (old).

A. There is a theory according to which attraction did not take place but two *ụ*'s developed, one from *b* and one from *u;*

the first one combined with *a* to form the diphthong while the second one became *v*, e.g., *habuit* > *\*abụit* > *\*auụe* > *houve*. With other consonants an anticipatory *ụ* is thought to have developed before the original *ụ* was lost, e.g., *placụit* > *\*plaụgụit* > *\*plauget* > *prougue*. See SpV, § 385; RHi, LXXVII, 73 ss.

4. The *s* of perfects in *-si* combined with a preceding [k] to become *ss* or [ʃ], according to § 92, 9 and § 92, 9 A: *dixit* > *disse*. A preceding *n* fell, according to § 12, 6: *\*prensī* > *\*prẹsị* > *pris* (old); *mansit* > *mas* (old).

5. There are three strong preterits in Portuguese which have the characteristic endings of weak preterits and might therefore be fittingly called pseudo-weak preterits. The third plurals of these preterits became paroxytones by syncope and not by a shift of accent: *lēgĕrunt* > *\*lẹgron* > *lẹram; \*rīdĕrunt* (for *rīsĕrunt*) > *\*rịdron* > *riram; vīdĕrunt* > *\*vịdron* > *viram*. In these forms and in all forms of the derived tenses the radical vowel became also the vowel of the ending and helped to give the tense the appearance of a weak preterit. The vowel resulting from contraction after the fall of intervocalic *d* (or *g*) in certain other forms contributed also to this appearance, e.g., *lēgistis* > *lẹẹstes* > *lêstes; \*rīdistī* (for *rīsistī*) > *rịịste* (§ 35, 4) > *riste; vīdistī* > *vịịste* (§ 35, 4) > *viste*. As a result of this partial resemblance, analogical third singular forms, viz., *lẹu, riu* and *viu*, developed.

The preterit (and derived tenses) of *dar* developed in the same way, that is, by syncope in some forms, e.g., *dĕdĕrunt* > *\*dẹdron* > *dẹram*, and through the fall of intervocalic *d* in others, e.g., *dĕdistis* > *\*deestes* > *dẹstes*. But resemblance to weak preterits is found only in the first and third singular because of the radical *ẹ* of the other forms.

A. The preterit of *crer* belongs only apparently to this group as it is a regular weak verb of the Portuguese second conjugation with contraction of the radical vowel and the vowel of the ending, e.g., *crēdĭ(dĕ)runt* (§ 166, 3) > *\*crẹdẹron* > *crẹẹrom* > *crẹram*.

B. The preterit of *ser* (and *ir*) does not have the characteristic vowel of the endings of weak or strong preterits, inasmuch as it lost the vowel of the ending in Vulgar Latin and its radical vowel is ǫ (GVL, § 431), e.g., *fǫrunt* > *fǫram*.

**168. Pluperfect Indicative.**

1. The endings of the pluperfect indicative of verbs of the first conjugation in Classical Latin and Portuguese are:

| Classical Latin | Portuguese |
|---|---|
| -āram | -ara |
| -āras | -aras |
| -ārat | -ara |
| -ārāmus | -áramos (§ 154, 1) |
| -ārātis | -árades (§ 154, 1) > -áreis (§ 155, 1 and 2) |
| -ārant | -aram [arẽ] > [arẽw] (§ 157, 2) |

For the Latin endings, see § 165.

2. The endings of the pluperfect indicative of verbs of the fourth conjugation in Classical Latin, Vulgar Latin and Portuguese are:

| Classical Latin | Vulgar Latin | Portuguese |
|---|---|---|
| - īeram | *-ịra | -ira |
| -īeras | *-ịras | -iras |
| -īerat | *-ịrat | -ira |
| -īerāmus | *-ịramus | -íramos (§ 154, 1) |
| -īerātis | *-ịrates | -írades (§ 154, 1) > -íreis (§ 155, 1 and 2) |
| -īerant | *-ịrant | -iram [irẽ] > [irẽw] (§ 157, 2) |

For the Vulgar Latin endings, see § 165.

3. The Classical Latin forms of the pluperfect indicative of the *dare* component of compounds of *dare*, their Vulgar Latin derivatives and the endings which developed from them in Portuguese and became the weak pluperfect indicative endings of the conjugation resulting from the fusion of the Classical Latin second and third conjugations are given below.

| Classical Latin | Vulgar Latin | Portuguese |
|---|---|---|
| -dĭdĕram | *-dę(de)ra | -ęra |
| -dĭdĕras | *-dę(de)ras | -ęras |
| -dĭdĕrat | *-dę(de)rat | -ęra |
| -dĭdĕrāmŭs | *-dę(de)rámus | -êramos (§ 154, 1) |
| -dĭdĕrātĭs | *-dę(de)rátes | -ęrades (§ 154, 1) > -êreis (§ 155, 1 and 2) |
| -dĭdĕrant | *-dę(de)rant | -ęram [erę̃] > [erę̃w] (§ 157, 2) |

For the spread and development of these forms, see § 166, 3. The syllable -de-, which fell by haplology, is indicated by inclusion in parentheses, while the Portuguese endings are given with the d detached, as they spread to verbs whose stem does not end in d.

4. The endings of the Classical Latin, Vulgar Latin and Portuguese pluperfect indicative of verbs which have strong preterits are:

| Classical Latin | Vulgar Latin | Portuguese |
|---|---|---|
| -ĕram | *-ę́ra | -ęra |
| -ĕras | *-ę́ras | -ęras |
| -ĕrat | *-ę́rat | -ęra |
| -ĕrāmŭs | *-erámus | -éramos (§ 154, 1) |
| -ĕrātĭs | *-erátes | -érades (§ 154, 1) > -éreis (§ 155, 1 and 2) |
| -ĕrant | *-ę́rant | -ęram [erę̃] > [erę̃w] (§ 157, 2) |

In the whole singular and the third plural the accent shifted to the penult by analogy with weak pluperfects. Thus arose the accented ę of these endings. Compare the development of the third plural of strong preterits (§ 167, 1).

1st and 2d pl.: The e of the first and second plural, which, being unaccented for a time, may have tended to become close, remained open by analogy with the whole singular and the third plural.

**169. IMPERFECT SUBJUNCTIVE.**

1. The endings of the Classical Latin pluperfect subjunctive and the Portuguese imperfect subjunctive of verbs of the first conjugation are:

| Classical Latin | Portuguese |
|---|---|
| *-assem* | *-asse* |
| *-asses* | *-asses* |
| *-asset* | *-asse* |
| *-assēmŭs* | *-ássemos* (§ 154, 1) |
| *-assētĭs* | *-ássedes* (§ 154, 1) > *-ásseis* (§ 155, 1) |
| *-assent* | *-assem* (§ 46, 11) |

For the Latin endings, see § 165.

2. The endings of the Classical Latin pluperfect subjunctive and the Portuguese imperfect subjunctive of verbs of the fourth conjugation are:

| Classical Latin | Portuguese |
|---|---|
| *-īssem* | *-isse* |
| *-īsses* | *-isses* |
| *-īsset* | *-isse* |
| *-īssēmŭs* | *-issemos* (§ 154, 1) |
| *-īssētĭs* | *-issedes* (§ 154, 1) > *-isseis* (§ 155, 1) |
| *-īssent* | *-issem* (§ 46, 11) |

For the Latin endings, see § 165.

3. The Classical Latin forms of the pluperfect subjunctive of the *dare* component of compounds of *dare*, their Vulgar Latin derivatives and the endings which developed from them in Portuguese and became the weak imperfect subjunctive endings of the conjugation resulting from the fusion of the Classical Latin second and third conjugations are given below.

| Classical Latin | Vulgar Latin | Portuguese |
|---|---|---|
| *-dĭdĭssem* | *\*-(dę)dęsse* | *-ęsse* |
| *-dĭdĭsses* | *\*-(dę)dęsses* | *-ęsses* |
| *-dĭdĭsset* | *\*-(dę)dęsset* | *-ęsse* |
| *-dĭdĭssēmŭs* | *\*-dę(dę)ssémus* | *-êssemos* (§ 154, 1) |
| *-dĭdĭssētĭs* | *\*-dę(dę)ssétes* | *-ęssedes* (§ 154, 1) > *-êsseis* (§ 155, 1) |
| *dĭdĭssent* | *\*-(dę)dęssent* | *-ęssem* (§ 46, 11) |

For the spread and development of these forms, see § 166, 3. The syllable *-de-*, which fell by haplology, is

indicated by inclusion in parentheses, while the Portuguese
endings are given with the *d* detached, as they spread to
verbs whose stem does not end in *d*.

4. The endings of the Classical Latin pluperfect subjunctive and the Portuguese imperfect subjunctive of verbs which
have strong preterits are:

| Classical Latin | Portuguese |
|---|---|
| -ĭssem | -ęsse |
| -ĭsses | -ęsses |
| -ĭsset | -ęsse |
| -ĭssēmŭs | -éssemos (§ 154, 1) |
| -ĭssētĭs | -éssedes (§ 154, 1) > -ésseis (§ 155, 1) |
| -ĭssent | -ęssem (§ 46, 11) |

The *ę* of all these endings in Portuguese developed by
analogy with the third plural preterit, the whole singular
and the third plural pluperfect indicative, and the whole
future subjunctive of verbs which have strong preterits.

**170. FUTURE SUBJUNCTIVE.**

1. Classical Latin writers often confused the future perfect indicative and the perfect subjunctive, with the result
that the two tenses became alike except in the first singular
(Sommer, 583–584). Even this difference disappeared in
Vulgar Latin when the two tenses fused into one, with the
-*o* of the first singular of the future perfect indicative
(Tempuslehre, § 282–284). This -*o* survived in Spanish
until the end of the fourteenth century and was the basis
of analogical forms in other tenses, e.g., *quisiesso* (Cid, I,
§ 92). It became *e* by analogy with the third singular
of this tense, the first singular of the personal infinitive
and the first singular of the imperfect subjunctive. This
*e* then fell in Portuguese according to § 46, 2. It is obvious
that the future perfect indicative was dominant in the fusion,
since the perfect subjunctive was much less common than
the future perfect indicative in future conditions and since

the type of conditional sentence formed by the Portuguese (and Spanish) future subjunctive is "more vivid." The "Glosas Silenses" (M-P, Orig, 10–27) abound in examples of the Spanish future subjunctive used to translate the Latin future perfect indicative.

2. The endings of the Classical Latin future perfect indicative and the Portuguese future subjunctive of verbs of the first conjugation are:

| Classical Latin | Portuguese |
|---|---|
| -*āro* | -*ar* (section 1 above) |
| -*āris* | -*ares* |
| -*ārit* | -*ar* (§ 46, 2) |
| -*ārĭmŭs* | -*armos* (§ 154, 2) |
| -*ārĭtĭs* | -*ardes* (§ 154, 2; § 155, 1) |
| -*ārint* | -*arem* (§ 46, 11) |

For the Latin endings, see § 165.

3. The endings of the Classical Latin and Vulgar Latin future perfect indicative and the Portuguese future subjunctive of verbs of the fourth conjugation are:

| Classical Latin | Vulgar Latin | Portuguese |
|---|---|---|
| -*ĭero* | *-*įro* | -*ir* (section 1 above) |
| -*ĭeris* | *-*įres* | -*ires* |
| -*ĭerit* | *-*įret* | -*ir* (§ 46, 2) |
| -*ĭerĭmŭs* | *-*įremus* | -*irmos* (§ 154, 2) |
| -*ĭerĭtĭs* | *-*įretes* | -*irdes* (§ 154,2; §155, 1) |
| -*ĭerint* | *-*įrent* | -*irem* (§ 46, 11) |

For the Vulgar Latin endings, see § 165.

4. The Classical Latin forms of the future perfect indicative of the *dare* component of compounds of *dare*, their Vulgar Latin derivatives and the endings which developed from them in Portuguese and became the weak future subjunctive endings of the conjugation resulting from the fusion of the Classical Latin second and third conjugations are given below.

| Classical Latin | Vulgar Latin | Portuguese |
|---|---|---|
| -dĭdĕro | *-de̜(de)ro | -e̜r (section 1 above) |
| -dĭdĕris | *-de̜(de)ris | -e̜res |
| -dĭdĕrit | *-de̜(de)rit | -e̜r (§ 46, 2) |
| -dĭdĕrĭmŭs | *-(de̜)de̜remus | -e̜rmos (§ 154, 2) |
| -dĭdĕrĭtĭs | *-(de̜)de̜retes | -e̜rdes (§ 154, 2; § 155,1) |
| -dĭdĕrint | *-de̜(de)rent | -e̜rem (§ 46, 11) |

For the spread and development of these forms, see § 166, 3. The syllable -de-, which fell by haplology, is indicated by inclusion in parentheses, while the Portuguese endings are given with the d detached, as they spread to verbs whose stem does not end in d.

1st and 2d pl.: The open e of these endings became close by analogy with the whole singular and the third plural, with the third plural perfect, and with the whole pluperfect indicative and the whole imperfect subjunctive.

5. The endings of the Classical Latin and Vulgar Latin future perfect indicative and the Portuguese future subjunctive of verbs which have strong preterits are:

| Classical Latin | Vulgar Latin | Portuguese |
|---|---|---|
| -ĕro | *-e̜ro | -e̜r (section 1 above) |
| -ĕris | *-e̜res | -e̜res |
| -ĕrit | *-e̜ret | -e̜r (§ 46, 2) |
| -ĕrĭmŭs | *-e̜remus | -e̜rmos (§ 154, 2) |
| -ĕrĭtĭs | *-e̜retes | -e̜rdes (§ 154, 2; § 155,1) |
| -ĕrint | *-e̜rent | -e̜rem (§ 46, 11) |

In the whole singular and the third plural the accent shifted to the penult by analogy with weak future subjunctives. Thus arose the accented e̜ of these endings. Compare the development of the third plural of strong preterits (§ 167, 1).

**171.** IMPERATIVE.

1. The endings of the second singular and second plural imperative of verbs of the first conjugation in Classical Latin and Portuguese are:

| Classical Latin | Portuguese |
|---|---|
| *-a* | *-a* |
| *-āte* | *-ade* > *-ai* (§ 155, 1) |

2. The endings of the second singular and second plural imperative of verbs of the second and third conjugations in Classical Latin and of the conjugation resulting from their fusion in Portuguese are given below.

| Classical Latin 2d Conjugation | Classical Latin 3d Conjugation | Portuguese |
|---|---|---|
| *-ē* | *-e* | *-e* |
| *-ēte* | *-ĭte* | *-ẹde* (§ 148, 1 b) > *-ei* (§ 46, 6; § 155, 1) |

A. The Classical Latin second singular imperative of *dīcĕre*, *facĕre* and *dūcĕre* were *dīc*, *fac* and *dūc*, without the ending *-e*. But the full forms *dīce*, *face* and *dūce* were also used (GVL, § 412). The forms *dīc*, *fac* and *addūc* became *di*, *fa* (Fal, 17) and *adu* in Old Portuguese (§ 97, 2), while *dīce*, *face* and *addūce* became *diz*, *faz* and *aduz* (§ 46, 2) and *dize*, *faze* and *aduze* by analogy with other verbs of the Portuguese second conjugation (§ 152, 2). The forms *diz*, *faz* and *aduz* are still used colloquially.

3. The endings of the second singular and second plural imperative of verbs of the fourth conjugation in Classical Latin and Portuguese are:

| Classical Latin | Portuguese |
|---|---|
| *-ī* | *-i* (old) > *-e* (§ 47, 1) |
| *-īte* | *-ide* > *-i* (§ 46, 9; § 155, 1) |

**172. FUTURE INDICATIVE.**

1. The Classical Latin future indicative was replaced in Vulgar Latin by a periphrastic future consisting of the present indicative of *habēre* and the infinitive. Such futures, in which the order of the two elements is not fixed, still exist in Modern Portuguese (Grund, I, 1023). But two futures with fixed order soon became more common. One was made by placing *de* plus the infinitive after

the forms of the present indicative of *haver*, e.g., *hei de ir*, while the other was made by adding as suffixes to the infinitive the forms of the present indicative of *haver* (minus the element *hav-* of the first and second plural). The endings of the simple future indicative are, accordingly, *-ei*, *-ás*, *-á*, *-emos*, *-eis*, *-ão*. Its simple nature is shown by the loss of the accent of the infinitive component in a few verbs in Old Portuguese, e.g., *salrei* (from *\*salīre-aio*), while its compound nature is shown by constructions found in the early Cancioneiros consisting of two futures formed with one ending, e.g., *direy e non estar* (RF, XXV, 673) and by the continued use of pronoun infixes.

A. In dialectal Portuguese other words besides pronouns are sometimes infixed, e.g., "Qu'eu apartar-me não hei" (Opúsculos, II, 465).

B. In dialectal Portuguese the *de* of analytical futures sometimes became attached to the forms of *haver* and the inflectional ending was transferred to it, e.g., *has de > hades; hão de > hãodem* and *hadem*. See AStNS, CLXX, 231–234.

2. In addition to *salrei* other Old Portuguese futures in which syncope took place as a result of loss of the accent of the infinitive component are: *terrei* (from *\*tenere-aio*), *porrei* (from *\*ponere-aio*), *marrei* (from *\*manere-aio*), *verrei* (from *\*venire-aio*), *querrei* (from *\*quaerere-aio*), *ferrei* (from *\*ferire-aio*), *valrei* (from *\*valere-aio*), *adurei* (from *\*aducere-aio*), *trarei* (from *\*tracere-aio*), *jarei* (from *\*jacere-aio*). These futures (except *trarei*) were replaced by analogical futures re-formed with the infinitive.

A. For the intermediate forms *\*aduzrei*, *\*trazrei*, and *\*jazrei*, see Comp, 333; Manual, § 123, 2.

B. The short infinitives found in *farei* and *direi* originated probably in Vulgar Latin (GVL, § 406).

## 173. CONDITIONAL.

The conditional arose in Vulgar Latin (Tempuslehre, § 29). It was made like the future indicative except that

the imperfect of *haver* (minus the element *hav-*) instead of
the present indicative was used. The endings of the conditional are, accordingly, *-ia, -ias, -ia, -íamos, -íeis, -iam*.

A. The conditional is practically unknown in popular speech
today; the imperfect indicative is taking its place even in the
literary language (Estudos, I, 83–84).

## RADICAL-CHANGING VERBS

**174.** RADICAL-CHANGING VERBS.

Practically all Portuguese vowel sounds vary according
as they are accented or unaccented. Hence, practically all
Portuguese verbs are radical-changing verbs. And most
verbs with radical *e* and *o* of the Portuguese second and
third conjugations display a variation of the radical vowel
even when it is accented; this variation is due to the action
of yod and the action of metaphony.

**175.** RADICAL-CHANGING VERBS WITH RADICAL *a*.

1. Radical *a* is generally pronounced [a] when accented
(§ 33, 1) and [ɐ] when unaccented (§ 40, 1): *fabŭlo > fạlo;
partit > pạrte; fabulāmus > fạlamos; partīmus > pạrtimos*.

A. Verbs with radical *a* followed by a nasal are not radical-
changing verbs because the *a* has become close even when
accented (§ 33, 6): *amo > ạmo; amāmus > ạmamos*.

2. The radical *a* of a few verbs has changed to *ai* in the
first singular present indicative and the whole present subjunctive because of a following yod (§ 33, 2; § 40, 2): *parĭo
> pairo; capĭo > caibo; sapiāmus > saibamos; *aprĭo* (for
*apĕrĭo*) > *aibro* (popular; cf. Moraes, 158).

**176.** RADICAL-CHANGING VERBS WITH RADICAL *e* AND *o*.

1. The following paradigms show the changes of the
present indicative singular of *vertĕre* and *servīre* from
Classical Latin to Modern Portuguese.

| Classical Latin | Old Portuguese | Modern Portuguese |
|---|---|---|
| vẹ̆rto | vẹrto | vẹrto (§ 100, 6) |
| vẹ̆rtis | vẹrtes | vẹrtes |
| vẹ̆rtit | vẹrte | vẹrte |
| sĕrvĭo | sẹrvo (§ 34, 2) | sirvo (§ 100, 6) |
| sĕrvis | sẹrves | sẹrves |
| sĕrvit | sẹrve | sẹrve |

In Old Portuguese there was presumably no change in the first singular of verbs of the Portuguese second conjugation while ę was closed to ẹ by yod in the first singular of verbs of the Portuguese third conjugation. At least, *servo* is the spelling which at first replaced the older *servio*, found in the early Cancioneiros. In the transition to the modern forms through the action of metaphony, *sẹrvo* became *sirvo* and *vẹrto* became *vẹrto*. Thus the vowel of the first singular of verbs of the Portuguese second conjugation was closed one step by the action of metaphony while the vowel of the first singular of verbs of the Portuguese third conjugation was closed two steps by the successive action of a yod and of metaphony. Language, X, 146–147.

The whole singular and the third plural present subjunctive almost always had the same root as the first singular present indicative. Following this general and well-established relationship and in spite of the metaphonic effect of final *a* (§ 100, 4), *vẹrta* became *vẹrta* and *sẹrva* became *sirva*. Such is the force of analogy in its triumph over the force of a phonological change. In verbs of the Portuguese third conjugation this analogical development was supported by analogy with the first and second plural present subjunctive, in which the development of *i* was phonological, e.g., *sĕrvĭāmus > sirvamos* (§ 41, 3).

A. Foerster (ZRPh, III, 505) suggests that vowel variation in the Portuguese third conjugation may have begun in verbs with original radical ọ (Cl. L. ō and ŭ) and spread later to verbs with radical ę (Cl. L. ĕ), e.g., *sŭbĕo* became *subo*, then *sĕrvĭo*

became *sirvo* by analogy with *subo*. His alternate suggestion
that the verb *frigir* may have been the basis for the analogy
seems to be founded on the erroneous assumption that Lat.
*frigere* has radical $\breve{\imath}$ instead of $\bar{\imath}$, and disregards the fact that
none of the verbs supposed to be modeled on *frigir* is conjugated
like it (see section 4 below).

D'Ovidio assumes that the $\rho$ of verbs of the Portuguese third
conjugation with original radical $\rho$ (Cl. L. $\bar{o}$ and $\breve{u}$) developed by
analogy with the $\ell$ of verbs with radical $\ell$ (Cl. L. $\breve{e}$) while the *i*
of verbs with radical $\ell$ (Cl. L. $\breve{e}$) developed by analogy with the
*u* of verbs with original radical $\rho$ (Cl. L. $\bar{o}$ and $\breve{u}$). Thus *sŭbit*
became *spbe* by analogy with *sęrve* (from *sĕrvit*) while *sĕrvio*
became *sirvo* by analogy with *subo* (from *sŭbĕo*). D'Ovidio, 44.

Cornu (Grund, I, 940) assumes that the paradigm of radical-
changing verbs of the Portuguese third conjugation arose first in
verbs with radical $\ell$ (Cl. L. $\bar{e}$ and $\breve{\imath}$) and $\rho$ (Cl. L. $\bar{o}$ and $\breve{u}$) and was
adopted analogically by verbs with radical $\ell$ (Cl. L. $\breve{e}$) and $\rho$ (Cl.
L. $\breve{o}$). The objection to this explanation is that verbs of the
Portuguese third conjugation with original $\ell$ did not fall into this
class, with the possible exception of *despir*, which may have come
from *dē-expedīre* or from *dĕspuīre* (for *despuĕre*) (see Nascentes,
s.v. *despir*). Besides, Cornu's assumption that final *e* opened the
radical vowel and final *a* was neutral in its effect is not only
contrary to the facts as found, for example, in *êste* (from *ĭste*)
and *ęsta* (from *ĭsta*) but has no rational phonetic foundation.
Final *e* is certainly more likely to be neutral in its effect on a
radical *e* than final *a*, in a phenomenon which is clearly one of
vocalic assimilation.

Almeida Cavacas holds that yod closed $\ell$ as well as $\ell$ to *i* in
verbs of the Portuguese third conjugation, e.g., *sĕrvio* > *sirvo*,
while it closed $\ell$ but one step to $\ell$ in verbs of the Portuguese
second conjugation, e.g., *vĕrtĕo* > *vęrto* (Cavacas, 115 and 122).
Cf. ZRPh, IX, 143. But it is impossible to accept a rule of phonology which operates in two ways without provision for a
principle of differentiation. The yod of verbs of the Classical
Latin second conjugation generally disappeared (§ 148, 1 a) and
the hypothetical spread of this yod to verbs of the Classical Latin
third conjugation in forms like *vĕrtĕo* destroys a dissimilarity
originally existing between *vĕrto* and *sĕrvio*, which is the basis

for the dissimilarity in the final outcome.    Even where the yod
of verbs that joined the Portuguese second conjugation actually
survived for a time in Old Portuguese, it had no effect on the
radical vowel in the modern form, which is analogical: *recĭpĭat
> recebia* (Lições, 69, A.D. 1214) > *recęba*, instead of *\*reciba*.

Nunes (Comp, 297, n. 1) explains that in the infinitive radical
*e* became *i* by assimilation to the *i* of the ending and that the
change then spread to the whole indicative and subjunctive.
He also suggests that the change from *e* to *i* may have been due
to the influence of Spanish.    But neither of these explanations
accounts for the differentiation between the first singular present
indicative and the rest of the singular and third plural, for
example, between *sirvo* and *sęrves*.

B. The development of the conjugation of the Spanish verbs
*servir, vestir*, etc. has been variously explained by Menéndez
Pidal (Manual, § 114), Hanssen (Hanssen, § 27, 6), and Fouché
(RHi, LXXVII, 25–44).    But none of these explanations would
account for the development of these verbs in Portuguese.    The
type of verb (with Cl. L. *ē* or *ĭ*) on which Menéndez Pidal bases
his analogy does not fall into this class in Portuguese (e.g.,
*\*mētĭo > męço*) and often does not belong to the third conjugation (e.g., *conceber*); this is true of the type of verb (with Cl. L. *ī*)
on which Hanssen bases his analogy (e.g., *dizer, rir*, in which
dissimilation of the unaccented radical vowel did not take place);
and the phonological phenomenon on which Fouché bases his
argument, viz., *ĕ > ie*, is notably lacking in Portuguese.

C. Metaphonic forms are rare in the early Cancioneiros.    The
form *sirvo* is found twice in an anonymous poem of the "Cancioneiro da Ajuda" (CA, I, No. 307).    In the "Cancioneiro
Geral" they have greatly increased but have not entirely replaced
the older forms.

D. The verb *seguir* (from *\*sĕquīre* for *sĕqui*) is a radical-
changing verb of the *servir* type.    However, it is not clear how
it developed, as it did not have a yod in the first singular present
indicative and in the present subjunctive.    The differentiation
between the first and second singular present indicative could
not be explained by the *y* as this *y* originally existed in all forms
and fell in all forms as a regular phonological change (§ 93, 3)

except in the present subjunctive, where it fell by analogy with the rest of the verb (§ 151, 6). It could not be explained by analogy with the *servir* type because the fully developed forms occur too early, e.g., in the rime *amiga : siga : diga* (CV, No. 404). Perhaps the *i* of *sigo* and *siga* developed through the influence of *digo* and *diga* in the almost equivalent expressions *digo* and *sigo* (*dizendo*), *diga* (impv.) and *siga* (*dizendo*).

E. In some radical-changing verbs of the Portuguese third conjugation radical *ę* (Cl. L. *ĕ*) became *i* in the second and third singular present indicative, third plural present indicative, and second singular imperative through the influence of the first singular present indicative and the whole present subjunctive: *\*aggrĕdis* (for *aggrĕdĕris*) > *agrides*.

2. Verbs with Classical Latin radical *ŏ* had a similar development to that of verbs with Classical Latin radical *ĕ*. The following paradigms show the changes of the present indicative singular of *volvĕre* and *dormīre* from Classical Latin to Modern Portuguese.

| Classical Latin | Old Portuguese | Modern Portuguese |
|---|---|---|
| *vŏlvo* | *vǫlvo* | *vǫlvo* (§ 100, 7) |
| *vŏlvis* | *vǫlves* | *vǫlves* |
| *vŏlvit* | *vǫlve* | *vǫlve* |
| *dŏrmĭo* | *dǫrmo* (§ 37, 2) | *durmo* (§ 100, 7) |
| *dŏrmis* | *dǫrmes* | *dǫrmes* |
| *dŏrmit* | *dǫrme* | *dǫrme* |

A. Hiatus of radical *o* and the vowel of the ending did not interfere with the regular development of radical-changing verbs of the Portuguese second conjugation: *mŏlo* > *môo; mŏlis* > *mǫes*. Cf. section 6 A, below.

3. Verbs with Classical Latin radical *ē* (or *ĭ*) and *ō* (or *ŭ*) have developed in Portuguese by analogy with verbs with Classical Latin radical *ĕ* and *ŏ* (sections 1 and 2 above). They, accordingly, have *ę* and *ǫ* in the first singular present indicative, unaffected by metaphony, e.g., *mĭtto* > *męto; cŭrro* > *cǫrro*, or *u* because of a following yod, e.g., *sŭbĕo* >

*subo; tŭssĭo* > *tusso*, and non-phonological *ę* and *ǫ* in the second and third singular present indicative, third plural present indicative, and second singular imperative, e.g., *mĭttit* > *męte; dēbet* > *dęve; cŭrrit* > *cǫrre; sŭbit* > *sǫbe; tŭssit* > *tǫsse*.

A. This change took place in inchoative verbs: *\*parēscit* > *paręce; \*merēscit* > *meręce*. But where a following consonant group beginning with *n* developed (according to § 78, 5), the vowel was prevented by the nasal from opening (section 8 below): *\*pertĭnēscit* > *pertĕece* > *pertęnce*.

The radical vowel of the second and third singular and third plural present indicative and second singular imperative of two inchoative verbs became *ę* by a regular phonological change, namely, assimilation and contraction (§ 99, 3 A): *\*adcalēscit* > *acaece* > *aquęęce* > *aquęce; \*excadēscit* > *escaece* > *esquęęce* > *esquęce*. This vowel became *ę* in the first singular present indicative also, the assimilating force of the first *e* (from *a*) being apparently greater than the forces of metaphony and of analogy combined: *\*adcalēsco* > *aquęço; \*excadēsco* > *esquęço*. This was the situation as described by Gonçalves Vianna in 1883 (Rom, XII, 77) but in 1920 Almeida Cavacas finds a tendency in these forms to follow the analogy of radical-changing inchoative verbs (Cavacas, 119): *aquęço* > *aquęço; esquęço* > *esquęço*.

B. In many verbs of the Portuguese third conjugation radical *ǫ* (Cl. L. *ō* or *ŭ*) became *u* in all weak forms through the influence of the first singular present indicative and the whole present subjunctive: *sŭbĭmus* > *subimos*. As pretonic *o* is pronounced [u] (§ 43, 1), this change is merely orthographic.

C. Verbs with Classical Latin *ĭ* and *ŭ*, followed by *ng*, have *i* and *u* in all forms in Portuguese and are, therefore, not radical-changing verbs: *cĭngo* > *cingo* (§ 35, 10) > *cinjo* (§ 151, 2); *cĭngāmus* > *cingamos* (§ 41, 11) > *cinjamos* (§ 151, 2); *jŭngo* > *jungo* (§ 38, 12) > *junjo* (§ 151, 2).

D. In the second singular imperative of a few verbs of the Portuguese third conjugation accented radical *ǫ* (Cl. L. *ō* or *ŭ*) was closed to *u* by the *ĭ* of the ending (§ 38, 6): *\*fŭgī* (for *fŭge*) > *fuge* (old and dialectal); *sŭbī* > *sube* (old). These forms have been replaced by forms that developed through the influence of the second singular present indicative: *fǫge; sǫbe.*

4. The verbs *frigir* (from *frīgĕre*) and *sumir* (from *sūmĕre*) have developed in Portuguese by analogy with verbs with Classical Latin radical *e* and *o* (sections 1, 2 and 3 above). They have *ę* and *ǫ* in the second and third singular present indicative, third plural present indicative, and second singular imperative, e.g., *frīgit* > *fręge; sūmit* > *sǫme.* Unlike the *servir* type, *frigir* has radical *i* in all weak forms.

A. In popular speech the verb *luzir* (from *lūcēre*) had the same analogical development, e.g., *lūces* > *lǫzes.*

5. In Old Portuguese a diphthong developed in verbs in which the radical vowel and yod were separated only by a short *r* or *m: fĕrio* > *feiro* (§ 34, 2 A); *\*mŏrio* (for *mŏrior*) > *moiro* (§ 37, 2 A); *cŏmĕdo* > *comio* > *coimo* (§ 37, 2 A). Later *feiro* was replaced by *firo* by analogy with the *servir* type; *moiro* was replaced by *mǫrro* by analogy with the *volver* type, the infinitive being *morrer;* and *coimo* was replaced by *cǫmo* by analogy with the *volver* type, the remaining forms of the present indicative and present imperative that are accented on the radical vowel conforming to this type by regular phonological development, e.g., *cŏmĕdis* > *comees* > *cǫmes.*

This change obviously took place also in the whole present subjunctive (in the first and second plural, according to § 41, 3 A and § 43, 2 A), but here too the phonological forms were replaced by analogical forms.

6. Metaphony did not take place in the first singular present indicative of verbs of the first conjugation. In these forms radical *ę* (Cl. L. *ĕ*) and *ǫ* (Cl. L. *ŏ*) remained open by analogy with the second and third singular and third plural present indicative and present subjunctive and the second singular imperative: *lĕvo* > *lęvo; rŏgo* > *rǫgo.* But cf. the noun *rôgo.*

A. In verbs of the first conjugation, accented radical *o* (Cl. L. *ŏ* or *ō*) in hiatus with *a* or *o* of the ending became or remained *ǫ*:

*corōno* > *corôo; perdōnat* (Du Cange) > *perdôa; cōlat* > *cǫa; sŏno* > *sôo; vŏlat* > *vôa.*  The usual open vowel was avoided in order to prevent assimilation and contraction (according to § 99, 3), which would have destroyed the characteristic *a* of the ending. Analogical *ǫ* is found in the strong forms of the present subjunctive of these verbs: *sŏnet* > *sôe; vŏlet* > *vôe.*

7. Radical *ę* (Cl. L. *ē* and *ĭ*) and *ǫ* (Cl. L. *ō* and *ŭ*) became open in the whole singular and third plural present indicative and present subjunctive and in the second singular imperative of verbs of the first conjugation by analogy with verbs with radical *ę* (Cl. L. *ĕ*) and *ǫ* (Cl. L. *ŏ*): *spēro* > *espęro; cŭrto* > *cǫrto.*

A. Not affected by analogy or metaphony was the form *pesa* (from *\*pesat < pensat*) in the expression *pęsa-me, pęsa-lhe,* etc. and the noun *pêsame.*

B. Verbs with radical *ę* followed by a palatalized consonant were not affected by analogy or metaphony; *\*adconsĭliat* > *aconsęlha* (§ 35, 2 c).  This is also true of one verb with radical *ę* preceded by a palatalized consonant: *plĭcat* > *chęga.*

8. Accented radical *ę* (Cl. L. *ĕ*) and *ǫ* (Cl. L. *ŏ*), followed by a consonant group beginning with *m* or *n*, became close in verbs of all three conjugations (§ 34, 9 and § 37, 6): *vĕndit* > *vęnde; sĕntit* > *sęnte; cŏmpŭtat* > *cǫnta; abscŏndit* > *escǫnde.*

A. These verbs are radical-changing verbs in certain dialects (Rom, XII, 74, n. 1; AStNS, CXXV, 390).

B. A few verbs have analogical forms in which *ē* changed to *ī* and *ō* to *ū*.  Thus the forms *sinto, sinta,* etc. and *minto, minta,* etc. are analogical.  First *\*mentĭo* (for *mentĭor*) became *mença* and *sentĭo* became *sença* (§ 89, 3).  Then *mença* and *sença* were replaced by *mento* and *sento* by analogy with the *servir* type. Finally, when *servo* became *sirvo, mento* and *sento* became *minto* and *sinto,* forms which are first found early in the fifteenth century (Grund, I, 941).  The verb *cumprir* (from *\*complīre* for *complēre*) developed at first by analogy with the *dormir* type; then the *u* spread to all forms of the verb.

9. It seems that there was no metaphony in verb forms whose stems were otherwise differentiated. Thus, *pŏssum* became *pǫsso*, the rest of the tense having the stem *pǫd-*. This is an important factor in the development of the present indicative and present subjunctive of *pedir* and *medir*. There was no metaphony in the first singular present indicative of these verbs: *\*pĕtĭo* > *\*pẹço* (§ 34, 2); *\*mētĭo* (for *mētĭor*) > *\*mẹço* (§ 35, 2 c). In the subjunctive, however, metaphony took place: *\*pĕtĭam* > *\*pẹça* (§ 34, 2) > *pęça* (§ 100, 4); *\*mētĭam* (for *mētĭar*) > *\*mẹça* (§ 35, 2 c) > *męça* (§ 100, 4). Then *\*pẹço* became *pęço* and *\*mẹço* became *męço* through the influence of the whole singular and third plural present subjunctive. The *ę* of the indicative forms *mędes, męde, mędem* and the imperative form *męde* developed by analogy with radical-changing verbs; that it developed early is shown by the rime *pędes : mędes* (CV, No. 942).

10. In radical-changing verbs of all three conjugations, unaccented radical *e* and *o* are generally pronounced [ə] and [u] respectively: *levāmus* > *levamos; rogāmus* > *rogamos; dēbēmus* > *devemos; movēmus* > *movemos; servīmus* > *servimos; dormīmus* > *dormimos*. In the first and second plural present subjunctive of radical-changing verbs of the Portuguese third conjugation, unaccented radical *e* became *i* (§ 41, 3): *sĕrvĭāmus* > *sirvamos;* and unaccented radical *o* became *u* (§ 43, 2): *dŏrmĭāmus* > *durmamos; sŭbeāmus* > *subamos*.

A. An unaccented radical *e* resulting from contraction of secondary tonic *ę* and intertonic *ę* became *ę* (§ 60, 2): *praedĭcāmus* > *preegamos* > *prègamos*. The same development took place in the weak forms of the two inchoative verbs *aquecer* and *esquecer*. First, secondary tonic *a* in hiatus with intertonic *e* became *e* in imitation of the strong forms, in which the *a* in hiatus with tonic *e* regularly became *e* (section 3 A above), e.g., *\*adcalescēbam* > *acaecia* > *aqueecia*. Then, the two *e*'s contracted to *ę* (§ 60, 2):

*aqueecia* > *aquęcia.*   Similarly: *\*excadescēbam* > *escaecia* > *esqueecia* > *esquęcia.*

B. Unaccented radical *e* and *o*, followed by a consonant group beginning with *m* or *n*, became [ẽ] and [õ] respectively in verbs of all three conjugations (§ 41, 10; § 43, 6): *vĕndēbam* > *vęndia; sĕntīmus* > *sęntimos; cŏmputāmus* > *cǫntamos; abscŏndēbam* > *escǫndia.*

C. Unaccented radical *e*, followed by a palatalized consonant became *e* [ị] in verbs of all three conjugations (§ 41, 3 A): *\*adconsiliāmus* > *aconselhamos; mĭscēmus* > *mexemos; vĕstīmus* > *vestimos.*   This change took place also in one verb with unaccented radical *e* preceded by a palatalized consonant: *plĭcāmus* > *chegamos.*

D. Unaccented radical *o*, followed by *l* plus a consonant, became [o] in verbs of the first and second conjugations (§ 43, 7): *fŏllicāmus* > *fǫlgamos; vŏlvēbam* > *vǫlvia; \*soltāmus* (Comp, 140, n. 1) > *sǫltamos.*

11. Verbs with radical *ę* (Cl. L. *ē* or *ĭ*) in hiatus with the vowel of the ending display a different kind of radical change. If the radical vowel was accented and in hiatus with *a* or *o*, it became *ei* (§ 35, 7): *cēno* > *ceio; \*recēlat* > *receia; crēdo* > *creio.* If the radical vowel was unaccented and in hiatus with *a*, it became *e* [j] (§ 99, 5): *cēnāmus* > *ceamos* [sjɐmuʃ].

A. Strong and weak forms in which the radical vowel was in hiatus with *e* developed analogically: *cēnet* > *ceie*, instead of *\*cem* (§ 78, 2); *\*recēlem* > *receie; cēnēmus* > *ceemos* [sjemuʃ]; *cēnāvī* > *ceei* [sjɐj].   In the phonological development the two *e*'s would have contracted.

B. Verbs with Classical Latin radical *ĕ* in hiatus with the vowel of the ending did not become radical-changing verbs in Portuguese: *crĕat* > *cria* (§ 34, 6); *crĕāmus* > *criamos* (§ 99, 5). The first singular present indicative and the whole present subjunctive developed by analogy with forms in which the radical vowel was in hiatus with the *a* of an ending: *crĕo* > *crio; crĕet* > *crie; crĕēmus* > *criemos.*

## UNCLASSIFIABLE VERBS

**177.** Ptg. *aduzir*, OPtg. *aduzer* (Cl. L. *addūcĕre*).

1. General: Intervocalic *c* with *e* or *i* following (§ 73, 2). Intervocalic *dd* (§ 81, 1). Shift to the Portuguese third conjugation (§ 148, 2).

A. In the fusion of the Classical Latin second and third conjugations this verb also adopted in Old Portuguese the endings derived from the Classical Latin second conjugation in the infinitive, the whole plural present indicative, and the second plural imperative (§ 148, 1 b and c), e.g., *aduzer*, *aduzemos*, etc.

2. Present Indicative: 1st sg. *addūco* > OPtg. *adugo* (§ 151, 4 A), replaced by *aduzo* (§ 151, 4). 3d sg. *addūcit* > *aduz* (§ 152, 1). 3d pl. *addūcunt* > *aduzem* (§ 162, 2).

3. Imperative: 2d sg. *addūc* > OPtg. *adu* (§ 171, 2 A); and *addūce* > OPtg. *aduz* and MPtg. *aduze* (§ 171, 2 A).

4. Future Indicative: 1st sg. *\*addūcere-ai̯o* > OPtg. *adurei* (§ 172, 2), replaced by analogical *aduzirei*.

5. Preterit: 1st sg. *addūxī* > OPtg. *adusse* and *aduxe* (§ 92, 9 A), replaced by analogical *aduzi*.

**178.** Ptg. *benzer* (Cl. L. *benedīcĕre*).

1. General: Intervocalic *n* (§ 78, 5); intervocalic *d* (§ 74, 1); intervocalic *c* with *e* or *i* following (§ 73, 2). Fusion with second conjugation (§ 148, 1).

In weak forms of this verb a secondary accent fell on the final vowel of the *bene* component; the *i* of these forms became, accordingly, a yod in early Portuguese, e.g., *benedīcendum* > *bẽéi̯zéndo*. The vowel group *ẽéi* then had the same development as in the past participle (section 7 below): *bẽéi̯zéndo* > *bẽezendo* > *benzendo*. The same change took place in the first and second plural present subjunctive except that a velar *n* developed, e.g., *benedīcāmus* > *bẽeigamos* > OPtg. *bengamos* (§ 78, 6).

In strong forms the accent stood at first on the *i* of the three vowels in hiatus, e.g., *benedīco* > *\*bẽeigo; benedīcis* >

*bĕeízes; it then shifted to the middle vowel by analogy with the weak forms: *bĕeígo > bĕéigo > OPtg. bengo (§ 78, 6); *bĕeízes > bĕéizes > benzes. Cf. RL, XXIII, 13, s.v. bĕeiga.

2. Infinitive: benedĭcĕre > benzer (§ 158, 1).

3. Present Indicative: 1st sg. benedīco > OPtg. bengo, replaced by benzo (§ 151, 4). 1st pl. benedīcĭmus > benzemos (§ 162, 2). 2d pl. benedīcĭtis > benzeis (§ 162, 2). 3d pl. benedīcunt > benzem (§ 162, 2).

4. Imperative: 2d pl. benedīcĭte > benzei (§ 171, 2).

5. Present Subjunctive: 1st sg. benedīcam > OPtg. benga (cf. bengo in section 1), replaced by benza (§ 151, 4). 1st pl. benedīcāmus > OPtg. bengamos (§ 78, 6), replaced by benzamos (§ 151, 4).

6. Preterit: benzi, benzeste, benzeu, etc. are all analogical.

7. Past Participle: benedĭctum > bĕeito > bento (§ 92, 7 A).

**179.** Ptg. *caber* (Cl. L. *capĕre*).

1. General: Intervocalic p (§ 72, 4). Fusion with second conjugation (§ 148, 1).

2. Infinitive: capĕre > caber (§ 158, 1).

3. Gerund: capiendum > cabendo (§ 160).

4. Present Indicative: 1st sg. capĭo (§ 162, 2) > caibo (§ 33, 2). 1st pl. capĭmus > cabemos (§ 162, 2). 2d pl. capĭtis > cabeis (§ 162, 2). 3d pl. capĭunt > cabem (§ 162, 2).

5. Imperative: 2d pl. capĭte > cabei (§ 171, 2).

6. Present Subjunctive: 1st sg. capĭam (§ 163, 2) > caiba (§ 33, 2). 1st pl. capĭāmus > caibamos (§ 40, 2).

7. Preterit: 1st sg. capuī (GVL, § 428) > coube (§ 167, 3). 3d pl. *capuĕrunt (§ 167, 1) > coubĕram (§ 167, 3).

**180.** Ptg. *cair*, OPtg. *caer* (Cl. L. *cadĕre*).

1. General: Intervocalic d (§ 74, 1). Fusion with second conjugation (§ 148, 1). Second conjugation forms have

survived in dialectal Portuguese, where the *a* of the weak forms has been assimilated to the *e* of the endings (according to § 99, 3), e.g., *queer* (RL, XXIII, 15, s.v. *caer*) and *quel* (RL, XXXI, 201). The shift to the Portuguese third conjugation took place in the fourteenth century.

2. Infinitive: *cadĕre* > OPtg. *caer* (§ 158, 1), replaced by *cair* (§ 148, 2; § 99, 4).

3. Present Indicative: 1st sg. V. L. *cadĕo* (for *cado*) > *caio* (§ 89, 5 a). Perhaps [ʒ] was prevented from developing in this form and in the present subjunctive through the influence of the other forms of the present indicative (RL, XXXIII, 198). 3d sg. *cadit* > *cae* > *cai* (§ 99, 5). 1st pl. *cadimus* > *caemos* (§ 162, 2), replaced by *caímos*. 2d pl. *caditis* > *caedes* (§ 162, 2), replaced by *caides*, which became *caís*. 3d pl. *cadunt* > *caem* (§ 162, 2). For OPtg. *caim*, see § 156, 2 c.

**181.** PTG. *crer* (CL. L. *credĕre*).

1. General: Intervocalic *d* (§ 74, 1). Fusion with second conjugation (§ 148, 1).

2. Infinitive: *credĕre* > *creer* (§ 158, 1) > *crer* (§ 99, 2).

3. Present Indicative: 1st sg. *credo* > *creo* > *creio* (§ 35, 7; § 176, 11). 3d sg. *credit* > *cree* > *crê* (§ 46, 4). 1st pl. *credimus* > *creemos* (§ 162, 2) > *cremos*. 2d pl. *creditis* > *creedes* (§ 162, 2) > *credes* (§ 155, 4). 3d pl. *credunt* > *crêem* (§ 162, 2; § 156, 1).

4. Imperative: 2d pl. *credite* > *creede* (§ 171, 2) > *crede* (§ 155, 4).

5. Present Subjunctive: 1st sg. *credam* > *crea* > *creia* (§ 35, 7; § 176, 11). 1st pl. *credamus* > *creamos* [krjɐmuʃ] (§ 99, 5; § 176, 11).

6. Imperfect Indicative: 1st sg. *credebam* > *creia* (§ 164, 2) > *criia* (§ 99, 3) > *cria*.

7. Weak Preterit: 1st sg. *credidi* > *credei* (§ 166, 3) > *creii* (§ 35, 4) > *crei* > *cri* (§ 99, 3). 3d sg. *credidit* > *creu* (§ 166, 3). 3d pl. *credidĕrunt* > *crederon* > *crerom* > *creram* (§ 166, 3). See § 167, 5 A.

8. Strong Preterit: 1st sg. *crēduī (M-L, Intro, § 191) >
crẹvị (§ 93, 7) > OPtg. crive (§ 35, 4; § 47, 1).   Cf. Hanssen, § 31, 13.   3d sg. *crēduit > OPtg. crẹve (§ 93, 7).
3d pl. *crēduĕrunt (§ 167, 1) > OPtg. crevẹrom.

The forms accented on the ending, of this tense and the
derived tenses, e.g., creverom, disappeared before the time
when pretonic e was dissimilated to i as in fizeram and
estiveram.   That the endings of these forms had the ẹ of
the strong preterit and derived tenses is shown by numerous
rimes in the early Cancioneiros, e.g., creverdes : poderdes
(CV, No. 421), quysesse : ouvesse : crevesse (CV, No. 120).

**182.** PTG. dar (CL. L. dare).

1. Present Indicative: 1st sg. dō > dou by analogy with
vou.   This form has also been explained as coming from a
Vulgar Latin hypothetical form: *dao (M-L, Intro, § 188)
> dou, according to § 33, 4.   Algarvio dom developed by
analogy with som (RL, III, 264, n. 3).   3d pl. dant > dam
> dão (§ 157, 2).

2. Present Subjunctive: 1st sg. dĕm > de > dê.   2d sg.
dēs > dês.   3d sg. dĕt > de > dê.   2d pl. dētis > deis
(§ 155, 4).   3d pl. dent > dem > dêem (§ 156, 1).

The e of the first and third singular was open in Old
Portuguese, as is shown by rimes in the early Cancioneiros;
it became close through the influence of the second singular
(RL, XXIII, 24, s.v. dar).

3. Preterit: 1st sg. dĕdī > dei.   A dialectal form di (RL,
II, 27) developed by analogy with the first singular of weak
preterits of the Portuguese second and third conjugations.
2d sg.  dĕdĭstī > *dẹẹstị  (§ 7) > *dẹstị > diste  (§ 35, 4;
Crest, 50), replaced by dẹste by analogy with the first and
third plural.   3d sg. dĕdit > dey (Fab, 108; RL, XXIII,
24, s.v. dar), replaced by dẹu by analogy with the endings
-ou, -ẹu, and -iu.   That the e was open is shown by rimes
in the early Cancioneiros (RF, XXV, 650; BF, I, 301, n. 2).
Then dẹu became dẹu by further analogy with the ending

-*ęu* of weak verbs.   An old and dialectal form *dou* (FM, I,
xxxvi; RL, XXIII, 24; RL, XXVIII, 228; Comp, 334, n. 3)
developed by analogy with the ending of the third singular
preterit of verbs of the first conjugation.   1st pl. *dĕdĭmus*
> *dęmos* with fall of -*di*- by haplology.   2d pl. *dĕdĭstĭs* >
\**dęęstes* > \**dęstes*, replaced by *dęstes* by analogy with the
first and third plural.   3d pl. *dĕdĕrunt* (Lindsay, 532) >
\**dędron* (§ 167, 5) > *dęram* (§ 86, 1).

Similarly some forms of the derived tenses developed by
syncope, e.g., *dĕdĕram* > \**dędra* > *dęra*, some through the
fall of intervocalic *d*, e.g., *dĕdĭssem* > \**dęęsse* (§ 7) > \**dęsse*
> *dęsse* with *ę* by analogy with forms of the preterit, the
pluperfect indicative and the future subjunctive (cf. § 169, 4).

**183.** Ptg. *dizer* (Cl. L. *dīcĕre*).

1. General: Intervocalic *c* with *e* or *i* following (§ 73, 2).
Fusion with second conjugation (§ 148, 1).

2. Infinitive: *dīcĕre* > *dizer* (§ 158, 1).

3. Present Indicative: 1st sg. *dīco* > *digo*.   3d sg. *dīcit*
> *diz* (§ 152, 1).   1st pl. *dīcĭmus* > *dizemos* (§ 162, 2).   2d
pl. *dīcĭtis* > *dizeis* (§ 162, 2).   3d pl. *dīcunt* > *dizem* (§ 162, 2).

4. Imperative: 2d sg. *dīc* > OPtg. *di;* and *dīce* > *diz* and
*dize* (§ 171, 2 A).   2d pl. *dīcĭte* > *dizei* (§ 171, 2).

5. Future Indicative: 1st sg. \**dīre* (GVL, § 406) + *aįo*
> *direi*.

With the pronoun infix the long infinitive was used until
the end of the fourteenth century, e.g., *dizer-me-ha*.

6. Preterit: 1st sg. *dīxī* > *dixe* (old) and *disse*.   See
§ 92, 9 A.

7. Past Participle: \**dīctum* (GVL, § 166) > *dito* (§ 92,
7 B).

**184.** Ptg. *estar* (Cl. L. *stāre*).

1. General: Prosthetic *e* (§ 71, 1).   For dialectal loss of
prosthetic *e*, see RL, II, 40; RL, VII, 47.   The development
of this verb was greatly influenced by forms of *ser*.

2. Present Indicative: 1st sg. *stō* > *estou* by analogy with *vou*. This form has also been explained as coming from a Vulgar Latin hypothetical form: *\*stao* (M-L, Intro, § 188) > *estou*, according to § 33, 4. Dialectal *stom* (Comp, 335, n. 2) developed by analogy with *som*. 1st pl. *stāmus* > *estamos*. Dialectal *stemos* (RL, IV, 46) developed by analogy with *semos* and dialectal *estomos* (RL, XXVI, 254) by analogy with *somos*. 3d pl. *stant* > *estam* > *estão* (§ 157, 2).

3. Present Subjunctive: 1st sg. *stĕm* > *este*, replaced by *esteja* by analogy with *seja*. For the open tonic *e* of *este*, see rime *este : e* (CV, No. 702).

The forms *este*, *estes*, etc. lasted throughout the sixteenth century (FM, I, xxxvii, n. 1).

4. Preterit: 1st sg. *stĕtī* > *estẹvị* > *estive*. There was presumably an Old Portuguese form *\*stẹdi;* cf. 3d sg. *stede* (Eluc). And forms with *d* were common in Old Spanish (Cid, I, § 96, 2). But in Old Portuguese the forms with *d* of this tense and the derived tenses were replaced at an early date by the forms with *v* by analogy with *sẹvị, sevesti*, etc. (Hanssen, § 31, 13). Radical *e* in forms in which it was unaccented became *i* by dissimilation, e.g., *estevẹrom* > *estivẹram*.

**185.** PTG. *fazer* (CL. L. *facĕre*).

1. General: Intervocalic *c* with *e* or *i* following (§ 73, 2). Fusion with second conjugation (§ 148, 1).

2. Infinitive: *facĕre* > *fazer* (§ 158, 1).

3. Gerund: *faciendum* > *fazendo* (§ 160).

4. Present Indicative: 1st sg. *facĭo* (§ 162, 2) > *faço* (§ 89, 2). Dialectal *fazo* developed by analogy with the other forms of the indicative. 3d sg. *facit* > *faz* (§ 152, 1). 1st pl. *facĭmus* > *fazemos* (§ 162, 2). 2d pl. *facĭtis* > *fazeis* (§ 162, 2). 3d pl. *faciunt* > *fazem* (§ 162, 2).

5. Imperative: 2d sg. *fac* > OPtg. *fa* (Fal, 17); and *face* > *faz* and *faze* (§ 171, 2 A). 2d pl. *facĭte* > *fazei* (§ 171, 2).

6. Imperfect Indicative: 1st sg. *faciēbam* > *\*facēbam* (§ 164, 2) > *fazia*.

7. Future Indicative: 1st sg. *\*fare* (GVL, § 404) + *ai̯o* > *farei*.

8. Preterit: 1st sg. *fēcī* > *fiz* (§ 35, 4; § 152, 1). 3d sg. *fēcit* > *fêz* (§ 152, 1). 3d pl. *\*fēcĕrunt* (§ 167, 1) > *fezẹrom* > *fizẹram*.

Radical *e* when pretonic became *i* by dissimilation in this and the derived tenses.

A. The Old Portuguese forms *fige*, *figeste*, etc. developed by analogy with OPtg. *quige*, *quigeste*, etc.; or they may be of dialectal origin, in regions where [z] became [ʒ] (cf. Ent, 302).

B. For the first and third singular forms *fize* and *feze*, see § 143, 3 c.

9. Past Participle: *factum* > *feito* (§ 33, 3).

**186.** PTG. *haver* (CL. L. *habēre*).

1. General: Intervocalic *b* (§ 72, 1).

2. Present Indicative: 1st sg. V. L. *\*ai̯o* (M-L, Intro, § 188) > *\*ai̯* (Manual, § 116, 2) > *hei* (§ 40, 2). 2d sg. V. L. *\*as* (M-L, Intro, § 188) > *has*. 3d sg. V. L. *\*at* (M-L, Intro, § 188) > *ha*. 1st pl. *habēmus* > *havemos*. Dialectal *hamos* developed by analogy with *estamos*. 2d pl. *habētis* > *haveis*. Dialectal *hendes* developed by analogy with *tendes*. 3d pl. *\*hant* (GVL, § 401) > *ham* > *hão* (§ 157, 2).

A. In Baixo-Beirão and in some of the southern dialects, *hade*, formed by the agglutination of the preposition *de* to the third singular, was taken to be a simple verb form. From it a new analogical second singular and a new analogical third plural were formed: *hades*, *hadem*. The latter, through the influence of *hão*, became *hãodem*.

B. OPtg. *hai* was formed by the agglutination of *i* (from *ibī*) to the third singular. An analogical plural of *hai* has been noted in dialectal Portuguese, viz., *haiẽ* (RL, XX, 166).

3. Imperative: 2d sg. *habē* > OPtg. *ave*.   MPtg. *há* was formed from the present indicative by analogy with *está*.

4. Present Subjunctive: 1st sg. *\*aįam* (Manual, § 116, 2) > *haja* (§ 73, 5).

5. Preterit: 1st sg. *habuī* > *houve* (§ 167, 3).   3d pl. *\*habuĕrunt* (§ 167, 1) > *houvęram* (§ 167, 3).

**187.** PTG. *ir* (CL. L. *īre*).

1. General: This verb is composed of parts of Lat. *īre*, *vadĕre* and *esse*.   Intervocalic *d* in forms of *vadĕre* (§ 74, 1).

2. Gerund: Cl. L. *eundum* did not survive; it was replaced by *indo*, formed on the analogy of gerunds of the Portuguese third conjugation (cf. § 160).

3. Present Indicative: 1st sg. *vado* > *\*vao* > *vou* (§ 33, 4 F).   Dialectal *vom* (RL, VII, 46; Opúsculos, II, 115) developed by analogy with *som*.   2d sg. *vadis* > *vais* (§ 99, 5).   3d pl. *vadĭt* > *vai* (§ 99, 5).   Dialectal *vas* and *va* arose either through the regular development of *ai* to *a* (Esquisse, § 56 f) or by analogy with *estás* and *está*.   1st pl. *vadĭmus* > *vamos* by analogy with *estamos* (cf. Manual, § 106, 4 c). Old and dialectal *vomos* (BF, III, 249; RL, VII, 46) developed by analogy with *somos*.   2d pl. *ītĭs* > *ides* (§ 155, 4).   Alto-Beirão *ídes* developed in imitation of *vindes*.   3d pl. *vadunt* > *vão* (§ 157, 2).

4. Imperative: 2d sg. *vade* > *vai* (§ 99, 5).   2d pl. *īte* > *ide* (§ 155, 4) and OPtg. *i*, e.g., *hii* (BF, IV, 92 and 99).

5. Present Subjunctive: 1st sg. *vadam* > *vaa* > *va*.   2d pl. *vadātis* > *vaades* > *vades* (§ 155, 4); 3d pl. *vadant* > *vão* (§ 157, 2 A).

6. Imperfect Indicative: 1st sg. *ībam* > *ia* (§ 164, 3). Dialectal *inha* (RL, IV, 46; RL, VII, 47) developed in imitation of *vinha*.

7. Preterit: This tense and the derived tenses are forms of *ser* (§ 198).   Their use as forms of *ir* resulted from the confusion of place-where and place-whither (Hanssen, § 31, 20).   Cf. French colloquial *j'ai été* for *je suis allé*.

**188.** PTG. *jazer* (CL. L. *jacēre*).

1. General: Intervocalic *c* with *e* or *i* following (§ 73, 2).

2. Present Indicative: 1st sg. *jacĕo* (§ 148, 1 A) > OPtg. *jaço* (§ 89, 2), replaced by analogical *jazo*. 3d sg. *jacet* > *jaz* (§ 152, 1).

3. Imperative: 2d sg. *jacē* > *jaz* (§ 152, 1) and analogical *jaze*.

4. Future Indicative: 1st sg. *\*jacere-aio* > OPtg. *jarei* (§ 172, 2), replaced by *jazerei*.

5. Preterit: 1st sg. *jacuī* > *\*jagui* > *\*jaugi* > *jougue* (§ 167, 3), replaced by *jouve*, which developed by analogy with *houve*, and by *jazi*.

**189.** PTG. *ler* (CL. L. *lĕgĕre*).

1. General: Tonic radical *ę* became *ẹ* through the influence of the corresponding forms of *crer*. Pretonic radical *ę* became *ẹ* (§ 7). Intervocalic *g* with *e* or *i* following (§ 73, 4). Intervocalic *g* with *a* or *o* following (§ 73, 3 A). Fusion with the second conjugation (§ 148, 1).

2. Infinitive: *lĕgĕre* > *lẹẹr* (§ 158, 1) > *ler* (§ 99, 2).

3. Present Indicative: 1st sg. *lĕgo* > *lẹo* > *leio* (§ 35, 7; § 176, 11). 2d sg. *lĕgĭs* > *lees* > *lês*. 1st pl. *lĕgĭmus* > *leemos* (§ 162, 2) > *lêmos*. 2d pl. *lĕgĭtis* > *leedes* (§ 162, 2) *lẹdes* (§ 155, 4). 3d pl. *lĕgunt* > *lêem* (§ 162, 2; § 156, 1).

4. Imperative: 2d pl. *lĕgĭte* > *leede* (§ 171, 2) > *lẹde* (§ 155, 4).

5. Present Subjunctive: 1st sg. *lĕgam* > *lẹa* > *leia* (§ 35, 7; § 176, 11). 1st pl. *lĕgāmus* > *leamos* [ljɐmuʃ] (§ 99, 5; § 176, 11).

6. Imperfect Indicative: 1st sg. *lĕgēbam* > *lẹia* (§ 164, 2) > *liia* (§ 99, 3) > *lia*.

7. Preterit: 1st sg. *lēgī* > *\*lẹi* > *lii* (§ 35, 4) > *li*. 3d sg. *lēgit* > *lẹu* with *-u* by analogy with weak preterits. 1st pl. *lēgĭmus* > *lẹẹmos* > *lêmos*. 2d pl. *lēgĭstis* > *lẹẹstes* > *lêstes*. 3d pl. *lēgĕrunt* (Lindsay, 532) > *\*legron* > *lẹram*. See § 167, 5.

**190.** Ptg. *morrer* (Cl. L. *mŏrī*).

1. General: Change to active endings in Vulgar Latin (§ 13, 4 b).   Fusion with the second conjugation (§ 148, 1). The double *r* of the stem of this verb probably spread from the infinitive, where it developed as follows: *mŏrĕre* (Rönsch, 298) > *morre* (SN, XIX, 167–168) > *morrer,* with an added *r* and shift of accent to conform to verbs of the Portuguese second conjugation (Grund, I, 1029). Cf. V. L. *essĕre* (from *esse,* GVL, § 419). The primitive *morre* is found in the Old Portuguese future *morrei* (cf. Comp, 341, n. 2).

2. Gerund: *mŏriendum* > *morrendo* (§ 160).

3. Present Indicative: 1st sg. *\*mŏrio* (for *mŏrior*) > OPtg. *moiro* (§ 162, 2; § 37, 2), replaced by *mọrro* (§ 176, 5).   1st pl. *\*mŏrimus* (for *mŏrimur*) > *morremos* (§ 162, 2). 2d pl. *\*mŏritis* (for *mŏrimĭnī*) > *morreis* (§ 162, 2).   3d pl. *\*mŏriŭnt* (for *mŏriuntur*) > *morrem* (§ 162, 2).

4. Imperative: 2d sg. *\*mŏre* (for *mŏrĕre*) > *morre.*   2d pl. *\*mŏrĭte* (for *mŏrimĭnī*) > *morrei* (§ 171, 2).

5. Present Subjunctive: 1st sg. *\*mŏriam* (for *mŏriar*) > OPtg. *moira* (§ 163, 2; § 37, 2), replaced by *mọrra* (cf. 1st sg. pres. ind.).   1st pl. *\*mŏriāmus* (for *mŏriāmur*) > *moira-mos* (§ 43, 2), replaced by *morramos.*

6. Future Indicative: 1st sg. *morere* + *ai̯o* > *morrei* (FM, I, xxxviii; CGC, Glossary), replaced by *morrerei.*

7. Past Participle: *mŏrtŭum* > *mŏrtum* (GVL, § 226) > *mọrto* (§ 100, 7); *mŏrtŭam* > *\*mŏrtam* (by analogy with *mŏrtum*) > *mọrta.*

**191.** Ptg. *perder* (Cl. L. *perdĕre*).

1. General: Fusion with second conjugation (§ 148, 1).

2. Infinitive: *perdĕre* > *perder* (§ 158, 1).

3. Present Indicative: 1st sg. *\*perdĕo* > *perço* (§ 89, 6), replaced by *perco.*   The *c* [k] of the Modern Portuguese form *perco* has been explained as due to the influence of the antonyms *venco* (old) and *merco* (Huber, § 378, 17), as due

to the influence of verbs ending in -*sco* (ZRPh, XXXII, 310, n. 2), and as arising in the subjunctive in the curse *Que Deus te perca* through the influence of the antonym *parca* (subjunctive of *parcir*, from Latin *parcĕre*) in the blessing *Que Deus te parca* (ZRPh, XIX, 530; RL, XXIII, 66; H-MP, III, 462–463). 1st pl. *perdĭmus* > *perdemos* (§ 162, 2). 2d pl. *perdĭtis* > *perdeis* (§ 162, 2). 3d pl. *perdunt* > *perdem* (§ 162, 2).

A. Popular and dialectal *perdo* does not come from Cl. L. *perdo* but is doubtless a late analogical development.

4. Imperative: 2d pl. *perdĭte* > *perdei* (§ 171, 2).

5. Present Subjunctive: 1st sg. *\*perdĕam* > *perça* (§ 89, 6,), replaced by *perca* (cf. 1st sg. pres. ind.).

**192.** PTG. *poder* (CL. L. *posse*).

1. General: Intervocalic *t* (§ 74, 2). This verb was partly regularized on the model of verbs of the second conjugation (GVL, § 403; M-L, Intro, § 187).

2. Infinitive: V. L. *pŏtēre* (GVL, § 403, 1) > *poder*.

3. Present Indicative: 1st sg. *pŏssum* > *pǫsso* (§ 176, 9). 2d sg. *pŏtes* > *pǫdes*. 3d sg. *\*pŏtet* (GVL, § 403, 1) > *póde*. 1st pl. *\*pŏtēmus* (GVL, § 403, 1) > *podemos*. 2d pl. *\*pŏtētes* (GVL, § 403, 1) > *podeis*. 3d pl. *\*pŏtent* (GVL, § 403, 1) > *pǫdem*.

4. Present Subjunctive: 1st sg. *\*pŏssam* (for *pŏssim*) > *pǫssa*. 2d sg. *possas* (Sommer, § 346, 4) > *pǫssas*. This tense adopted the endings -*a*, -*as*, etc. by analogy with verbs of the second conjugation.

5. Imperfect Indicative: 1st sg. *potēbam* (GVL, § 403, 1) > *podia*.

6. Preterit: 1st sg. *pŏtuī* > *\*poudi* > *\*pǫdį* (§ 37, 4) > *pude* (§ 38, 6). Cf. ZRPh, III, 506; M-L, Gram, II, § 284. 3d sg. *pŏtuit* > *poude* > *pôde* (§ 37, 4). 3d pl. *\*pŏtuĕrunt* (§ 167, 1) > *podęrom* (§ 43, 5) > *pudęram*.

The change of pretonic radical *o* to *u* in this tense and the derived tenses took place in imitation of the form *pude*. As pretonic *o* had long been pronounced [u], this change was purely orthographic.  See § 167, 3.

**193.** PTG. *pôr*, OPTG. *poer* (CL. L. *pŏnĕre*).

1. General: The modern forms of the infinitive, first and second plural present indicative, and second plural imperative are accented on the same syllable as the Classical Latin forms, but the Old Portuguese forms show the usual shift of accent which verbs of the Classical Latin third conjugation underwent in the fusion of this conjugation with the second conjugation (§ 148, 1); see the rimes *responder : poer* (CV, No. 27) and *cometer : pôer* (CV, No. 663).  Cf. Sp. *poner*.

The change to the modern forms took place early in the sixteenth century.  Fernão de Oliveira says in 1536 that *poer* is still heard "a alghũs velhos" (Oliv, 104).  This extraordinary recession of the accent arose probably in dialectal Portuguese.  Nunes finds an example of *pôr* in an Algarvio document of 1450 (RL, VII, 264).  And corresponding derivatives of *dolēre*, *solēre* and *molēre* are found today in other dialects, viz., *dôr*, *sôr* and *môr* (RL, XIII, 367).

Perhaps *pomos* and *pondes* developed by analogy with *somos* and *sondes;* and *pôr*, *ponde* and also *pondo* followed the analogy of *pomos* and *pondes*.  Cf. dialectal *estomos* and *entromos* (RL, XXVI, 254, n. 2).  The forms *posto*, *posta*, etc., with accented radical *o*, may have contributed also to the shift of accent in all these forms.

A. Meyer-Lübke assumes that *sodes* became *sondes* by analogy with *pondes* (M-L, Gram, II, § 214) but Carolina Michaëlis de Vasconcellos's observation that *sondes* appeared before the time when *poēdes* became *pondes* (ZRPh, XIX, 516, n. 4) shows the invalidity of this assumption and at the same time the possibility at least of the contrary assumption, namely, that *pondes* developed by analogy with *sondes*.

B. Nunes explains *pôr* as a back-formation from the old future *poerei* in which the *e* was practically silent; he points to the colloquial pronunciation *posia* of the word *poesia* as an example of the same change (Comp, 342, n. 3).   But the *o* of these forms is pretonic whereas the *o* of the forms in question is accented. Nobiling explains the recessive accent as due to analogy with the corresponding forms of *ter* and *vir* (RF, XXV, 710).

2. Infinitive: *pŏnĕre* > *põer* (§ 158, 1) > *poer* > *pôr*.

3. Gerund: *pōnendum* > *poendo* > *pondo*.

The accent of the noun *poente* (from *pōnentem*) did not shift to the radical vowel as this word was not affected by the analogy of the forms *pomos* and *pondes*.

4. Present Indicative: 1st sg. \**pŏnĕo* (for *pōno*) > *ponho* (§ 89, 9).   2d sg. *pōnis* > *pões* (§ 78, 3).   3d sg. *pōnit* > OPtg. *pom* (§ 46, 2), replaced by *põe* by analogy with *pões*. For the Old Portuguese form, see the rime *pon : son* (CV, No. 1201).   1st pl. *pŏnĭmus* > *poemos* (§ 162, 2) > *pomos*. 2d pl. *pŏnĭtis* > *poēdes* (§ 155, 4; § 162, 2) > *pondes*.   3d pl. *pōnunt* > *põe* and *põem* (§ 162, 2; § 156, 1).

5. Imperative: 2d sg. *pōne* > OPtg. *pom* (§ 46, 2), replaced by *põe* by analogy with the second singular present indicative.   2d pl. *pōnĭte* > *poēde* (§ 155, 4;   § 171, 2) > *ponde*.

6. Present Subjunctive: 1st sg. \**pŏnĕam* (for *pōnam*) > *ponha* (§ 89, 9).   1st pl. \**pŏneāmus* (for *pōnāmus*) > *ponhamos* (§ 43, 2 A).

7. Imperfect Indicative: 1st sg. *pōnēbam* > *ponia* (§ 164, 2) > *poīa* > *poinha* (§ 78, 4 B) > *puinha* (§ 99, 6) > *púinha* > *punha*.   The last two changes are characteristic of certain dialects of the northeast, e.g., *moinho* (from *mŏlīnum*) > *múinho* (RL, V, 161) and *munho* (Opúsculos, II, 451 and 456).   See § 38, 4 A.

8. Future Indicative: 1st sg. \**pōnere-aįo* > *ponrei* > *porrei* (§ 172, 2), replaced by analogical *poerei* and later *porei*.

9. Preterit: 1st sg. *pŏsuī* > *\*pousi* > *\*pọsị* (§ 37, 4) > *pus* (§ 38, 6; § 152, 1). But cf. Comp, 322, n. 2; RHi, LXXVII, 70. 3d sg. *pŏsuit* > *\*pouse* > *pôs* (§ 37, 4; 46, 2; § 152, 1). 3d pl. *\*pŏsuĕrunt* (§ 167, 1) > *posẹrom* (§ 43, 5) > *pusẹram*.

The change of pretonic radical *o* to *u* in this tense and the derived tenses took place in imitation of the form *pus*. As pretonic *o* had long been pronounced [u], this change was purely orthographic. See § 167, 3.

A. The Old Portuguese forms *puge*, *pugeste*, etc. developed by analogy with OPtg. *quige*, *quigeste*, etc. Or they may be of dialectal origin, in regions where [z] became [ʒ] (cf. Ent, 302). They have also been explained as coming from *posịị*, etc. (Grund, I, 961).

B. For the development of a first singular form *puse* and a third singular form *pose*, cf. § 143, 3 c.

10. Past Participle: *pŏsĭtum* > *pọsto* (§ 8; § 100, 7); *pŏsĭtam* > *pọsta* (§ 8).

**194.** PTG. *querer* (CL. L. *quaerĕre*).

1. General: Fusion with second conjugation (§ 148, 1).

2. Infinitive: *quaerĕre* > *querer* (§ 158, 1).

3. Present Indicative: 1st sg. *quaero* > *quẹro*. It is not clear why metaphony did not take place in this form. 3d sg. *quaerit* > *quer* (§ 46, 2), replaced by *quere* (§ 152, 2). Assimilation of the final *r* of *quer* to the *l* of the direct object pronoun took place in Old Portuguese (according to § 109, 3), e.g., *que-lo* (CV, No. 832). 1st pl. *quaerĭmus* > *queremos* (§ 162, 2). 2d pl. *quaerĭtis* > *quereis* (§ 162, 2). 3d pl. *quaerunt* > *querem* (§ 162, 2).

4. Imperative: *quaere* > *quer* (§ 46, 2) and *quere* (§ 152, 2). 2d pl. *quaerĭte* > *querei* (§ 171, 2).

5. Present Subjunctive: 1st sg. *\*quaerĭam* (for *quaeram*) > *queira* (§ 34, 2). 1st pl. *\*quaeriāmus* (for *quaerāmus*) > *queiramos* (§ 41, 3).

6. Future Indicative: 1st sg. *quaerere-aịo > querrei
(§ 172, 2), replaced by quererei.

7. Preterit: 1st sg. quaesiĭ > *quẹsịị > quige (§ 89, 10),
replaced by quis and quiz (an orthographic variant) in
imitation of pris and fiz. The radical ẹ was closed two
steps to i by the double action of yod (§ 34, 2) and final ị
(§ 35, 4). See D'Ovidio, 46, n. 4. 2d sg. quaesiĭstī >
*quẹsịesti > quigeste, replaced by quiseste. In the weak
forms of this tense and the derived tenses, the radical
vowel closed to ẹ because it was pretonic (§ 7); then ẹ
closed to i because of the yod (§ 41, 3). This radical i
existed in the earliest Portuguese and is therefore unlike
the i of fizeste, estiveste, etc., which is of comparatively late
development and due to dissimilation. 3d sg. quaesiĭt >
*quege, replaced by quige and later by quis. The i of this
form developed by analogy with all other forms of this
tense and the derived tenses.

8. Past Participle: *quaestum (GVL, § 436) > *questo >
quisto by analogy with visto (M-L, Intro, § 195, n. 3), or
through the relation quis : quisto by analogy with the relation pôs : posto (RL, VII, 72–73); quisto was replaced by
analogical querido.

**195.** Ptg. rir (Cl. L. rīdēre).

1. General: Intervocalic d (§ 74, 1). Shift to the Portuguese third conjugation (§ 148, 2). Cf. Sp. reír. Some
forms, such as the third singular present indicatĭve and
the whole imperfect indicative, may have come directly
from the Classical Latin forms without the shift of conjugation.

2. Infinitive: *rīdīre (for rīdēre) > riir > rir.

3. Gerund: rīdendum > riindo (§ 160) > rindo.

4. Present Indicative: 1st sg. *rīdo (for rīdĕo) > rio
(§ 162, 3). 2d sg. rīdes > *ries > riis > ris (§ 99, 3). 3d
sg. rīdet > *rie > rii > ri (§ 99, 3). 1st pl. *rīdīmus (for
rīdēmus) > riimos > rimos. 2d pl. *rīdītis (for rīdētis)

> *riides* > *rides* (§ 155, 4).   3d pl. *rīdent* > *riem* > *riim* > *rim* (§ 99, 3), e.g., *rijn* (RL, XXV, 145).   But *riem* has survived as the standard form in Modern Portuguese (§ 156, 1).

5. Imperative: 2d sg. *rīdē* > *\*rie* > *rii* > *ri* (§ 99, 3). 2d pl. *\*rīdīte* (for *rīdēte*) > *riide* > *ride* (§ 155, 4).

6. Present Subjunctive: 1st sg. *\*rīdam* (for *rīdĕam*) > *ria*.

A. The form *rija* (CV, No. 1106), mentioned by Nobiling as coming from *rīdĕam* (RF, XXV, 700), is probably a variant spelling of *riia*, in which two *i*'s were used in imitation of other forms such as *riir* and *rii*.

7. Imperfect Indicative: 1st sg. *rīdēbam* > *riia* (§ 164, 2) > *ria*.

8. Preterit: 1st sg. *\*rīdī* (for *rīsī*) > *rii* > *ri*.   2d sg. *\*rīdīstī* > *rịịste* (§ 35, 4; § 47, 1) > *riste*.   3d sg. *\*rīdit* > *riu* by analogy with verbs of the Portuguese third conjugation.   1st pl. *\*rīdĭmus* > *\*riemos* > *riimos* > *rimos* (§ 99, 3).   2d pl. *\*rīdĭstis* > *\*riestes* > *ristes* by analogy with verbs of the Portuguese third conjugation.   3d pl. *\*rīdĕrunt* (Lindsay, 532) > *\*rịdron* > *riram*.   See § 167, 5.

9. Pluperfect Indicative: 1st sg. *\*rīdĕram* > *\*rịdra* > *rira*.   1st pl. *\*rīderāmus* > *\*rịdramos* > *riramos* (§ 154, 1).

10. Imperfect Subjunctive: 1st sg. *\*rīdĭssem* > *\*riesse* > *risse* by analogy with verbs of the Portuguese third conjugation.   1st pl. *\*rīdĭssēmus* > *\*riessemos* > *rissemos* (§ 154, 1) by analogy with verbs of the Portuguese third conjugation.

11. Future Subjunctive: 1st sg. *\*rīdĕro* > *\*rịdro* > *rir* (§ 170, 1).   1st pl. *\*rīdĕrĭmus* > *\*riermos* (§ 154, 2) > *rirmos* by analogy with verbs of the Portuguese third conjugation.

12. Past Participle: *\*rīdītum* (for *rīsum*) > *riido* > *rido*.

**196.** PTG. *saber* (CL. L. *sapĕre*).

1. General: Intervocalic *p* (§ 72, 4).   Fusion with second conjugation (§ 148, 1).

2. Infinitive: *sapĕre* > *saber* (§ 158, 1).

3. Gerund: *sapiendum* > *sabendo* (§ 160).

4. Present Indicative: 1st sg. *\*sai̯o* > *\*sai̯* (Rom, XLI, 252) > *sei* (§ 33, 2). The popular form *sabo* developed in imitation of the other forms of the present tense. And dialectal *saibo* developed in imitation of the forms of the present subjunctive. 1st pl. *sapĭmus* > *sabemos* (§ 162, 2). 2d pl. *sapĭtis* > *sabeis* (§ 162, 2). 3d pl. *sapiunt* > *sabem* (§ 162, 2).

5. Imperative: 2d pl. *sapĭte* > *sabei* (§ 171, 2).

6. Subjunctive: 1st sg. *sapĭam* (§ 163, 2) > *saiba* (§ 33, 2). 1st pl. *sapiāmus* > *saibamos* (§ 40, 2).

7. Preterit: 1st sg. *sapuī* (GVL, § 428) > *soube* (§ 167, 3). 3d pl. *\*sapuĕrunt* (§ 167, 1) > *soubĕram* (§ 167, 3).

**197.** Ptg. *sair* (Cl. L. *salīre*).

1. General: Intervocalic *l* (§ 75, 1).

2. Present Indicative: 1st sg. *salĭo* > *saio*. Perhaps [ʎ] was prevented from developing in this form and in the present subjunctive through the influence of the other forms in which there was no yod (§ 89, 8 в). In Modern Galician there is a form *sallo*, i.e., *salho*. 3d sg. *salit* > OPtg. *sal* (§ 46, 2), replaced by *sai* (§ 152, 2).

3. Imperative: 2d sg. *salī* > OPtg. *sal* (§ 47, 2), replaced by *sai* (§ 152, 2). 2d pl. *salīte* > *saide* > *saí* (§ 171, 3).

4. Future: 1st sg. *\*salīre-ai̯o* > OPtg. *salrei* (§ 172, 1), replaced by *sairei*.

**198.** Ptg. *ser* (Cl. L. *sĕdēre*).

1. General: OPtg. *ser* at first meant "to sit," e.g., "hūa seeda . . . em que *sija* hūu rrey" (RL, VIII, 258) and "cadeiras . . . em que *sijam*" (RL, VIII, 260). But it appeared at an early date with the sense of "to be," e.g., "séé en scrito" (AHP, IV, 386, A.D. 1267). And a pun based on the two meanings is found in CV, No. 365; "ben

sej'acá, non quero seer melhor" (RL, XXIII, 82, s.v. *seer*).
The verb derived from *sĕdēre* was conjugated in its entirety
in Old Portuguese but many of its forms were soon replaced by forms of Lat. *esse* (cf. D'Ovidio, 37; AStNS,
LXV, 49, s.v. *sê*; RL, XXIII, 82, s.v. *seer*).　See also RL,
XXVII, 69; RPh, II, 34–48.　Intervocalic *d* in forms of
*sĕdēre* (§ 74, 1).

2. Infinitive: *sĕdēre* > *seer* > *ser*.

3. Present Indicative: 1st sg. *sĕdĕo* > *sejo* (old).　2d sg.
*sĕdes* > *sees* (old).　3d sg. *sĕdĕt* > *sęę* > *sę* (old).　The
open *e* of *se* is shown by the rimes *fe : sse* (CV, No. 636)
and *é : ssé : fé* (CSM, I, p. 55).　1st pl. *sĕdēmus* > *seemos* >
*semos* (old and dialectal).　2d pl. *sĕdētis* > *seedes* > *sedes*
(old) > *sendes* (old and dialectal) with nasal by analogy
with *tendes*.　3d pl. *sĕdent* > *seem* (old).

Except *semos* and *sendes*, which were preserved in dialectal Portuguese through the influence of *temos* and *tendes*
(Esquisse, § 75 l), these forms did not survive but were
replaced by forms of *esse* as follows:

1st sg. *sŭm* > OPtg. *som* or *sõ* > OPtg. *são* (according
to § 157), replaced by *sou* by analogy with *vou* and *estou*.
The form *sõ* became *sõo*, with a second *o* adopted by
analogy with the first singular of other verbs (Theoria, 22;
ZRPh, XIX, 516, n. 7).　Cf. It. *sono*.　Fernão de Oliveira
mentions four forms of the first singular present indicative,
viz., *som*, *são*, *sou* and *so*, and says he prefers the last
(Oliv, 103).　2d sg. *es* > *es*.　3d sg. *est* > *\*es* (§ 97, 7) > *é*.
Final *s* fell because of the relation of this form to the second
singular *es* by analogy with the relation between the third
singular and the second singular of the present tense of all
other verbs in the language (Theoria, 82–83; M-L, Gram, II,
§ 209 and § 214; RF, XX, 593; RF, XXII, 409; Language,
XI, 243).　In the early Cancioneiros the Latin form *est* is
sometimes used; it generally became *este* (with paragogic *e*)
when standing before words beginning with a consonant
(RL, XXIII, 36).　1st pl. *sŭmus* > *somos*.　Old and dia-

lectal *samos* developed by analogy with *estamos*. 2d pl.
**sŭtis* (GVL, § 419, 1) > *sodes* > *sois* (§ 155, 1). The form
*sodes* also became *sondes*, in which the nasal developed
through the influence of the first and third plural (Grund,
I, 1029; ZRPh, XIX, 516, n. 4). See § 193, 1 A. 3d pl.
*sŭnt* > *som* > *são* (§ 157, 2).

4. Imperative: 2d sg. *sĕdē* > **sẹẹ* > OPtg. *sei* (§ 99, 5),
replaced by analogical *sê*. OPtg. *sei* has been explained as
coming from **sĕdī* (Grund, I, 1026) and as developing by
analogy with *vai* (Huber, § 149). 2d pl. *sĕdēte* > *seede* >
*sêde* (§ 155, 4).

5. Present Subjunctive: 1st sg. *sĕdĕam* > *seja* (§ 34, 2;
§ 89, 5). See SpV, § 181. 1st pl. *sĕdeāmus* > *sejamos*
(§ 41, 3 A).

6. Imperfect Indicative: 1st sg. *sĕdēbam* > *sedia* (§ 164,
2) > *sẹia* > *siia* (§ 99, 3) > *sia* (old). The tense thus
formed was replaced by forms of *esse*: 1st sg. *ĕram* > *ẹra*.

7. Future Indicative: 1st sg. **sedere-aịo* > *seerei* > *serei*.
Cf. M-L, Gram, II, § 317.

8. Preterit: 1st sg. **sēduī* (GVL, § 428) > *sẹvị* (§ 93, 7)
> OPtg. *sive* (§ 35, 4; § 47, 1). Cf. Hanssen, § 31, 13. 3d
sg. **sēduit* > OPtg. *sẹve* (§ 93, 7). 3d pl. **sēduĕrunt* (§ 167,
1) > OPtg. *sevẹrom*.

The forms accented on the ending, of this tense and the
derived tenses, e.g., *severom*, disappeared before the time
when pretonic *e* was dissimilated to *i* as in *estiveram*. That
the endings of these forms had the *ẹ* of strong preterits is
shown by the following rimes: *seuesse : teuesse : ouuesse :
esteuesse* (CV, No. 214); *desse : possesse* (i.e., *pusesse*) :
*seuesse* (CSM, I, p. 525).

This tense and the derived tenses were replaced by forms
of *esse* as follows:

1st sg. *fŭī* > *fui* (§ 38, 6). Confusion of *fui* and *foi* was
common in Old Portuguese and still is in certain dialects
(CD, 114). 2d sg. **fọstị* (GVL, § 431) > *fusti* (§ 38, 6) >
*fuste* (RL, XX, 197), replaced by analogical *fọste*. 3d sg.

*fŭit* > *\*foe* > *foi* (§ 46, 10).   1st pl. *\*fǫmos* (GVL, § 431) > *fǫmos.*   2d pl. *fŭstis* (Bourciez, § 210 c) > *fǫstes.*   3d pl. *\*fǫrunt* (GVL, § 431) > *fǫrom* > *fǫram.*   See § 167, 5 b.

A. The dialectal imperfect subjunctive *sêsse* and future subjunctive *ser* (RL, I, 200) are not derived from *sēdissem* and *sēdĕro* but were formed on the analogy of verbs of the second conjugation.

**199.** Ptg. *ter* (Cl. L. *tĕnēre*).

1. General: Intervocalic *n* (§ 78).

A. The compound *entreter* is conjugated in certain dialects as a regular verb of the second conjugation (RL, IV, 45; RL, VII, 47; RL, XXVIII, 232).

2. Infinitive: *tĕnēre* > *tēer* > *ter.*

3. Present Indicative: 1st sg. *tĕnĕo* > *tenho* (§ 34, 2; § 89, 9).   2d sg. *tĕnes* > *tēes* (§ 46, 3) > *tens* (§ 78, 2).   3d sg. *tĕnet* > *tem* (§ 46, 2; § 98, 4; § 34, 10).   1st pl. *tenēmus* > *tēemos* > *temos* (§ 78, 7).   2d pl. *tenētis* > *tēedes* > *tendes* (§ 78, 5; § 155, 4).   3d pl. *tĕnent* > *tēem* (§ 156, 1).

4. Imperative: 2d sg. *tĕnē* > *tem* (§ 46, 2; § 34, 10).   2d pl. *tenēte* > *tēede* > *tende* (§ 78, 5; § 155, 4).

5. Present Subjunctive: 1st sg. *tĕnĕam* > *tenha* (§ 34, 2; § 89, 9).   1st pl. *teneāmus* > *tenhamos* (§ 41, 3 a).

6. Imperfect Indicative: 1st sg. *tenēbam* > *\*tenia* (§ 164, 2) > *tęia* > *tiia* (§ 99, 3) > *tinha* (§ 78, 4 b).   See MLN, XLIII, 469–470.

7. Future Indicative: 1st sg. *\*tenere-aio* > *tenrei* > *terrei* (§ 172, 2), replaced by analogical *teerei*, which became *terei.* An early occurrence of *teerei* is found in CV, No. 540.

8. Preterit: 1st sg. *tĕnui* > *tive* by analogy with *sive* and *estive.*   Meyer-Lübke has endeavored to explain the change from *tĕnui* to *tive* as a phonological change (M-L, Gram, II, § 284).   According to his explanation it would have been necessary for intervocalic *n* to fall before the time when *u* in hiatus with a following vowel became *ụ*.   But we know

that the change of *u* to *ų* had taken place by the first century of our era (GVL, § 224) and that the fall of intervocalic *n* (or at least the nasal resonance left by *n*) did not take place until the Portuguese language was well developed (HR, I, 243). Even in the earliest Portuguese no form of this tense or the derived tenses is found with the radical vowel nasalized. See Hanssen, § 31, 13. For the radical vowel of *tive* and *teve*, see *sive* and *seve* (§ 198, 8) and for the radical vowel of forms accented on the ending, see *estiveram* (§ 184, 4).

9. Past Participle: *\*tenūtum* (§ 159, 1) > *tẽudo* (old) and *teudo* (old), replaced by analogical *tido*.

**200.** PTG. *trazer*, OPTG. *trager* (CL. L. *trahĕre*).

1. General: This verb had apparently two different stems in Vulgar Latin, viz., *\*trac-* and *trag-* (GVL, § 417; RL, II, 269 and 349). Cf. RL, XXIII, 90. *Trager* and its forms have disappeared in Modern Portuguese. In Old Portuguese it was preferred perhaps as more literary to *trazer*, which may have been considered popular. Intervocalic *c* with *e* or *i* following (§ 73, 2). Fusion with the second conjugation (§ 148, 1).

2. Infinitive: *\*tracĕre* > *trazer* (§ 158, 1).

3. Present Indicative: 1st sg. *\*traco* > *trago* (§ 73, 1). 3d sg. *\*tracit* > *traz* (§ 152, 1). 1st pl. *\*tracimus* > *trazemos* (§ 162, 2). 2d pl. *trahĭtis* > OPtg. *treides* (§ 148, 1 B), replaced by *trazeis* (§ 162, 2).

4. Imperative: 2d sg. *trahe* > OPtg. *trei* (§ 33, 2 c). See RL, III, 188. And *\*trace* > *traz* and *traze* (cf. § 171, 2 A). 2d pl. *trahĭte* > *treide* (§ 148, 1 B), replaced by *trazei* (§ 171, 2).

5. Future Indicative: 1st sg. *\*tracere-aįo* > *trarei* (§ 172, 2).

6. Preterit: 1st sg. *\*tracuī* > *\*tragui* > *\*traugi* > OPtg. *trougue* (§ 167, 3). And *\*traxuī* > *\*trauxi* > *trouxe* [trosə]

(§ 92, 9).   Cf. RF, XX, 597; M-L, Gram, II, § 291.   Old and dialectal *trouve* developed by analogy with *houve*.

7. Past Participle: *tractum* > OPtg. *treito* (§ 33, 3), replaced by analogical *trazido*.

**201.** Ptg. *valer* (Cl. L. *valēre*).

1. General: The preservation of intervocalic *l* in forms of *valer* has been explained as due to analogy with forms in which the *l* had ceased to be intervocalic a) because of the development of a yod, e.g., *valho*, *valha*, etc., b) because of the development of *ŭ*, e.g., OPtg. *valvera*, etc., c) because of the fall of the intertonic vowel, e.g., OPtg. *valrei*, etc., and d) because of the fall of the final vowel, e.g., OPtg. *val* (3d sg. pres. ind. and 2d sg. impv.).   See Grund, I, 971; RL, XXIII, 91; RL, XXVIII, 24; Lições, 292; Comp, 112; Huber, § 251, 4.

Perhaps the *l* was kept by preservative analogy.   For if it had fallen, the development of the infinitive would have been: *valēre* > \*vaer > \*veer (§ 99, 3) > \*ver.   Similarly, *valēmus*, *valētis*, and *valendum* would have become respectively \*vemos, \*vedes, and \*vendo.   And *vales* would have become \*vais, identical with the second singular present indicative of *ir*.   Although confusion with forms of *ver* would not have been the immediate result of the fall of *l* (because of the intermediate stage before the assimilation of pretonic *a*), it is possible that the *l* did fall and was later restored to prevent this ultimate confusion.

The Spanish forms doubtless had some influence because of the constant use of this word in commerce.   This influence is seen in the noun *valor*.

2. Present Indicative: 1st sg. *valĕo* > *valho* (§ 89, 8).   3d sg. *valet* > OPtg. *val*, replaced by *vale* (§ 152, 2).

3. Imperative: 2d sg. *valē* > OPtg. *val*, replaced by *vale* (§ 152, 2).

4. Present Subjunctive: 1st sg. *valĕam* > *valha* (§ 89, 8).

5. Future Indicative: 1st sg. *valere-aio > valrei (§ 172, 2), replaced by analogical valerei.

The analogical forms of the future and conditional of this verb began to appear in the early Cancioneiros, e.g., valeredes (CV, No. 655).

6. Preterit: Although forms of the strong preterit (from valuī) are not found, forms of the tenses derived from the strong preterit, viz., valvera, valvesse, valver, are fairly common in the early Cancioneiros. That the endings of these forms had the ę of the strong preterit and derived tenses is shown by rimes in the early Cancioneiros, e.g., valvesse : quisesse (CV, No. 145), mester : valver (CA, No. 31). A strong preterit probably existed, to be replaced at an early date by the analogical weak preterit vali, valęste, etc. (see Huber, § 403, 5). See sections 7, 8, and 9 below.

7. Pluperfect Indicative: 1st sg. *valuĕram > OPtg. valvęra (§ 93, 6; § 168, 4), replaced by analogical valęra.

8. Imperfect Subjunctive: 1st sg. valuissem > OPtg. valvęsse (§ 93, 6; § 169, 4), replaced by analogical valęsse.

9. Future Subjunctive: 1st sg. valuĕro > valvęr (§ 93, 6; § 170, 5), replaced by analogical valęr.

**202.** Ptg. *ver* (Cl. L. *vĭdēre*).

1. General: Intervocalic *d* (§ 74, 1). For contraction of the vowels, see RF, XXV, 666–667.

2. Present Indicative: 1st sg. vĭdĕo > vejo (§ 35, 2 c; § 89, 5). 2d pl. vĭdētis > veedes > vêdes (§ 155, 4). 3d pl. vĭdent > vêem (§ 156, 1).

3. Imperative: 2d pl. vĭdēte > veede > vêde (§ 155, 4).

4. Present Subjunctive: 1st sg. vĭdĕam > veja (§ 34, 2; § 89, 5). 1st pl. vĭdeāmus > vejamos (§ 41, 3 a; § 89, 5).

5. Imperfect Indicative: 1st sg. vĭdēbam > vęia (§ 164, 2) > viia > via (§ 99, 3).

6. Preterit: 1st sg. vīdī > vii > vi. 2d sg. vĭdĭstī > viiste (§ 35, 4; § 47, 1) > viste. 3d sg. vīdit > viu by anal-

ogy with verbs of the Portuguese third conjugation. 1st pl. *vīdĭmus* > *\*viemos* > *viimos* (§ 99, 3) > *vimos*. 2d pl. *vīdĭstis* > *\*viestes* > *vistes* by analogy with verbs of the Portuguese third conjugation. 3d pl. *vīdĕrunt* (Lindsay, 532) > *\*vịdron* > *viram*. See § 167, 5.

7. Pluperfect Indicative: 1st sg. *vīdĕram* > *\*vịdra* > *vira*. 1st pl. *viderāmus* > *\*vịdramos* > *víramos* (§ 154, 1).

8. Imperfect Subjunctive: 1st sg. *vīdĭssem* > *\*viesse*. > *visse* by analogy with verbs of the Portuguese third conjugation. 1st pl. *vīdĭssēmus* > *\*viessemos* > *víssemos* (§ 154, 1) by analogy with verbs of the Portuguese third conjugation (D'Ovidio, 46, n. 5).

9. Future Subjunctive: 1st sg. *vīdĕro* > *vịdro* > *vir* (§ 170, 1). 1st pl. *vīdĕrĭmus* > *\*viermos* (§ 154, 2) > *virmos* by analogy with verbs of the Portuguese third conjugation.

10. Past Participle: *\*vīstum* (§ 159, 3) > *visto*.

**203. Ptg. *vir* (Cl. L. *vĕnīre*).**

1. General: Intervocalic *n* (§ 78).

2. Infinitive: *vĕnīre* > *vẹ̄ir* > *vīir* > *vir* (§ 99, 3).

3. Gerund: *vĕniendo* > *\*venindo* (§ 160) > *\*vẹ̄indo* > *viindo* > *vindo* (§ 99, 3).

4. Present Indicative: 1st sg. *vĕnĭo* > *venho* (§ 34, 2; § 89, 9). 2d sg. *vĕnīs* > *\*venes* (§ 162, 3) > *vẽes* (§ 46, 3) > *vens* (§ 78, 2). 3d sg. *vĕnit* > *vem* (§ 46, 2; § 98, 4; § 34, 10). 1st pl. *venīmus* > *vẹ̄imos* > *viimos* (§ 99, 3) *vimos* [vimuʃ] and [vimuʃ]. 2d pl. *venītis* > *vẹ̄ides* > *viides* (§ 99, 3) > *vindes* (§ 78, 5; § 155, 4). 3d pl. *vĕnĭunt* > *\*vĕnent* (§ 162, 3) > *vẽem* (§ 156, 1).

5. Imperative: 2d sg. *vĕnī* > *\*vẽi* > *vem* [vẽj] (§ 47, 3 A). 2d pl. *venīte* > *vẹ̄ide* > *viide* (§ 99, 3) > *vinde* (§ 78, 5; § 155, 4).

6. Present Subjunctive: 1st sg. *vĕniam* > *venha* (§ 34, 2; § 89, 9). 1st pl. *veniāmus* > *venhamos* (§ 41, 3 A).

7. Imperfect Indicative: 1st sg. *venībam* (§ 164, 3) > *venia* > *vẹia* > *vīia* (§ 99, 3) > *vinha* (§ 78, 4 B). See MLN, XLIII, 469–470.

8. Future Indicative: 1st sg. *\*venire-aịo* > *venrei* > *verrei* (§ 172, 2), replaced by analogical *vēirei*, which became *vīirei* and then *virei*.

9. Preterit: 1st sg. *vēnī* > *vẹi* (RL, XXIII, 93, s.v. *vin*) > *vii* (§ 35, 4; § 47, 4 A) > *vim*. 2d sg. *vēnĭstī* > *vịistị* (§ 35, 4; RL, XXVII, 78, s.v. *viir*), replaced by *vẹẹste* (§ 167, 1), which became *vịẹste* (§ 99, 5). 3d sg. *vēnit* > *veno* (common in OSp.) > *vēo* > *veo* (Miscelânea, II, 61) > *veio* (§ 35, 7; § 149, 3 c). 1st pl. *vēnimus* > *vẹẹmos* (167,1) > *vịẹmos* (§ 99,5). 2d pl. *vēnĭstis* > *vẹẹstes* (§ 167,1) > *vịẹstes* (§ 99, 5). 3d pl. *\*vēnérunt* (§ 167,1) *vẹẹrom* > *vịẹrom* > *vịẹram* (§ 99,5). See RR, XXII, 42-43.

A. For the dialectal forms *vinheste, vinhera*, etc., see § 78, 4 c.

10. Past Participle: *\*venūtum* > OPtg. *vịudo* (§ 99, 6) and *\*venītum* > *vẹido* > *vịido* (§ 99, 3) > *vindo* (§ 78, 5).

# ABBREVIATIONS AND LIST OF BOOKS AND ARTICLES CITED

| | |
|---|---|
| Abraham | Richard D. Abraham, *A Portuguese Version of the Life of Barlaam and Josaphat, Paleographical Edition and Linguistic Study*, Philadelphia, 1938. Codex Alcobacensis 266; Tôrre do Tombo. |
| AGI | *Archivio Glottologico Italiano*, 1873 ff. |
| XIII, 361–446 | F. d'Ovidio, "*scoglio, maglia, veglia* e simili." |
| AHP | *Archivo (Arquivo) Historico Portuguez*, 10 vols., 1903–1916. |
| Ainsworth | Robert Ainsworth, *Thesaurus Linguae Latinae Compendarius* (4th ed.), London, 1761. |
| ALLG | *Archiv für lateinische Lexikographie und Grammatik*, 1884–1908. |
| I, 204–254, 539–557 | Gustav Gröber, "Vulgärlateinische Substrate romanischer Wörter." |
| V, 453–486 | Gustav Gröber, "Vulgärlateinische Substrate romanischer Wörter." |
| Alm | J. Leite de Vasconcellos, "Linguagem Portuguesa de Alamedilla ou 'Almedilha'," in *Estudios Eruditos in Memoriam de Adolfo Bonilla y San Martín*, II, Madrid, 1930, pp. 627–631. |
| Apostilas | A. R. Gonçalvez Viana, *Apostilas aos Dicionários Portugueses*, 2 vols., Lisbon, 1906. |
| ApPr | Wendelin Foerster, "Die *Appendix Probi*," in *Wiener Studien*, XIV, 278–322. |
| AStNS | *Archiv für das Studium der neueren Sprachen und Literaturen*, 1846 ff. |
| LXV, 1–52 | Carolina Michaëlis de Vasconcellos, "Ein portugiesisches Weihnachtsauto." |
| CXXIV, 332–345 | O. Nobiling, "Berichtigungen und Zusätze zum portugiesischen Teil von Körtings Lateinisch-romanischem Wörterbuch." |

| | |
|---|---|
| AStNS | *Archiv für das Studium der neueren Sprachen und Literaturen* (continued). |
| CXXV, 373–392 | Gustav Rolin, "Beiträge zur Kenntnis portugiesischer Orthoepie." |
| CXXV, 393–397 | O. Nobiling, "Berichtigungen und Zusätze zum portugiesischen Teil von Körtings Lateinisch-romanischem Wörterbuch." |
| CXXVI, 424–432 | O. Nobiling, "Berichtigungen und Zusätze zum portugiesischen Teil von Körtings Lateinisch-romanischem Wörterbuch." |
| CXXVII, 181– 188, 371–377 | O. Nobiling, "Berichtigungen und Zusätze zum portugiesischen Teil von Körtings Lateinisch-romanischem Wörterbuch." |
| CLXX, 229–234 | H. Sten, "Zur portugiesischen Syntax (I. Wiederholung des Verbums als Antwort. II. *haver de*)." |
| Barbosa | Jeronymo Soares Barbosa, *Grammatica Philosophica da Lingua Portugueza*, (2d ed.), Lisbon, 1830. |
| Barreto | Joam Franco Barreto, *Ortografia da lingua portugueza*, Lisbon, 1671. |
| Barros | *Compilação de varias obras do insigne portuguez Joam de Barros*, Lisbon, 1785. (1st ed. 1539–1540.) Contains the following works: *Grammatica da lingua portuguesa*, 71–177; *Da orthografia*, 178–206; and *Dialogo em louver da nossa linguagem*, 207–237. |
| Bauer | Charles F. Bauer, *The Latin Perfect Endings* -ere *and* -erunt, Philadelphia, 1933. |
| Bausteine | *Bausteine zur romanischen Philologie*, Halle a. S., 1905. |
| 581–586 | Pedro A. d'Azevedo, "Dois Fragmentos de uma Vida de S. Nicolau do Sec. XIV em Português." Early fourteenth century; Tôrre do Tombo. |
| 676–682 | J. Leite de Vasconcellos, "Dois Textos Portugueses da Idade-Media." *Auto de partilhas*, dated 1192, Tôrre do Tombo; and *Testemunho de confesso*, dated 1293, National Library of Lisbon. |
| Behr | Fritz Behr, *Beiträge zur portugiesischen Lautgeschichte*, Halle a. S., 1903. |

BF                        *Boletim de Filologia*, 1932 ff.

I, 3–7                    José Maria Rodrigues, "Sôbre o Uso do Infinito Impessoal e do Pessoal em *Os Lusíadas*."

I, 40–52, 125–162         Abílio Roseira, "*Vida do cativo monge confesso*."
                          Codex Alcobacensis 181, dated 1416; National Library of Lisbon.

I, 163–165                Rodrigues Lapa, "Transposição e Dissimilação Nasal."
                          Review of article in Language, VII, 142–143.

I, 177–184                José Maria Rodrigues, "Sôbre o Uso do Infinito Impessoal e do Pessoal em *Os Lusíadas*."

I, 199–234                Rodrigues Lapa, "Livros de Falcoaria."

I, 273–356                Rudolf Rübecamp, "A Linguagem das *Cantigas de Santa Maria* de Afonso X o Sábio."

II, 1–2                   José Maria Rodrigues, "Sôbre o Uso do Infinito Impessoal e do Pessoal em *Os Lusíadas*."

II, 105–140               Joseph M. Piel, "Os Nomes Germânicos na Toponímia Portuguesa."

II, 141–152               Rudolf Rübecamp, "A Linguagem das *Cantigas de Santa Maria* de Afonso X o Sábio."

II, 185–191               Joseph M. Piel, "Harri Meier, *Beiträge zur sprachlichen Gliederung der Pyrenäenhalbinsel . . .*, Hamburg, 1930."

II, 207–223, 315–328      Rodrigues Lapa, "A *Vida e feitos de Julio Cesar*."
                          Middle of fifteenth century; Library of the Escorial.

III, 54–58                Abílio Roseira, "*Vida do cativo monge confesso*."

III, 59–76                Jean-Baptiste Aquarone, "A *Vida e feitos de Julio Cesar*."

III, 77–98                R. de Sá Nogueira, "Subsídios para o Estudo da Assimilação em Português."

BF — *Boletim de Filologia* (continued).

III, 153–165 — Abílio Roseira, "Documentos Velhos Brigantinos."
Documents from the Archives of the District of Bragança, circa 1300.

III, 207–217 — Jean-Baptiste Aquarone, "A *Vida e feitos de Julio Cesar.*"

III, 243–280 — Abílio Roseira, "Costumes de Semide."
Study of a dialect, partly Beirão but chiefly Estremenho.

III, 331–332 — Rodrigues Lapa, "Edwin B. Williams, The Portuguese final -ão."
Review of article in Language, IX, 202–206.

III, 350–366 — Jean-Baptiste Aquarone, "A *Vida e feitos de Julio Cesar.*"

III, 395–399 — Abílio Roseira, "Quási Nada de Dialectologia Estremenha."

IV, 6–13 — F. Rebêlo Gonçalves, "Os Filólogos Portugueses do Séc. XVI."

IV, 92–108, 341–357 — Jean-Baptiste Aquarone, "A *Vida e feitos de Julio Cesar.*"

V, 197–198 — Edwin B. Williams, "Uma carta a propósito do ditongo -*ão.*"

BHi — *Bulletin Hispanique*, 1899 ff.

VII, 140–196 — Carolina Michaëlis de Vasconcellos, "Algumas palavras a respeito de púcaros de Portugal."

XXXIX, 397–400 — Jean Bourciez, "Notes sur quelques Faits de la Diphthongaison portugaise."

Biblos — *Biblos* (Faculdade de Letras da Universidade de Coimbra), 1925 ff.

VII, 512–521 — Joseph M. Piel, "Da Evolução dos Grupos Consonânticos com 'L' em Português e Espanhol, a propósito de Duas Etimologias *cocha* e *cascho.*"

VIII, 95–101 — Joseph M. Piel, "Da Vocalização do 'l' em Português."

Bourciez — E. Bourciez, *Éléments de Linguistique romane* (4th ed.), Paris, 1946.

BSC — *Boletim da Segunda Classe* (Academia das Sciências de Lisboa), 1898 ff.

V, 319–335 — Gabriel Pereira, "Trechos Portugueses dos Séculos XIV e XV."

VII, 187–192 — Pedro de Azevedo, "Influência Francêsa em Portugal até 1100."

VII, 334–338 — Cândido de Figueiredo, "Transformações Vocabulares."

VIII, 72–93 — José Maria Rodrigues, "O Imperfeito do Conjuntivo e o Infinito Pessoal no Português."

X, 812–860 — J. J. Nunes, "Convergentes e Divergentes."

XII, 312–331 — Carolina Michaëlis de Vasconcellos, "O Imperfeito do Conjuntivo e o Infinito Pessoal no Português."

BSLi — *Bulletin de la Société de Linguistique de Paris*, 1870 ff.

XXII, 87–88 — A. Meillet, "J. J. Nunes—*Compêndio de gramática histórica portuguesa* . . . Lisbonne, 1919."

CA — Carolina Michaëlis de Vasconcellos, *Cancioneiro da Ajuda* (*edição critica e commentada*), 2 vols., Halle a. S., 1904.

CA-Carter — Henry H. Carter, *Cancioneiro da Ajuda* (*A Diplomatic Edition*), New York, 1941.

Caix-Can — *Miscellanea di Filologia e Linguistica* (*In Memoria di Napoleone Caix e Ugo Angelo Canello*), Florence, 1886.

113–166 — Carolina Michaëlis de Vasconcellos, "Studien zur hispanischen Wortdeutung."

217–229 — J. Cornu, "Recherches sur la Conjugaison espagnole au XIII$^e$ et XIV$^e$ siècle."

263–269 — J. Leite de Vasconcellos, "Etymologias Populares Portuguesas."

Carnoy — A. J. Carnoy, *Le Latin d'Espagne d'après les Inscriptions* (2d ed.), Brussels, 1906.

Carter — Henry H. Carter, *Paleographical Edition*

*and Study of the Language of a Portion of*
Codex Alcobacensis 200, Philadelphia,
1938.

Castelo            *Castelo Perigoso*
Codex Alcobacensis 199, first half of fifteenth century;
original in National Library of Lisbon; photographic
copy in Library of Congress.

Cavacas            Augusto d'Almeida Cavacas, *A Língua
Portuguesa e a sua Metafonia*, Coimbra,
1920.

CB                 Enrico Molteni, *Il Canzoniere Portoghese
Colocci-Brancuti (pubblicato nelle parti che
completano il codice vaticano 4803)*, Halle
a. S., 1880.

CD                 Henry R. Lang, *Das Liederbuch des Königs
Denis von Portugal*, Halle a. S., 1894.

Cd'A               J. J. Nunes, *Cantigas d'Amigo dos Trova-
dores Galego-Portugueses*, 3 vols., Coimbra,
1926–1928.

CG                 E. H. v. Kausler, *Cancioneiro Geral (Alt-
portugiesische Liedersammlung des edeln
Garcia de Resende)*, 3 vols., Stuttgart,
1846–1852.
Other editions: Archer M. Huntington, *Cancioneiro de
Resende (facsimile of the edition of 1516)*, 1904; A. J.
Gonçálvez Guimarãis, *Cancioneiro Geral de Garcia de
Resende*, 5 vols., Coimbra, 1910–1917.

CGC                Henry R. Lang, *Cancioneiro Gallego-
Castelhano*, New York-London, 1902.

Chron              F. George Mohl, *Introduction à la Chrono-
logie du Latin vulgaire*, Paris, 1899.

Cid                R. Menéndez Pidal, *Cantar de Mio Cid*,
3 vols., Madrid, 1908–1911.

C–L                D. Luis Caetano de Lima, *Orthographia da
Lingua Portugueza*, Lisbon, 1736.

Comp               J. J. Nunes, *Compêndio de Gramática Histórica Portuguesa* (3d ed.), Lisbon, 1945.

Cortesão           A. A. Cortesão, *Subsídios para um Diccionário Completo (Histórico-Etymológico)
da Língua Portuguêsa*, 2 vols. and supple-
ment, Coimbra, 1900–1901.

CPh                *Classical Philology*, 1906 ff.

II, 444–460 — Frank F. Abbott, "The Accent in Vulgar and Formal Latin."

CR — *The Classical Review*, 1887 ff.

XV, 311–314 — Carl D. Buck, "The Quantity of Vowels before *gn*."

Cr Cond — Mendes dos Remedios (ed.), *Chronica do Condestabre de Portugal Dom Nuno Alvarez Pereira*, Coimbra, 1911.

Crest — J. J. Nunes, *Crestomatia Arcaica* (2d ed.), Lisbon, 1921, (3d ed.), Lisbon, 1943. Introduction, text and glossary.

Cr Tr — Andrés Martínez Salazar and Manuel R. Rodríguez, *Crónica Troyana (Códice Gallego del Siglo XIV)*, 2 vols., Corunna, 1900.

CSM — *Cantigas de Santa Maria de Don Alfonso el Sabio*, 2 vols., Madrid, 1889.

CV — Ernesto Monaci, *Il Canzoniere Portoghese della Biblioteca Vaticana*, Halle A. S., 1875.

CVB — Theophilo Braga, *Cancioneiro Portuguez da Vaticana (edição critica)*, Lisbon, 1878.

Dauzat — Albert Dauzat, *Histoire de la Langue française*, Paris, 1930.

DC — João Pedro Ribeiro, *Dissertações Chronologicas e Criticas*, I, Lisbon, 1810.

Deux — A. R. Gonçalves Vianna, *Deux Faits de Phonologie historique portugaise*, Lisbon, 1892.

DL — J. J. Nunes, *Digressões Lexicológicas*, Lisbon, 1928.

Dois Problemas — Theodoro Henrique Maurer Jr., *Dois Problemas da Língua Portuguesa—O Infinito Pessoal e o Pronome SE*, São Paulo, 1951.

Dottin — Georges Dottin, *Manuel pour servir à l'Étude de l'Antiquité celtique*, Paris, 1906.

D'Ovidio — F. D'Ovidio, *Portoghese e Gallego (Grammatica)*, Imola, 1881.

Dozy — R. Dozy and W. H. Engelmann, *Glossaire*

|  | *des Mots espagnols et portugais dérivés de l'Arabe* (2d ed.), Leyden, 1869. |
|---|---|
| Du Cange | C. Dufresne Du Cange, *Glossarium Mediae et Infimae Latinitatis*, 7 vols., Paris, 1840–1850. |
| Dunn | Joseph Dunn, *A Grammar of the Portuguese Language*, Washington, D. C., 1928. |
| Eluc | Fr. Joaquim de Santa Rosa de Viterbo, *Elucidario das palavras, termos e frases que em Portugal antigamente se usaram e que hoje regularmente se ignoram* (2d ed.), Lisbon, 1865. |
| Ent | William J. Entwistle, *The Spanish Language* (*together with Portuguese, Catalan and Basque*), London, 1936. |
| Esquisse | J. Leite de Vasconcellos, *Esquisse d'une Dialectologie portugaise*, Paris-Lisbon, 1901. |
| Est Tr | Jules Cornu, "*Estoria Troyãa, acabada era de mil et quatrocentos et onze annos (1373)*," in *Miscellanea Linguistica in Onore di Graziadio Ascoli*, Turin, 1901, pp. 95–128. National Library of Madrid. |
| Estudos | Júlio Moreira, *Estudos da Lingua Portuguesa*, Lisbon, vol. I (2d ed.), 1922; vol. II, 1913. |
| Fab | J. Leite de Vasconcellos, *O Livro de Esopo* (*Fabulario Português Medieval*), Lisbon, 1906. Fifteenth century copy of fourteenth century manuscript, National Library of Vienna. Originally published in RL, VIII, 99–151 and IX, 5–109. |
| Facciolati | Facciolati and Forcellini, *Totius Latinitatis Lexicon*, 2 vols., London, 1828. |
| Fal | Rodrigues Lapa, *Livro de Falcoaria de Pero Menino*, Coimbra, 1931. |
| Fig | Frederico Francisco de la Figanière, *Catalogo dos manuscriptos portuguezes existentes no museu britannico*, Lisbon, 1853. |
| Fink | Oskar Fink, *Studien über die Mundarten der Sierra de Gata*, Hamburg, 1929. |
| FL | A. Braamcamp Freire, *Primeira Parte da Crónica de D. João I por Fernão Lopes*, Lisbon, 1915. |

Flor — J. J. Nunes, *Florilégio da Literatura Portuguesa Arcaica*, Lisbon, 1932.

FM — J. J. Nunes, *Crónica da Ordem dos Frades Menores*, 2 vols., Coimbra, 1918.

Fifteenth century manuscript; National Library of Lisbon.

G–D, C — Vicente García Diego, *Elementos de gramática histórica castellana*, Burgos, 1914.

G–D, G — García de Diego, *Elementos de gramática histórica gallega*, Burgos, 1909.

GilVi — J. Mendes dos Remedios, *Obras de Gil Vicente*, 3 vols., Coimbra, 1907–1914.

Other editions: J. V. Barreto Feio and J. G. Monteiro, *Obras de Gil Vicente*, 3 vols., Lisbon, 1843; *Obras completas de Gil Vicente (Reimpressão "fac-similada" da edição de 1562)*, Lisbon, 1928; Marques Braga, *Obras Completas*, Coimbra, 1933.

GIt — Charles H. Grandgent, *From Latin to Italian*, Cambridge, Mass., 1927.

GPr — Charles H. Grandgent, *An Outline of the Phonology and Morphology of Old Provençal*, Boston, 1909.

Graal — Karl von Reinhardstoettner, *A Historia dos Cavalleiros da Mesa Redonda e da Demanda do Santo Graall*, Berlin, 1887.

National Library of Vienna.

Grund — Gröber's *Grundriss der romanischen Philologie* (2d ed.), 2 vols., Strassburg, 1897–1914.

I, 451–497 — W. Meyer-Lübke, "Die lateinische Sprache in den romanischen Ländern."

I, 916–1037 — Jules Cornu, "Die portugiesische Sprache."

GVL — Charles H. Grandgent, *An Introduction to Vulgar Latin*, Boston, 1908.

Now available in 2d ed. (1952) of Spanish translation by Francisco de B. Moll.

G–V, Port — A. R. Gonçalves Vianna, *Portugais*, Leipzig, 1903.

Hampson — R. T. Hampson, *Medii Aevi Kalendarium*, 2 vols., London, 1841.

Hanssen — Friedrich Hanssen, *Spanische Grammatik*, Halle a. S., 1910.

| | |
|---|---|
| H–MP | *Homenaje a Menéndez Pidal*, Madrid, 1925. |
| I, 607–615 | J. Leite de Vasconcellos, "Observações Gramaticò-lexicais." |
| III, 441–473 | Carolina Michaëlis de Vasconcellos, "Miscelas Etimológicas." |
| HR | *Hispanic Review*, 1933 ff. |
| I, 1–23 | Henry R. Lang, "The Text of a Poem by King Denis of Portugal." |
| I, 243–244 | Edwin B. Williams, "The Preterit of Portuguese *ter*." |
| II, 153–155 | Edwin B. Williams, "The Posttonic Penult in Portuguese." |
| V, 349 | Edwin H. Tuttle, "Spanish *Caja, Quejar, Quijada*." |
| VI, 264–265 | Norman P. Sacks, "Two Portuguese and Spanish Etymologies." |
| VI, 350 | James E. Iannucci, "The Origin of Portuguese *lho* and *lhe*." |
| Huber | Joseph Huber, *Altportugiesisches Elementarbuch*, Heidelberg, 1933. |
| Ineditos | Fr. Fortunato de S. Boaventura, *Collecção de ineditos portuguezes dos seculos XIV e XV*, Coimbra, 3 vols., 1829. |
| JdeV | Juan de Valdés, *Diálogo de la Lengua*. Madrid, 1928. |
| JREL | *Jahrbuch für romanische und englische Literatur*, 1859–1876. |
| VI, 218–220 | A. Mussafia, "*tj = ć* im Altportugiesischen." |
| Jud | Jacob Jud, "Die Zehnerzahlen in den romanischen Sprachen," in *Aus romanischen Sprachen und Literaturen (Festschrift Heinrich Morf)*, Halle a. S., 1905, pp. 233–270. |
| Kent | Roland G. Kent, *The Sounds of Latin (A Descriptive and Historical Phonology)*, Baltimore, 1932. |
| KJ | *Kritischer Jahresbericht über die Fortschritte der Romanischen Philologie*, 1890–1912. |
| IV (Part I), 321–347 | Carolina Michaëlis de Vasconcellos, "Portugiesische Sprache, 1891–1894." |
| Language | *Language*, 1925 ff. |

| | |
|---|---|
| VII, 142–143 | Edwin B. Williams, "Nasal Dissimilation and Transposition in Portuguese." |
| IX, 202–206 | Edwin B. Williams, "The Portuguese Final -ão." |
| X, 145–148 | Edwin B. Williams, "Radical-changing Verbs in Portuguese." |
| XI, 243 | Edwin B. Williams, "Portuguese *ser* in the Third Singular Present Indicative." |
| XI, 243–244 | Edwin B. Williams, "Hiatus in the Third Plural of Portuguese Verbs." |
| XII, 134–135 | Isidore Dyen, "Portuguese *nosso* and *vosso*, *nós* and *vós*." |
| XIII, 145–146 | Roland G. Kent, "Latin *tepidus*, Spanish-Portuguese *tibio*." |
| XIV, 205 | Edwin B. Williams, "Omission of Object Pronoun in Portuguese." |
| LBl | *Literaturblatt für germanische und romanische Philologie*, 1880 ff. |
| XIII, 197–206 | H. Schuchardt, "Michaëlis de Vasconcellos, Caroline, Der portugiesische Infinitiv. Sonderabdruck aus den *Romanischen Forschungen*, Band VII. Erlangen, 1891." |
| LEW | Walde-Hofmann, *Lateinisches Etymologisches Wörterbuch*, Heidelberg, 1930 ff. |
| Lexique | F. G. Mohl, *Études sur le Lexique du Latin vulgaire*, Prague, 1900. |
| L–F | M. Lugrís Freire, *Gramática do Idioma Galego* (2d ed.), Corunna, 1931. |
| Lições | J. Leite de Vasconcellos, *Lições de Filologia Portuguesa* (2d ed.), Lisbon, 1926. |
| Lindsay | W. M. Lindsay, *The Latin Language*, Oxford, 1894. |
| LP | *A Lingua Portuguesa*, 1929 ff. |
| I, 69–72 | J. J. Nunes, "Particípio Perfeito ou Passivo." |
| I, 188–196 | R. de Sá Nogueira, "Curso de Filologia Portuguesa." |
| I, 246–263 | João da Silva Correia, "A Rima e a sua Acção Lingüística, Literária e Ideológica." |
| III, 273–278 | Frazão de Vasconcelos, "Ortografistas Portugueses dos Séculos XVI a XVIII." |

254 ABBREVIATIONS, BOOKS, AND ARTICLES

| | |
|---|---|
| V, 120–129 | Alexandre de Carvalho Costa, "Pronúncia e significação de alguns vocábulos populares do Alto Alentejo." |
| LRW | Gustav Körting, *Lateinisch-romanisches Wörterbuch*, Paderborn, 1891. |
| Lusíadas | Epiphanio da Silva Dias, *Os Lusíadas de Luis de Camões* (2d ed.), 2 vols., Oporto, 1916–1918. |
| Manual | R. Menéndez Pidal, *Manual de gramática histórica española* (10th ed.), Madrid, 1958. |
| M–C | Fr. Luis do Monte Carmelo, *Compendio de orthografia*, Lisbon, 1767. |
| Md'Ar | W. H. Maigne d'Arnis, *Lexicon Manuale ad Scriptores Mediae et Infimae Latinitatis*, Paris, 1890. |
| Meier | Harri Meier, *Beiträge zur sprachlichen Gliederung der Pyrenäenhalbinsel und ihrer historischen Begründung*, Hamburg, 1930. |
| Meillet | A. Meillet, *Linguistique historique et linguistique générale*, Paris, 1926. |
| Miscelânea | *Miscelânea de Filologia, Literatura e História Cultural à Memória de Francisco Adolfo Coelho,* 2 vols., Lisbon, 1949–1950 (BF, X and XI). |
| II, 61 | Edwin B. Williams, "Old Portuguese -*eo* (A Note on the History of Portuguese Orthography)." |
| II, 115–132 | Harri Meier, "A Génese do Infinito Flexionado Português." |
| M–L, Gram | W. Meyer-Lübke, *Grammaire des Langues romanes*, 4 vols., Paris, 1890–1906. |
| M–L, Intro | W. Meyer-Lübke, *Introducción a la lingüística románica* (*Versión de la tercera edición alemana con notas y adiciones por Américo Castro*), Madrid, 1926. |
| M–L, It | W. Meyer-Lübke, *Italienische Grammatik*, Leipzig, 1890. |
| MLN | *Modern Language Notes*, 1886. |
| XLIII, 468–471 | Edwin B. Williams, "Three Irregular Portuguese (and Galician) Imperfects." |

L, 16–17     Edwin B. Williams, "Portuguese Intervocalic *n*."

Mont     Francisco Maria Esteves Pereira, *Livro da Montaria feito por D. João I, rei de Portugal*, Coimbra, 1918.

Moraes     João de Moraes Madureyra Feyjó, *Orthographia ou arte de escrever e pronunciar com acerto a lingua portugueza*, Coimbra (1st ed. 1734), 1739.

MP     *Modern Philology*, 1903 ff.

XI, 347–353     Edwin H. Tuttle, "The Romanic Vowel-System."

XII, 187–196     Edwin H. Tuttle, "Hispanic Notes."

XXVII, 297–302     Edwin B. Williams, "The Portuguese and Spanish Preterit."

M–P, Orig     R. Menéndez Pidal, *Orígenes del español* (3d ed.), Madrid, 1950.

MT     Muller and Taylor, *A Chrestomathy of Vulgar Latin*, Boston, 1932.

Mus     *Le Muséon*, 1881 ff.

III, 209–221     A. R. Gonçalves Vianna, "J. Cornu, Études de Grammaire portugaise." Review of article in Rom, X, 334–345 and XI, 75–96.

Nascentes     Antenor Nascentes, *Dicionário Etimológico da Língua Portuguesa*, Rio de Janeiro, 1932. Vol. II (Nomes Próprios), Rio, 1952.

N–L, Origem     Duarte Nunes de Lião, *Origem da Lingoa Portuguesa*, Lisbon, 1606.

N–L, Orth     Duarte Nunes de Lião, *Orthographia da Lingoa Portugueza*, Lisbon, 1576.

NS     *Die Neuren Sprachen*, 1888 ff.

XI, 129–153     O. Nobiling, "Die Nasalvokale im Portugiesischen."

XXXIV, 456–459     Heinrich Wengler, "Bemerkungen zur Aussprache des heutigen Portugiesischen."

Nyrop     Kristoffer Nyrop, *Grammaire historique de la Langue française*, 6 vols., Copenhagen, 1899–1930.

Oliv      Fernão de Oliveira, *Grammatica da lingoagem portuguesa.* (*Terceira edição feita de harmonia com a primeira (1536) sob a direcção de Rodrigo de Sá Nogueira, seguida de um estudo e de um glossário de Anibal Ferreira Henriques*), Lisbon, 1933.

Onís      Federico de Onís, "Notas sobre el dialecto de San Martín de Trevejo," in *Todd Memorial Volumes*, II, New York, 1930, pp. 63–69.

Opúsculos      J. Leite de Vasconcellos, *Opúsculos*, 4 vols., Coimbra, 1928–1931.

Palestras      A. R. Gonçálves Viana, *Palestras Filolójicas* (2d ed.), Lisbon, 1931.

Pereira      Bento Pereira, *Ars Grammaticae*, Lyons, 1672.

PhM      J. Leite de Vasconcellos, *Estudos de Philologia Mirandesa*, 2 vols., Lisbon, 1900–1901.

PMH      *Portugaliae Monumenta Historica (a saeculo octavo post Christum usque ad quintum decimum, iussu Academiae scientiarum olisiponensis edita*, Lisbon, 1856–1917.

     Published in the following divisions: *Scriptores; Leges et Consuetudines* (2 vols.); *Diplomata et Chartae; Inquisitiones.*

PMLA      *Publications of the Modern Language Association of America*, 1884 ff.

     XX, 1–151      W. H. Chenery, "Object-Pronouns in Dependent Clauses: a Study in Old Spanish Word-Order."

     LI, 636–642      Edwin B. Williams, "*Dialogo em Defensam da Lingua Portuguesa.*"

     Edition of the work of Pedro de Magalhães de Gandavo.

     LV, 360–395      Henry H. Carter, "Paleographical Edition of an Old Portuguese Version of the Rule of Saint Bernard (Codex Alcobacensis 200)."

Pope      M. K. Pope, *From Latin to Modern French with Especial Consideration of Anglo-Norman*, (*Phonology and Morphology*), Manchester, 1934.

| | |
|---|---|
| Questões | F. Adolfo Coelho, *Questões da Lingua Portugueza*, Oporto, 1874. |
| RA | *Revista de Archivos*, 1871 ff. |
|   VII, 112–129 | R. Menéndez Pidal, "Poema de Yúçuf (Transcripción en caracteres latinos)." |
|   XIV, 128–172, 294–311 | R. Menéndez Pidal, "El dialecto leonés." |
| Rad | Clemens Radermacher, *Lautlehre zweier altportugiesischen Heiligenleben (Euphrosyna und Maria Aegyptiaca)*, Bonn, 1899. |
| RB | John M. Burnam, *An Old Portuguese Version of the Rule of Benedict* (paleographical edition), Cincinnati, 1911. (Univ. of Cincinnati Studies, Ser. 2, VII, No. 4.) |
| | Codex Alcobacensis 231; National Library of Lisbon. |
| RC | *Revista da Universidade de Coimbra*, 1912 ff. |
|   VI, 341–371 | Manuel Paulo Merêa, "A Versão Portuguesa das *Flores de las Leyes* de Jácome Ruiz." |
|   XI,[1] 84–93 | Johan Vising, "Bemerkungen zur Geschichte des intervokalen *N* im Portugiesischen." |
|   XI,[1] 1120–1130 | Oliveira Guimarães, "Da Palatização de Grupos Consonantais Próprios em Português." |
| REL | *Revue des Études Latines*, 1923 ff. |
|   IV, 115–119, 212–217 | A. Burger, "Le Parfait latin en -*uī* et le Problème des Formes 'Contractes'." |
| | On the relationship and the relative frequency of the long and short weak endings in Classical Latin. |
| REW | W. Meyer-Lübke, *Romanisches Etymologisches Wörterbuch* (3d ed.), Heidelberg, 1935. |
| RF | *Romanische Forschungen*, 1883 ff. |
|   VI, 299–398 | Richard Otto, "Der portugiesische Infinitiv bei Camões." |
|   VII, 49–122 | Carolina Michaëlis de Vasconcellos, "Der portugiesische Infinitiv." |
|   XX, 560–599 | A. Gassner, "Die Sprache des Königs |

---

[1] RC, XI was published also as *Miscelânea de Estudos em honra de D. Carolina Michaëlis de Vasconcellos.*

Denis von Portugal (Einleitung; Vokalismus; Konsonantismus).''

XXII, 399–425    A. Gassner, "Die Sprache des Königs Denis von Portugal (Formenlehre).''

XXIII,[2] 175–178    J. Leite de Vasconcellos, "Fórmas verbaes arcaicas no Leal Conselheiro de el-rei D. Duarte.''

XXIII,[2] 339–385    Oskar Nobiling, "Zu Text und Interpretation des *Cancioneiro da Ajuda*.''

XXV, 641–719    Oskar Nobiling, "As Cantigas de D. Joan Garcia de Guilhade, Trovador do seculo XIII.''

RFE    *Revista de Filología Española*, 1914 ff.

VII, 57–60    Américo Castro, "Sobre *-tr-* y *-dr-* en español.''

XIX, 117–150,    E. Gamillscheg, "Historia lingüística de
229–260    los visigodos.''

RG    Ernst Gamillscheg, *Romania Germanica*, 3 vols., Berlin, 1934–36.

RHi    *Revue Hispanique*, 1894–1930.

I, 1–21    A. R. Gonçalves Vianna, "Les Langues littéraires de l'Espagne et du Portugal.''

II, 117–119    J. Leite de Vasconcellos, "Remarques sur quelques Vestiges des Cas latins en portugais.''

V, 417–429    J. Leite de Vasconcellos, "Notas Philológicas, II.''

V, 430–434    Julio Moreira, "Étymologies portugaises.''

LXXVII, 1–171    P. Fouché, "Études de Philologie hispanique.''

RL    *Revista Lusitana*, 1887 ff.

I, 30–34    G. de Vasconcellos Abreu, "A Gradação Prosódica de *A.*''

I, 64–65    J. Leite de Vasconcellos, "Para a Historia do *L.*''

I, 68–69    Julio Moreira, "Prolepse Phonetica.''

I, 133–142    F. Adolpho Coelho, "A Etymologia Popular.''

[2] RF, XXIII was published also as *Mélanges Chabaneau*.

| | |
|---|---|
| I, 158–166 | A. R. Gonçalves Vianna, "Materiaes para o Estudo dos Dialectos Portugueses (Fallar de Rio-Frio)." |
| I, 179 | A. Epiphanio Dias, "*Eno = em no.*" |
| I, 192–194 | J. Leite de Vasconcellos, "Português." |
| I, 195–226, 310–319 | A. R. Gonçalves Vianna, "Materiaes para o Estudo dos Dialectos Portugueses." |
| I, 332–345 | F. Esteves Pereira, "Vida de Santo Aleixo." |

I, 332–345 — Codex Alcobacensis 181, first half of fifteenth century (1416), National Library of Lisbon, with variants in Codex Alcobacensis 266, middle of fifteenth century, Tôrre do Tombo.

| | |
|---|---|
| II, 15–45 | J. Leite de Vasconcellos, "Dialectos Alemtejanos." |
| II, 97–120 | J. Leite de Vasconcellos, "Dialectos Trasmontanos." |
| II, 180–181 | A. R. Gonçalves Vianna, "Etymolojia de *Moleiro.*" |
| II, 241–252 | A. Alfredo Alves, "Notas sobre a Linguagem Vulgar da Aldeia de Santa Margarida (Beira-Baixa)." |
| II, 267–272 | J. Leite de Vasconcellos, "Etymologias Portuguesas." |
| II, 344–346 | L. Lucien Bonaparte, "Notas sobre a Classificação de alguns Dialectos Romanicos." |
| II, 347–350 | J. Leite de Vasconcellos, "Notas Philologicas." |
| III, 19–50 | J. Leite de Vasconcellos, "Curso de Lingua Portuguesa Archaica." |
| III, 57–74 | J. Leite de Vasconcellos, "Dialectos Trasmontanos." |
| III, 97–120 | F. M. Esteves Pereira, "Visão de Tundalo." |

III, 97–120 — Codex Alcobacensis 211, circa 1400; National Library of Lisbon.

| | |
|---|---|
| III, 129–190 | Carolina Michaëlis de Vasconcellos, "Fragmentos Etymologicos." |
| III, 251–307 | J. J. Nunes, "Phonetica Historica Portuguesa." |

| | |
|---|---|
| III, 325–329 | Joaquim de Castro Lopo, "Linguagem Popular de Valpaços." |
| IV, 13–77 | J. Leite de Vasconcellos, "Dialectos Alemtejanos." |
| IV, 122–134 | J. Leite de Vasconcellos, "Noticias Philologicas." |
| IV, 134–142 | Pedro A. d'Azevedo, "As Festas dos Imperadores." Documents from Chancery of King Manuel. |
| IV, 188 | José Augusto Tavares, "Linguagem Popular de Ligares." |
| IV, 197–215, 315–324 | Pedro A. d'Azevedo, "Superstições Portuguesas no Sec. XV." |
| IV, 215–246 | J. Leite de Vasconcellos, "Dialectos Alemtejanos." |
| RL | *Revista Lusitana* (continued). |
| IV, 272–278 | J. Leite de Vasconcellos, "Noticias Philologicas." |
| IV, 324–338 | J. Leite de Vasconcellos, "Dialectos Algarvios." |
| V, 52–55 | Sousa Viterbo, "Ourivezeiros." |
| V, 58–62 | J. Leite de Vasconcellos, "Noticias Philologicas." |
| V, 114–136 | Pedro A. d'Azevedo, "O Trovador Martim Soares e seu Filho João Martins." Documents dated from 1269 to 1310, from various archives. |
| V, 137–147 | J. Leite de Vasconcellos, "Dialectos Extremenhos." Contains brief historical account of the dialect. |
| V, 161–174 | Felicio dos Santos, "Lingoagem Popular de Trancoso (Notas para o Estudo dos Dialectos Beirões)." |
| VI, 151–188 | J. J. Nunes, "Subsidios para o Romanceiro Português." |
| VI, 261–268 | Pedro A. d'Azevedo, "A Respeito da antiga Orthographia Portuguesa." |
| VI, 332–346 | Otto Klob, "Dois Episodios da *Demanda do Santo Graal*." Extracts from *Historia dos Cavalleiros da Mesa Redonda e da Demanda do Santo Graal*, fifteenth century; National Library of Vienna. |

VII, 33–55 — J. J. Nunes, "Dialectos Algarvios."

VII, 59–65 — Pedro A. d'Azevedo, "Documentos Antigos da Beira."
Dated 1236, 1275, 1280, 1281.

VII, 68–73 — J. Leite de Vasconcellos, "Etymologias Portuguesas."

VII, 73–75 — Pedro A. d'Azevedo, "Tres Documentos em Português antigo."
Dated 1281, 1281, and 1309.

VII, 104–125 — J. J. Nunes, "Dialectos Algarvios."

VII, 133–145 — J. Leite de Vasconcellos, "Linguagens Fronteiriças de Portugal e Hespanha."

VII, 189–198 — F. M. Esteves Pereira, "Martyrio dos Santos Martyres de Marrocos."

VII, 244–264 — J. J. Nunes, "Dialectos Algarvios."

VIII, 35–45 — Pedro A. d'Azevedo, "Documentos Antigos da Beira."
Dated 1270, 1271, 1274, 1292, 1293.

VIII, 69–70 — J. Leite de Vasconcellos, "*Antre*."

VIII, 80–84 — Pedro A. d'Azevedo, "Testamento, em Português, de D. Affonso II."
Dated 1214. Cf. Lições, 67–100.

VIII, 159–170 — J. Leite de Vasconcellos, "Aula de Philologia Portuguesa."

VIII, 179–183 — Epiphanio Dias, "Notas Criticas a Textos Portugueses (I.Vida de Santa Euphrosina, Vida de Santa Maria Egypcia)."
Texts published in Rom, XI, 357–390.

VIII, 239–262 — J. J. Nunes, "A Visão de Tundalo ou o Cavalleiro Tungullo."
Codex Alcobacensis 266, late fourteenth century; Tôrre do Tombo.

IX, 119–128 — Julio Moreira, "Notas Philologicas."

IX, 135–138 — J. J. Nunes, "Testamento da Infanta D. Leonor Affonso."

IX, 184–186 — J. Leite de Vasconcellos, "Nota sobre o antigo Pronome *che*."

IX, 259–276 — Pedro A. d'Azevedo, "Documentos Portugueses do Mosteiro de Chellas."
Middle and late thirteenth century.

X, 177–190     J. J. Nunes, "Vida de Santa Pelagia."
*Codex Alcobacensis 266, late fourteenth or early fifteenth century; Tôrre do Tombo.*

X, 336–344     J. J. Nunes, "Die Sprache des Königs Denis von Portugal."
*Review of study in RF, XX, 560–599 and XXII, 399–425.*

XI, 79–95     Pedro A. d'Azevedo, "Documentos Portugueses de Pendorada do Século XIII."
*Late thirteenth century.*

XI, 139–145     Carlos A. Monteiro do Amaral, "Tradições Populares e Linguagem de Atalaia (Linguagem Popular: Phonetica e Morphologia)."
*The dialect is Baixo-Beirão.*

XI, 210–222     J. J. Nunes, "Vida de Tarsis, Vida de uma monja, Morte de S. Jeronimo."
*Codex Alcobacensis 266, late fourteenth or early fifteenth century; Tôrre do Tombo.*

XVI, 1–40     J. J. Nunes, "Textos Antigos Portugueses (Glossario; Observações Literarias e Filológicas; Anotações)."

XVI, 41–80     Sousa Viterbo, "As Candeias na Religião, nas Tradições Populares e na Industria."
*Contains documents of fourteenth and fifteenth centuries.*

XVI, 81–100     A. Gomes Pereira, "Gramatica e Vocabulario de Fr. Pantaleão d'Aveiro."
*Second edition of Itinerario, dated 1596.*

XVI, 101–111     Pedro A. d'Azevedo, "Duas Traduções Portugueses do Século XIV."
*Codex Alcobacensis 270 and a fragment, middle of fifteenth century; both in Tôrre do Tombo.*

XVII, 203–206     Pedro A. d'Azevedo, "Nova Leitura da 'Noticia de torto' (Texto do Século XIII)."
*In Tôrre do Tombo.*

XIX, 63–75     J. J. Nunes, "Textos Antigos Portugueses."
*Codex Alcobacensis 270, end of fifteenth century; Tôrre do Tombo.*

XIX, 163–216     F. Alves Pereira, "Glossario Dialectologico do Concelho dos Arcos de Val de Vez (Alto-Minho)."
*Contains "Observações Gramaticais," 171–177.*

| | |
|---|---|
| XX, 165–166 | J. Leite de Vasconcellos, "'Haver' (impessoal) no Plural." |
| XX, 183–205 | J. J. Nunes, "Textos Antigos Portugueses (Vyda de Sancta Maria egiciaca e do sancto homem Zozimas)." <br> Codex Alcobacensis 270, end of fifteenth century; Tôrre do Tombo. |
| XXI, 89–145 | J. J. Nunes, "Textos Antigos Portugueses, (Regra de S. Bento)." <br> Codex Alcobacensis 44, early fifteenth century; National Library of Lisbon. |
| XXI, 246–279 | Pedro d'Azevedo, "O Trovador Martim Soares e sua Familia (Documentos)." |
| XXII, 138–169 | J. J. Nunes, "Textos Antigos Portugueses (História de Dom Rodrigo, último rei godo)." <br> Extract from Portuguese translation of the *Crónica general de España*, now in the Library of the Academy of Sciences of Lisbon, fifteenth century. |
| XXIII, 1–95 | Carolina Michaëlis de Vasconcellos, "Glossario do Cancioneiro da Ajuda." |
| XXV, 5–28 | J. Leite de Vasconcellos, "História da Língua Portuguesa (Origem e Vida externa)." |
| XXV, 128–147 | Pedro A. d'Azevedo, "Uma Versão Portuguesa da História Natural das Aves do Séc. XIV." |
| XXV, 231–250 | J. J. Nunes, "Textos Antigos Portugueses." <br> One extract from *Vidas dos Padres Sanctos*, and one from *Dialogos de San Gregorio*. Probably late fourteenth or early fifteenth century. |
| XXVI, 111–146 | J. Leite de Vasconcellos, "Observações ao *Elucidario* do Pe. Viterbo." |
| XXVI, 247–259 | J. Leite de Vasconcellos, "Linguagem de San Martín de Trevejo (Cáceres: Hespanha)." |
| XXVII, 5–79 | J. J. Nunes, "Contribuição para um Dicionario da Lingua Portuguesa Arcaica." <br> Based on text, part of which was published in RL, XXV, 231–250. |
| XXVII, 86–197 | Celestino Monteiro Soares de Azevêdo, "Ervedosa: Linguagem popular de Ervedosa do Douro." |

XXVII, 243–276    J. Leite de Vasconcellos, "Observações ao *Elucidario* do Pe. Viterbo."

XXVIII, 16–41    "Inéditos de D. Carolina Michaëlis."

XXVIII, 87–244    José Diogo Ribeiro, "Linguagem Popular de Turquel."

XXXI, 164–275    J. Leite de Vasconcellos, "Português Dialectal da Região de Xalma (Hespanha)."

XXXII, 275–293    J. Leite de Vasconcellos, "Ementas Gramaticais (Para a história da língua portuguesa)."

XXXIII, 193–213    J. Leite de Vasconcellos, "Ementas Gramaticais."

XXXIV, 300–312    Rodrigues Lapa, "Joseph Huber, *Altportugiesisches Elementarbuch.*"

RLiR    *Revue de Linguistique Romane*, 1925 ff.

II, 25–112    Joseph Brüch, "Die bisherige Forschung über die germanischen Einflüsse auf die romanischen Sprachen."

R-M    Gerhard Rohlfs, *Manual de Filología Hispánica—Guía bibliográfica, crítica y metódica (Traducción castellana del manuscrito alemán por Carlos Patiño Rosselli)*, Bogotá, 1957.

Contains a large section on Portuguese.

Rom    *Romania*, 1872 ff.

II, 281–294    F. Adolfo Coelho, "Formes Divergentes de Mots portugais."

IX, 580–589    J. Cornu, "Portugais *er ar* = Fr. *re*."

X, 334–345    J. Cornu, "Études de Grammaire portugaise (De l'influence des labiales sur les voyelles aiguës atones)."

XI, 75–96    J. Cornu, "Études de Grammaire portugaise (L'*a* prothétique devant *rr* en portugais, en espagnol et en catalan)."

XI, 357–390    J. Cornu, "Anciens Textes portugais (Vie de sainte Euphrosyne, Vie de sainte Marie Egyptienne, fragments pieux)."

Codex Alcobacensis 266; Tôrre do Tombo.

XII, 29–98        A. R. Gonçalves Vianna, "Essai de Phoné-
                  tique et de Phonologie de la Langue portu-
                  gaise d'après le Dialecte actuel de Lis-
                  bonne."

XII, 243–306      J. Cornu, "Phonologie syntactique du
                  *Cancioneiro Geral*."

XIII, 285–297     J. Cornu, "Mélanges espagnols (Re-
                  marques sur les Voyelles toniques)."

XXII, 71–86       R. J. Cuervo, "Las segundas personas de
                  plural en la conjugación castellana."

XXX, 504–518      Otto Klob, "A Vida de Sancto Amaro
                  (Texte portugais du XIV^e Siècle)."
                  Codex Alcobacensis 266; Tôrre do Tombo.

XLI, 247–259      Georges Millardet, "Sur le traitement de
                  *a + yod* en vieil espagnol."

Romão             José Romão e J. Diogo Correia, *Vocabu-
                  lário Português Abreviado (Em harmonia
                  com a ortografia oficial)*, Lisbon, 1935.

Rönsch            Hermann Rönsch, *Itala und Vulgata*,
                  Marburg u. Leipzig, 1869.

RPh               *Revista de Philologia e de Historia*, Rio de
                  Janeiro, 1931 ff.

  I, 35–39        J. J. Nunes, "Nasalamento."

  II, 34–48       Sousa da Silveira, "Étimo de *Ser*."

RPS               Karl von Reinhardstoettner, *Grammatik
                  der Portugiesischen Sprache*, Strassburg,
                  1878.

RR                *Romanic Review*, 1910 ff.

  III, 310–312    Henry R. Lang, "Spanish and Portuguese
                  *orate*."

  XXI, 142–145    Edwin B. Williams, "The Second Person
                  Plural in Portuguese."

  XXII, 42–43     Edwin B. Williams, "The Preterit of
                  Portuguese *vir*."

  XXVI, 139       Edwin B. Williams, "Shift of Stress in
                  Proparoxytonic Verb-Forms of the First
                  Conjugation in Portuguese."

S–A               Juan A. Saco Arce, *Gramática Gallega*,
                  Lugo, 1868.

Sachs
Georg Sachs, *Die germanischen Ortsnamen in Spanien und Portugal*, Jena u. Leipzig, 1932 (Berliner Beiträge zur Romanischen Philologie, II, No. 4).

Said
M. Said Ali, *Grammatica Historica da Lingua Portugueza*, (2d ed.), São Paulo, 1931.

SaM
Carolina Michaëlis de Vasconcellos, *Poesias de Francisco de Sâ de Miranda*, Halle a. S., 1885.

S–B
Schwan-Behrens, *Grammaire de l'ancien français* (*traduction française par Oscar Bloch*), Leipzig, 1932.

S–D, Gram
A. Epiphanio da Silva Dias, *Grammatica Portuguesa Elementar* (10th ed.), Lisbon, 1899.

Seelmann
E. Seelmann, *Die Aussprache des Latein*, Heilbronn, 1885.

S–G
Schultz-Gora, *Altprovenzalisches Elementarbuch*, Heidelberg, 1906.

SM
*Studi Medievali*, 1904 ff.

  I, 171–234
Alessandro Sepulcri, "Le alterazioni fonetiche e morphologiche nel latino di Gregorio Magno e del suo tempo."

  I, 612–615
Alessandro Sepulcri, "Intorno a *bistia* e *ustium* nel latino volgare."

SN
*Studia Neophilologica*, 1928 ff.
  XIX, 167–168
Bertil Maler, "Portugais *morrer*."

Sommer
Ferdinand Sommer, *Handbuch der lateinischen Laut- und Formenlehre* (2d and 3d ed.), Heidelberg, 1914.

Spaulding
Robert K. Spaulding, *Syntax of the Spanish Verb*, New York, 1931.

SpV
Armin Gassner, *Das Altspanische Verbum*, Halle a. S., 1897.

Studies
Aubrey F. G. Bell, *Studies in Portuguese Literature*, Oxford, 1914.

TA
J. Leite de Vasconcellos, *Textos Arcaicos* (3d ed.), Lisbon, 1923.

TAPA — *Transactions and Proceedings of the American Philological Association*, 1869 ff.

XLVII, 145–152 — Albert J. Carnoy, "Some Obscurities in the Assibilation of *ti* and *di* before a Vowel in Vulgar Latin."

Tempuslehre — Ernst Gamillscheg, "Studien zur Vorgeschichte einer romanischen Tempuslehre," in *Sitzungsberichte der Kaiserlichen Akademie der Wissenschaften in Wien (Philosophisch-Historische Klasse)*, vol. CLXXII.

Theoria — F. Adolfo Coelho, *Theoria da Conjugação em Latim e Portuguez*, Lisbon, 1870.

Thurneysen — Rudolf Thurneysen, *Das Verbum être und die französische Conjugation*, Halle, 1882.

Traité — Maurice Grammont, *Traité de Phonétique*, Paris, 1933.

Vaughan — H. H. Vaughan, *The Dialects of Central Italy*, Philadelphia, 1915.

VO — A. R. Gonçalvez Viana, *Vocabulário Ortográfico e Ortoépico da Língua Portuguesa*, Lisbon, 1909.

Vok — Hugo Schuchardt, *Der Vokalismus des Vulgärlateins*, 3 vols., Leipzig, 1866–1868.

VPN — A. R. Gonçalves Vianna, *Exposição da Pronuncia Normal Portuguesa*, Lisbon, 1892.

Wechssler — Eduard Wechssler, "Giebt es Lautgesetze?" in *Forschungen zur romanischen Philologie (Festgabe für Hermann Suchier)*, Halle a. S., 1900, pp. 349–538.

Wern — H. Wernekke, *Zur Syntax des portugiesischen Verbs*, Weimar, 1885.

ZRPh — *Zeitschrift für romanische Philologie*, 1877 ff.

III, 481–517 — W. Foerster, "Beiträge zur romanischen Lautlehre—Umlaut (eigentlich Vocalsteigerung) im Romanischen."

IV, 591–609 — Carolina Michaëlis de Vasconcellos, "Wilhelm Storck, *Luis de Camoens'* Sämmtliche Gedichte, Paderborn, 1880."

V, 249–322 — H. Schuchardt, "Die Cantes Flamencos."

VIII, 82–105     Fr..d'Ovidio, "I riflessi romanzi di *viginti, triginta, quadraginta, quinquaginta, sexaginta, sept(u)aginta, oct(u)aginta, nonaginta \*novaginta.*"

VIII, 205–242     W. Meyer-Lübke, "Beiträge zur romanischen Laut- und Formenlehre (Die Behandlung tonloser Paenultima)."

IX, 143–146     W. Meyer-Lübke, "Zu den Auslautgesetzen."

IX, 223–267     W. Meyer-Lübke, "Beiträge zur romanischen Laut- und Formenlehre (Zum schwachen Perfectum)."

XIII, 213–224     H. R. Lang, "Notas de Philologia portuguesa."

XIX, 513–541     Carolina Michaëlis de Vasconcellos, "Zum Liederbuch des Königs Denis von Portugal."

XIX, 578–615     Carolina Michaëlis de Vasconcellos, "Henry R. Lang: *Das Liederbuch des Königs Denis von Portugal.*"

XXI, 313–334     W. Meyer-Lübke, "Zur Stellung der tonlosen Objektspronomina."

XXVIII, 602–603     W. Meyer-Lübke, "Portug. *colaga.*"

XXXII, 129–160, 290–311, 385–399     H. R. Lang, "Zum Cancioneiro da Ajuda."

XLI, 555–565     W. Meyer-Lübke, "Beiträge zur romanischen Laut- und Formenlehre (Die Entwicklung von zwischensilbischem *n*)."

XLII, 227–230     Josef Brüch, "Die Entwicklung von *gr* im Spanischen und Portugiesischen."

LVII, 629–633     Harri Meier, "Joseph Huber, *Altportugiesisches Elementarbuch.*"

## SUPPLEMENTARY SELECTIVE BIBLIOGRAPHY

Most of these items are not quoted in the present work but the list is offered as a guide to those who may desire further orientation in the field of Old and Modern Portuguese.

## Manuscript Collections

António Anselmo, *Os Códices Alcobacenses da Biblioteca Nacional* (I. *Códices Portugueses*), Lisbon, 1926.

Frederico Francisco de la Figanière, *Catalogo dos Manuscriptos Portuguezes Existentes no Museu Britannico*, Lisbon, 1853.

Henry A. Grubbs, *The Manuscript Book Collections of Spain and Portugal*, New York, 1933.

Gerhard Moldenhauer, "Bibliographischer Wegweiser zu den Handschriftenbestände in Portugal," *Zentralblatt für Bibliothekswesen*, XLII (Leipzig, 1925), pp. 25–31.

Alfred Morel Fatio, *Catalogue des Manuscrits espagnols et des Manuscrits portugais de la Bibliothèque Nationale*, 2 vols., Paris, 1882–92.

Pedro Tovar, *Catálogo dos Manuscritos Portugueses ou relativos a Portugal existentes no Museu Britânico*, Coimbra, 1932.

## Paleography

John M. Burnam, *Palaeographia Iberica (Fac-Similés de Manuscrits Espagnols et Portugais avec Notices et Transcriptions)*, 3 vols., Paris, 1912–1925.

## Bibliography

Aubrey F. G. Bell, *Portuguese Bibliography*, Oxford, 1922.

Fidelino de Figueiredo, *Textos Portugueses Medievaes (Subsidio para um Inventario Bibliographico)*, Madrid, 1934. (Reprint from *Las Ciencias*, Madrid, Año I, No. 4.)

Innocencio Francisco da Silva, *Diccionario Bibliographico Portuguez*, Lisbon, 1858 ff.

## Syntax

A. Epiphânio da Silva Dias, *Syntaxe Historica Portuguesa* (2d ed.), Lisbon, 1933.

## Portuguese Literature

Aubrey F. G. Bell, *Studies in Portuguese Literature*, Oxford, 1914.

Aubrey F. G. Bell, *Portuguese Literature*, Oxford, 1922.

Hernâni Cidade, *Lições sôbre a Cultura e a Literatura portuguesas*, Coimbra, 1933.

Mendes dos Remédios, *História da Literatura Portuguesa* (6th ed.), Coimbra, 1930.

Jole Ruggieri, *Il Canzoniere di Resende*, Geneva, 1931.

Carolina Michaëlis de Vasconcellos and Theophilo Braga, "Geschichte der portugiesischen Literatur," in *Gröber's Grundriss der romanischen Philologie*, II, Part 2 (2d ed.), Strassburg, 1897, 129–382.

Rodrigues Lapa, *Das Origens da Poesia Lírica em Portugal na Idade-Média*, Lisbon, 1929.

Rodrigues Lapa, *Lições de Literatura Portuguesa*, Lisbon, 1934.

Albino Forjaz de Sampaio (ed.), *História da Literatura Portuguesa, Ilustrada*, 3 vols., Paris-Lisbon, 1929–32.

### DICTIONARIES

J. Y. da Silva Bastos, *Diccionário Etymológico, Prosódico e Orthográphico da Lingua Portugueza* (2d ed.), Lisbon, 1928.

Raphael Bluteau, *Vocabulario Portuguez e Latino*, 10 vols., Coimbra and Lisbon, 1712–1727.

F. J. Caldas Aulete, *Diccionario Contemporaneo da Lingua Portugueza* (2d ed.), 2 vols., Lisbon, 1925.

Cândido de Figueiredo, *Novo Diccionário da Língua Portuguesa* (4th ed.), 2 vols., Lisbon, 1926.

Augusto Magne, *Dicionário da Língua Portuguesa* (*Especialmente dos Períodos Medieval e Clássico*), Vol. I (A-AF), Rio de Janeiro, 1950.

H. Michaëlis, *A New Dictionary of the Portuguese and English Languages*, New York, 1945.

Marcial Valladares Nuñez, *Diccionario Gallego-Castellano*, Santiago, 1884.

Bento Pereyra, *Prosodia in Vocabularium Bilingue Latinum, et Lusitanum Digesta* (9th ed.), Evora, 1741.

Francisco Javier Rodríguez, *Diccionario Gallego-Castellano*, La Coruña, 1863.

James L. Taylor, *A Portuguese and English Dictionary*, Stanford, Calif., 1958.

Leonel Vallandro and Lino Vallandro, *Dicionário Inglês-Português*, Rio de Janeiro, 1954.

Domingos Vieira, *Grande Diccionario Portuguez ou Thesouro da Lingua Portugueza*, 5 vols., Porto, 1871–1874.

Volume I contains in the *Introducção* a study entitled *Sobre a Lingua Portugueza* by Adolpho Coelho.

## SELECTIVE BIBLIOGRAPHY OF ITEMS PUBLISHED SINCE 1938 AND NOT LISTED ABOVE

Abraham, Richard D. "Omission of the Pronoun *o* with Third Singular Weak Preterits in Old Portuguese." HR, VII, 248–250.

Allen Jr., J. D. H. *Portuguese Word-Formation with Suffixes,* Baltimore, 1941.

Allen Jr., J. D. H. *Two Old Portuguese Versions of* THE LIFE OF SAINT ALEXIS—*Codices Alcobacenses* 36 *and* 266, Urbana, Ill., 1953.

Carter, Henry H. "A Fourteenth-Century Latin–Old Portuguese Verb Dictionary." Romance Philology, VI, 71–103.

Cintra, Maria Adelaide Valle. "Bibliografia de textos medievais portugueses publicados." BF, XII, 60–100.

Domincovich, Ruth. *Portuguese Orthography to* 1500, Philadelphia, 1948.

Learned, Erma. *Old Portuguese Vocalic Finals, Phonology and Orthography of Accented* -ou, -eu, -iu *and* -ao, -eo, -io. Baltimore, 1950.

Magne, Augusto. *A Demanda do Santo Graal,* 3 vols., Rio de Janeiro, 1944.

> Edition of the whole Vienna manuscript. Vols. I and II contain a generous sampling in facsimile of pages of the codex.

Magne, Augusto (ed.). *Ludolfo Cartusiano, O LIVRO DE VITA CHRISTI em Linguagem Português* (*Edição Fac-similar e Crítica do Incunábulo de* 1495 *Cotejado com os Apógrafos*), Vol. I, Rio de Janeiro, 1957.

Mattoso Câmara Jr., Joaquim. *Dicionário de Fatos Gramaticais,* Rio de Janeiro, 1956.

Nykl, A. R. *Cronica Del Rey Dom Affomsso Hamrriquez por Duarte Galvão,* Cambridge, Mass., 1942.

Paiva Boléo, Manual de. *Introdução ao Estudo da Filologia Portuguesa,* Lisbon, 1946.

Roberts, Kimberley S. *Orthography, Phonology and Word Study of the* LEAL CONSELHEIRO, Philadelphia, 1940.

Roberts, Kimberley S. *An Anthology of Old Portuguese,* Lisbon, no date.

Russo, Harold J. *Morphology and Syntax of the* LEAL CONSE-LHEIRO, Philadelphia, 1941.

Sacks, Norman P. *The Latinity of Dated Documents in the Portuguese Territory,* Philadelphia, 1941.

Silva Neto, Serafim da. *Fontes do Latim Vulgar (O Appendix Probi),* Rio de Janeiro, 1946.

Silva Neto, Serafim da. *História da Língua Portuguêsa,* Rio de Janeiro, 1952.
    External history of the language.

Silva Neto, Serafim da. *Textos Medievais Portuguêses e seus Problemas,* Rio de Janeiro, 1956.

Sletsjøe, Leif. *Le développement de l et n en ancien portugais. Etude fondée sur les diplômes des Portugaliae Monumenta Historica.* Oslo and Paris, 1959.

Spitzer, Leo. "Omission of Object Pronoun in Portuguese." HR, VIII, 58–62.

Sten, Holger. *Les Particularités de la Langue Portugaise,* Copenhagen, 1944.

Williams, Edwin B. "The Old Portuguese Versions of the Life of Saint Alexis: A Note Based on the Chronology of Old Portuguese Orthography." HR, IX, 214–215.

## REVIEWS OF THE FIRST EDITION OF "FROM LATIN TO PORTUGUESE," PHILADELPHIA, 1938

Bourciez, Edouard. BHi, XLI (1939), 375–378.

Coester, Alfred. Hispania, XXII (1939), 227.

Entwistle, William J. HR, VII (1939), 260–264.

Fernández, Xavier A. RR, XXXI (1940), 95–97.

Ford, J. D. M. Language, XV (1939), 257–260.

Machado, José Pedro. BF, VI (1940), 481–484.

Meier, Harri. RF, LIII (1939), 242–244.

Mulertt, Werner. LBl, LXII (1941), columns 60–61.

Rohlfs, Gerhard. AStNS, CLXXIX (1941), 85–86.

Silva Neto, Serafim da. *Bibliografia Filológica,* 1943, 7–14.

Silva Neto, Serafim da. *Manual de Filologia Portuguesa (História, Problemas, Métodos),* Rio de Janeiro, 1952, 153–164.

Spitzer, Leo. MLN, LIV (1939), 376–378.

# INDEX

References are to paragraphs, sections, and sub-sections (in a few cases to footnotes). The index is a combined subject and word index. Subjects are in roman. Words, graphs, letters, and groups of letters are in italics, their language being indicated unless it is Old or Modern Portuguese. A few definitions are included in this section.